HAIG:
THE GENERAL'S
PROGRESS

1241824　　MORRIS, R.

973.927
Haig: the general's progress
MORRIS. R.
£8.95
1241824

10/82

PA

HAIG:
THE GENERAL'S PROGRESS

Roger Morris

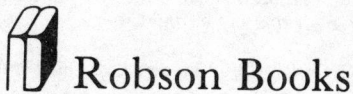 Robson Books

FIRST PUBLISHED IN GREAT BRITAIN IN 1982 BY
ROBSON BOOKS LTD., BOLSOVER HOUSE,
5-6 CLIPSTONE STREET, LONDON W1P 7EB.
COPYRIGHT © 1982 BY ROGER MORRIS

British Library Cataloguing in Publication Data

Morris, Roger
    Haig.
    1. Haig, Alexander
    I. Title
    973.927'092'4   E838.5

ISBN 0-86051-188-X

Design by Tere LoPrete

Printed in Great Britain by Biddles Ltd, Guildford, Surrey

For Kat
Friend, Lover, Example, Critic, Patriot

"I may be dangerous," he said, "but I am not wicked. No, I am not wicked."

Henry James, *The American*

CONTENTS

ACKNOWLEDGMENTS

This book owes a creative debt to Charles Sopkin of Seaview Books and Playboy Press who encouraged it from the beginning, yet patiently allowed me to do the book I drew from his inspiration. If there is a public service here, it is very much his.

For sources, I am grateful to the Zimmermann Library of the University of New Mexico for its impressive collection and cooperation; to the cheerful staff of the New Mexico State Library who at one point must have thought me a strange new fixture in the reading room, casting over forgotten battles and scandals; and not least to the Fogelson Library Center of the Christian Brothers' College of Santa Fe, which lent me its substantial resources and a quiet, scenic refuge in which to write—invaluable courtesies. These fine libraries, far from either coast, are heartening proof that work in contemporary politics and diplomacy need no longer be the preserve of a narrow section of the country, if only the opportunities are used. The people whose purses and sons share the fateful costs of foreign policy ought, after all, to share in understanding it as well.

This is also a chance to acquit publicly an old professional debt to Lawrence Eagleburger, now undersecretary of state for political affairs and, from the moment we met in 1966 as aides to Dean Acheson, a patron and friend who was instrumental in my staying on the National Security Council staff through my own personal experience with both Alexander Haig and Henry Kissinger. Now working for the general and always happily to my right in political matters, Larry will no doubt find some of this book unpalatable, and he is responsible, Secretary Haig should be assured, for none of its conclusions. Still, ironically, at least some of the insights here would not have been possible without his bipartisan nurturing of my government service, and despite our considerable and honest differences of view then and now. I acknowledge that gift in affectionate and admiring memory.

For Playboy Press, Susan Friedland gave generously of her talent and patience in the crucial last stages of editing, and Nat Sobel was a thoughtful, dynamic promoter.

I must thank, too, several friends and colleagues in New Mexico who so stoically understood my total seclusion from urgent common enterprises in journalism. Devoted to making democracy work out here on this desert, they abided my preoccupation from the Yalu to the Fulda Gap, when all the time they knew that a decent foreign policy begins at home.

To my sons, David and Peter, loving gratitude for tolerating so well all the quiet hours, distractions, abbreviated football games, and late nights at the library. Anything positive out of these efforts is for them, and for Zoë and Ethan and Dylan.

And finally there is my wife, whose contribution I cannot properly acknowledge here, who sheltered, listened, read, debated, softened, sharpened, improved—and left the surviving flaws to my willfulness.

ROGER MORRIS

Santa Fe
April 1982

PREFACE

This is the story of an ascent to power, with no pretense to complete biography. My purpose is to draw an informed, thoughtful portrait of the relatively unknown man who became secretary of state in the Reagan administration and who moved through the highest levels of American government for more than a decade before. It is a portrayal of who he is, what he represents, and how he rose to high office; of the forces and experiences that shaped him; of the quality of his mind and of his public service; of what we might expect of a career and potential still unfinished. The narrative traces the general's progress to the Senate confirmation in early 1981, and deals only incidentally with the events of the first year in the State Department.

Rummaging through the last thirty-five years of the Haig rise, I have been very conscious of the limits in trying to compose such contemporary and unsettled history. As biographers of the future will ruefully discover, it is the essence of the bureaucratic life, of people like Haig who increasingly populate the great offices of government, to leave few palpable tracks to begin with. Moreover, because we are in that special sanctum of foreign policy, important parts of the record are shrouded in official secrecy as well as self-protection, and sometimes both, perhaps indistinguishably.

Of the last decade in particular, the bodies, and scandals, are still warm. The memoirs and memories of the Nixon regime and Watergate have been prodigal yet selective, the more we learned somehow leaving all the sharper sense of what we had not yet been told. The diary and telephone-conversation transcripts of Henry Kissinger, for instance, oozed only discreetly through the first thick volume of Kissinger's testimonial to those years. That redolent little archive, candid snatches of Alexander Haig and others, will apparently for everyone's sake await some distant release when the men and the public reaction no longer matter. Trackless bureaucrats, secrets, and awkward personal papers aside, some of the record of this turbulent era, of crucial participants such as Haig, may be lost for good to the shredder and the furnace— the modern statesman's ultimate precautions against unwanted history.

Yet for all those recognized obstacles, the stakes were too high not to write seriously about Haig from the many sources already available. He is, after all, secretary of state in an administration where the foreign-policy expertise he is thought to have is clearly at a premium and his influence as a result potentially enormous. He wields that authority in a time, too, of chronic international crises, from Warsaw to San Salvador, and when the costs of foreign policy have come home for Americans as never before—from the inflationary ravages of the Vietnam

War to a new draft registration for their sons, from a
swelling military budget at the expense of social services
to the price of a gallon of Arab, African, or Latin gas at
the local station. If there seem any unarguable lessons
from the story that follows, it is that the quality of leaders
and their decisions in foreign affairs are indeed life-and-
death matters, and that Alexander Haig tends to use the
power at hand.

Beyond the man and his present importance, though,
there is still another, perhaps larger reason for this preliminary portrayal, especially of the more than twenty
years of public service before Haig became a Nixon White
House prodigy. For Haig was witness, actor, product of
so much history before the Nixon presidency. In revealing ways, his early career joined and embodied the great
currents—some now willfully forgotten, some never understood—of America's post–World War II torment with
the world. It is an unexpected bonus in Haig's prominence
that his career takes us again across that fateful ground,
with a new chance—who knows?—to learn something.

In tracing such treacherously recent history, I had
frankly hoped to make good use of the oral, sometimes
unnamed source, the scourge of officialdom while often
the necessary salvation of a writer opening the drapes on
the closed society of national security. Yet many of those
sources were inclined to speak reflectively about a general retired or resting in Arlington, and only vapidly or
obsequiously about one now in the cabinet and a possible
future president. Nor was there a shortage of unnamable
venomous critics. "Subtly ambitious with just the right
amount of ruthlessness," Lloyd Shearer, an early and im-
pressionable interviewer wrote of Haig in 1972, apparently

presuming his readers knew, like the general, the dosage in "just the right amount."

Of Haig's excesses, in any case, several inside sources had no doubt. There were the predictable apocrypha of CIA conspiracy, stinging anecdotes and lurid personal iniquity, tales with neither much substance nor relevance that tended only to turn back on the tellers. "This is a cruel town," Haig once remarked bitterly about Washington with its ubiquitous rumors, and even an author avidly on his trail would have to agree (though along the way Haig himself was evidently not above the murmured attacks he now finds so unfairly launched at an innocent secretary of state).

Hearing so little responsible testimony between the idolatry and cruelty, however, I have labored to discard both, and especially not to indulge the petty or personal. As it is, Haig's public record speaks amply to his relevant flaws as an official. The quoted comments about the man in what follows are largely from written, documented material, and from clearly attributable, on-the-record sources, much of it from Haig himself.

With the same discrimination, I hoped to avoid the fatuous detail and official pap that frequently clutter current biographies—especially, it seems, of living soldiers. So I have not been all that concerned to describe the view from Haig's quarters in Tokyo or Carlisle Barracks, but rather the historical or career setting, and what it meant to be there. Nor, having been in government and witnessed its habitual laxity with the truth, could I rely on efficiency ratings or even battle citations, no more than congressional testimony or press releases, as primary, indubitable sources.

Finally, there is my own personal perspective to be acknowledged. For a year and a half, I worked around Haig on the National Security Council staff, sometimes at close range and usually on cordial personal terms whatever our policy differences, when he was Henry Kissinger's still obscure if upwardly mobile outer-office aide. Though fourteen years his junior, I felt then and recognize now in his past, like baggy old clothes, the ambitions, experiences, and relationships we shared at the time but now no longer. Some of my friends were, or have become, Haig's Haigs, and I have benefited in this book from their firsthand knowledge as from my own. Yet after that same intense exposure, I gave up longtime dreams of diplomacy, left government, and deliberately chose, with not much anguish, a very different life and quite another ethic of public service. That background in an author is obviously a special vantage point and genealogy, of which readers are entitled to be forewarned.

However different our paths and places today, I confess, in writing this book about Haig's climb, a nostalgia for what we thought we were—or perhaps even for what else we might have become in a different bureaucratic culture. If being high inside government gave me an acute sense of the squalor and of the shrunken reality of men there, I could not have tried to recapture that world, in part once my chosen profession, without as well some empathy, and compassion, for the subject. It is what Alexander Haig evokes of our past, after all, that makes his rise to power so important—and in many ways so disturbing.

PROLOGUE

A gray, humid August morning in Washington. On the south lawn of the White House, poised at the end of a red carpet, an army helicopter waits for its final passenger. The familiar, slightly stooped figure climbs to the doorway of the craft, pauses, turns for a last time to the small, silent crowd gathered near the house at the edge of the lawn, thrusts his arms up and out once more in characteristic, now defiant and poignant "V" for victory signs, and vanishes inside. The helicopter lifts slowly and wheels away to the south. Olive-drab against the overcast, it soon recedes in the distance beyond the chalky spike of the Washington Monument, and then, suddenly, is out of sight.

It is the finale of a disgraced presidency, the close of a remarkable era in American government, and there is a sense of anticlimax and irony about the event. To one onlooker, the historic passenger with all the turmoil he embodied "seems to have just floated away." Long afterward, the new president, an earnest but vulnerable successor, remembered another symbolic ending as he turned away from the disappearing helicopter, and the "guards rolled up the red carpet behind us."

Yet inside the White House, later that day, there is still another last act. In the small private secretary's room adjacent to the Oval Office, cool and air-conditioned against the rising heat outside, an aide to the new president smells the acrid, unmistakable odor of papers burned in the fireplace. That evening, the office of the ex-President's chief of staff and most trusted aide is crowded with bulging "burn bags." Routinely sealed and then shredded and burned, such sacks ostensibly hold duplicates or other superfluous classified material. This August night, however, there are far more documents to be destroyed than any day's official effluence. At the end of the worst, most corrosive political scandal in modern American history, a scandal swarming with deception and vital missing evidence, the chief of staff has clearly purged his files.

When the new president is anxiously warned about the ominous bags, he wearily shuns what may be discovered. "I don't want to know about that," he is said to tell an assistant. "Just let him get 'em out of this house."

The day is August 9, 1974, and Richard Nixon has been driven at last from the White House by Watergate, leaving the wreckage and the red carpet to Gerald Ford.

The keeper of the abundant burn bags left in Nixon's wake is Alexander Meigs Haig, Jr. Nearly fifty, he has been for the last fifteen months perhaps the most powerful man in America, regent to a dazed, scandalized, alcohol-besotted president whose mind is sometimes so moiled that his successor, knowing only a fraction of what Haig knows, will pardon the resigned leader in part for fear that otherwise he will commit suicide.

Haig's has been a regency of awesome, unstable authority. On one night the previous autumn, while the president lay soddenly asleep, thought unable to command, Haig and other unelected, constitutionally unempowered officials had furtively taken it on themselves to order United States forces to worldwide alert, and to the edge of war. Later, there loomed the dark silhouette of a veritable military coup to keep the disgraced regime in power, and nearby troop units were warned by the worried Pentagon to question any unusual orders from the White House. Added to this are the still entombed remains of Watergate, and of the foreign-policy practices that so resembled it, the further excesses and complicities of a government toppled by its already visible abuse of power. Haig has had several secrets to keep. The burn bags this night are a fitting emblem.

Haig's rise in this haunted regime, even before his regency, has been almost without parallel in the nation's military or political history, from obscure colonel to full general, four stars in four years, promotions comparable only to Dwight Eisenhower's in the tumult of World War II. In a sense, however, his importance has never been in grade or prominence or open achievement, but in the largely unseen, unacknowledged back-room power of the aide, the special assistant, whose cachet depends on the peculiar strengths, and weaknesses, of the men he serves. "None of MacArthur's men," remarked one of them who, like the young Haig, worked in the famous general's orbit, "can risk being first-rate." Whether by calculation

or plain human limits, that has been true of Haig regardless of the patron of the moment. Through the most important of twenty-seven years in government, he has
served a number of MacArthurs *manqués*. His career
has been spent much of the time in some retinue, and he
has been increasingly rewarded for it.

"The facts of Alexander Haig's rise to power are familiar enough," *The New York Times* would write about him
later, content with a résumé. But his experience as a
retainer is hardly perfunctory. He talks to newsmen with
throaty bravura about being at "the vortex." Few realize
how much his officer's career has been a prism of the
times, of America's postwar experience, its anguish and
portent. The forces that shaped and elevated him have
been historic. Over the quarter-century before Watergate
and Nixon's aberrance, he has been present, not as a
witness to edifying military triumphs or statesmanship,
but rather to a succession of debacles: the bitter retreat
from the Yalu, the peacetime bureaucratic rot of the army,
the doomed imperium of Kennedy and Johnson. He has,
nonetheless, enjoyed personal success amid national frustration, defeat, and virtual rebellion, almost as if his
service has been somehow vindicated in the surrounding
disaster. His reaction to this history—and, most of all, his
lack of it—says much about the man. Among other effects,
his past has produced in Haig, despite all his rewards, a
barely concealed resentment, a belligerence of pose and
policy, and an angry, elastic ethic of self-belief if not
self-esteem.

His career is studded with paradox. Raised to general
and eventually to the highest Allied command in defense
of the West, he has never fought in a victorious war,

never led a military unit larger than a brigade, and that for only a few weeks. While he commands a sophisticated, computer-armed NATO force in the 1970s and is celebrated as an authority on the alarming might of the Russian arsenal versus the imputed dangerous weakness of his own, his last training in the surging technology of modern war was a tank school in the early 1950s. Though he has been decorated for battlefield valor several times, his commendations later seem marred by arguable discrepancies in the record and by what is sadly discovered to be the army's larger profligacy with medals in a corrupting war. With Henry Kissinger, he has been at the center of American foreign policy for four years. He has come to such grave responsibility with no practical experience in diplomacy and apparently meager sophistication in the subject. Later, as secretary of state, he will be called the "most knowledgeable" about foreign affairs in the Reagan administration, though his public statements betray too clearly the hyperbole and incoherence of the half-educated. His work with Kissinger has been far more clerical, bureaucratic, and political than the formulation of policy.

Smooth, sometimes pandering, and rarely critical in person with his succession of demanding chiefs, he can be coarse and acidly contemptuous of the same men out of their presence. Few have been so deeply embroiled, so sternly loyal in the desperate White House efforts to block and stave off Watergate justice. Almost no one so integral (save his cohort Kissinger) will survive the calamity so well, with such career immunity and rewards, while other men go to jail and ignominy.

Conservative by background, temper, and conviction,

clearly at home if not always welcome on the right of the Republican party, he owes his rescue from oblivion, the subsequent turning point in his career, and still later his political revival once again, to the Democrats. To become Richard Nixon's ultimate loyalist, he has been propelled into the halls of power by Nixon's lasting nemesis, John Kennedy, and by the bravado, pretense, and lethal amateurism of the Kennedy era. He is the offspring of an elite incest, of a bipartisan rule and often misrule over foreign policy that is classically American. In many ways he is a scion of Camelot come to sit at the head of Ronald Reagan's cabinet.

Party politics aside, he will later aspire to the highest elected office, with an abiding disdain for and mistrust of both press and public. These are the marks of Haig the bureaucrat, who in the Nixon White House and elsewhere similarly loathes and strives to undercut the bureaucracy, not least the State Department he will someday head. To those who knew and worked with him along the way, he was among the last men expected to succeed to such high position. Yet when it came, his elevation seemed, on a closer look at his record, almost natural and predictable. Apparently a special figure with unique experience, he is a bureaucratic everyman in modern government. To understand Haig, his passions and limits, is to understand what has happened to all of us.

But now, this August night in 1974, still in his ornate White House suite only footsteps away from the Oval Office but his regency at an end and his prospects uncertain, not all of these ironies and paradoxes are yet clear. What is more plain is his gritty, almost imperious claim on some return. "We'll be back. Believe me, we'll

be back," he tells a Kissinger aide, who thinks it the empty
boast of a man whose power is done.

But this Watergate disaster, too, like others in his past,
Haig will survive. As the burn bags and the wary new
president attest, he inters failure, absorbs and ignores it
—at least, he is able to do that so long as it does not become his own. One by one he has watched his patrons fall,
until little more was left of their power than to anoint
him for a new, higher position. Still planning, waiting . . .
soon it will be his turn.

Part One

APPRENTICE

Must I not serve a long apprenticehood
To foreign passages, and in the end,
Having my freedom, boast of nothing else
But that I was a journeyman to grief?
                    Shakespeare, *Richard II*

Part One

APPRENTICE

A half-mile hard outside Philadelphia's western city limits, Bala-Cynwyd anchors the lower end of the Main Line, launching the trains on their fashionable run out through the wealthy suburbs and counties beyond. It is hardly an ordinary railroad town, of course, astride the route whose name became synonymous with affluence and social standing. As novelist John O'Hara described his fictional but similar Gibbsville, Pennsylvania, these were communities where "the expression 'the wrong side of the tracks' never caught on."

By 1930 Philadelphia had grown to nearly two million, swollen by Irish and German migrations in the middle decades of the nineteenth century, and by succeeding waves of poor whites and blacks from the American South as well as southern and eastern Europeans. As the city then went through the familiar cycle of influx, political neglect, and decay, the nearby Main Line hamlets became discreet, upper-middle-class islands. The closest, Bala-Cynwyd, was still an ample eight miles from the teeming city center and dingy Delaware River, while happily segregated by income and ethnic makeup as well as from other, less exclusive outskirt communities like Manayunk's working-class Italians and Poles to the north.

With its substantial homes, leafy avenues, open spaces, and prospering white gentile professionals, it was among the more prized and insulated of the fresh American suburbs of the 1920s and 1930s, yet uncrowded, unthreatened, relatively unpaved. When the Bala Golf Club published its directory in those years, a virtual census, by address, of the town's few hundred families, the houses per street were notably sparse. Altogether, O'Hara explained of the Main Line amenities, it was "a matter of pride with the best people . . . to live comfortably."

Not surprisingly, politics along the Main Line tended to follow its social comforts. Bala-Cynwyd, like the succeeding stops, was largely conservative. Even pulsing Philadelphia was firmly in the grip of a Republican machine that had ruled the metropolis under the yoke of a state legislative charter since the Civil War, and would continue its dominion until 1951. Though Depression breadlines curled about the historic downtown, though jobless hoboes and their pathetic camps sheathed the Pennsylvania Railroad's corridors in every direction, Philadelphia was the only one of the nation's twelve largest cities in 1932 not carried by Franklin Roosevelt.

More than a decade before that exceptional Roosevelt defeat, an ambitious young lawyer named Alexander Haig had settled in Bala-Cynwyd. Haig was in many ways typical of the slowly growing Main Line population after the First World War. Though not independently wealthy, he traced a respectable Scotch-English lineage in Philadelphia; was an educated, well-paid professional when such credentials were at least a partial mark of class distinction; and had Republican connections in the city, where he would serve for a time as assistant solicitor.

Hardworking and well liked; he seemed a successful man on the local way up.

Perhaps the most interesting asset Haig brought to those very respectable suburbs, however, was a strong and beautiful wife. A half-century later, her well-known son would tell a reporter that Regina Anne Murphy Haig was "lace curtain Philadelphia Irish." The description was apt enough in part. The Murphys were parvenu, Catholic Republicans, Regina's brothers going into medicine and law, her sister marrying an engineer who would be politically prominent and become her far more prominent son's first patron. Yet the label does not capture fully what by all accounts was the woman's lively sense of duty to both the past and future, and an apparent belief in good breeding that went beyond the lace at the window.

The Haigs had three children: the first a girl, named Regina for her mother; the last a boy christened Frank in 1928. In between, in Bala-Cynwyd on December 2, 1924, came another son, Alexander Meigs Haig, Jr. The family lived in a solid, three-story stone house on Bryn Mawr Avenue close to the city line. Haig, Jr., recalls their existence as "well-to-do, upper-middle-class," invariably with the prefix "upper."

Through the false boom of the Twenties and the early Depression, the father's law practice was steadily profitable, affording summer vacations in Atlantic City as well as their life in Bala-Cynwyd. There is a grainy family snapshot, expressive of the times, of a cherubic four- or five-year-old Alexander, Jr., in Buster Browns, short-pants sailor suit and hat, placidly sitting on a blanket on the sand in front of a boardwalk cottage, with what seems a large toy pistol grasped in both hands. Less charming, less memorable, was the social exclusion of it all. No blacks shared such beach idylls, much less Bala-Cynwyd, which then concentrated its bigotry in anti-Semitism. "One Jewish family finally moved in during those years," recalled Philip Nolan, a boyhood friend who went to parochial grade school with young Alexander, "and I remember hearing a lot of disparaging remarks in the town. There was a great deal of prejudice."

Then, suddenly, in 1935, part of that world shattered for the Haigs. Only thirty-eight, Alexander, Sr., died of cancer, leaving his ten-year-old namesake and the rest of the family in what loomed as respectable poverty. "He was a breadwinner who overextended himself," Haig says, almost as if his father had collapsed of overwork rather than dying of a dread, then still usually unannounced disease. At any rate, the legacy of the once easy affluence and promising career was "a minimum estate, just enough to carry us five years," says Haig. "It was a tough time for us when my father died. It brought our family together, what was left of it," Haig once said, providing in that last phrase, almost forty years after the event, the child's sense of decimating, irreplaceable loss.

About precisely what was left and what then happened to young Alexander's life, there would be slightly different memories among the family, with tellingly different points of emphasis. "Ours was a typical childhood, a typical adolescence," recalls Frank, the young son reminiscing about older brother Al who was an altar boy in Bala-Cynwyd and taught him how to swim and box. To Regina Haig, Alec (as a cadet he would be Alex, Al to his friends and later to prominent sponsors, and ever

Alec to his mother) "was the leader," always with "a houseful of boys around." One of those boys, Philip Nolan, remembered too the sports and Haig's "leadership."

From such descriptions, it was, despite the tragedy, an almost typical growing up. Yet when Haig himself looks back on those years, what endures most vividly is the hardship, the burden, spoken of with both boasting and a trace of bitterness, a sense of an heir's responsibility larded with some self-pity. If younger Frank evokes sacristies and swimming pools, Al remembers "working always."

"I had to pretty much fend for myself in terms of economics." . . . "I had to be self-reliant and fend for myself," Haig repeated nearly verbatim to two different reporters more than a year apart. "Whatever hopes I had for my own future were going to be shaped largely by me," he echoed in a separate television profile, then reeling off a series of menial jobs "to support myself"—a paper route, stints for the post office and the local Atlantic Richfield, a time at a well-known Philadelphia department store: "I even worked as a floorwalker in the ladies' department of John Wanamaker's."

Haig's autobiographical interviews on the fatherless future general, toiling and self-made, commonly omitted two crucial early influences outside himself. The first was clearly his mother. Witnesses from the years after her husband's death remember Regina Haig variously as "very wonderful" and doting, or daunting and "in control," but in any case as the strong single parent holding the family together, and a dominant personality in Alexander's life, to whom he grew ever closer. "Whatever it is that a mother is supposed to do, she did," Frank Haig says of her. "If there was something we wanted, she'd say, 'Well, yes. Now, how will we go about getting it?'" Whether transferring to the children dashed hopes for a dead husband or simply taking his place, whether following naturally her own Irish pride and class pretense or all this and more, Haig's mother by every account nurtured in all her children, and in "Alec" particularly, who responded for his own reasons, the expectations, the sense of achievement and entitlement, that might have been lost with the senior Haig's premature death. It was in that Bryn Mawr Avenue house, with its omnipresent missing figure, that young Alexander's avid, later notorious, ambition was first fired and fused.

While mother and son worked their chemistry, it was more than a part-time paper route or floorwalker's salary that eked out the Haig's dwindling estate and kept the family in a decent if diminished manner in Bala-Cynwyd through the Depression. The benefactor, and obvious other force in Haig's beginnings, was John H. Neeson, Regina's brother-in-law and, more than ten years older, already in the mid-1930s a powerful, prosperous Philadephia bureaucrat. Another of the city's native Irish professional caste, Neeson had played football at Notre Dame and graduated from its engineering school in 1903 straight into municipal service. He rose by 1928 to be chief of surveys and zoning, and in 1940 to director of public works, managing along the way such major projects as garbage collection, sewer laying, the city's WPA program, and the construction of both Philadelphia airports. It was a period of throbbing urban growth, the repair of a town long left derelict, fostering what one observer remembers as "the golden age of Philadelphia graft." And while Neeson was generally regarded among his fellow governors of the posh Penn Athletic and Union Clubs as an upright civil servant amid the City Hall chicanery, his prominence and means were plain.

"Our uncle did a lot to support the family," Frank later remarked of the vital and continuing subsidies from Neeson to the Haigs after the senior Alexander' death. Though never at a loss to talk about those "tough times" and his own sacrifice and contributions, it was another acknowledgment Alexander, Jr., would not easily make, and the first of much such patronage.

Together, the mother's bolstering drive and the uncle's money eventually underwrote remarkable achievement in the Haig children, whose future had seemed so precarious in 1935. The oldest, Regina, became a successful attorney, like her father. Frank Rawle Haig became a Jesuit priest with a Ph.D. in physics and a career of honors and clerical administrative posts leading to the presidency of a Catholic college. For Alexander, his mother's ambition ran to the law as well, and almost certainly to the success and security she had known and lost. But "Al knew when he was twelve years old that he wanted to go to West Point," his brother remembers, and Regina Haig, skeptical but ever supportive, would be once again a quietly decisive influence on her son's rise, along with her brother-in-law.

The boy walked the three blocks to parochial elementary school at St. Matthias, where his classmates recalled him as shining at sports and grades in a tiny class of eight boys and thirteen girls. From there he won a scholarship to the Jesuit St. Joseph's Preparatory nearby in Philadelphia, and to the severity and narrowness of that sort of Catholic education at the end of the Thirties. But after two lackluster years at the prep school, his scholarship went unrenewed. "Athletic, vigorous, gregarious," in Frank's words, "but not a scholar," Haig was forced to finish in public school at the suburban Lower Merion Senior High in 1942, his hopes for the military academy already dimmer. "Al is definitely not West Point material," Lower Merion's principal is said to have told Regina Haig when she came round to urge her son's recommendation.

The Haigs later delighted in recounting the story of that remark—and of how, forty years before, another Lower Merion principal passed the same rash judgment on the school's other noted alumnus, Air Force General "Hap" Arnold of World War II fame. A renowned Al Haig would even someday receive the Air Force Association's "Hap Arnold Award." But in the spring of 1942, it was no laughing matter. As the principal thought, Haig could not qualify for the academy.

The failure was in a sense sharper and more personal than any he would know again for decades, and it produced a vague hiatus, what his brother saw as "the closest he ever came to having a spiritual crisis." Ultimately, he applied and was accepted at John Neeson's alma mater, Notre Dame, where the uncle was on the board of lay trustees and had been honored by the school for his alumni boosterism. Haig's record at South Bend shows nine routine liberal arts courses for 1943, and again no visible academic distinction. His family noticed, however, a new maturity "from an adolescent to a man," and a new seriousness of mind, the young Catholic college student impressing his brother, the future priest, by "coming home and seriously discussing evolution and God, and how to reconcile them."

Meanwhile, he applied again to West Point. Later, reminiscing with reporters, Haig termed going to the academy a "financial necessity" due to his family's straitened circumstances and their tradition of self-reliance. But at nineteen, facing the draft in the middle of a world war, it seems unlikely that his influential uncle would not somehow have helped to see him through at Notre Dame. More important than college fees, he no doubt wanted to be an officer. And as it was, Neeson did even better for his sister-in-law's first son. When Alexander, in another try, passed the ordeal of the entrance exams, the director of public works flexed his substantial Philadelphia muscle —"pulled strings," as the *Wall Street Journal* subsequently put it—and secured him a political appointment to the entering class in 1944.

When Neeson died the next year, there was a suitable obituary in *The New York Times* and later a Notre Dame scholarship in his memory for deserving Philadelphia boys, but no mention when his most famous beneficiary reflected on his own rise. For her part, Regina Haig, though at the time she had obviously welcomed the patronage appointment for her son, was rueful. When "Alec" was White House chief of staff, at the center of power and atop an astonishing career climb, she still had regrets. "If he had followed my advice years ago, he'd be a senator by now. I wanted him to be a lawyer. The army is such a slow procedure, and you can't make any money," said the mother, still bearing the marks of the young widow in Bala-Cynwyd. "Money is the thing you want as you get older."

The West Point that Alexander Haig entered belatedly in the summer of 1944 was in wartime flux, but still largely confined to the old encrusted mold of a military seminary. In a nation that admired and even craved such tradition, while at the same time harboring a healthy distrust of any military caste, the academy was a reflection of the isolation and inertia of the prewar army. Though swollen to almost 2,500 cadets during the war, the corps remained (like Bala-Cynwyd) a white middle- and upper-middle-class preserve. Before an integration order in 1951, only thirteen blacks had attended. If anything, Haig was something of an anomaly for being Catholic. World War I had spurred changes in military training, but there was the complacency of the victors even then, and but modest updating and expansion in the sciences, engineering, and social studies. Only in 1947, the year Haig graduated, would West Point auction off its horses, signaling two years after Hiroshima the reluctant end of the cavalry era as well as the annual horse show and polo matches with the local Hudson Valley squirearchy.

Behind the pomp and ceremony on the famous Plain was a society still mostly hidden to all but its initiates. Like a dark-side moss that survived public sunlight and periodic surgery, hazing continued to be harsh, the virtue of discipline hiding a multitude of petty cruelties. The harassment and rigidity, thought to instill battlefield dependablity whatever the orders, began with the plebe's aptly named Beast Barracks under the tyranny of upper-classmen in the sticky New York summer before his first academic term, and continued through succeeding years in the person of the staff tactical officers, the despised "tacs" who were career army men and commonly grad-uates of the academy, handpicked by the commandant to enforce the ritual in each unit of the corps. Yet the rigors hardly guaranteed seriousness of mind to match the ostensible mission. When a cadet diary purported to be typical and "true" was published in 1943, *The Collected Works of Ducrot Pepys* (edited by Roger Hilsman, class of '43, later a ranking State Department official presiding over Vietnam policy for John Kennedy), the result was a journal of unrelieved trivia and sophomoric absorption in the oppressive routine. "Unless the pictures in the mess hall stop winking at me," read the entry for Sunday, December 7, 1941, in its entirety, "I am not going to eat there any more."

To feed the war's appetite for officers, the academy's four-year curriculum was reduced to three in 1942, and dominated by a new "fit to fight" course, intensive field-combat training for the corps. It barely rescued West Point from imminent War Department plans to close the academy down and convert it to one more quick officer candidate school just as Haig was struggling to enter. The saving course, however, put Haig and fellow cadets of the era under packs and helmets as no classes before them. They moved through rugged and graphic exercises and obstacle courses with tactical maneuvers, demolition, artillery, tanks, and assorted military engineering, a basic infantryman's program far more practical than such pre-war training. War beyond its gates also had the salutary effect of temporarily replacing with more responsive civilian teachers some of the academy's mostly alumni faculty now called to other duty, the latter group tending to be characterized by the instructor who told an inquiring cadet, "I'm not here to answer questions but to mark you."

Besides those gains, however, Haig's West Point in the mid-Forties suffered the one wartime casualty it could least afford—a thinning of its already spotty and stunted academic standards. The new hours in the field came at the expense of study time and, as one future general remembered, "over the dead bodies of academic professors." Shaving four years to three was accomplished mainly by reducing courses in English, the social sciences, and even military history in a curriculum already nine-tenths engineering, and in which nearly half of the few remaining courses labeled "humanities" were in narrow vocational subjects like military correspondence or the law of courts-martial. Electives such as applied psychology or national-security studies were added only after the war. It amounted to a basic educational deficiency, not least in writing and speaking English, of which Haig would always bear the mark.

The regimen, pressure, and shrunken scholarship often produced predictable results in officers about to graduate into the complexities and frustrations of the post-1945 cold-war world. "Here at West Point we learn to think in straight lines," a cadet told a visitor at the time. The celebrated ideal, much of what boys like Haig "wanted" in the academy, was soon to be discovered painfully at odds with the reality. General Maxwell Taylor, war hero made academy superintendent in 1945 and later a chief of staff as well as a prominent figure in Vietnam policy, could pronounce the famous West Point honor system and the resulting character training the academy's "crowning glory." Meanwhile, beginning in Haig's plebe year 1944–45 and continuing through the Taylor superintendency, the school basked in the prestige of Army football teams that swept five of six undefeated seasons and two national championships. Two years after Taylor moved on, in August 1951, the uglier truth appeared in a football-team cheating scandal that left ninety cadets cashiered but touched only the surface. The academic corruption had been "rife," a later study concluded, with hundreds of cadets involved in cheating that had gone on "for years." With a gift for dubious claims on behalf of his clients, then and later in Saigon, Taylor had also extolled the "catholic," broadly educated "interests" of the new postwar West Pointer. Ten years after Haig graduated, an army review board found that the same "catholic" training he had been given "is designed for the mediocre student and does not challenge the really good student."

It was, at any rate, challenging enough for Haig. He nearly failed to graduate with the class of 1947 after running afoul of one of the myriad regulations. The details of what happened are lost in the mists of West Point inanities, but the mere incident is worth noting in light of Haig's conduct as a career officer on the other side twenty years later, in a dispute with a cadet over regulations. He got over his own "rough times" at the academy "by going to chapel," according to Frank, who is prone to remember his brother's youthful piety at this stage. In a class of 310, he finished deep in the third quarter at 214th, with no apparent aura of success. "He was the last

man in his class anyone expected to become the first
general," thought Lieutenant General William Knowlton,
who placed 7th in an earlier wartime class and later became superintendent. Knowlton and 230 other senior
officers were passed by Haig in rank in 1973. There were
others with him at the academy, both more and less apt,
whose careers would cross Haig's. Nixon White House
Counsel Fred Buzhardt was in the class ahead. Above
Haig at a respectable 86th in the class of '47 stood Brent
Scowcroft, another future general and Henry Kissinger's
successor as presidential national security adviser under
Ford. The Point yearbook shows the toddler on the beach
at Atlantic City become a young man, cadet "Alex" Haig,
with a pleasant, smooth, open face, dark wavy hair, and
at least some clue to the future in the characteristics attributed to him under the picture: "Strong convictions
and even stronger ambitions."

He would return to West Point twice again in his career; and as both alumnus and staff officer of the academy,
he was to see it hotly attacked, sometimes by fellow grad-
uates, for pursuing "an ideology, not an education," and
for its "anointed . . . access to America's ruling elite." Yet
the flaws of the academy in his era went deeper than
politics and political access. West Point had been traditionally conservative, traditionally powerful in the place-
ment of its graduates. But in the wartime cheating and
later such incidents, in classes that would lead America
into another, more furtive war, there was a seed of the
army's inner corruption and atrophy in Vietnam. And in
the shallowness and dilution of learning, the absorption
in routine and technique, there was the precondition to a
military generation's sterile careerism and the savage arro-

gance and ignorance of later policies, a "blissful obliviousness," as two former teachers at West Point wrote later,
by "industrious professionals whose success has little connection with either a greater social good or an ethical
imperative."

Perhaps even more than the two complaisant decades
before, the 1940s were to prove in that sense the locust
years of American military education. The irony was that
in the America that greeted Second Lieutenant Alexander
Haig, Jr., in June 1947, the disillusion was still distant,
and the military profession, fresh from a triumphant war,
rarely in higher repute. For Haig and others, that was part
of what would make the eventual reckoning so bitter.

Haig spent his first months as an officer in a round of
routine postacademy training. First came several months
at army's ground general school at Fort Riley, a dull relic
of the Indian Wars on the central Kansas plain. Having
chosen the cavalry, he was then sent to steamy Fort Knox,
south of Louisville, for the basic armored course in tank
tactics and repair. It was a period of remote postings and
political-military interregnum for an eager young West
Pointer who had joined the service at the height of world
war, and now graduated apparently too late for the battlefield, with its glory and swifter promotion.

Beyond the forts' gates in Kansas and Kentucky, the
nation had demobilized and was returning gladly to
peacetime. There was only a dawning awareness of the
emerging cold war, though its omens punctuated this
first year and a half of Haig's duty. Winston Churchill
had made the "iron curtain" speech while Haig was still

at the academy. The Truman Doctrine, the Marshall Plan, Whittaker Chambers's accusation against Alger Hiss, the Berlin blockade, the Communist coup in Czechoslovakia —all now unfolded while he was at Riley and Knox, inaugurating the rivalry that would ever after channel and propel his career. But the larger shape of that contest was hardly visible in these early postwar days. NATO was yet to be formed, and the vast military budgets and bureaucracies a future undreamed of. The action and plum for shavetails were the occupation forces, and Haig like others managed an assignment. Promoted to first lieutenant, he was ordered to Japan at the end of 1948 to command a First Cavalry rifle platoon.

In Japan, he wore the bright yellow scarf of the famous "First Cav," played on the division football team, and for a time settled into the uneventful, untaxing garrison life of a victorious legion, an occupation languor that army commanders were soon to have reason to regret. Without an old army name and family, without wartime heroics and contacts, academy distinction, or even an elite postwar unit like the paratroops behind him, Haig lacked at the beginning the marks of military caste that might have singled him out, and up, in that setting. But in less than eighteen months after his arrival in Japan, his status as one more occupation-army lieutenant changed dramatically, and with the change his rise began.

At a Tokyo musical recital he met Patricia Fox, a pretty and talented young American pianist. "She was playing Chopin. She was quite good and I was impressed both by the piano playing and her looks," as Haig recalls it, "so I made a point of getting to know her." After a brief courtship, they were married in May 1950, an army photograph of the moment capturing the trim bride in gown and veil beside the earnest, smiling groom in his Eisenhower-jacketed tan uniform, a step slightly ahead as they leave the chapel under crossed swords. Before the ceremony, he had called home, shouting into the trans-Pacific line, "Mother, I'm going to get married!" And back from Regina Haig, her face suddenly tightened as she held the phone, came the anxious, perhaps instinctive Bala-Cynwyd question in a similar shout: "Is she Japanese?"

His mother need scarcely have worried: By the measure behind the question, Patricia Fox Haig was clearly a proper match, the daughter of a high-ranking army general for whom Alexander was now aide-de-camp, and in whose train Haig first entered the heady, coveted halls of high command.

Then fifty-four, Alonzo Fox came from a St. Louis Catholic background, was educated at a parochial academy and college, and, after commission as a lieutenant in the First World War, rose largely by staff skills through the ranks of the interwar and World War II army to major general. In 1947, Fox was assigned to Tokyo as deputy chief of staff to the supreme commander, Allied powers (SCAP), Douglas MacArthur, with whom he first served briefly in the Philippines in the early Twenties. One of the worshipful MacArthur entourage in the Dai Ichi, SCAP's landmark headquarters building in Tokyo, Fox was a dutiful if unexceptional officer on the staff, typically dispatched to Washington to assure a congressional subcommittee in April 1950, two and a half months before the Korean War, that MacArthur's occupation policies had communism in Asia "on the very definite decline."

That spring of his daughter's wedding, such service

had placed Fox, with his powerful chief's patronage, in
line for reward and likely promotion as the new commandant of the prestigious Command and General Staff
School at Fort Leavenworth, one of the army's stepping-
stone jobs from which the last occupant had gone on to
the European Command. Altogether it was a promising
ascent on which he might well have taken along at some
stage his aide and new son-in-law, with rather different
career results for both men. But the Fox appointment to
Leavenworth was announced June 23, 1950. Two days
later, the North Koreans attacked the South, and transfer
was frozen by the war, never to be revived in the ensuing
political turmoil.

If not to Leavenworth or Europe, General Fox did take
Haig across Tokyo into the Dai Ichi at its remarkable
bureaucratic and political zenith. There in 1949–50, Haig
was a junior orderly like any other, drawing up schedules,
assembling and filing documents, laying out and rolling
up maps, observing the routine and prickly pecking order
of the other staff officers, and, above all, catering to the
personal and professional whims of his superiors. The
significance was much less his role or rank than that he
was simply present to see and hear, with the singular
privy access of the aide-de-camp, the conversations, con-
ceits, and general climate of the extraordinary MacArthur
headquarters. It was a decisive early experience for the
young officer, the influence and echoes of that time reaching across twenty years to another, similar "headquarters"
of Richard Nixon.

At the Dai Ichi, Haig enters at least a vaguely familiar
history. In popular imagery, it is that recognizable, not-
so-distant era of wide-lapeled civilians in baggy trousers

standing uncertainly next to generals in well-pressed suntans, some of them Haig's models and superiors. Yet
behind the newsreels and wire photos, the reality of the
men and the politics, as it would be so often in his career,
was far different from the public portrait. Haig called it
the "inner sanctum," and the name is fitting. The demigod
at its center was General of the Army Douglas Mac-
Arthur. The "last of the great colonial overlords," William
Manchester, his biographer, called MacArthur in Tokyo,
and his position *was* awesome. Operating with characteristic latitude under a broad presidential order that "our
authority is supreme" and that he was to exercise it "as
you deem proper," MacArthur ruled with a pervasive, absolute control over the beaten nation of seventy million. No
corner of Nipponese life was beyond his dictate. Empowered as no American officer before or after, he wielded
his civil and military supremacy in sweeping reform and
regeneration of Japan.

The effect on the country was historic, and no less evident on MacArthur's already legendary ego and megalomania. Asked once to brief foreign diplomats in Tokyo,
the general dismissed the request with the imperious
aside, "And why, as a sovereign, should I?" Though technically subordinate to the president and Joint Chiefs back
in Washington, on the scene in the Dai Ichi MacArthur
was nothing less than "a head of government," wrote
William Sebald, the ranking U.S. diplomat in occupied
Japan. In that sense, Haig was given a taste of both the
pomp and the politics of a veritable presidency two
decades before he joined the White House staff.

The essence of the MacArthur achievement in Japan
was a paradox of benevolent despotism. A preening auto-

crat, he nurtured liberal democracy, dissolving the feudal bonds of the old Japan, forging a model constitution, preempting and isolating the local Communists. At the same time, few questioned the military regime's tyrannical grip on the press. Japanese papers were tightly reined, and American reporters could be barred, too, at SCAP's pleasure. "They were there," concluded one historian of the occupation press, "to be used." Nor was there much reflection, then or afterward, on the special, relatively fortuitous setting for the MacArthur "miracle" when set beside Europe or the rest of Asia—the comparative weakness of indigenous Japanese Communists to begin with and their virtual abandonment by the Soviets, who were engaged elsewhere; the spiritual depth of Japan's defeat and the malleability of a subdued culture; the momentary chemistry between MacArthur the natural proconsul and a nation bred to imperial obedience.

Later, when Asia gradually turned from showcase to burial ground for the American army's prestige, those factors that made the Japanese occupation unique, and much of its success inimitable, were often forgotten. For his part, Haig remembered that aspect of the Dai Ichi as a valuable political education. "I was always interested in politics and started early in Japan with a rather sophisticated view of how the military ran it," he told a White House reporter during Watergate. "There was a strong communist influence then," he went on, "and our major consideration was the kind of government which was going to evolve." It had not been "test tube" stuff, he remembered. "This was formed in the vortex of the political situation."

Much of the seething in that "vortex," Haig neglected

to recall, was the jealous, ceaseless jockeying and maneuvering of high-level aides around MacArthur, staff politics
of the sort described in William Manchester's MacArthur
biography *American Caesar* as "more appropriate in Medi-
cean Florence." Ever competing in flattery as well as suspicion of SCAP's enemies in Washington and elsewhere,
MacArthur's twin insatiable appetites, they "poured it
on," said one eyewitness, "and the general ate it up."
They were an uncommon group, these headquarters courtiers for and around whom the young Haig worked. Of
those closest to MacArthur, one openly extolled military
dictatorship, another lionized Franco and his Spanish
fascism, while a third spied on his fellow staff officers. All
joined in a naked cult of MacArthur, whose choice of
subordinates ipso facto was "not reassuring," as one
chronicler put it.

This senior circle included Fox and, still closer to the
throne, Major General Edward "Ned" Almond, who pronounced MacArthur quite simply "the greatest man
alive," and who was to be yet another notable Haig patron. From an old Blue Ridge family of Alsatian ancestry,
Almond traced a career through Virginia Military Institute, the sleepy postings of the Twenties and Thirties, and
a record of gallantry in both world wars, including command of the all-black Ninety-second Division during its
dash through western Italy in 1944. In 1947 he was made
deputy chief of staff of the Far East Command (FECOM
being the U.S. Army's Tokyo headquarters alongside the
separate but analogous allied SCAP, with both under the
supreme commander), and rose to chief of staff two years
later at age fifty-seven, having proved himself a Mac-
Arthur favorite. Variously described by peers and re-

porters as "bilious," "vitriolic," "an insufferable martinet" who "drives himself hard and his subordinates only a shade less," the gray-haired, ruddy Almond was given to addressing other senior officers nearly his own age as "son," and was generally reputed to be "no man to trifle with." To observers of headquarters politics, he was also "the man who hates correspondents," who looked upon both American and foreign diplomats as an "unholy nuisance," and who had thus "taken onto himself some of his autocratic chief's characteristics." A military historian summed up his working formula in simple terms: "When MacArthur proposed, Almond agreed." In the sharp-spoken chief of staff seemed to converge the more dubious characteristics of the Dai Ichi—its slavishness and arrogance, the brusque contempt for civilian authority and the press.

Earlier in 1948, only months before Haig arrived in Japan, such officers around SCAP had been arguing earnestly over which cabinet posts they should choose in Washington after MacArthur took the White House. They were "riding the political horse so vigorously," said Sebald looking on, "that they already had jobs picked out." The pastime ended only with the burst of the general's presidential bubble in that year's Wisconsin primary, though it was typical of a mentality and larger pretense that endured.

This was Haig's first, impressive schooling in the politics of command and administration. Imagine him as the alert, attentive, agreeable young adjutant his superiors found him, listening quietly to the staff gossip about the daily intrigues and exotica of the Dai Ichi, crisply preparing the conference table for meetings and then sitting

in the back of the room to watch the exchanges, standing
dutifully in his boss's office as the general privately vented
his spleen at fellow staff, at Washington, at Haig himself
—taking it all in. As no other headquarters in the army,
it was a novitiate in the arts of the courtier, in fawning
and deceit and self-promotion, amid an arbitrary power
over a submissive public and with open scorn and distrust
of other institutions outside itself, of anyone outside the
sanctum. Everywhere—in the rule of Japan and in the
presidential and cabinet ambitions in Washington—there
was the political presumption, almost prerogative, claimed
by the senior officers, an utter blurring of the American
constitutional boundary between civil and military. If
much later his White House colleagues would wonder at
Haig's phlegmatic acceptance of the outrageous, at his
tolerance of the bizarre as routine, and his seizure of that
routine's opportunities as an intensely political officer, no
one seemed to remember, save Haig himself, that other
sun court of the Dai Ichi.

Absorbed in their staff satrapy, MacArthur and his aides
presided in the spring of 1950 over a slack occupation
army that was unready and understrength for the ordeal
that lay ahead. Two skeleton corps, a field commander
wrote later of units like Haig's First Cavalry, "had been
fat and happy in occupation billets, complete with Japanese girl friends, plenty of beer, and servants to shine
their boots." The postwar army promised its recruits "all
conceivable advantages," recorded one of its official historians, "but never suggested that the principal business of
an army is to fight." When North Korea lunged across the
38th Parallel on June 25, the South's ill-led soldiers were
routed. The U.S. troops that were rushed into the line

from their Japanese pleasures reeled back to a bare foot-
hold around the port of Pusan, retching over their rations
in a dung-spread Korean countryside that in the summer,
as a military writer described it, "steamed and stank like
a giant diaper pail."

In the defeats of these reluctant, unprepared GIs was
the foretaste of a war in which one in three captured
Americans collaborated, and two of every five POWs died,
many at the hands of fellow prisoners. Haig once referred
in passing to the outbreak of the conflict. "I could watch
the factors contributing to the Korean War," he told an
interviewer about the benefits of working in the Dai Ichi.
But there would be no inkling that he saw the larger picture—the land reforms that solidified communist rule in
the North, or the opportunities offered in what was judged
a "harsh and inept" U.S. occupation in the South—and
no trace, then or afterward, of sensibility to the burrowing
decay of army morale and leadership first visible in Korea.

General Almond, whose only son had been killed in Germany two months before the end of World War II, would
periodically rebuke his Korean War aides, among them
Haig, with the bitter question "Why are you alive and he's
dead?" In Haig's case, the literal answer in part was that
he had been spared the early rout and bloody siege of the
Pusan perimeter because he had become aide-de-camp to
his father-in-law. While his original unit, the First Cavalry,
was plugged that summer into the desperate front on the
edge of the peninsula where its infantry platoons and
young officers suffered heavy casualties, Haig and an entourage of twenty-four other staff aides were accompanying Fox on a mission to Formosa to set up, in the wake of

a controversial MacArthur visit there, a liaison mission with Chiang Kai-shek.

"I had to go to Taiwan," Haig once said, without elaboration, to explain what he had done after his Japanese honeymoon. As it happened, the mission was also vintage Dai Ichi politics. SCAP imperiously neglected to inform Secretary of State Dean Acheson of the "details" of its highly political embassy to a foreign government. It led, of course, to a further poisoning of the military-civil rivalry, and was scarcely the last time Alexander Haig as an obscure deputy was to know about crucial foreign-policy moves and fateful diplomacy well before the secretary of state.

He entered the war in the autumn of 1950 in a flurry of new patronage. To command the newly formed X Corps marshaling to land at Inchon, MacArthur named his favorite, Almond, who in turn was Fox's friend. Haig now promptly moved from his father-in-law to work for the churlish Almond in a coveted aide's job on the "handpicked" X Corps headquarters staff. A military history of the subsequent battles judges the appointment of Almond and his Dai Ichi retinue "an act of military nepotism" in which MacArthur "erred gravely." But for the moment there seemed only dash and glory as the general prepared to hurl the X Corps onto the beach at Inchon, just west of Seoul and 150 miles behind enemy lines, in a daring flanking move that would, at a stroke, reverse and win the war. Haig's Korea was to be a war of movement and drama in its first months, before the fighting wore into the savage stalemate of the last two years. Inchon was the high point of that opening period.

As usual with MacArthur, there were bureaucratic as well as martial exploits. From the vantage point of the corps staff, Haig watched the general wave aside, then win over, a formidable array of doubting officers from the Joint Chiefs, navy and marines who opposed the landing for strategic or topographical reasons. To those who brought their misgivings to Almond, the new commander muttered a terse, typically acid "not interested," and the invasion plans proceeded. It was yet another demonstration, with thousands of lives at stake if not the fate of the war, of the Dai Ichi's iron sway.

In the event, the Inchon assault at dawn on September 15, 1950, was a brilliant vindication of their power—and, of its kind, the last. As MacArthur expected, the First Marines swept through a surprised enemy to capture the key Kimpo Airport in two days, and the army's Seventh Infantry pursued to cut off Seoul and the North Korean Army to the south. About Haig's own role in the landing there were two common stories. The first, which he later enjoyed telling younger men as an illustration of a staff officer's sacrifices, was that he had waded ashore at Inchon, water up to his chest, holding aloft MacArthur's sleeping bag, only to find that the general would not sleep there that night, and later to catch pneumonia from the soaking. According to the second, Almond, Haig, and other aides stopped ashore to pose for a combat photographer. Moments after the party moved on, an enemy shell exploded where they had stood, what one magazine writer called "the first of several near-misses" in Haig's "charmed life."

In fact, MacArthur, the seventy-year-old supreme commander, never planned to camp out on the beachhead. And it was almost less credible that Haig, a X Corps junior aide now relatively removed from the general's suite, and with the corps headquarters staff aboard an entirely different transport in the Inchon Harbor, would have carried any of SCAP's baggage in any case. (The bag might have been Almond's, though he, too, was billeted more comfortably with MacArthur apart from his X Corps staff, slept aboard ship the first night, and was not so Spartan a general. But then even with Almond, the story, and Haig's relation to MacArthur, would have been much less impressive.)

Nor do several official or other detailed accounts of the operation corroborate Almond's, and Haig's, near-miss after a photograph. The documented reality seems more prosaic, less heroic but nonetheless expressive. In this, Haig's first combat operation, his father-in-law, General Fox, was nearby, along with Almond attending MacArthur aboard the brass-laden flagship *Mt. McKinley*. Moreover, when the X Corps headquarters later disembarked, the fighting having moved miles inland from Inchon, it landed with Almond's personal van, "rigged," a marine colonel recorded, "with refrigerator, hot running water, electricity, shower and flush toilet," albeit apparently no sleeping bag. There were also, according to corps records, other "amenities" as Almond and his aides took command ashore, including "fine Japanese china" for which fresh food was brought daily from navy ships in the harbor, and "a spit-and-polish ceremonial honor guard."

Inchon was a stunning victory, "a twentieth-century cannae ever to be studied," conceded a high-ranking army skeptic back in Washington. But the sequel Haig saw from X Corps headquarters was bloodier than necessary, and

campaign histories were not kind to Almond and his Dai
Ichi–hatched staff. Still intent on the bold stroke, "or at
least the announcement of it," as one analyst wrote, Almond pressed on Seoul and its fanatic defenders rather
than investing the city and more slowly forcing its surrender at less cost. "A political undertone underlay all the
tactical planning," a marine aide remembers of Almond's
staff conferences. The result was savage house-to-house
fighting with nearly a thousand U.S. casualties days after
the city's capture had been announced, "a holocaust," said
one account, "through which the First Marine Division
had to pass."

On September 25, the day of Almond's bitterly premature claim on Seoul, Haig was winning a Bronze Star for
valor—though that, too, would be somewhat at odds with
later records. Impatient with the advance of leading
marine units, Almond ordered the army's Thirty-second
Infantry across the Han River south of Seoul, and Haig to
reconnoiter "observation posts and routes of advance." In
the dawn crossing, Haig was afterward cited by Almond
for "outstanding heroism" and "fearless conduct in a position of great responsibiilty" while securing the observation
posts and routes of advance in "areas which were under
enemy machine gun, sniper, and mortar fire."

If the words of the official citation suggested pitched
battle, however, Robert Heinl's *Victory at High Tide: The
Seoul-Inchon Campaigns*—a history drawn from eyewitness accounts, other official documents, and Almond's own
subsequent recollections—leaves another picture. "Resistance was negligible," Heinl recounts of the initial cross-
ings; once on the other bank, they encountered "no enemy

resistance"; and a following South Korean regiment "also crossed with scant opposition."

The official army history similarly recounts that the Han crossing "surprised the North Koreans," was accomplished "without loss of personnel or equipment," that enemy "works" in the area were "lightly manned," and that major action did not take place until a predawn counterattack against the U.S. forces well across the river the following morning. The question of Haig's citation seems all the more nagging given Almond's headlong political pursuit of X corps headquarters glory in Seoul, in which the vigor and decorations of his own staff were reflected on the commander. Then, too, there would soon be another noted incident in the war in which Almond hurriedly pinned on decorations for his own reasons, whatever the actual circumstances.

Meanwhile, Almond continued the fight in and around Seoul, his headquarters later to incur critics' wrath for a "poor record" in providing combat support, "dilatory" coordination of his divisions, and even "a novice's blunder" in issuing orders for a potentially disastrous night attack outside the capital "with totally faulty map coordinates." With the final taking of the city, the Truman White House singled out several commanders for praise, but not Almond, confirming the orthodox Dai Ichi staff view of Washington's myopia. And beyond this unappreciated victory for Haig's current patron, worse was yet to come.

Caught between Almond's Inchon force and the U.S. Eighth Army breaking out of the Pusan perimeter, the North Korean invading army broke and its battered relics fled back across the 38th Parallel. Plunging north after

them in fateful pursuit went first the South Koreans at the
beginning of October, and then their American deliverers.
The decision to take the war into the satellite state and
to the frontier of China would be long and acidly debated
afterward, but at the time it was no act of battlefield
caprice. Washington's intelligence agencies as well as
MacArthur discounted Chinese intervention, and the subject was raised only perfunctorily at an astonishingly fey
Wake Island meeting between Truman and MacArthur,
both men fixed on their respective political and bureaucratic prerogatives. When U.S. troops sped north that
autumn after a fleeing enemy, it was also with the formal
blessing of both the Pentagon and the ostensible political
sponsor, the United Nations. The point would be worth
remembering when the ensuing debacle brought the inevitable blame in which Haig's army saw its own blunders
less clearly, and its self-exonerating civilian critics as all
the more treacherous, for the original decision's having
been unanimous. Said one cooler observer looking back:
They had all suffered "a bad case of victory fever."

Strategically cursed from the start, the invasion plan
pushed the Eighth Army up the western side of the Korean
peninsula while Almond's X Corps climbed north along
the eastern rim, the two forces sidling together to join on
the Yalu River bordering China. In hostile territory, the
already jealous, uncoordinated commands would be di-
vided by the central massif of North Korea, violating one
of the oldest axioms of war and inviting a concentrated
blow at either or both of the separate columns. With
palpable "tension" between the two "snarling" staffs that
would later dot the historians' postmortem, Almond and
his aides embarked from Inchon in a sealift of the corps

around Korea, setting up headquarters on October 20 at the captured eastern port of Wonsan, a hundred miles north of the Parallel, and later at Hungnam, another port fifty miles further up the coast. There Haig tended to the commander's well-stocked headquarters billet, rolled out the maps, and, with the ten officers and thirty enlisted men of the corps staff, watched the disaster unfold.

What followed can be traced in a brief chronolgy. In the days after his October 20 arrival, Almond sent his force of 84,000 men, one-third Korean, in a series of scattered files up the narrow valleys rising north from the coastal plain. So confident were the Americans that the First Cavalry, Haig's former unit now similarly advancing in the west, returned some of its equipment to Japan for an expected victory parade in Tokyo on Thanksgiving Day. On October 26, Almond ordered the X Corps onward, though the night before a South Korean corps had been virtually annihilated in a pocket of the western front by what was thought to have been not retreating North Koreans but a major Chinese unit. Three days later, as the bomber command in Tokyo announced it had "run out of targets," the X Corps took Chinese prisoners in its own eastern sector, quilted soldiers who spoke neither Japanese nor Korean and whom Almond interrogated personally, cabling MacArthur that the Chinese "might" have crossed the Yalu in "division strength."

In fact, the captives were part of four Chinese armies which had crossed the river before Almond and Haig disembarked at Wonsan, a force swelling to 180,000 by the end of October and soon to 300,000. Through the first three weeks of November, the fighting sank into a deceptive lull as MacArthur's intelligence stoutly denied the evidence of an enemy it had already precluded. "If, as General Almond says, these people turn out to be Chinese—" a Dai Ichi staff officer began at a November conference at X Corps headquarters. "What do you mean 'if'?" Almond barked back. "They *are* Chinese!" But the signs would go on being misread, excused, ignored.

On November 21, an American unit reached the Yalu, and Almond, with a cable of "heartiest congratulations" from MacArthur, exultantly left Haig's billet and flew up to stand for photographers on the heights above the river, peering at the Chinese village and its sentries fifty yards away. Over the next few days, in the valleys and plateaus to the southeast around the Chosin Reservoir, the fragmented American columns walked forward in temperatures diving to 10 or 20 degrees below zero, freezing food, weapons, plasma, and flesh on a rock-hard ground. Fretting over their advance, Almond hurried them on.

The blow fell on November 27. Under what survivors remembered as a great "gibbous" moon, ten Chinese divisions slammed into the First Marines and an army task force of the Thirty-second Infantry, the unit that had crossed the Han so uneventfully two months before with Haig's reconnaissance. After a night and day of furious fighting, Almond helicoptered into the task force command post the afternoon of the 28th. In a brief conference, he told the colonel leading the force that he had three Silver Stars in his pocket, one for the colonel and the rest for anyone he selected. Bitterly, the colonel picked the first men within reach, a wounded lieutenant and a mess sergeant, and as the three stood at attention with other battle-dazed men behind them, Almond pinned on the medals with a remarkable little speech. "The enemy who is delaying you for the moment is nothing more than the remnants of Chinese divisions fleeing north," he told the stricken unit. In the Dai Ichi staff mind, there would be no other but Chinese divisions "fleeing north," much as diplomats were a "nuisance" and the press to be "hated." "We're still attacking and we're going all the way to the Yalu," Almond finished. "Don't let a bunch of Chinese laundry-men stop you."

As Almond's helicopter rose to leave, the colonel ripped off the decoration and flung it into the snow, muttering to an aide, "You heard him, remnants fleeing north!"

"I got me a Silver Star," the wounded lieutenant cried to a friend nearby, "but I don't know what the hell for."

Within hours the colonel was dead, and the task force, nearly half its 2,500 men lost, dissolved under the Chinese assault.

His headquarters at last stirred, Almond flew off that same evening for an emergency midnight conference at the Dai Ichi, where he was told to "consolidate" his forces and halt the U.S. "advance." At another Tokyo council three days later, he and his staff were "ever-sanguine" and talked quixotically of some flanking blow in the Chinese rear. On December 6, Army Chief of Staff J. Lawton Collins flew into X Corps headquarters, which Haig and the other staff had moved inland to Hamhung. There, on the edge of the mountains where his American army was trapped, Collins found Almond "confident."

It was all empty posturing. In the forty miles to the north, 20,000 marines and GIs were desperately running a frozen bloody gauntlet of 100,000 Chinese troops in one of the most brutal retreats in history. They survived, not by the generalship that put them there but by constant precious air support, extraordinary bravery, and bold junior leadership. They broke out miraculously, carrying their wounded and dead as well as weapons and vehicles. And as they marched, some sang a black, incredibly prophetic song to the tune of the old British "Bless 'Em All." "But we're saying goodbye to them all, we're Harry's police force on call," went the lyric, "so put back your pack on, the next stop is Saigon. Cheer up, me lads, bless 'em all." When they came down to the sanctuary of the coastal perimeter on December 9, the toll was ghastly. In a typical company there were 23 men left out of 180. "Everyone was wrong," Collins reflected tersely on the Chinese attack.

At Hungnam, where Almond had moved Haig and the headquarters once again, the X Corps prepared for its Dunkirk. Shielded by air cover and naval gunfire, over 100,000 troops, nearly that many civilian refugees, and tons of materiel were air- and sea-lifted out of the surrounded port, which was fired and left to the enemy on Christmas Eve 1950. But before the debacle was complete, there was one last Haig story to be played out. As Haig told it, the headquarters billet had an impressive tile bathtub, and at the last moment of evacuation he had been ordered to brave enemy fire to go back and throw a grenade in the tub "so no stinking Chinese general would get a bath that night." Once again, in Haig's version he was aide to MacArthur and it was the supreme commander's tub, though obviously it could only have been Almond's. In his later Korean tales, he would almost always be MacArthur's aide. There is no military history depicting the young aide dashing back through the burning, abandoned Hungnam with a grenade to pitch in a bathtub while the navy waited anxiously in the harbor.

Perhaps. Apocryphal or not, it almost fits the character of that doomed campaign.

Almond and his aides were evacuated to Pusan, where the X Corps was placed in humbled reserve to its rival and equally routed Eighth Army, and where the Eighth's new commander, Matthew Ridgeway, found Haig and his colleagues the day after Christmas a "dispirited command" with "a gloomy foreboding, a spirit of apprehension as to what the future held."

By February, though, the corps was back at the front in central Korea, the battle line having sagged in the winter retreat some fifty miles or more below the 38th Parallel. Here, in action covering the same week in mid-February, Almond was promoted to lieutenant general, Haig was given by his commander a Silver Star for gallantry in "repeated flights at low altitudes in a light-type aircraft over enemy-infested territory" amid "repeated exposure to hostile enemy [sic] fire." Three months later, as the front crept northward in a slow cadence of attack and counterattack that now became the pattern of the war, he won a second Silver Star from Almond. Once again it was for a reconnaissance flight "in a light unarmed aircraft at low altitude subjecting himself to enemy small arms and automatic weapons fire," and this time with the record showing the commander at his side. Flying over the front and finding Chinese troops ahead of a U.S. tank patrol, Almond and Haig ordered their spotter plane landed near the patrol and turned over to the tank-platoon leader for an aerial look himself at the enemy positions. Then, according to the citation, while Haig and Almond stayed with the tanks, a Chinese machine gun opened fire on the column, and the aide "accompanied the Commanding

General in directing the tank fire which silenced the weapon." Of the eight medals he would later wear for valor in Korea and Vietnam, four would come, like this one, while Haig "accompanied" a senior officer.

A month before, however, on April 11, 1951, came the event that had been perhaps inevitable since the war began: Truman's dismissal of MacArthur. The immediate cause was the general's public scorn for the restrictions on the bombing of Manchuria and the "unleashing" of Chiang Kai-shek, but the issue went deeper than tactics, to matters of national policy, presidential power, and personal rancor. The climax of lapse and folly on both sides, the recall was one of those acts by which eras are marked, in this case the poisoning of domestic politics for a generation by a stymied war and the new frustrations of foreign policy. Ironically, in Haig's case, it produced a political frenzy in America—what he might have called later a "fire storm"—largely unmatched until more than twenty-two years later, when Haig and *his* president would relieve Special Prosecutor Archibald Cox to a similar public outcry. Among its far-reaching implications was the further impetus it lent at the time to a coming young senator from California. "The happiest group in the country," Richard Nixon said typically of MacArthur's recall, "will be the Communists and their stooges."

In Korea, the impact was swift. For Almond, as for other creatures of the Dai Ichi, the news was "sickening" and his career predetermined in the harsh patronage politics of the army. In July he was relieved from the X Corps, served briefly as commandant of the Army War College, and soon went into obscure retirement, where he lived to eighty-six and to see Haig command NATO. Fox was similarly

shunted to a superfluous Pentagon job, never again to hold
a high staff command, though later in some position still
to help his son-in-law along. Haig himself, ill with hepatitis, returned from Korea in 1951 within weeks of his
patrons. The war bled on for two more years, hemorrhaging casualties along a fixed front that MacArthur had
sought to avoid, and ending nearly on the prewar boundary demarking petty tyrannies typical of the two sides'
client states: in the drab North, brutal party zealots; in
the tawdry South, military dictators.

"I learned a lot out there," Haig would say of his time
in Japan and Korea. Watching his later White House style
from a polite distance, the *Washington Post* thought his
"penchant for round-tabling issues with many people" was
a reaction to what he had "regarded as the excessively
hierarchal staff system used by MacArthur." But there was
little evidence of either the "penchant" or the opinion.
Instead, when he spoke of MacArthur, he waxed nostalgic
for the stature and autonomy of SCAP. "He was one of a
dying breed of American bureaucrats," Haig told one
interviewer, using in praise a term MacArthur threw only
derisively at his Washington enemies. "He was a very accomplished American leader, at the end of a generation of
leaders who could operate largely on their own." They had
been "highly independent, self-assured, competent, and
become the focal point of policy in that part of the world,"
he went on. "They were able to operate with a degree of
independence no longer acceptable. Faster communications and public communications—the press—changed all
this. It's a worrisome phenomenon to me," he concluded.
"It's more difficult for our system to produce this kind of
guy, or for him to survive." As for Truman, Haig thought

him "one of the greatest presidents," though "some of his decisions in the Korean conflict . . . gave me gas pains."

It was at best a revealing but spare reflection on what he had seen so closely in the Dai Ichi and in the field, from Inchon to Hungnam to the recall—the lying and evasion with the press; the bickering and megalomania of his superiors; the rewards of seemingly blind, cynical, loyalty to men who were later the contemptuous butt of war stories; the blunders and blunderers hidden.

The unwon battle in Korea was the unwelcome harbinger of a new postwar world and the beginning of ambiguity and uncertainty for young officers like Haig, of brokered, political wars that reeked of defeat. It was not only or even mainly the military, of course, that derived ominous lessons from what was yet so strange and so threatening. From the specter of stalemate and a "lost" Asia, the deposed Democratic party would draw back in a self-conscious chauvinism, virtually never to recover. But it was the army, Haig's army, that took its "defeat" hardest. Korea set the stage for the decade of "massive retaliation" with its unheroic missiles and retrenchment of field forces. And in the army's eclipse, there grew a new theology of limited war, a new preoccupation with bureaucratic advantage, and a further moldering of the military art, which would make Korea a parent of Vietnam. It was to be a melancholy destiny for West Point classes like "Alex" Haig's. Trained to the command posts of a victorious army, thrusting confidently across the plains of Europe, they would find themselves instead in the bitter hills or unconquerable jungles of mainland Asia, fighting not crusades or even campaigns, but furtive, haunted colonial skirmishes with only uncertain backing at home.

In the end, however, there would be perhaps one nice irony, almost a vindication, though MacArthur and Almond would not live to see it. One day in the very seat of their nemesis, the Achesons and the meddling civilian bureaucrats at State, would be one of their own boys, a graduate of the Dai Ichi, the young aide who, it was said, had gone back there in Hungnam to take care of Ned Almond's tile tub.

In the hegira of officers after Korea, Haig spent more than a decade in obscure army postings. It was the itinerant life of the junior professional soldier in peacetime, restlessly · moving where promising slots were open or where assignments dictated. Intent on the upward career man's résumé sum of experiences, credentials, and contacts rather than on any sustained accomplishment, he was never more than two years in any single job and rarely that long. In the now grim, now decent officers' housing along the way, the Haigs quickly had their children— Alexander, Brian, and Barbara—over the five years after their father's return from the war.

On the surface, the 1950s would be a relatively placid era, a foreign-policy Thermidor after the traumas of Korea. Europe, where no unwieldly client armies marched against the status quo, became again the more manageable, more reassuring focus of attention. Berlin threats, the Hungarian uprising, Suez, the marines in Lebanon—all came and went for America as limited spasms, essentially confirming the new limits of action on both sides of the cold war. France's distant torment in Indochina was soon papered over by Geneva diplomacy and supplanted by Algeria.

Cuba was for most of the period still a raucous vacation spot and investment opportunity in the Caribbean. Washington orthodoxy took for granted Stalinist ferocity by his successors, who in their weakness were about to soften it, and the solidity of the Sino-Soviet Alliance, which was already badly cracking.

At home, the outwardly torpid Eisenhower regime, emblem of the decade, quietly ignited CIA intrigues in a half-dozen places from Guatemala to Saigon. Thought by administration critics to be part of the apparent lassitude, the Pentagon grew relentlessly as both arsenal and bureaucracy, what a former defense secretary wearily called "a glandular thing." For the army, too, its budgets shriveled, this seemed a time of disuse. Military after-dinner speakers were fond of quoting the old British epitaph: "In time of peace when all is righted, God is forgotten and the soldier slighted." Yet the instrument itself was believed invincible, and the Korean stalemate the fault of political meddling. Of the army's basic World War II prestige there was still in the Fifties no widespread doubt, if only the mission were clear.

Meanwhile, as one mordant participant watched, the Democrats' foreign-policy makers in opposition anxiously competed to show their own post-Korean, anticommunist stoutness in contrast to the appeasements of Eisenhower and Dulles. It was a "thought-denying process," John Kenneth Galbraith remembered of the periodic meetings with Acheson and others to plan the policies of the next, hoped-for Democratic president, "not that the issue was debated and the wrong position taken; it was rather that there was no debate." Looking back on such shadow government, and on the illusion and reality of the decade against what followed, journalist Theodore White was to characterize the 1950s as "incubating the storm."

In Haig, like the country, the events of the otherwise dull decade took on importance in terms of the unexpected moment and turbulence in his future. In the ten years after Korea, he got in swift succession his only real administrative experience with an organization, as apart from being a personal aide, before being charged to run the White House staff and later the State Department; his sole practice as a working negotiator with a foreign power before becoming America's foreign minister; his only command of troops before being given more than a thousand men to lead in the midst of a war; his sole exposure to Europe before being made supreme Allied commander for the Continent.

Promoted to captain the previous October in the flush days before the retreat from North Korea, and still weakened by hepatitis, he returned to the U.S. later in 1951, once again to Fort Knox, to take command of a tank company of the 131st Armored Tactical Battalion. There he stayed through 1952, one more Korean veteran despite his lofty headquarters background. In 1953, he went through the thirty-six-week advanced armored school at the fort— a sequel to his prewar training there in the tactics and technology of the tank. But in the early Fifties, with conventional nuclear weapons still largely on the drawing board, the course devoted only a few hours to nuclear warfare, the subject that would dominate tank tactics two decades later when Haig, with no added training in it, was to command whole armored divisions in NATO. For a time it seemed he might remain in armor, drawing another company command. But at West Point, a much-decorated

Korean veteran was the new commandant and looking for tactical officers with "enviable combat records." Boosted by Almond, who knew the current academy superintendent, Blackshear Bryan, a former West Point football coach and frontline general in Korea, Haig got one of the jobs in the summer of 1953.

The school where he now became a disciplinary officer with the 1802 Cadet Regiment had changed little since Haig left it. The major curriculum reforms of the decade were still ahead under a more reflective superintendent than the hale Bryan. The corps was still excessively harried in the perpetual cycle of hazing by its vengeful upperclassmen and young graduate drillmasters like Haig, for whom their conformity, however pointless or distracting, now meant career advancement. Confined as well to a narrow, shallow academic channel, cadets and the officers they became were at least freed, as a former academy professor put it, "from the frequently troublesome chore of deciding for themselves what is worth doing."

From Haig's individual record as a "tac" during the Fifties, there was the enduring image of an ordinary spit-and-polish army martinet, with no apparent quality of mind to mark him as a future general. Surveying the factors in army success, writer Maureen Mylander found young officers in the early Seventies—Haig's former company cadets from these years—who were "surprised" at his later rapid promotions. "Practically the only thing he talked about as a tactical officer was shining shoes," remembered one of them. "He had a fixation on appearance as a way to get ahead in the army, and the cadet perception of Haig was, you know, this guy is strictly in left field," his former student told Mylander. "He'll never make it [we thought] . . . lieutenant colonel, full colonel maybe, that sort of thing. But smarts! We thought he was non-intellectual. . . ."

In his own official State Department biography, Haig hurried over these two West Point years with the phrase "a variety of military assignments." At the same time, he would be at pains to point out that he had "'pursued graduate studies in business administration at Columbia University in 1954–55." A part-time course sandwiched between his duties up the Hudson, the record of his enrollment later lost in the maw of Columbia records, the term "graduate studies" clearly stretched a point, and apparently would have surprised the cadets he was policing. But like so much else, it would be there ever afterward, impressive if vague in Haig's file. It was one more certifying jot for future employers looking for an earnest, cerebral young officer, and who would not see that other, more intimate and caustic cadet view of his mediocrity.

From West Point he moved briefly to Annapolis to become an "executive officer," or, more prosaically, a staff aide in the school administration during the academic year 1955–56. One of the junior interservice jobs that dot the military bureaucracy, honoring unification of the branches on paper and in the breach, the duty was trivial but another line of apparent breadth on the record. Like West Point, Annapolis changed its stolid seminary tradition, said a scholar, only "with painful hesitancy," and Haig passed through it well before the post-1959 reforms stirred by *Sputnik* and the piercing criticism of a powerful alumnus impatient with the academic backwardness, Admiral Hyman Rickover. A few years later at either academy, Haig might have experienced a fresh ferment and questioning, even as a lower-grade staff man with no academic role. At that, there is no reason to assume the changes at the institutions would have altered his own views; twenty years later when Vietnam released a torrent of military soul-searching and self-criticism, much of it by officers of Haig's rank and age, he would stand cautiously and almost obliviously aside. But in that sense the West Point and Annapolis years were still—though the reality was again unseen in the résumé—missed opportunities.

In the summer of 1956, he was posted to Europe for what would be three years abroad and, unaccountably, another chunk of his background he rarely advertised. He omitted Europe altogether, for instance, from his biography in later editions of the *West Point Register of Graduates*, the much-thumbed career chart for academy alumni. During the first year, he held a low-level assignment, routine for his rank, as operations officer of the 899th Tank Battalion. A promotion to major came on schedule while he was on battalion staff in May 1957, the yield of his unblemished rounds at Knox and the academies. Otherwise, the tour was uneventful.

Both the quiet and the promotion were tokens of the time. The American army in Europe, a Senate committee would learn much later in officers' testimony, was becoming "a dragon with a huge tail and tiny teeth," with a preference for relatively "soft living" on the Continent and a surplus of special duty and rank. There had been a lieutenant colonel in charge of hunting and fishing in Europe, for example, and a brigadier general commanding the rigors of the post-exchange system. With far fewer men overall and a much smaller percentage of combat forces, the army of the 1950s was also on the way to having thousands more officers at every grade than at the height of World War II. From the bloat begun in these years, of which Haig's promotions were part, officers in Vietnam, as observers noted, would later be "literally tripping over each other."

As it happened, Haig's only mark in Europe involved matters of economy, albeit not in excess officers. In mid-December 1957, he was transferred to be a staff officer at the headquarters Logistics Division of the U.S. European Command near Stuttgart. There he was thrown into banal but barbed negotiations over the exchange of facilities between the U.S. forces and the rebuilding West German Army: At a moment when money and space were tight, the Germans were being pushed by Washington to retrain and rearm, even at the expense of what had been American installations.

The talks and trading consumed nearly a year and a half. When Haig left the job in the spring of 1959, he had won a commendation medal for what the citation called in typical army prose "remarkable foresight, ingenuity, and mature judgment" in dickering with the Germans and in helping to develop "a more . . . realistic picture of the overall utilization of facilities" and "an improvement in the percentage of utilization." Beyond the question of space loomed much more serious logistics issues between Bonn and Washington, future quarrels over offsetting the costs of U.S. forces in Germany and coordination of weaponry and policy. Such issues were only a glimmer at the close of the Fifties, and Haig at most could have only glimpsed them. Yet his functional experience in Stuttgart juggling billets with German staff counterparts was to be the only authentic task of diplomatic bargaining and actual administration of men and materiel in his background before he became both a celebrated diplomat and administrator. Henceforth, his diplomacy and management would be confined to the intimate inner offices of Washington.

Haig's nomadic career in the Fifties reflected what was happening in a large sense to the post-Korea military. There was "no substitute for victory," MacArthur had written a congressman in the letter that finally prodded Truman to fire him. But the army now found one, at least in part, in the warm bath of a careerist, managerial ethic. Ruled increasingly over the century by its multiplying bureaucracy of modern war, and correspondingly inhospitable to the officer as individual, the army had already become, of course, a vast, sclerotic organization. But the eclipse after Korea seemed to give that process a new intensity. Vaguely yet suddenly unsure of itself in the postwar armed peace, the profession struggled to redefine its place, and reassure its survival. Beginning with the striving for class rank at the academy, or merely for a West Point ring, that struggle in the 1950s created more and more what one critic called the "formlessly ambitious" officer, climbing in the army and coming to treat it as any other corporate organization, "as eager to become chairman of the board . . . as to make general. . . ."

In a sense, it was a hoary military tradition, what Charles de Gaulle had deplored in the French Army between the world wars as "the passion for rank and honors" that was "only careerism." To that, the American army now added the fetish and pseudoscience of "management," commanded by a warrior astride desks, paper flow, and the new numerology of budgets and weapons systems. "The pursuit of the good staff life, rather than troop command, became the goal of nearly every aspiring young career officer," said Edward King, a colonel who reflected on these trends in the Fifties, and who entitled his book accordingly *The Death of the Army*. "Duty, honor, country," the academy credo, was replaced, wrote another high-ranking participant in the process, "by the need to be in the right job at the right time."

Known as "ticket punching" by its practitioners and victims, the prescribed formula for success included all the rites of passage of the old army, such as obedient wives, conformity, and contacts, along with the modern attributes of graduate degrees, high-level staff duty, a variety of assignments (thought to ensure versatility), and what one embittered combat colonel later called "a necessary but minimal amount" of field duty. The unsurprising products were officers pursuing rank as an end in itself, who in their cultivated superficiality had little sense of what it might be for, other than to reach the next rung. While grasping, everyone agreed, there was one immutable law of survival: Cover your ass.

The toll in integrity and sophistication was equally plain. Where credentials were merely accumulated, officers' efficiency reports became uniformly inflated and meaningless. Service graduate schools like the War Colleges became pro forma, and sank to the "usually superficial and vapid," found an inquiring observer. Most of all, management itself, the faith and practice of the new creed, became the first casualty of the institutional shallowness and self-protection. Winners in the system grew inevitably cynical, losers contemptuous of superiors, nongraduates often and justifiably training their disillusion on a West

Point they mocked as the South Hudson Institute of Technology—SHIT.

Outwardly led by the shining and creased airborne clique from World War II, the army of the Fifties was being eaten away by an atrophy of both ethics and the military art. There would be no Clausewitz in that army, said Ward Just surveying its wreckage a decade afterward, "because the writing of *Von Krieg (On War)* took time and serious thought." This postwar bureaucratic decadence and decay overtook several great arms of government, not least the State Department and Foreign Service, where the effects were similar and the introspection and honesty afterward ironically less open and even less cleansing than that of the military. But then, Haig's was not simply another organization or bureaucracy. As Vietnam was soon to demonstrate, such craven ethos in an army—whose business, Korea had reminded its recruits, is to fight—would be lethal.

This inner withering of the army shaped one condition of Haig's rise in and beyond the 1950s. A fifty-eight-year-old retired general, Haig's former academy superintendent, satisfied another. Under the presidency of a man who perhaps knew his army too well, the Eisenhower years had been the golden age of the air force in national strategy and budgets. As missiles and bombers collected behind the policy of "massive retaliation," army force levels, appropriations, and prestige declined by comparison. But it was only "the old air power dogma set forth in Madison Avenue trappings," grumbled a former army chief of staff who set out to prove the national peril in slighting his branch.

As Haig returned from Europe at the close of the Fifties,

the army's ideological search for a new post-Korean mission centered on Maxwell Davenport Taylor, a Missouri country boy made good by way of West Point; Japanese-language training; accidental transfer to, and subsequent heroism in, the vaunted airborne; post-MacArthur command of the Eighth Army in Korea; and accession to the Joint Chiefs in the mid-1950s. Taylor, rather like Haig, was an officer of ordinary capacities destined nonetheless for extraordinary authority and influence. Handsome, beribboned, pensive-looking, at ease in mufti and with civilians, he was a reputed military intellectual who could unabashedly speak of the shah's repressive Iranian troops as among "the armies of freedom" and of a wider world in which, as he told a West Point audience on the eve of the Vietnam debacle, "the ascendancy of American arms and American military concepts is accepted as matter of course." Taylor, as David Halberstam wrote, was the "right officer," his powerful political patrons would believe, "for the American century."

He proposed to correct the errors of "massive retaliation," and incidentally rescue the army, by a new orthodoxy of "limited wars" fought with a "strategy of flexible response." He defined his breakthrough in his celebrated 1959 book *Uncertain Trumpet* as "the need for a capability to react across the entire spectrum of possible challenge, for coping with anything from general atomic war to infiltration and aggressions such as threaten Laos and Berlin in 1959." On whether the United States could practically or should politically cope "with anything," Taylor did not elaborate. The point, after all, was "capability" (read bigger, better army), and limited wars, or newly created forces chafing to be used, would presumably take care of themselves. It would be necessary, though, "to deter or win quickly" in limited wars, he wrote, dictating an overwhelming application of men and weaponry to smother the "brush fire." "Otherwise," the book continued in a passage Taylor and his admirers tended to overlook, "the limited war which we cannot win quickly may result in our piecemeal attrition. . . ."

The theme, minus this gloomy caveat, enjoyed swift vogue with the new Democratic candidate in 1960, and once in the White House, John Kennedy summoned Taylor to become a special adviser. Its crippling careerism still too close to be seen, Haig's army thus readied itself in theory to fight the neglected prospect, a limited war of attrition. And if Haig's old idol of the Dai Ichi, the ghostly MacArthur now in retirement in New York's Waldorf-Astoria, recalled the virtues of maneuver against huge, lumbering forces, and the inherent political limits on such peripheral wars, no one seemed to notice.

Haig came home from the logistics negotiations in Stuttgart in the summer of 1959 for one of the stints of schooling recommended for the new, eclectic managerial officer. Of twelve years on duty since leaving West Point, he had spent more than a third of his assignments in military courses or staff jobs around the academies. Excepting the part-time business study at Columbia, though, this would be his first postgraduate education that could be called academic. At thirty-five, he put on the prescribed civilian clothes and joined the junior class of the command and staff course at the Naval War College, where one in five students was non-navy and his earlier Annapolis contacts had eased his entry.

The oldest of the war colleges, the school was the scene of historic lectures by Captain Alfred Thayer Mahan, whose prolix naval theories had propelled American jingoists into Asia and the Caribbean at the turn of the century. The reservation was a graceful interlude of weathered white stone architecture, manicured lawns, and the obligatory ornamental cannon, all situated on the islet of Coasters Harbor across a causeway from Newport, Rhode Island. But also typical of the service colleges, the ten-month junior course, which concentrated on naval warfare and staff routine, was unremarkable. Beyond the incremental status for him in simply having been there, Haig and the college left no lasting trace on one another. While at Newport, he did press the Pentagon for further time to go on for a master's degree in international affairs—an increasingly common punch in the ticket—and when approvals came through in the spring of 1960, he prepared to enroll the following autumn at Georgetown University in Washington.

A Jesuit school on the bluffs above the Potomac in northwest Washington, Georgetown was known in Haig's chosen field mainly for its School of the Foreign Service, a prescribed four-year undergraduate curriculum for prospective diplomats that was reminiscent of the military academies in its vocational approach and never in the first rank of such university programs. The institution would enjoy something of a revival in the mid-1970s in basketball teams and in foreign-policy prominence, with an influx of conservative money and accompanying academics, some of whom would later advise Secretary Haig. But in 1960, Georgetown lacked even that distinction in international studies, the school's chief virtue being the unacademic contacts in the Washington bureaucracy, down the river.

Haig moved through an undemanding master's program with average performance. He got the degree at the beginning of 1962 and was remembered by younger fellow students as a sometimes "condescending" officer of decided views. This time, however, he left behind as well a more tangible trace, his master's thesis. Written on the threshold of his entry into the Pentagon on at least the fringes of policy making, Haig's Georgetown thesis was remarkably prophetic and expressive of the man he had become by his late thirties, with clues to his limits, style, strivings, and the professional animus that wound through his later record.

He chose as his theme, boldly and topically enough, the role of the military man in the making of national-security policy. Calling for a "new breed of military professional" who could "continually appraise military policy in terms of its political implications," and who should occupy "a seat at the pinnacle" among presidential advisers, the thesis was in a way both advertisement and argument for himself, or at least the officer he thought himself someday becoming, in part for writing on the topic to begin with. That he went in fact to the "pinnacle" so soon, and so politically, was of course nowhere foreshadowed in the study, but it lends certain parts of it today a curious quality almost of premonition.

Read in hindsight with Haig standing on the seventh floor of the State Department, what may be most recognizable in the thesis is the mere language, echoes of which have become one of his distinguishing marks, or scars, with Congress and the press. Characteristically, the thesis is sprinkled with such phrases as "interpretative vagaries," "thought modes," a "permeating nexus," and that old Haig favorite, "vortex"—in this case, as in "vortex of total war." They are the words and often wandering syntax of a man whose college English was cut short and who was striving here to be heard in a certifying jargon—a sad effort he has never abandoned. Even the term he was thought to have coined as secretary of state, the "vicar of foreign policy," with its supposed overtones of a Catholic cast of mind, turns out in the thesis to be unoriginal, cited there from a speech in the early 1960s by then Pentagon official (and now one of Haig's negotiators) Paul Nitze, and obviously borrowed for Haig's Senate confirmation. Much more important, however, is what he actually said in this trademark style. Regardless of the origin of the term, Haig in 1962 denounced with an infidel's zeal the very "vicarage" he would later claim.

In the thesis, he surveys the civil-military relationship in policymaking past and present. The tone is frequently subdued, the phrases carefully oblique. On the surface, the point seems unexceptionable—that the military should play its "proper" role—yet at closer look the theme is strident and the bias plain. Over most of the thesis's 133 pages pour his strictures against distrust and exclusion of the soldiers. Along the historical way, he deplores the civilians' "constant interference" in the Mexican War; pronounces the First World War "successful" for President Wilson's having "left matters of strategy" to the military; says General George Marshall conceded too many political considerations to "his civilian superiors" in World War II; notes "unfortunately" that Korea had "further repelled political leadership from reliance on conventional war," while MacArthur's recall was a "further strengthening of statutory civilian control"; and portrays the National Security Council that was soon to employ him so advantageously as representing a rotten compromise between government forces "rather than a rational formula" adequately including the military and "induced for the estimated challenges of the future." All this led to "useless civilian incursions" on what military authority was left, he argues, adding a little apocalyptically that the "non-professionals" might get away with running the system, "so long as the sword is not put to the test."

Yet Haig thought the "test" inevitable, "the free world–communist confrontation" being "the overriding environmental factor dominating the current scene." Spared any awkward conflict between the appropriate strategy and what was good for his army, he embraced passionately Maxwell Taylor's doctrine of flexible response as well as the "new Administration's defense team," some civilians having apparently learned their lesson. And here his ingratiation with the current masters of the Pentagon flashes nakedly. They were, he tells his prospective readers, "a balance of intellectual theorists and skilled management operators," and flexible response was a "transmutation in basic strategy [that] is a tribute to the new civilian leadership and a testimony to its exceptional competence in military affairs." Along with repeated paeans to one future employer, Defense Secretary Robert McNamara, he even includes footnote praise for another who approved the new policy, "intellectual and educational" strategist Henry Kissinger.

There are fleeting touches of self-consciousness, nearly

apology. "No doubt this contention will find many violent dissenters," he says in footnoting a point about policy being given a military "frame of reference." But then, the dissenters would be "among those who fail to grasp the overriding significance of the East-West confrontation." The crisis "also explains, though hardly justifies," he goes on, "the difficulties some patriotic soldiers are having in divorcing themselves from what were formerly political areas." But there is no apparent hesitation in his conclusion. The State Department "supremacy in the politico-military field," the "unfortunate monstrosity" of a system where the secretary of state is the president's "vicar" in "inter-departmental politico-military matters," must be ended. The military should adopt "the single chief of staff concept," a military czar permanently at the president's side, unencumbered by "non-professionals" and giving his counsel in a worldwide "challenge which is essentially militant [sic] in nature."

As for other institutions resisting this, the key was clearly the presidency. "Throughout history Congress has gladly relinquished most of the reins to the Executive in times of peril." For its part, the cabinet "has never been a key policy making body." Citing McNamara's moves at the Pentagon, he also thought major changes might be effected quietly, "achieved without fanfare or congressional action."

Having dismissed "indictments" of excessive military power as "fraudulent," having taken for granted the central importance of the cold war and the urgent need for the "fullest participation" of the great military adviser ensconced at the elbow of a beleaguered president, he pauses for only one qualification about American politics

on the eve of the Vietnam War. It would be an epitaph
for much that followed. "Professional counsel at the summit of decision bears great weight," he remarks, "but in
democratic government it cannot consistently shape policy
if it is at odds with the prevailing consensus."

Fresh from his thesis reflections and just promoted to
lieutenant colonel, on the strength of both his European
efficiencies and postgraduate study, Haig was assigned in
February 1962 to a staff job in the murky reaches of the
Pentagon. He remained there and rose significantly over
just short of two and a half years, through some of the
fateful policy junctures of the 1960s. Once more he owed
the essential first step in part to patronage, and now again
to his father-in-law the general. Fox had survived the
MacArthur purge well enough to hang on in the late
Fifties as adviser then deputy to the Pentagon's civilian
assistant secretary for international affairs. Even after retiring from the army and the change of administration, he
was still, at sixty-seven, a consultant on disarmament to
Defense Secretary McNamara in 1961–62, when he backed
Haig's new posting.

Haig's first Pentagon job sounded impressive—the staff
of the International and Policy Planning Division, Strategic Plans and Policy Directorate, for the Army's Deputy
Chief of Staff for Operations. It appeared to stake the sort
of military claim on foreign affairs Haig the erstwhile M.A.
candidate had urged, and later his biography described it
as "work on top level European and Middle Eastern
affairs."

Actually, however, in this division, as others in that

bloated bureaucracy, he was one of a crowd of officers at the overpopulated middle grades, in Haig's case shuffling, reshuffling, meeting and meeting again over army contingency planning for Berlin or other trouble spots. Like all such "planning," it remained for both better and worse on the fringe of policy, though it was also Haig's first brush with the Washington process, and the sixteen months he spent there left him with decided views on the new doctrine of flexible response he had lauded at Georgetown.

"There was sterility in massive retaliation. But the applications of the Taylor philosophy were something else," he said ten years afterward in a rare recorded comment about the moral he had learned in 1962–63. "The Cuban missile crisis, Berlin and contingency plans—they involved minuscule escalation. Do the minimum necessary during confrontations to minimize a nuclear holocaust—that was the thinking." For Haig, the practice was clearly not as tough as he expected from the theory. "You never applied one iota of force. I was against this," he went on. "It provided incentive to the other side to up the ante. I had a serious problem with it. It gave me gas pains." That the Russians had not "upped the ante" in Berlin or the Cuban blockade, that the crises of the early Sixties passed in fact through "the minimum necessary" without catastrophe, apparently did not then or later relieve his chronic "gas."

There was one slightly bizarre footnote to his planning job. Telling a reporter in 1973 about the unusual breadth of his background, Haig would claim he had experience with every part of government, "even the judicial process when I was with Bobby Kennedy during the Cuban missile crisis." In that tense October of 1962, he was one of many young briefing and liaison officers sent swarming over Washington to keep principal actors, like Robert Kennedy, abreast of the army's throbbing "operational plans" for a possible invasion of Cuba if the blockade diplomacy failed. But the duty was scarcely "with Bobby," as he implied—a strange, revealing exaggeration in a man who, when he made that statement, had truly been "with" so many notables, and was at the very moment chief of staff to a president. Then, at that, there was the added bland assertion that an attorney general advising his brother in a missile crisis was somehow "the judicial process." It was rhetorical and constitutional confusion, even nonsense, of the sort he would proclaim so shakingly and so embarrassingly in 1981, when the subject was presidential succession and Haig was "in charge" moments after Ronald Reagan was shot.

The lasting importance of the Pentagon slot was that he would simply be there in the summer of 1963, when the Democrats rescued him from the army's oblivion, and granted him perhaps the most decisive patronage of his career. His patrons were archetypes of the polish and all too common shallowness and bravura of the Kennedy regime, the technocracy of style and credentials and caprice which then seemed an adequate equivalent of genuine knowledge or sophistication about government or the world beyond.

Asked after JFK's election which service secretary he wanted to be, Cyrus Vance, then a general-practice lawyer in his mid-forties with patrician origins, political ties to then vice-president Lyndon Johnson, and no cluttering experience with policy, replied that he "guessed" the navy, since that's where he was in the war. As it turned out, though, as the jobs fell open he eventually got the army instead. Meanwhile, Vance hired as assistant and then army general counsel another young New York lawyer, Joe Califano, whose Italian Catholic background was rather more modest than Vance's but whose grasp and qualifications were otherwise similar. When Vance gave his counsel the task of assimilating into the army some of the ransomed Cuban-exile veterans of the Bay of Pigs, Califano cast about for his own military aide to help, one of the fashionable "new breed of officers," he remembered later, "liberal, renaissance kind of men." After several interviews among the surfeit of Pentagon staffers, he thought Haig "the brightest," and hired him in July 1963, beginning one of the era's most obscure personal and political connections, yet also one of the longest and most historic. "And, Jesus!" Califano exclaimed over his discovery in Haig. "He was more of a workaholic than I was." In any case, the Kennedy men recalled, it was quality that counted in the service of Vances and Califanos on their way up. In 1963 they had been looking for and found, Califano said, one of "the Maxwell Taylors of tomorrow."

The Army Secretary's Office in 1963–64 was thus a virtual hatchery of the famous-to-be—in Vance, Califano, and Haig, all starting there at once, two future White House advisers and three cabinet members, including two secretaries of state. Haig was obviously the junior aide, the military assistant who typically helped route the paper, attended meetings with Califano's and, as needs be, Vance's proxy, and generally handled some of the secretary's special projects as well as a portion of the daily flow of business. Of how they all worked beyond that—who did precisely what and when in their odd conjunction of stars—there is little trace now clear of Pentagon secrecy and careful memories. More visible are the shards of policy they left behind.

A "fiasco," "calamitous and abortive," Haig had called the Bay of Pigs episode in his thesis, attributing the failure in large part to "lack of continuous and readily available military counsel." Now in 1963 he dealt directly with the aftermath of the invasion and missile crisis on the working staff of a special Defense Department group created by McNamara and chaired by Vance to formulate a "long-range policy toward Cuba." After months of meetings, the group produced no way out of the impasse in Cuba-U.S. relations, leaving American diplomacy in sterile hostility and Havana with every incentive for anti-U.S. subversions for a dozen years, until Henry Kissinger put out the first secret though unsustained feelers to Castro in 1975.

Meanwhile, as Haig and his colleagues approved the operations, the CIA "boom and bang" campaign of covert raids and sabotage against the island, as several agents later testified, was going "full blast" in 1963. (In yet another odd early connection of men whose futures would be somehow linked, one of the CIA saboteurs in those raids was Eugenio Martinez, who was later arrested for burglary inside the Watergate Hotel, Haig having reason in the end to regret the burglary if not the "boom and bang" nine years before.

Other policies, where Vance was the outward face and Califano and Haig the inner-office executors or prompters, fared little better, and the record of results was at best mixed. In January 1964, for example, Vance flew off armed with his aides to quell a Panama Canal Zone riot. But the violence eventually petered out without benefit of his diplomacy, while the underlying crisis of sovereignty at the canal remained to bedevil Vance (and give Ronald Reagan a campaign issue) during the Carter administration.

The Office of the Secretary of the Army seemed insistently courageous in 1963–64 in trying to end racial discrimination in military-base housing, yet equally blind to the malignant institutional rot of the army's runaway careerism.

Similarly, they claimed a special watching brief, and the influence that went with it, over policy toward the Dominican Republic. In the post-Trujillo turmoil of 1963–64, the elected regime of Juan Bosch was overthrown, military factions veered into bloody civil war, and later scholars found "an undermining" of the State Department's support for civilian rule "by the Defense Department." Now acquiring repute as a "troubleshooter," Vance flew to Santo Domingo in the spring of 1965 to mediate between the warring sides, and, having settled on a conservative U.S. "candidate" to run the country, left behind a crisis that dragged on long and savagely after he returned to Washington. When 22,000 U.S. troops intervened in the Dominican Republic in April 1965, the record would show that Vance and Co. recommended and approved it with alacrity. With what expertise they acted would always be hard to say. According to Ambassador John Bartlow Martin, probably the most knowledgeable American about the Dominican scene, he had spoken to the vague, amiable Vance exactly twice, and to Califano not at all. But when that intervention seemed to work, when the left seemed thwarted, and despite the savagery of the rightist military and continuing chaos, the precedent lured everyone deeper into the same "quiet" military remedy to such problems in South Vietnam.

Cuba and the Dominican Republic offered fleeting glimpses of Haig's attitude toward Latin America, important as a portent of his controversial policy in 1981–82 toward the civil war in El Salvador. Bitterly, a former Latin friend of the United States christened Washington's approach to the Caribbean in the mid-Sixties "Pentagonism." Those shaping American policy, a disillusioned Juan Bosch wrote from exile, were "bureaucrats and functionaries, not leaders." With other priorities, Califano had a rather different verdict on aggressive, hardworking young colonels like Haig around the office. "We wound up outstaffing the State Department . . . with these kinds of officers," he concluded, as if they had indeed heeded Al Haig's thesis admonition about who ought to have "politico-military" supremacy. "We put the State Department in the bush leagues."

In February 1964, Haig and Califano went along to the Office of the Secretary of Defense when Vance was promoted by McNamara to be deputy secretary. Two years after he came to the building, Haig was now working atop the Pentagon. He sat "at McNamara's right hand," Haig said later. Again, he promoted himself in retrospect. He was not one of McNamara's closest aides, but instead some crusty layers removed as military assistant in Califano's Office of the Special Assistant. Still, his responsibilities were bureaucratically important and his vantage point unique. While a staff officer—reading, perhaps amending, passing on the usual run of documents to the senior men—

he also acted as a liaison or simply a courier, carrying the views of the civilian defense secretaries both to the Joint Chiefs and to the Johnson White House. En route, he watched as relatively few others the furtive descent into full-scale war in Southeast Asia.

A brief chronology of that descent—set against Haig's position, what he knew, did or did not do—puts the relatively obscure man in the more familiar history, a history of which he was very much a part.

From *Frebruary 1964,* the date of Haig's arrival at the secretary's office, to *June,* the *Pentagon Papers* showed McNamara and his aides steadily involved in plans for and reports of covert raids against North Vietnam and readying U.S. escalation.

August 1964 saw the Gulf of Tonkin attacks on U.S. vessels and the resulting congressional resolution supporting the war policy. While Haig and others as close knew that there had been secret attacks by South Vietnamese forces in the gulf for the last six months, that secret diplomatic threats had been made to Hanoi, and that there were plans to "seek" such congressional endorsement, McNamara publicly denied knowledge of any provocative raids against the North, and the resolution appeared spontaneous. ("Officials exaggerated the facts and distorted them," concluded one study of the Tonkin incident.)

By *November 1964,* the Joint Chiefs proposed the introduction of U.S. ground troops into South Vietnam.

In *February 1965,* Johnson having been elected to a full term, the Vietcong rocketing of Pleiku brought U.S. bombing reprisals on Hanoi, with the backing of both Vance and McNamara and without dissent by their aides.

By *March,* two marine battalions were deployed in Vietnam, and the bombing of the North began again with full approval of the Office of the Secretary of Defense.

In *July,* U.S. troops would rise to 125,000, on the way to half a million. Beyond McNamara's clearances, however, the official analysts of the *Pentagon Papers* would find "so little of him in the files," the secretary and his personal staff on the record in the fatal buildup "more clearly for good management than for any policy judgment."

Watching it all, passing on the proposals and the conflicting intelligence, witnessing the government's vast deception of the public, the Congress, and itself, Haig offered no brake, no check or pause. In an archive of warmaking, in which the recommendations of the military were almost wholly unquestioned by 1965, his chief legacy would be a "tough" memorandum that summer to Vance and McNamara urging that the chairman of the Joint Chiefs be invited regularly to the weekly "Tuesday lunch of high-level advisers at the White House, lest the military be excluded from "key decision-making . . . on the war."

By then eager to get to Vietnam himself for its wartime promotions and ticket-punching combat commands, his tour at the Pentagon already extended a year by Califano, who pronounced him the "ultimate professional," Haig prepared to leave his desk in June 1965 with a Legion of Merit for his "outstanding" staff performance. Then as later, he would be memorable for his stamina, and absolved of what he did with it. The more prominent men he worked for and around—the men of the inner offices, those too visible in the seats at the conference tables while the Haigs sat in the discreet back rows—paid later for the

Vietnam policies and deceits of 1964–65 with their reputations and careers. Even aides at his level in Saigon or
Washington, men too doubtful about the war or too rashly
in favor of it, paid as well. But he went on unscathed.

Like Vance's, the job Haig held was deemed important
for one's credentials, a cachet. The deputy, the special
assistant or aide, disposed a subtle power in government.
No policy was purely theirs alone, yet the bureaucrats
below could not propose without going through them, and
superiors rarely decided without them. In the trust and
sheer proximity of the decision-maker, theirs was the
power to shade, to change, to initiate, and, even more
formidably, to delay, to plant doubts or nuance or complexity blanched out by a bureaucracy abhorring and ignoring them all, to protect the boss from blunder by
stampede or default of independent judgment. Most of all,
the power was *part* of the process, symbiotic in the orga-
nism of policy, inseparable—mainly because if the aide
were not so intimate and crucial, he would be replaced
by someone to fill that necessary role. Yet somehow, at the
same time, Haig bore no more responsibility for folly, or
his knowledge of it, than a junior orderly. Then as later,
the press and Congress did not seem quite to understand
how it all really worked, the breadth and depth of accountability in power—and happily for Haig, did not care to
discover. He was to go on to wield far greater power
without public responsibility. "I've served in many administrations," he once told an interviewer. "I have strong
views . . . but it's not an excessive burden to restrain them."
In the bellicose Democratic Pentagon of Califano, Vance,
and McNamara, as they took the nation into war, apparently it was not so hard at all.

. . .

He paused before Vietnam in 1965–66 to pick up the
forty-two week course at the Army War College at Carlisle
Barracks in the quiet charm of the southern Pennsylvania
hills. Among the hundred students (here, too, as at the
Naval College, dressed in civilian clothes), Haig was in a
tradition of alumni such as Omar Bradley, Generals Collins
and Ridgeway whom he had seen in Korea, and, of course,
Maxwell Taylor. Now one more way station in the army's
career trail of certificates, however, the college had lost
much of its rigor and prestige. After largely elementary
courses in geopolitics and strategy, the officer's best chance
for originality and fresh thought lay in the obligatory
thesis or final paper in the spring. But in practice, as a
faculty member told a visiting researcher, "thesis" was "a
highly dignified term" to give the War College papers,
which were "almost always high-school-level in length and
content." At least some students chose provocative topics
on the district advisory program in Vietnam, or pacification, or even peace negotiations.

Haig chose a less heated subject, "Military Intervention:
A Case Study of Britain's Use of Force in the 1956 Suez
Crisis." It was a paper of the common level, and not one
he particularly would want remembered. London's disastrous colonial reflex at Suez, a War College teacher remembers him concluding, had been "justified" in "its own
terms."

He arrived in Vietnam in July 1966 as G-3, an operations planning officer for the First Infantry Division at Lai
Khe just north of Saigon. In the year he'd spent at Carlisle,
the American war begun on paper in the Pentagon had

started in earnest with over 350,000 U.S. troops in South
Vietnam, 5,000 of whom would die there in 1966 alone.
The First Infantry had come the previous October, been
bloodied in the Ia Drang Valley a month later, and was
now about to embark on the huge, thrashing search-and-
destroy missions that were the hallmark of U.S. strategy.

Forces like the First were commanded overall from
Saigon by General William Westmoreland, whom a Pentagon official at the time described as a "thoroughly decent,
moderately intelligent product of the army system" who
was "precluded" from serious comparison to great generals
"by an unmistakable aura of Boy Scoutism." In American
mobility and sheer massive firepower, the same official recalled, Westmoreland and his staff "had discovered the
military answer" to what they saw as "endless Asian man-
power and the Oriental indifference to death." But strategy
was shrouded, too, by the costly lesson of Korea, or what
that lesson seemed to be. From the success of Inchon and
the icy debacle on the Yalu, there grew the myth that
somehow, without the Chinese coming in, a war was manageable, that the army could handle the tributaries if not
the Middle Kingdom. The uncertain Chinese trumpets had
haunted the Pentagon planners in 1964–65, and having
decided that those trumpets would not blow here, they
launched an American army and reckoned to get away
with it. Far more than Korea, of course, it would be a
wrong war, fought, as is the wont of generals, in the wrong
way from the unlearned lessons of the last.

Only a month in the country, Haig won the first of what
were to be three Distinguished Flying Crosses in this helicopter war. Sitting beside his division commanding
general, William Depuy, "in an exposed position," and "dis-

regarding . . . heavy fire" when their chopper took several
hits on its third pass over the site of a U.S. heliborne
assault, Haig was cited for "gallant actions" in "pinpoint-
ing" the enemy, "advising the general," and "repeatedly"
risking his life to advise ground commanders as well. Soon
afterward he added an oak leaf cluster with a second DFC
awarded when his command chopper dipped onto a rice-
paddy dike to pick up a wounded guerrilla for intelligence
questioning. When Haig leaned out, as he told it later, to
"scroff this fellow up," the Vietnamese blew himself up
with a hand grenade, and a fragment flew into the corner
of Haig's right eye. Stunned but still conscious, and bleed-
ing profusely, he thought he had lost the eye until the
shrapnel was removed at a field hospital. "God, piece of
thing looked like spaghetti," he remembered. ". . . It just
curved around miraculously. Right around the bone ridge.
Never touched the optic nerve. But you do get fatalistic,"
he went on, telling the story to *Esquire* more than ten
years later. "I was in Korea and there are so many who
get it and those that don't."

In November, he received yet another decoration, this
one the National Order of Vietnam, Fifth Class, for his
"initiative, organizational skill and solid military experience" in helping plan Operation Attleboro. The largest
sweep of its kind to date, Attleboro sent 22,000 U.S. troops
through fitful, inconclusive encounters near the Cambodian border northwest of Saigon, with statistics that
were virtual parodies of the war of numbers. The attack
claimed 1,080 Vietcong killed, 42 captured, but only 122
individual weapons taken. Throughout the war, such body
counts (and the "success" they represented for officers like
Haig) would far outnumber the enemy weapons taken, as

if, for those who looked closely, the Americans faced a phantom-armed force whose guns disappeared in death.

Already well decorated and well connected at First Infantry headquarters, he now lobbied for and got his own combat command. After Attleboro, he took over the First Battalion of the division's Twenty-sixth Infantry Regiment, late in November, just in time for even larger assaults in the same vein, operations code-named after the hometowns of division martyrs—Cedar Falls and Junction City. Less than twenty-five miles northwest of Saigon, a historic guerrilla sanctuary and long-Vietcong-controlled territory, the area known as the Iron Triangle was "aimed," said Robert Leckie, a military writer, "like a dagger at the heart of South Vietnam." Cedar Falls' first target was a village of 3,500 called Ben Suc on the western point of the Triangle. To a young U.S. medic in Haig's division who had been there "a dozen times before" to give medicine to the people, the place was simply "a very nice old village in a beautiful setting by the river," where "nobody had ever shot at us, nobody even bothered us." But to the South Vietnamese, the village was a political embarrassment; and to the American command, a "fortified supply and political center . . . ensuring the dominance of the VC in the Iron Triangle," and thus beckoning to Westmoreland's planners.

Now, as in the Cambodian invasion three years later, the Americans were ever lured on to find the siren of the COSVN, the Vietcong's own legendary headquarters command. Kept even from the South Vietnamese until the last moment for security reasons, the U.S. plan called for a "swift, decisive strike" to eliminate the village once and for all as a VC refuge. The new operation revised the usual method, thought *New Yorker* correspondent Jonathan Schell, who went along. "This time," he wrote, "they would destroy first and search later." The battalion chosen to lead the surprise assault on Ben Suc was Alexander Haig's.

Haig and his men were airlifted on January 7 to the staging area nearby, where he and other officers got a final briefing by Colonel James Grimsley, commander of the battalion's parent Second Brigade. The object was rapid control, with about ten seconds to empty each troop-carrying helicopter, Grimsley told them. Their job would be to seal off the village and all escape. "Now, of course, if it's just a bunch of women and children wandering down through the woods, who obviously don't know what they're doing, don't fire," Schell recorded Grimsley saying, "but otherwise you'll have to take them under fire." Haig and the others had no questions. They silently filed out of the colonel's tent, Schell recalled, into the camp's night sounds of whining artillery, the "smothered thumping" of a distant B-52 raid, and the reassuring "roaring of one of the diesel generators" on this "little island of safety." "Each man," he wrote, "seemed to want to be alone with his thoughts."

The next morning they breakfasted and boarded their aircraft in the predawn darkness. Sixty helicopters then swooped out of the sunrise at treetop level onto the surprised village, in what a First Division newspaper account later characterized as "a fantastic mess . . . beautifully coordinated and planned." The landings were unopposed. But the events of the next two hours would be recorded, typically, in conflicting accounts.

Schell saw Haig's men without warning shoot down one unarmed Vietnamese man riding a bicycle at the edge of the village, and watched as troopers later senselessly machine-gunned a water buffalo. Other news accounts described General John Hollingsworth, division deputy commander, personally directing helicopter fire to kill seven people fleeing across the nearby Saigon River. Yet Schell, questioning officers on the scene, reported forty-nine captured weapons in Ben Suc, all found in caches in tunnels beneath the village rather than on the more than forty dead villagers or with prisoners. By midmorning, Schell wrote, the village was quiet, there were "no friendly casualties reported," and "in the middle of this relaxed, almost drowsy scene," Haig and his men set up a "temporary command post . . . humming with activity," as villagers were assembled for questioning and eventual deportation. At the same time, according to the official army version, at least five American soldiers were casualties to enemy mines, there was Vietcong sniper fire around the village, and all those Vietnamese killed were hostiles. "What do you mean, 'Were they carrying a weapon?'" one of Haig's junior officers barked at Schell. "Anyone killed by this outfit was carrying a weapon."

About the sequel to these first hours of the assault, however, there would be no dispute. As Haig and other officers looked on, villagers were interrogated, often tortured, by South Vietnamese forces, and then the entire population was deported to a "new-life" hamlet, "which for all practical purposes," remembered an American soldier who watched, "was a concentration camp." Ben Suc, its houses, fields, and graveyards, would be fired and bulldozed until, in the words of the army's official summary, "it no longer existed." The First Division medic who had known the village wrote later, "The whole thing was turned into a big parking lot." The story was told in Schell's book, *The Village of Ben Suc,* and the incident became a symbol of the cruelty and distortion of U.S. tactics. But the destruction and forced deportation were also the substance as well as a symbol of military stupidity. Encircled and herded into camps so briskly by the U.S. Army, the refugees of Ben Suc and other "eliminated" villages became a bitter horde the South Vietnamese regime could not manage, eventually spilling into the shantytowns of the cities where they further drained and despised the regime Haig and his men were fighting to preserve.

Meanwhile, his First Battalion had been relieved in Ben Suc on January 10, and over the next few days helped search the nearby Than Dinh forest as part of the continuing Cedar Falls thrust. Finding caches of rice but no enemy, Haig was soon ordered back to a base camp, where he ran perimeter defense, made occasional road forays, and awaited the planned replica of Cedar Falls' celebrated "success," Operation Junction City.

In late March, Haig was alerted to prepare for a helicopter assault still deeper into a traditional Vietcong area beyond the Iron Triangle near Ap Gu, a tiny village west of An Loc and just south of the Cambodian border. The plan was to secure a landing zone and adjacent defensive area, drawing out enemy forces, as such operations rarely did, for a punishing, set-piece battle.

Poor weather delayed the attack, but by early afternoon on March 30, 1967, Haig's battalion touched down in an uncontested landing, patroled briefly, and then dug in to spend an uneventful night. Another battalion arrived without incident and took up positions a few kilometers away early the next morning. A forty-two-year-old lieutenant colonel, Haig was now in the field in war-time, in relatively independent command, and with responsibility as never before in his military career. At sunup, he sent out a small reconnaissance platoon toward the Cambodian border, and larger companies to the south and the east. Almost immediately the reconnaissance group found evidence, as an army history put it, that they were "expected." Hanging from the trees were small signs in English warning that Americans who went beyond would not return. Told about the signs, Haig ordered the patrol continued. At one o'clock, and five miles from Cambodia, the platoon ran into a major enemy force. Its point man was hit, and the lieutenant in command mortally wounded.

Back at his base, Haig heard the first radio reports of the action. Calling in artillery support and bombing, he boarded his helicopter to help coordinate the strikes. Meanwhile, one of his companies, without coordination, had heard the reports as well and rushed to the relief of the now desperate platoon, where it, too, was soon pinned down. In the air over the fighting, within range of both Vietcong ground fire and "friendly" artillery, Haig continued to advise and observe the defense through the afternoon as the U.S. position steadily worsened.

Once more, what followed would yield separate records, with subtle yet notable differences.

In the citation awarding Haig a second oak leaf cluster to his DFC, he decided to take personal command on the ground and ordered his pilot to land. His helicopter was then hit and forced to make a crash landing at almost six o'clock, after which he took command and pulled out the heavily engaged troops.

In another version, he "crawled out" of the crashed

helicopter, stayed with his besieged men alone for four hours until nearly ten o'clock that night, some 700 yards outside the base perimeter, and made it back to camp in the darkness. "He never wanted to lose a soldier," said General Hollingsworth, who put Haig in for a Distinguished Service Cross for the action. "It was the most gallant and extraordinary heroism I've even seen in the field."

Yet according to still another account—the official army history of the battle by Lieutenant General Bernard Rogers, a First Division staff officer who would be Haig's superior later at West Point and still later his successor at NATO—Haig simply "landed near the point of contact" and sent an aide aloft to direct fire in an apparently airworthy helicopter, "electing to stay with his units when he found the platoon lieutenant dead and the company commander "wounded and in mild shock." Then, the army history goes on, they were rescued and relieved by another, fresh company, which moved through to "gain fire superiority over the enemy force." And as "the intensity and accuracy of artillery and air strikes increased," the Americans pulled back to their camp, all by five o'clock that afternoon.

Whatever the time sequence, helicopter landings, or Haig's definite gallantry, the day's action ended with seven of his men dead, thirty-eight wounded, and the battle not yet over.

During the fighting, another battalion had reinforced Haig directly, and the two units now dug in together for the night. At nearly five the next morning, April 1, there was the champagne-cork pop of a single mortar round over the American lines. Haig accurately heard it as registering fire for a coming barrage and attack, and both ordered an alert of the camp and called in air and artillery strikes. "There were indicators that the battle would be resumed that morning," Haig later told Rogers the historian. If not attacked, he would have attacked himself to exploit "a fairly successful action the day before."

Within moments of the enemy mortar barrage, Haig's lines were hit by a fierce assault. The Vietcong tore a hole in the American perimeter the size of a football field. There was hand-to-hand combat rare for Vietnam. So frantic was the fighting, so desperate Haig's position, that air strikes were sometimes called within sixty feet of his troops. By daylight, though, the VC forces had begun to falter under massed American firepower of cluster bombs, artillery and helicopter gunships hovering overhead. At 8:00 A.M. the U.S. forces broke out of the perimeter to counterattack briefly, and the enemy units melted away. In the mists of the morning, 17 Americans had been killed, 102 wounded. Though official reports had 609 enemy dead, 80 percent of them from air and artillery strikes, only 50 weapons were captured.

A dispatch on the battle two days afterward in *The New York Times* proclaimed an impressive U.S. victory, credited Haig with sensing the mortar round as the prelude to attack, and proceeded to report only half the actual American casualties. (That same weekend the *Times* in other articles had noted Ronald Reagan "reasonably pleased" with his first three months as governor of California, and Vice President Hubert Humphrey departed for Europe, where he would give the pope a leatherbound official propaganda booklet on U.S. policy in Vietnam.) Commenting for the army's official history,

Haig thought the enemy commanders not up to the battle. "When you get belly to belly with a large VC force, they are not sufficiently flexible to react especially intelligently," he concluded. Meanwhile, back in Washington, a few disenchanted Pentagon civilians worried increasingly about the course of the war in 1967, and what one of them called "sanguinary inconclusive battles in remote border regions."

On the evening of April 1, after Ap Gu, Haig had taken temporary command of the Second Brigade when Grimsley was wounded. But he saw no more action. By June he was sent home, where he was promptly promoted to colonel and assigned to command a cadet regiment at West Point. Much decorated, his courage seemed unquestioned. Yet in reality his combat record had been mixed. His planning at the First Division copied the sterile, lumbering pattern then in vogue—clumsy, conventional tactics doomed in guerrilla war. His men at Ben Suc trod the thin edge of atrocity. He had been saved from disaster at Ap Gu not by tactical flair or skillful deployment of his troops, nor even by his obvious personal bravery (whatever the circumstances of his flight and landing), but on both days by the typically profligate U.S. firepower of airplanes, artillery, and helicopters, without which his thin reconnaissance in a known enemy stronghold, and then the uncoordinated initial company-strength counterattack, would have ended in virtual annihilation of his command.

Hidden in the decorations and claimed victories were blunders far deeper and grander than any battalion commander's. The American soldier, General Rogers told a civilian audience that autumn, "looks with disgust at re-

ports of those back home who question his being and fighting in the far-off place." It was 1967, a year of 27,000 desertions from the United States Army in Vietnam. Writing
his history of Cedar Falls and Junction City at Westmoreland's order, Rogers even subtitled the book *A Turning Point.* Yet only weeks after Cedar Falls and the razing
of Ben Suc, as even the official history had to acknowledge, "the Iron Triangle was again literally crawling with
what appeared to be Vietcong." When the military lash
and crippling political blow of the Tet Offensive fell
"belly-to-belly" on unprepared U.S. forces a year later, it
would come in large measure from Vietcong troops supposed to be dead, marshaling in the very areas where Haig
and his men had fought and supposedly won in 1967.

Nonetheless, fifteen years later, the victorious colonel
become secretary of state, other officers in other swooping
American helicopter gunships would look down on peas-
ant villages in El Salvador, promising a similar "turning
point."

Returning a war hero to West Point, Haig by the summer of 1967 was on the eve of his stunning rise to national
prominence. A year and a half later would come the call
from Henry Kissinger to join the White House staff, and a
history no one could have imagined for the brave, ambitious officer from Bala-Cynwyd. There had been about
his progress few of the earmarks of exceptional talent that
distinguished other soldiers destined for such heights—
not MacArthur's dash or brilliance, Stillwell's leadership,
Marshall's or Eisenhower's administrative genius, even

Taylor's fashionable bookishness. He had been largely a creature of patronage since the nomination his uncle secured for him at West Point, and a creature also of the post-Korea army whose careerist ethic was a substitute for the pageantry of simpler wars.

It was also a rise launched and schooled in defeat, in lost Asian campaigns, in a nation increasingly uncertain about world power it once took for granted, and in an officer corps not bred to battle but more often compelled to shuffle paper and politics with civilians of dubious competence or conviction. In that disappointing world, there was about Haig the vague common resentment at defeat, the "gas pains" at what seemed the dangerous new distrust of the military. At the same time, the great tides of the postwar era washed over him: Russia after Stalin; the historic Sino-Soviet schism; the emergence of the third world. If the new army changed its uniforms outwardly, he had remained intellectually in the suntans and simple anti-communism of the Dai Ichi.

What had distinguished him most was not ideology or ideal, but rather the capacity to adapt to the men he served, to absorb the lessons of advance in being near the top. For all the medals and promotions, there was about the man the unmistakable odor of limit and banality. He might have been any of hundreds of lucky, eager, valiant, well-connected officers—but for his unique experience with his masters. If Almond had been capricious and demanding, or MacArthur megalomaniac, if Fox and Califano had been formidable patrons, if the retreat from the Yalu or the Vietnam buildup or the raid on Ben Suc were given a comforting veneer for public consumption, if crises were buried and leadership often happened in a hidden squalor, mediocrity, and uncertainty of petty men, it was all now to be amazingly relevant. From that painful, cynical apprenticeship, what lay ahead in Richard Nixon's White House was perhaps the one battle for which Haig was fully prepared.

Part Two

CHAMBERLAIN

I can keep honest counsel, ride, run,
mar a curious tale in telling it,
and deliver a plain message bluntly:
That which ordinary men are fit for, I am qualified in,
and the best of me is diligence.

Shakespeare, King Lear

It began almost quietly. Early in December 1968, at his transition headquarters in New York's dignified Hotel Pierre on Fifth Avenue facing the park, President-elect Richard Nixon introduced to the press his choice as national security adviser, a relatively trim, still unfamiliar Harvard professor named Henry Kissinger. Typically, it began, too, with a little deceit on a matter that would prove monumental. Having vouchsafed to a gratified Kissinger beforehand that they would "run foreign policy from the White House," Nixon proceeded to announce to the reporters that his new assistant would confine himself to "planning" and properly leave diplomacy to a "strong secretary of state" about to be named. Out of "eagerness to deflect any possible criticism," Nixon's public pretense was "substantially at variance" with their private intention, as Kissinger delicately described it later in his memoirs. It was also, he might have added, an omen of much more such "variance" to come.

From the Pierre, Nixon and Kissinger fastened their absolute control over the governance of the country's international relations. They fashioned and implanted a new circuitry of decisionmaking in which all the impulses of foreign policy fused in the White House, shorting and flowing past the bureaucracy and cabinet secretaries. So complete, so exclusive was their control that soon the mechanism itself no longer mattered—only the men at the core of the vast, hoarded power. In the hotel that December, a time that Kissinger (if not his bureaucratic victims) remembered as a "moment of charmed innocence," those fateful consequences were scarcely apparent. It was an unlikely dyarchy, this German-born academic strategist with a fondness for applause and great power concerts, and the California politician of native suspicion and bigotry and a homegrown anticommunism. Least of all was there any foreshadow that their historic collaboration would produce one more unexpected figure; that as their arbitrary power waxed in Washington and the world, another unfamiliar face would be more and more often at their side in great affairs; and that the obscure third man, raised in the strange inner ferment of their regime, would eventually succeed to Kissinger's place and pretend to Nixon's. Like the seizure of power at the Pierre, that extraordinary rise of Alexander Haig in 1969–73 happened largely out of sight.

While his future employers were making their respective ways through electoral politics and establishment jockeying to the far-reaching rendezvous on Fifth Avenue, Haig had returned home in June of 1967 to vaguely uncertain prospects. Years later the *New York Post* called him "probably the only ranking officer to emerge from Vietnam stronger than when he went in," but that was distorted hindsight. The war laid bare the post-Korea decay of the army, and by that summer it was by no means clear what would be the ultimate toll or taint in careers. The system that in peacetime routinely ground out rhapsodic officer efficiency reports and denied its careerist decline had applied the same practiced reflexes to the surreal paper work of Saigon, fattening the Vietcong body counts that proved victory, falsifying the intelligence reports that discovered awkward numbers of enemy troops and with them the unwanted signs of another unwinnable war.

The fraud fed on itself until it had eaten deep into even the old honor of citations. By 1971, the 1,273,987 medals for bravery given out in Vietnam were already more than twice the number of awards in Korea and approaching the number of decorations in World War II with its ten million men in uniform. Guidelines were simply "ignored," wrote an eyewitness afterward, and especially for officers "it came to the point where medals were issued almost automatically." Citations were written for flying around frozen turkeys for Thanksgiving, sought for donating blood, and handed out routinely to generals whose valor in such numbers, wrote one veteran officer later, was "incomprehensible." The inflation was perhaps worst with regard to the once-respected Air Medal, roughly 800,000 of the total decorations and now presented for a "preset number of flights within a combat zone." Of course, all Vietnam was such a "zone," and almost any flight in the army's ubiquitous helicopters thus counted as an exploit.

Like a debased currency, ribbons for courage lost value as they accumulated, with awards bitterly called "gongs," oak leaf clusters termed "rat turds," and a sneering war joke about receiving a "twenty-seventh Air Medal." (Haig himself came away with seventeen.) "It was easy and it was cheap," said a chaplain of the debauchery in medals. "Some acted as if it were a play war, but elsewhere people were dying."

With the corruption of standards came the inevitable loss of morale. To officers, the obvious ignorance and widespread opportunism of their superiors made the war's generalship, as one colonel described it, "the dark ages in the army's history." To the men in the ranks, Vietnam's "grunts," this war was too often fought with their officers 2,000 feet up in the comparative safety of "eye in the sky" command helicopters rather than with their "ass in the grass" with their troops. The casualty figures were telltale. In over a decade of fighting, with more than 57,000 American dead, only four generals and eight colonels fell in combat—officer rank a safeguard of survival as for no other modern army at war. "The officer corps simply did not die in sufficient numbers or in the presence of their men often enough," concluded two postwar analysts of the army's "crisis in management."

Haig's own heroism in joining his embattled units on the ground at Ap Gu was plainly an exception to the rule. But his and authentic leadership by other officers were not enough to spare the army from the resulting Vietnam disintegration in the late Sixties—refusal of orders amounting to mutiny, desertions in the tens of thousands, the drug epidemic and race riots, the uncounted atrocities, even the assassination of officers and noncoms by their own men, the American army's internecine murder, which acquired its own ugly Vietnam word, "fragging." A subsequent war-college study concluded nimbly that there had been "a clear loss of military ethic" among the officer corps. Other scholars found more clinically and more bluntly that the army in Vietnam bordered on "an undisciplined, ineffective, almost anomic mass," its commanders high and low manifesting "severe pathologies."

All this provoked an exodus of disillusioned soldiers, many at Haig's grade. It also produced an unprecedented outpouring of public and internal criticism by officers and other observers. Officially, the crumbling of discipline and performance in Vietnam was blamed on on the scapegoats of antiwar agitation and the larger social turbulence of the Sixties. But the critics within saw as far more corrupting the army's own long-cultivated bureaucratic venality and incompetence.

Yet Haig had no part in the soul-searching or -airing, and remained sternly aligned with the system that had promoted him to middle management, disastrous wars notwithstanding. The West Point to which he returned once more in 1967 was, in its staff ranks at least, a bastion of orthodoxy, superintended by General Samuel Koster, who, when he was removed in 1969 for implication in the cover-up of My Lai atrocities, simply left a dining hall full of sympathetic cadets with the old Stilwell adage "Don't let the bastards grind you down." Of whom the "bastards" were, Haig had no doubt. The Vietnam War stories he told later to colleagues at the White House were not about army corruption or fragging, but about an old Vietnamese villager who approached his column one day with a concealed grenade and pulled the pin, killing himself and one of Haig's troopers.

"War enhanced my perception of professionalism," he said vaguely later. "The army has suffered a degree of damage to its standards due to Vietnam. . . . The army has its eye on the ball right now. There's introspection and assessment."

But when a war-college study of Vietnam "professionalism" had been completed in 1970 with implications, as one reader described it, "devastating to the image of the officer corps," it was promptly classified and effectively suppressed by Westmoreland, then promoted from Saigon to be chief of staff. While Haig spoke of "introspection," the counterattack on army critics had been long since vicious. "Overlong in battle and emotionally unbalanced," one favorite military journalist pronounced a colonel of legendary heroism who had publicly deplored the careerism in Vietnam. The tide of reform, as a 1978 study found, was "allowed to recede," and those officers "whose careers were deeply rooted in the policies and practices [of the war] finally prevailed."

The siege mentality of the Vietnam-tortured army may have been even more visible, though, in the account left of Haig's tenure at the academy in 1967–68 by one of his regimental cadets who ran afoul of him. Lucian K. Truscott IV was the offspring of an old army family who later left the service in disillusion to become a reporter and novelist, and his memoir in New York's *Village Voice* in May 1973 was predictably acid. Set against Haig's past as well as what followed with Nixon and Kissinger, however, it also seems in many ways a recognizable and trenchant portrait of the man and his culture on the eve of his White House rise.

At first impression in the autumn of 1967, Truscott's Haig was "a popular if enigmatic figure," grinning and snapping salutes at Third Regiment cadets whom he called by nicknames in a style "polished and magnetic" and apparently "a perfect mixture of ego and humility." No other staff officer, thought Truscott, seemed more a "soldier's soldier." Yet there was also the mark of the martinet that an earlier generation of cadets had seen in Haig as a tactical officer in the mid-Fifties. His "first action" on taking command of the regiment was to require it to march even more rigidly than regulations required, with elbows locked, fingers cocked at the second knuckle and thumb, and index finger "pointed like an arrow" to the ground. Ever present at fall drills, slapping yellow gloves against his leg to make constant corrections in the technique, Haig told his cadet officers, "If they can get that hand straight, that elbow stiff, then all the rest falls into place. Every directive becomes second nature," adding: "It's my way of putting my signature on a unit." Truscott saw the marching obsession as a leadership "gimmick" that "unsurprisingly . . . worked." It no doubt stemmed, too, from the West Point creed of discipline for its own sake. "Those leaders who seek perfection in time of peace," Haig said to an interviewer later, sounding like an academy manual, "provide an incalculable benefit in combat situations."

But the regimental commander's motives soon went beyond "signatures" and "perfection" in Truscott's account. Haig had "an almost maniacal desire," he wrote, to keep "within the regiment" and unknown to superiors "anything which he felt would reflect badly upon his command." When seven cadets were investigated for marijuana in the autumn of 1967, in a unit where Truscott called drug use "widespread," the seven were furtively punished by unexplained loss of summer leave and the incident was covered up because "neither Haig nor his superiors at the Academy wanted it known at the Pentagon that the Third Regiment harbored a bunch of junkies and perverts." Truscott similarly described a regimental cheating scandal in May 1968, an echo of Haig's own West Point days when cheating was "rife." Now the inquiry was cut short and the cadet company involved was told "to keep the whole thing quiet," a second "cover-up" over which "Colonel Haig presided with something less than glee."

Truscott's climactic clash with Haig began the same spring when he and other cadets complained to the colonel about mandatory attendance at chapel. Greeting the cadets heartily, Haig heard their complaint with a "frown" and then told them cheerfully that he would do them "a big favor" and send them back to their barracks before they "only hurt" themselves by bucking a regulation "bigger than us." Truscott and his fellow cadets retreated meekly. But a few months later they protested again, this time in writing, about arbitrary deductions of chapel "donations" from the small cadet pay. Soon they began to be "called in" by staff officers below Haig who asked them to resign or threatened courts-martial.

Haig had been named deputy commandant of cadets in June 1968, and in October he summoned Truscott to his new office, a "wood-paneled vault-like chamber" at the venerable brigade headquarters. Again according to the cadet's version, Haig at first struck an "informal, almost jovial" pose, in shirt sleeves, tie askew, asking "Mr. T." about alleged infractions and "laughing off" the charges as Truscott denied them. Haig then held up the chapel-donation complaints: "Know what this is, Mr. T?"

Once more he was going to do the cadets a "favor." He would route the paper work back to them, and Truscott and his buddies should "tear them up." Otherwise, "if these go up, Mr. T., you'll leave the Commandant with no choice but to eliminate you, all of you, from the Academy. Do you understand that? You're boxing him in, Mr. T., leaving him no choice."

When Truscott argued that expulsion was not an issue, that even West Point chaplains wanted no such compulsory donations, Haig "began to get agitated," tightening his tie and donning his beribboned coat. He had tried to "play ball," tried to "warn" and "protect" the cadets, but no more. "This is the end," Truscott remembered him saying. "You'd better watch your step from here on out, young man, because you're treading on some dangerous ground."

With Haig coming around the desk, Truscott flung his own defiant rejoinder ". . . if this is the way you want to play it . . ." and then "Haig exploded, driving himself across the blue carpet until he was inches from my face. His fists were clenched and one of them was raised next to my head. 'You little bastard,' he seethed between gritted teeth. 'I will personally see you out of here one way or another. Now get out of here. Get out of my sight. The next time I see you, it will be at the front gate of West Point, going out.'"

Over the following two months, before Haig was suddenly transferred to the White House, Truscott was hounded at every turn, had his room ransacked for "subversive" papers, and was threatened repeatedly with expulsion. According to the *Voice* article, when Truscott asked a staff major about the harassment, he was told,

"Surely you must know" why it was happening and that
feelings at headquarters were "running so high" that anyone who questioned the persecution would "ruin his
career." When by this account Truscott's father, himself a
colonel, West Pointer, and Vietnam veteran, went to see
Haig about the case, Haig denied having threatened the
cadet and told the father his son was "way beyond being
a hippie." Haig had been "obsessed" with power, the
younger Truscott concluded in his memoir, an "ultimate
action/reaction . . . addict" who saw power as the "simple
establishment of authority by any means necessary." He
was "unable to cope" with moral or psychological elements in the dispute, had shown "a peculiar anxiety"
about the challenge to authority, and in "the perfect
malleability of his personality" was "willing to go to any
length to achieve his ends"—all in all, thought Truscott,
a man in whom "there was never a core" and the "only
true authority, inner or outer, was the Action."

There were several curious, somewhat twisting sequels
to Truscott's colorful episode. Haig, of course, left soon
for Washington, where he commented in passing and with
disdain about the *Voice* article late in 1973. "This is a
young fellow who suffered a number of problems of
alienation," he said of "Mr. T." "I wouldn't presume to
know why. I didn't know the young man all that well."
As for the article, he went on, it "didn't embarrass me,
because, except for a few factual things, it was totally
incorrect. I didn't know what he was talking about." It
had been "chalk smears on an otherwise clean slate of
press attention to Haig," concluded the *Washington Post*
interviewer who asked him about Truscott then.

For his part, Colonel Truscott, the father, later went

into retirement, from which he apparently remembered his earlier encounter and wrote a 1974 magazine article entitled "The Hazard of Haig" about the latter's appointment to command NATO. Quoting Lloyd George, he said: "There is no greater fatuity than a political judgment dressed in a military uniform." Lucian Truscott IV, the third-generation West Pointer, went on to stir more controversy and accumulate more demerits at the academy, and graduated in 1969 largely because of the intervention of the commandant and Haig's former boss, General Bernard Rogers. Rogers afterward told a writer that he had been booed when he handed Truscott his diploma, but that he had erased the demerits because "I was willing to take the risk if there was a fifty-fifty chance he'd turn out all right."

Second Lieutenant Truscott was then posted to Fort Carson, Colorado, where Rogers himself soon became commander. According to the *Voice* article, Truscott asked the general if he had known what his deputy, Haig, had been up to. "Rogers told me that he was quite frankly flabbergasted to hear what Haig had carried off without his knowing it." Haig had appeared "completely loyal," Rogers reportedly told Truscott, but now Truscott's story "had given him a new perspective on the rapidly rising young star."

When Rogers subsequently talked about Truscott to author Maureen Mylander in 1973, however, he never mentioned Haig (then his senior), and instead related Truscott's continuing troubles with the army until the young officer resigned his commission in mid-1970. Whatever he knew about the West Point events, whatever he had told Truscott, Rogers was a Maxwell Taylor protégé

and bureaucratic adept who went on to be chief of staff
and Haig's successor at NATO. But he was also the author
of the army's official 1973 history of Ap Gu that left
subtle questions and discrepancies in the record of Haig's
battlefield performance.

The issue that set in motion all this intricate grinding
of personalities was later settled by a cadet suit and a
federal appeals court decision ending mandatory chapel
attendance at all academies, though not before one of
Nixon's military aides and a colleague of Haig's wrote
the West Point superintendent in September 1970 about
the "chapel lawsuit" and the army's "strong behind-the-
scene support from the President." Harassment of the sort
Truscott described came to light in other cases as well,
most notably a nineteen-month "silence" or official ostra-
cism imposed on one independent-minded cadet in the
early Seventies about a dubious charge of cheating. Nor
was Truscott the only cadet to report official suppression
of scandal. "We were taught to cover up anything that
reflects unfavorably on the army and particularly West
Point," a cadet from the Haig years later told a congressional committee.

As for the plausibility of Truscott's harsh profile of
Haig the man, there would be about his story in any event
a disquieting sense of déjà vu. The Haig who in the
Forties "got over his tough times" at the West Point
chapel was now enraged by less pious cadets. The officer
who had long been intent on "ticket punching" and
credentials now used his hard-won authority to stand off
what he naturally saw as a potential career embarrassment.
The Georgetown student who self-consciously extolled

the military perspective now bristled when confronted by a challenge to regulations by "hippies" and subordinates. Not least, there would be the mark of Truscott's martinet and practioner of cover-up in the White House: Haig would later participate in wiretaps on his colleagues, withhold evidence from Congress and prosecutors, and rail through clenched teeth at government dissenters that "your commander in chief has given you an order."

But while Haig went on to ever grander office after 1973, Truscott had his own last word as it were—a 1978 best-selling novel, *Dress Grey*, about a West Point scandal of sex, bureaucratic politics, and cover-up in which the chief villain, a commandant, bore an obnoxious resemblance to the Haig portrayed in the *Village Voice*. There was even a climax between the officer and the cadet hero with much the same setting and dialogue the author recorded having had with Haig ten years before. Truscott clearly found fiction more comforting than reality; in the novel, the Haiglike figure aspired only to the academy superintendency, was thwarted in the end, and was eased into an obscure Washington job somewhat short of Kissinger, Nixon, or secretary of state.

The hiring of Alexander Haig by Henry Kissinger took on afterward a kind of mystique in bureaucratic lore. West Point Superintendent Knowlton was fond of telling visitors years later how in December 1968 "a phone call came from New York City" and an otherwise obscure Colonel Al Haig was magically "summoned to the inner sanctum." It was his "favorite success story," Knowlton would say, proving that in today's army you just never knew where lightning might strike.

Public credit, or blame, for the lightning commonly went to Joe Califano, at the time Lyndon Johnson's chief counsel for domestic affairs, who, as Haig's fame grew, never tired of telling reporters how ardently and in what bipartisan spirit he had recommended his old aide when Kissinger came asking for counsel that winter. If Califano's recommendation was important, though, it was not original. Seldom given to soliciting Democratic house lawyers for general diplomatic advise, Kissinger called Califano like a dutiful personnel officer simply because he already had Haig's name and the Pentagon connection. The impetus was neither magic nor the cachet of any single patron, but came from deep within the half-accidental, half-incestuous politics of the military bureaucracy.

To begin with, the position for which Haig was considered was not one of the key roles on the staff of the National Security Council. As military aides to the presidential adviser, a train of officers had come and gone in deserved obscurity even during the Kennedy-Johnson revival of the NSC officialdom as a personal arm of foreign policy. Their duties were confined to acting as liaison between the council staff and the Joint Chiefs and Pentagon in general, while the bureaucrats on either side picked over each other's cables and memoranda in the endless trimming and compromise called policymaking. The incumbent under Walt Rostow, Air Force General Robert Ginsberg, thus carried back and forth the bombing scenarios, the blinded intelligence on Tet, troop deployments in the Middle East or Czechoslovakia, and other policy debris. It was exactly that filmy Washington sphere of errands, gossip, and assorted bureaucratic propitiations in which Haig had moved doing the same job for McNamara and Vance. So perfunctory was the assignment that it was not a matter of searching for the single most qualified candidate, but rather a rotating sinecure for the services, the new Nixon administration now being the army's or navy's turn after an air-force aide to Rostow. When Kissinger called Califano, he had the name of a naval officer as well as Haig's.

Nor, however trivial or important, did Nixon take a hand in the selection. In a gesture of seriousness that soon haunted both men, he gave Kissinger at the outset a free hand in choosing the NSC staff, the only White House Assistant so autonomous from political spoils or the nepotism of the powerful new presidential chief of staff, H. R. Haldeman. Kissinger's recruitment fell into two distinct categories. There were the key substantive men he wanted to handle particular areas or functions, and there were those selected not for expertise or intellectual distinction but out of bureaucratic patronage to fill what Kissinger saw as essential yet lesser clerical seats.

He went after the key men first: his old friend and State Department bureaucrat Helmut Sonnenfeldt to deal with Soviet affairs; Morton Halperin, a Pentagon official and erstwhile Harvard instructor, who was to coordinate the elaborate new NSC machinery funneling policy papers and power through Kissinger; Daniel Davidson, another State Department aide, who had discreetly kept Kissinger

abreast of Vietnam negotiations and now came to deal
with the same subject; planner Robert Osgood, a Washington academic whom Kissinger liked.

Ironically, some of the men in the second recruitment
category, though unknown, were to be among the most
important and longest with his regime. Lawrence Eagleburger, for example, his first executive assistant and
destined to be a close associate in later years (eventually
even one of Haig's assistant secretaries of state), he borrowed from the staff of Johnson undersecretary of state
and former Kennedy retainer Nicholas Katzenbach;
Eagleburger was an outer-office aide who composed the
muddle of paper and schedules for one boss as for another,
and rose accordingly. Such men, often invisible, sometimes fated for responsibility far beyond their capacities,
came with the government, as it were, like furniture and
limousines. And so it was with Haig.

When Kissinger cast about for a military assistant, he
turned naturally to the Pierre's resident general for the
transition. At fifty-three, gray-haired and slim with a
professorial countenance and a Princeton Ph.D. to match,
General Andrew Jackson Goodpaster was the Republicans' version of Max Taylor. He was another aide-de-
camp made good, singled out from other ambitious,
educated officers by having been Dwight Eisenhower's
assistant at Allied headquarters in Europe in 1950, and
then accompanying his patron to the White House, where
Goodpaster was defense liaison officer and a staff secretary and knew Vice President Nixon. A practitioner of
the very regime of bureaucratic consensus Nixon and
Kissinger were about to emasculate, he was at the Pierre
paradoxically and very politically to give his stamp of

Eisenhower respectability to the new NSC machinery, to help sell it to its cabinet prey, and then for his endorsement to be shunted off to the NATO Command. But before he stamped and departed, he responded to Kissinger by remembering Haig, whom Goodpaster had known when he himself worked as assistant to the chairman of the Joint Chiefs in 1962–66 and Haig was the courier for Vance, then McNamara. The general had been a deputy commander in Vietnam earlier in 1968, and would have known nothing of Haig's recent record at West Point, where Goodpaster would be superintendent in the late Seventies. The NSC slot was, after all, the sort of job they both understood—routine, and another useful post to have had.

Yet Goodpaster's was only one vote for Haig. Another was decisive, even exotic. While at his Pentagon staff desks, Haig had come in contact as well with one of the intramural legends of the building, Fritz Kraemer. Monocled, now sixty, with a large head, German education and accent, and Gothic affectations and political preferences that made him, much more than Kissinger, the Strangelove prototype, Kraemer had risen from a precocious army private in World War II intelligence to a Pentagon colonelcy and back-room advisory role as an Army Department "strategist." Far more important for Haig, Kraemer was also, as the press dubbed him later, "the man who discovered Henry Kissinger." Kraemer had picked out the young Kissinger, a fellow refugee and army private, for administrative duties in the German occupation, then encouraged him to go to Harvard and nurtured his later consultancies and contacts, including the vital connection with Nelson Rockefeller. His son had studied

under Kissinger at Harvard and was to join the NSC staff,
working for a time under Haig. No figure from Kissinger's
life was more influential in bringing him within range of
the Nixon White House, and none would remain closer or
more discreet. When Kissinger was sworn in as secretary
of state, it would be a small family gathering, and Kraemer
was there. By the sheer fates of the Pentagon corridors,
to which the door had been pushed ajar by his father-in-
law, Haig had impressed Kraemer as a diligent, suitably
loyal yet orthodox young adjutant. At any other moment,
with any other men, it would have made no more difference than thousands of such encounters in the bureaucracies. But now the conjunction suddenly pulled Haig
into history.

Despite this extraordinary patronage, there was still a
fleeting question at the Pierre that December about Haig's
job, and it would be still another dramatic twist in retrospect. For a moment it seemed that Haldeman had offered
the position to Alexander Butterfield, the man who later
revealed the Nixon taping system and at the time a decorated air-force acrobatic pilot and colonel. Butterfield had
not only served with Haig briefly as another aide under
Califano in that star-studded Pentagon office in 1966, but
also had gone with Haldeman to UCLA, where their
wives were sorority roommates. At the same time, it was
not the air force's round, and Butterfield was posted at
the moment in Australia with no prospect of a swift appearance at the Pierre and a personal interview with Kissinger that might have gotten him the post anyway in the
bustle and mounting staff needs of the transition. In any
case, when Haldeman ordered his old college friend's file
from the Pentagon and pushed him for the role, Kissinger

shied away, under the pull of prerogative, no doubt, as much as the influential recommendations behind Haig and the pressure to fill the vacancy. So the call was made early in December to the closer, perhaps more trustworthy, staff officer up the Hudson at West Point.

Whatever its weight, Kissinger's resistance to Haldeman's influence in the hiring would be one more irony, of course, considering Haig's later maneuvering among the two rivals. Butterfield, meanwhile, was offered instead a pivotal place as Haldeman's deputy, going on to witness the installation of the Oval Office tape recorders, and to find his own, somewhat different destiny.

The Butterfield interlude pointed up again the narrow conventional expectation of the job. "I told Henry that if he wanted somebody who could really become his deputy, it was Haig," Califano recalled more than a decade later. "No question. He took Haig."

But that was at best gilding the record. There was no precedent or thought at the Pierre for anything more—and Goodpaster and Kraemer had selected nothing else —than an experienced aide to act as military liaison, and by no means as Kissinger's deputy or alternate, with all that implied in political and intellectual peerage. Haig himself remembered the original writ more clearly when he told a 1972 interviewer that he'd been called by Goodpaster for the "military adviser" position. "When I met Dr. Kissinger, he asked some very brief questions," Haig went on about their thirty-minute interview. "He explained that he was interested in a military man who was a field soldier and a commander and not such a military intellectual."

The point is crucial in understanding what followed,

especially the chemistry of the men. In the jungle of ambition and calculation surrounding Kissinger, the common
presumption of the military assistant's limited brief, the
fact that he had not indeed been hired or groomed as the
NSC deputy, was a factor that in many ways made possible Haig's eventual claim to that powerful role. Not
least, he was to be an unthreatening "field soldier" and no
"military intellectual" to rival in that respect the adequately gifted Kissinger, who would later write eight
chapters and almost 250 pages into his detailed White
House memoirs before recalling an event involving his
military aide. Kissinger's preference for a simple, obscure
soldier was perhaps most ironic of all. For much the same
martial, nonintellectual qualities and background in Haig
that Kissinger saw as limits, as a natural weakness in any
potential rivalry for power, Richard Nixon would see as
attractive strengths.

But all that lay ahead. After a swift enlistment, Haig
was sent in mid-December to Washington, where he
routinely filtered back to Kissinger in New York daily
intelligence briefings from the bureaucracy for the president-elect and his staff, and where, unlike Halperin,
Eagleburger, and other aides, he missed altogether the
organizational coup hatching at the Pierre. There in the
old Executive Office Building next to the White House,
the lame-duck Rostow staff first saw him before Christmas
1968, a forty-four-year-old lined, ruddy, and leathery
colonel in tweedy hat, trench coat, and new dark business
suit with trousers slightly high-water. On one occasion,
leaving the building for a late supper with Eagleburger,
he rudely brushed past one of the NSC staff officers,

Harold Saunders, who knew Eagleburger and who had greeted them in the hallway. "It's okay, Al, he's one of ours," said Eagleburger, referring to Kissinger's decision to retain Saunders on the staff; at which Haig broke into a smile and clapped Saunders on the back, reminiscent, Truscott would have said, of handling "Mr. T."

From his stately "vaulted" office at West Point, he would soon move into the NSC quarters in the White House West Basement, a scene that a style-conscious staff lawyer named John Dean described a year later as surprisingly "dreary and overcrowded, jammed with cluttered desks and staffed by a few young military men wearing out-of-date civilian clothes." But its decor never reflected the significance of the office. What mattered there amid the clutter was the gathering, largely invisible power to command and exploit men elsewhere in government in much more impressive quarters, including those upstairs at the White House. And in that, Haig, schooled and elevated in a career of office-staff politics, would soon find himself in style.

Hearing its conversations, Elizabeth Drew described the Nixon White House, its atmosphere if not its refinement as "A place of suspicions . . . resembling the court of the Borgias." So vast was to be the ruin of the regime in Watergate, so anxious then were critics and defenders alike to find some consolation in its diplomacy, in the remnant glamour of Henry Kissinger, that few Americans saw how much of the squalor that bred scandal had been there in the inner politics of foreign policy from the beginning. Too powerful and unprincipled courtiers, weak cabinet ministers, a haunted, isolated president distrustful of everyone outside his chambers and some within; mixed with rare intensity were most of the ingredients of disaster —and of opportunity for Haig.

Kissinger's take-over was swift and sweeping. Within the first weeks of the new administration in 1969, while Haig sat in an adjacent office routinely sorting and passing through daily intelligence digests from the Pentagon and CIA, the new national security adviser came to dominate every issue and forum of foreign policy. Kissinger's intellect, his grasp of the issues, his bureaucratic instinct and political gifts would have made him a force at the higher levels of any government, but here his preeminence seemed inevitable. By all measures, his competition was sadly meager. At the State Department sat Secretary William Pierce Rogers, a congenial New York attorney and Nixon associate from the Eisenhower years. Rogers understood little of either the policies or politics at play, and his ambiguous personal relationship with the new president was no salvation and perhaps an added weakness. A more politically astute ex-congressman from the Wisconsin dells, Melvin Laird as defense secretary was only slightly better armed for the bureaucratic struggle. But his Capitol Hill prowess for press leaks and personal publicity only aroused Kissinger's superiority at the same arts, and Nixon's resentment. Behind both men were the usual, largely stagnant and self-protective bureaucracies whom Kissinger shrewdly flattered, co-opted, or ignored to outflank his rivals, and who watched his burgeoning power with habitual caution and the sullen forbearance of timeservers.

Meanwhile, though determined to dictate foreign policy through his NSC strategist, the new president was just as loath from the murkier depths of his personality to face his own cabinet officers with the unpleasant news—such a direct order, Kissinger wrote tartly, being "the one thing Nixon was psychologically incapable of doing." The pernicious result was a chief executive who was diffident and equivocal when personally confronted by his ministers, and who raged and schemed against them in private for thwarting his will. Having then deepened everyone's sense of insecurity and rancor, not least his own, he increasingly withdrew to leave the furtive, uneven bureaucratic battle to Kissinger. About this organic presidential distress with the rest of government and with Rogers in particular, Kissinger admitted in his memoirs that "I undoubtedly encouraged it," if only because he could hardly "reject opportunities" to have his own strong views "prevail." As for "less elevated motives of vanity and quest for power" in the process, he confessed it "unlikely that they were entirely absent."

Had all this stopped at the usual limits of bureaucratic jostling for authority, even with Nixon's evasions the result might have been simply another period of chafing personal dominance over American foreign policy, Kissinger's ascendancy comparable to that of John Foster Dulles, or Dean Acheson, strong secretaries of state. But what set this government and these men apart, what provided much of the strange yeast for Alexander Haig's rise, was the personal venom, the pervasive suspicion and sheer excess that soon descended over the White House in its stealthy new power, and came to poison the Nixon administration nearly throughout its upper reaches. The court found its style at one level early in 1969, for example, in savage slurs and gossip. Thus it was not enough for

Kissinger to best Rogers in policy issue after issue. There were also stories pandered with staff and press that the secretary of state was keeping a homosexual lover in Georgetown, a rumor that apparently amused more than angered Rogers's staff, who saw their handsome and conventional boss as rather a ladies' man, but which was nonetheless redolent of the White House climate. So, too, Kissinger said, with the same susceptible audience in mind, the secretary of defense was a veritable "traitor" whose Pentagon office was the "Laird-for-President" headquarters.

But equal or worse epithets were reserved for the new president himself who had recently hired him at the Pierre and now heeded his advice almost without exception. In his memoirs, Kissinger would publicly and compassionately remember a "spent, even fragile" Nixon at the inauguration, a politician tragically drained and embittered by his long quest for the office. Earlier, however, while an adviser to rival Nelson Rockefeller, Kissinger had less charitably pronounced Nixon "dangerous" and "unfit" for the presidency. And now in the opening months of 1969 as Nixon's chief foreign-policy adviser, he talked with his staff sneeringly about "our meatball president," or "my drunken friend," referring to Nixon's late-night losing bouts with gin. Closing the sordid circle, there were even recurrent and utterly baseless insinuations about Nixon's past relationship with Rogers, hiding something illicit, illegal, or both, and holding hostage the president of the United States.

Smut was one of Kissinger's weapons against his own consuming anxieties and against the bizarre setting in which he now found his opportunity of a lifetime of striving. One burden of statesmanship for which the Harvard professor was woefully unprepared was that Nixon indeed was a deeply flawed leader, his pettiness and impulsiveness as dangerous as his intelligence or boldness might be creative. His caprice, the maddening paradox of his strengths and unfitness, even came to be codified in White House staff practices, where Haldeman had prudently ordained "the staff officer's duty to ignore any clearly inappropriate demand, even if the President . . . insisted on it." Nixon's nightly drinking was fitful, never incapacitating by day, yet darkly ominous, leaving him to slur orders on the telephone, and his aides, like Kissinger or Haig, to act sometimes as de facto presidents when urgent matters came in after the president was asleep.

The early cost of having this tragic figure in the presidency was not some single act or negligence, but, far worse, the added erosion of integrity and restraint among the none too honorable men he had gathered about him. Nixon's weakness was an invitation to manipulation, and to abuse of authority, which his men did not resist because to most there seemed no other choice of governance, because there would be occasional mitigating accomplishment, because no one on the outside really knew anyway, and because, as Kissinger said, there were "opportunities." In foreign policy, the result was to exploit in the West Basement the power Nixon formally seized or which his method of rule made possible, and at the same time to shield that power from him when necessary. This created Kissinger's furtive world of personal diplomacy—leaks and back-channel communications; narrow, compressed decisions wrung from a bitter and distrusting president; and a general hypocrisy toward the barbarians at every gate. Elmo Zumwalt, a thoughtful young admiral raised by Laird to be chief of naval operations, later captured in his memoirs the flavor of it all in a mock bit of stage dialogue from a meeting with Kissinger in 1971:

> Scene: An office in the basement of the White House. HENRY KISSINGER, smiling and gesticulating, is escorting ELMO ZUMWALT out the door.
>
> KISSINGER: Bud, it is always a pleasure to talk to you. You are the only intellectual among the Chiefs, the only one able to take a broad view. We must have these talks more often.
>
> (They shake hands warmly. ZUMWALT exits. KISSINGER makes sure the door is shut tightly and ZUMWALT is out of earshot.)
>
> KISSINGER (rolling his eyes): If there's one thing I can't stand it's an intellectual admiral!

"In sum," the nation's naval adviser concluded, "I found that I could not believe what Henry told me."

Zumwalt was hardly alone, and Kissinger's devious technique not unique to the politics of foreign policy. Inevitably, the rancid practices turned back on the White House. Haldeman and his colleague, domestic affairs counselor John Ehrlichman, Kissinger's most formidable rivals on the Nixon staff, men whom the Oval Office tapes show talking to the president virtually as equals with few of the deferential "sirs" or "Mr. Presidents" of other inter-

locutors, thus became known in the West Basement as
"the Gestapo." Reciprocating with the house fixation on
homosexuality, Ehrlichman thought his friend Henry
"queer." From early in 1969 Kissinger faithfully recorded
all his telephone conversations with Nixon, senior aides,
and everyone else, the Dictabelts transcribed every day
(eventually under Haig's watchful eye) and salted away
in personal files to be removed from the White House to
Rockefeller's Pocantico Hills estate, Kissinger's insurance
against history as well as his fellow policymakers. "This
is not an honorable business conducted by honorable men
in an honorable way," he told an unsurprised staff later
that first year.

On it went. When he was hired as White House counsel,
the yet uninitiated John Dean thought it "strange" that
Haldeman told him he must now be loyal to Nixon and
not to his former boss, Attorney General John Mitchell.
Were they not after all in the same government and enjoying a "close relationship?" "Nobody is a friend of ours,
let's face it," Nixon would later answer the figurative
question in a passage from the tapes. What distinguished
domestic from foreign affairs was chiefly Kissinger's intellectual quality. "Your job is to do, not to think," Haldeman typically informed assistant Jeb Magruder, and
witnesses of Haldeman and Ehrlichman doing business
with the president thought Nixon was "never in danger of
being overstimulated." Meanwhile, though similar foreign-
policy deliberations would be forever shielded by "national security," the overall tenor seeped through in the
Watergate tapes in which "shit" was the mildest expletive
deleted, and the conversation in the highest office of the
American republic sounded, thought one longtime Wash-

ington observer, like "the back room of a second-rate
advertising agency in a suburb of hell."

Haig watched all this develop from an intimate vantage
point just outside Kissinger's office. His duties "varied
dramatically," he told his 1981 confirmation hearing, from
merely reading and transmitting documents to preparing
"a substantive analysis" to his later "more substantial
role" in the Vietnam negotiations. For most of the first
year and a half, however, it was very much the first,
essentially clerical job. He began by funneling intelligence reports to Kissinger, and through him to Nixon.
Then, as the stream of staff papers, cables, and bureaucratic studies rose with Kissinger's control, he joined
Eagleburger to read and transmit a share of those as well.
It began as an orthodox staff position, seeing that the dis-
orderly Kissinger disposed the papers and decisions expected of him, and that the outflow from Kissinger's desk,
on to the president, to the NSC staff, to the bureaucracies
beyond, ran without major snags. To that end he worked
fourteen-to-sixteen-hour days, though always on a schedule that necessarily stretched just before and beyond
Kissinger's, and rarely involving his own writing or reflection as distinct from waiting on and noting the work of
others. Like all such high-level government clerking, it
was an uneven rhythm of quiet and rush, late nights as
often the result of the lumbering inefficiency of the bureaucrats whose paper he processed, or of the fashionable
night hours thought *de rigueur* among key officials, as of
the actual significance or volume of a day's work. It was
one of the several little secrets staff men at these heady
reaches never vouchsafed to awestruck outsiders—that
you might be "at the office" all those hours, late for

dinner and never available, but that actually working all that time in the sense a surgeon or mechanic or waitress worked was altogether another matter.

Still, at what he did, Haig was indefatigable, and, even more important, was reputed to be. "Not smart but he's the quintessential staff man," the *New York Post* quoted an NSC staff colleague. There was the military bearing and sense of command to calm the perturbing disarray of paper, and not least the regular frenzies and abuse of underlings by Kissinger, whose office discourtesies were legend. "He pounds assistants into the ground," observed White House speechwriter William Safire. "Only some-one schooled in taking shit could put up with it," echoed Coleman Hicks, an appointments secretary who quit.

NSC colleagues and White House staff who dealt occa-sionally with Kissinger's office described the long-working colonel as "personable" or "likable." Safire, however, who as a writer worked around Kissinger and his assistants more than most presidential aides, judged Haig tellingly like Nixon, Haldeman, and Kissinger, all "loners, in a superficially gregarious way." Outwardly loyal to Kissin-ger with somber, low-toned deference, he could be in-gratiating with the staff officers who trooped through to see Kissinger or push their papers. Posing as their ir-reverent, sympathetic advocate in the West Basement, he was one more of Henry's victims, one of the boys. When Kissinger sent out a staff officer at the close of 1969 to conduct delicate secret negotiations with foreign factions in defiance of the State Department—a mission of doubt-ful success and high risk of bureaucratic explosion in which Kissinger could claim credit or else disavow the aide—Haig, with a sympathetic smile, passed the man a note after Kissinger had left a meeting. "He gets the diamonds," said the large scrawl. "You get the rocks."

Often the empathy was discreetly self-serving. When Anthony Lake, another outer-office aide close to Kissinger, resigned over the invasion of Cambodia in the spring of 1970, Haig was told by Kissinger to take Lake to lunch to try to rescind the resignation, though Haig could not have been more opposed to Lake's position. He should not leave, Haig told Lake as they sat down in the White House mess. Yet Haig then launched into a familiar, unbroken litany of how difficult and demeaning it was to work for Kissinger. "He was very subtly working on all the feelings I had about leaving, all the embers of my resentment," Lake told a reporter long afterward, having resigned as planned. "He knew what *he* wanted from me and he meant to get it."

Subtle or no, after Cambodia Haig could more readily exercise his preference. At the start, his rivalry with an often ambitious, self-important, and more cerebral NSC staff was careful and muted. As the new foreign-policy power of the presidential adviser rapidly became evident, there was the predictable and unseemly early jockeying in 1969 for the unspecified position as Kissinger's deputy, though Kissinger himself showed scant readiness to share even a slice of his title and role, jealously blocking staff contacts of any sort with Nixon. In any case, Haig, the processor of documents with no noticeable policy intellect, was then an outside choice at most. The more likely candidate was Halperin, the architect and staff coordinator of the new NSC system, and, before his later conversion by wiretap to civil libertarian and public opponent of the regime, one of the more grasping, calculating bureaucrats circling the West Basement.

While Halperin's ambition flashed nakedly, Sonnenfeldt, the old and much overestimated Kissinger friend in Soviet affairs, and equally predatory, sat in his office down the hall in the Executive Office Building sullenly joking about his potential rivals and waiting for the summons to be deputy himself. Eagleburger, Haig's peer if not slight superior in staff and rank and no admirer, might have been a third even stronger prospect. He was a practiced adjutant of little threatening substance to disturb Kissinger, and had a nervous compulsiveness that not only kept the office running but drove him more than once obsessively to change shirt and suit in the middle of the day he was to meet the president. Six years Haig's junior, he was better educated, shrewd, ambitious, and politically conservative, though also a chronic asthmatic with no matching stamina or patience. Haig would surpass these men in the first instance not by ingenuity, depth, or particular design (though they all typically saw the latter when it happened), but mainly by outlasting them. The historic opportunity at Kissinger's side he won more by accretion and indirection, almost by default, as his rivals, real and potential, fell by the way of their own weight.

Haig's first break in that respect came in midsummer 1969 when Eagleburger collapsed in the office and consequently was forced to leave the job altogether for a calmer posting as a NATO diplomat in Brussels. Bellowing for staff attention and service even as Eagleburger lay on an office sofa waiting for an ambulance, Kissinger soon replaced him with Lake, a thirty-year-old junior and liberal Foreign Service officer and another former aide to Katzenbach, at one stroke leaving Haig the senior and stronger figure on Kissinger's immediate staff. There, where routine and compliance far outshone any other abilities, Haig flourished by enduring. Within months, Halperin was gone under a shadow of the wiretap and questions of security, to be replaced by Richard Kennedy, an army colonel recruited by Haig and the modest beginning of his own coterie of men on the staff. The same political doubts hung over Sonnenfeldt as well, even though he stayed. When Lake had left, another possible rival had gone with him, Staff Secretary William Watts who had worked for Rockefeller. Of the men who followed them in Kissinger's personal orbit, none was strong or senior enough to rival Haig, and none would be so politically or personally compatible with the Nixon regime.

With that attrition and Haig's gradual emergence, rather like the junior officer who finds himself eventually commanding in a bloody battle, his further rise became all the more dependent on his relationship with Kissinger. It was another of the envious Sonnenfeldt's acid jokes that Henry Kissinger, the German-Jewish immigrant, only kept Haig, the all-American war hero from Philadelphia, to reassure the Joint Chiefs and, if necessary, testify for Henry someday at an imagined right-wing star chamber trial when Kissinger went too far with detente. The malice had a point: Kissinger did fear an eventual reaction to his diplomacy from the right and it did later materialize so formidably as to make Haig, but not his old boss, an acceptable secretary of state for Ronald Reagan.

The ties between the two men were more complex,

however. Haig's organizational contribution was crucial. "He never would have got anything read if it wasn't for Haig," Laird once said of Kissinger's disorder. As the national security adviser became theorist, bureaucratic politician, then renowned negotiator of the regime, Haig became his much-needed logistics and administrative officer, managing his growing empire with attention to the mundane but all too necessary details Kissinger spurned. With every new bureaucratic diplomatic conquest and its demands on Kissinger, with every cession of office management, every proxy in his absence, every bit of added knowledge about Kissinger's plans, vulnerabilities, needs, Haig's power accumulated.

MacArthur's biographer said that early assignments "didn't really matter; he would have risen anyhow." In Haig's case, however, it seems almost impossible to envision his prominence apart from Kissinger—and later Nixon—without the singular coincidence of men and moment. The very secrecy and aggrandizement of the Kissinger approach drew power into his own office, making Haig, or someone in that place, at that time, indispensable. But another temperament would not have put such a premium on Haig's clerical skills. A more secure man would not have found such comfort, or indeed necessity, in Haig's relative lack of intellect. Then, too, a diplomat of lesser gifts than Kissinger's would not as a one-man show have compensated so easily for a deputy of Haig's limits, could not have afforded them. Nor are they quite imaginable outside that particular regime. With all the genuine and phantom enemies about, Kissinger needed a Haig for reassurance with far more than the Joint Chiefs or reactionary politicians.

And that Haig provided. Safire records them together in typical interaction in 1971. In high dudgeon at a State Department inference that he could not leave Washington for fear of losing influence with Nixon, "Kissinger's voice broke a couple of times as he paced and talked, he was so worked up," while "Haig, standing in the corner, kept nodding in agreement or sympathy." It was an ironic twist on another moment when Kissinger would indeed be afraid to leave Washington lest Haig undermine him, but for now the general was simply nodding in the corner.

In a similar incident, Kissinger took Safire into Haig's office, demanding, "Where is that cable that shows how State is stabbing me in the back?" Whereupon Haig, "with a tight little smile," pulled the offending telegram immediately from his right-hand drawer. Moments before, Haig had been scouring the office for a lost document on strategic arms negotiations that an again infuriated Kissinger told Safire was "the most sensitive, the most top secret piece of paper that exists in the entire government at this moment." Haig was also, as one colleague put it, a "willing hostage," to Kissinger's now authentic, now contrived fears of political extremism, whether right or left, a ghost of Weimar Germany that prowled his mind. "He had a healthy sensitivity to the danger of being a scapegoat . . . and some justification for that," Haig told the *New York Post* in 1974 in talking about Kissinger's background. "No one can come to Washington and serve in a responsible position and not develop a degree of paranoia," he said later in the same interview, "which can also be diagnosed as excess complacency."

In the first few years they rarely argued, Haig insinuating his views in the traditional fashion of the staff assistant

—a cover note on certain memos, a puncturing question of another officer at a staff meeting, a remark about this man's pet cause and ambition or that one's dubious loyalty or insensitivity to Kissinger's plight. Dealing with an extraordinarily moody, busy, distracted, and ever suspicious superior, he might shape policy or its consideration without ever truly resorting to open advocacy or opposition. It was privileged access of the same kind Eagleburger enjoyed briefly in 1969 and much more in later years, that Lake wielded to a degree for a few months, and that Haig enjoyed most of all. And it had its special price, levied in terms of what was at once Haig's strength and weakness in Kissinger's aura: that he was a soldier. "I'm going to call the Pentagon to ask them to release you for a day's work on my staff," Kissinger would taunt him; or, in another variation: "There's no point in your coming, Al; the army doesn't have anything at stake in this meeting." Characteristically, Kissinger once remarked to Safire, "I don't need an intelligent, sensitive human being for an assistant. What I need is a good, smart robot."

Seeing him smile, Safire thought the great man was "only kidding," since Haig seemed a "highly intelligent" aide who understood Kissinger "better than he understood himself." At the same time, it seemed that Haig could not, as Safire remembered as well, "have gone to the bathroom without raising his hand and asking Henry." Forbearance was required, if not understanding—"taking shit," as the appointments aide had put it. With Haig in the room, Kissinger reportedly held forth for visitors on how military men were "dumb, stupid animals to be used." By similar accounts, he frequently berated Haig in front of the rest of the West Basement staff. In one instance, when fighter bombers did not attack Vietnam because of poor weather, Kissinger ranted about the need for "generals who could win battles . . . not good briefers like Haig."

There would be no shortage of such humiliating outbursts seen and recorded by several witnesses. As Haig was leaving for a trip to Cambodia in 1970, with a small crowd of aides and even reporters around the White House exit, Kissinger walked out with him. When Haig bent to enter the waiting car, Kissinger pulled him back and began to polish the single star on his shoulder. "Al, if you're a good boy," he said in stage conversation, "I'll get you another one." A witness of this and similar gestures described Haig at such moments as smiling thinly, looking off and "working his jaw and neck back and forth in a sharp tight motion . . . almost as if the man were trying to straighten his tie with no hands."

Sparing the rest of the staff such abuse, acting as a buffer, explained in part why Haig would be gradually accepted in his role as first among equals by NSC officers, and why the job as deputy, whatever its political rewards, lost much of its allure for others as Kissinger's personal oppressiveness at close range became known. It was with the staff as well that Haig had his whispered revenge, such as it was in the early years. Thus Henry could not see them just now, he was having "one of his fits." Or it would do no good to propose the cable tonight; he was "weak," "crazy," he was about to leave for a date and "his mind is in his pants."

If Haig first distinguished himself with Kissinger by sheer perseverance and seniority by survival, he took one office initiative in 1969–70 that was crucial to his progress.

In a time-honored feudal technique of bureaucracy as well as diplomacy and war, he formed a quiet precautionary alliance with his tormentor's nemesis, in this case Kissinger's White House adversary, Haldeman. As the single contact point between the two staffs (Kissinger did not trust his NSC officers dealing independently with his White House rivals any more than with the president or the rest of the government), Haig came to cultivate the Nixon inner circle with casual, then increasingly sympathetic, conversation about Kissinger's spreading notoriety, which both Nixon and his senior men viewed with mounting resentment.

To William Gulley, head of the White House Military Office and a close observer of staff politics, Haig had "found a way to make use of Bob Haldeman. He began to tell Haldeman little, intimate tidbits of gossip about Kissinger—he's screwing this or that broad in New York . . ." Gulley wrote in his memoirs. "Kissinger was hot copy and everybody wanted to be let in on the inside story, a story nobody but Haig could give out." It was "valuable currency," thought Gulley, and Haig "bought Haldeman's support with it."

Still another former colleague called Haig "Kissinger's man in Haldeman's office and Haldeman's man in Kissinger's office." But some of those accounts have an aroma of gossip as well, and the connection was never so simple as titillation or so immediately ambitious or structured as some aides feared. A more thoughtful former Nixon campaign aide called Haldeman and his faction, for all their imperious manner, "basically unsure of themselves, second-raters playing over their heads and fiercely resentful of anyone who dared approach them at eye level."

Haig now made that approach as a dutiful middle-level staff man giving them an entry into the one bureaucratic sanctum of the White House they did not control, and indirectly as well into a vault of Nixon's mind and the province of his major political triumphs—foreign policy —from which they had been barred.

Like most office politics, it tended to be a devious double gambit. When Kissinger sent Haig to Haldeman early in 1970 with one of what would become a series of periodic resignation threats provoked by tangible or suspected affronts, Haldeman would know from Haig that it was not serious but a petulant gesture. And when Haig returned with the reply that Henry should resign if he wished, Kissinger went into a funk that aides recall as lasting for days. But then Haig was also a source for an ever interested Kissinger on the ceaseless machinations around Haldeman and Ehrlichman. From his discreet forays upstairs at the White House, Haig brought back news of the rise and decline of a presidential counselor like Pat Moynihan, or later, more ominously, of the creation of Erlichman's plumbers and the fulminating obsession with internal security and domestic espionage that would bring down the government.

Only rarely was the liaison visible. As the White House rivalry turned steadily more rancorous, Haig was presumed to be Kissinger's man. Yet as Haig pinned on the second star of a major general in the spring of 1972, Haldeman bantered with him perhaps too easily, some thought, at the award ceremony. "Stop smiling, look hawkish," he said in mock command, to which Haig smiled even more broadly and quipped that working for Kissinger had been "a race between a second star and a cardiac." In the end, of course, the discreet relationship was revealed to have been no more than coldly expedient for both sides. Two and a half years after the ceremony, with Haig in Haldeman's job and the smiles wiped away by Watergate, the general would be calling the once-powerful chief of staff and his old spymaster "that criminal."

The most important and lasting benefit of the Haldeman tie was to cast Haig in a favorable light with his ultimate patron, Richard Nixon. There was little or no direct exposure to the president in those early months under a jealously watchful Kissinger, but when attention in the Oval Office turned to Kissinger's staff—and Haldeman and Nixon used questions about leaks and the loyalty of the NSC bureaucrats (recruited after all, including Haig, so largely with the blessing of the previous administration) to undermine or at least limit Kissinger—Haig would be a notable exception, the soldier who saw Kissinger's flaws as clearly as Haldeman. With that impression preparing the way, the relationship between Haig and the president developed "subtly," as the *New York Post* described it, and very much at Nixon's initiative.

There was a telling prophetic scene late in 1969 when Nixon, Kissinger, and a speechwriter were working in the president's hideaway EOB office and Haig was summoned to bring a piece of missing information. He brought a paper with the answer and was dismissed with a nod from Kissinger. But as Haig turned to go, Nixon suddenly said to him, "No, stay while we're doing this," adding to his staff writer in an aside, "Thought and action." The cryptic reference was to a favorite Nixon speech theme drawn from a passage by Woodrow Wilson about the dis-

tinction between "men of thought and men of action."
Nixon had given a 1966 campaign speech with the line
"The man of thought who will not act is ineffective; the
man of action who will not think is dangerous." The
maxim ran deep in the precarious self-image of a Nixon
who struggled to prove himself the suitable blend of the
two characteristics.

Safire, who recorded this incident and others like it,
observed that "the President—unknown to Kissinger—
saw that combination in Al Haig" and sought to encourage it. Nixon regarded Haig as "both a brave combat
soldier and a brilliant staff officer, whose morale would be
boosted by being treated not as a messenger but as an
advisor." Safire's revelation benefited from hindsight of
Haig as Nixon's closest aide in the Watergate finale. It
was unlikely Nixon had formed in late 1969 more than a
cursory perception of Haig, and that mostly from Haldeman. Yet it was probably enough that Haig, as decorated
veteran and loyal aide, *seemed* the part, and in any case
supplied in his background of "action" the ingredient
Nixon most doubted in himself. Later, when Nixon struck
out with ferocity in Cambodia and Vietnam to prove his
own decisiveness, Haig would be there always to lend the
advice of action, not thought—to fortify and indulge the
impulse to be "effective," not to temper the "dangerous."
Whatever he represented in that deeply forested interior
that was Nixon's mind, he would be a creature of the
president's inner turmoil as he was of Kissinger's, and of
the state of siege their rancor transposed to government
at large, answering peculiar needs other presidents and
advisers at other times in Washington would never have
felt.

Following that encounter, at any rate, their direct dealings became more common, and Nixon's regard more
open, in part as a conscious antidote to the coveted fame
and Washington acceptance of his national security adviser. "Haig's always down there," the president once
said, motioning to the West Basement in a bitter remark
to aides in the spring of 1970, "while Henry's off having
dinner in Georgetown." Another version delivered to reporters censored the "dinner in Georgetown" and Nixon's
old enduring rancor as the capital outsider. "When you
see the lights burning late in Henry's office, it's usually Al
Haig," the president said that same June.

The message in either rendition was clear enough. By
bureaucratic skill, doggedness, serpentine White House
politics, and Nixon's private imagery, Haig, after eighteen
months on the job, was showing through a dazzling
(sometimes too dazzling) Kissinger presence that had
blotted out much of the rest of government. On occasional nocturnal wanderings around the White House,
Nixon would stop by the lighted office and chat with
Haig, a few times asking for memos from Haig directly,
including one on the then proposed all-volunteer army.
In most cases, Haig was careful to tell Kissinger of the
request as if it had been made to the office in general,
and the responses went back upstairs signed with the
customary "HK." He ventured a few times, though, to
send his own paper quietly in and out of the Oval Office
through Haldeman, creating his private "chron-RN" file
kept from Kissinger and one more little intramural secret
of the West Basement.

As Kissinger increasingly became the regime's secret
and far-ranging diplomatic agent after the autumn of

1970, Haig's personal briefings and direct written reports to Nixon became all the more frequent. He acted as Kissinger's lone relay, often in matters of such exclusivity that only these three men in the entire American government knew the details. Several staff witnesses of the process thought it gave Haig ready opportunity to exploit the uneasy relationship between Nixon and Kissinger and to insert his own views, much as he played off Kissinger and NSC staff officers.

Haig was dealing with a Nixon so sensitive to the question of who actually conceived and directed his grand gestures of foreign policy that the president ordered the Oval Office to be bugged in part to prove his authorship, and doomed himself in the act. "So Haig gave Kissinger's messages a tilt . . . a little editing here and a little rephrasing there, making a suggestion that this or that point might fall in line better with the President's view of what should be done, rather than Kissinger's," reported Gulley from a cynicism educated by eleven years in the White House military office. "The result would be messages sent back in code with little changes, from Nixon, changes which in fact had been suggested by Haig purely in order to play up to Nixon's vanity. Al Haig was manipulating both players."

In 1972, Haig himself talked almost casually with Zumwalt over lunch about how he acted as an "intermediary" between the mutually suspicious Nixon and Kissinger. Yet once again, onlookers appear to have exaggerated both Haig's subtlety and the simplicity of the scheme. Tampering with Kissinger's cables on China or SALT or Vietnam would have been too easy to detect afterward

by Kissinger and his traveling aides, men who would
scarcely have spared Haig the consequences. Moreover,
Nixon was too involved by the time this triangle began,
too well versed in both the issues and Kissinger's approach
merely to pass over such manipulation. If Kissinger's recommendations or performance were at odds with the
president's view, Haig needed only to report it faithfully
and thoroughly, and sit back to await the predictable reaction, inserting his own comments with Nixon orally and
off the record.

It was another illustration of the recurring theme of
Haig's rise. He did not have to manufacture or conspire at
the condition, in this case the Nixon-Kissinger conun-
drum, but simply take advantage quietly of the chance to
ingratiate himself with a proud, touchy president while
maintaining "delicately," as one account worded it, his
primary relationship with Kissinger.

As always, while these personal factors shaped issues
of international moment, the service to Nixon had its
seamy, profoundly cynical side like almost every other
association at the higher levels of the regime. While dropping in on Haldeman or dutifully sitting in as the "man
of action" in Nixon's speechwriting, while chatting re-
spectfully with the presidential night stroller, Haig in
private with the NSC staff referred to Haldeman and
Company as "those shits," to Nixon as "our drunk," and
joked savagely—a variation on the Kissinger refrain—
about Nixon's "limp wrist" relationship with businessman
and White House "intimate" Bebe Rebozo. In 1969–70,
he would call over NSC colleagues to regale them with
what had come to be known as "Butterfieldgrams."

Before the recording devices were installed in February 1971, one of Butterfield's duties as Haldeman's deputy was to sit quietly in the Oval or EOB offices and record, nearly verbatim, random presidential utterings and instructions while Nixon read intelligence briefs or, more often, the press. The product was a weekly pile of two-to-three-line memos, many addressed to Kissinger from Butterfield, describing the president's thoughts, and usually the now comic, now pathetic virulence of rivalries in the administration. A typical batch reviled Laird while Haig sat smiling at the alternating shock and mirth of the staff men reading the memos. "Henry, Laird is up to his old tricks," a notation read after Nixon saw a critical article on defense policy. "Shut the bastard up." Or: "I see this goddamn c--- s------ story about troop levels, this is Laird again. The son of a bitch is up to his old games. What's he trying to do?" As for the State Department, "Stop this!" on a report of Rogers negotiating in the Middle East, or "They're trying to undercut us again," on reading about Undersecretary Elliot Richardson's congressional testimony. None of the instructions would be acted upon, as Haig and the staff men knew—just more proof of the disarray and veering sanity of the government, more morsels of gossip, in a sense, that Haig would share.

Of course "they" were crazy, Haig would tell incredulous or depressed colleagues reading such tidbits, but "no crazier than most." This was what one learned to expect working for great men. He might then tell the story of carrying MacArthur's sleeping bag ashore at Inchon or throwing the grenade in the tile bath. "I've got to get out of here," he said at other times to other men, talking wistfully about resuming his army career.

There were a few moments of what seemed deeper unease. One fellow assistant remembered him "silent and pretty upset" when it was evident during one of the administration's first crises—when the North Koreans shot down an EC-121 reconnaissance plane in the spring of 1969—that Nixon had been drinking during the hours of decision. And once, some months later, after reading a staff memo, he leaned forward and said softly, almost sadly, to the author, "God damn, if I could write that well, I wouldn't be doing this." But there would be no real pause, no sure sense of limit or of where to stop, of where service and acceptance crossed over into compromise and complicity.

He stayed, and was promoted, at the least resigned to the pettiness and megalomania and malevolence as occupational routine. "He moved me up, based on human chemistry," Haig once described his early rise with Kissinger, "not bureaucratic wiliness or all that." When Watts, the staff secretary, sent Kissinger an unusual memo early in 1970 "On Dealing with State," urging an end to the venom and harsher habits of rivalry, Haig openly ridiculed Watts with Kissinger and other officers. To many who saw him closely in 1969–70, he seemed to relish the utterances and maneuvers his fellow officers found appalling. "He was always perfectly comfortable doing what must be done," a coworker told a reporter.

Later, when there were vicious jokes and leaks about President Carter from NATO headquarters, when there was a year of savage rivalry and personal battle with security adviser Richard Allen in the Reagan administration, those who saw him in the West Basement wondered if Al Haig knew any other way to govern.

The malignant style of the administration tended to obscure the fact that the same people were engaged in the deadly serious business of foreign policy. For those who were there inside, for those who later studied the era and the personalities, there was a fascination with the ugly confederacy of power, and then with all the hypocrisy and connivance as omens of Watergate. Haig's fitness for even higher office came to be judged against that perverse standard: Had he been part of the worst excesses or only a staff retainer? Had he committed one of the outrages or somehow stood unknowing and apart. Finding no felonious evidence, the Senate Foreign Relations Committee would heartily endorse him as secretary of state. But behind the character scandals, the policies in the world beyond were real enough, and Haig's role in their making and conduct was another major influence in his rise.

Just as his sheer proximity to Kissinger spared his colleagues the worst of the temper tantrums or some of the more chilling glimpses of the squalor and incapacity upstairs in the West Wing, so too he became Kissinger's lone privy chamberlain as the most important decisions and the clandestine diplomacy shrank to Kissinger's person, often to the exclusion of the NSC staff as well as the remainder of government. Haig's power in their secret chamber was simply to know—not the issues or nuances of diplomacy so much as what had been done and who had recommended, ordered, opposed it. His advance in that power was propelled only in part by what he created or did himself, and as much or more by what he knew about the men, Nixon and Kissinger, he served so exclusively, what he had done for them that so many others could not be trusted to do, what he could be counted on never to tell—and rewarded for it.

Nor was it solely loyalty or ambition. He brought to policy, as his thesis and war-college papers forecast, a visceral, bristling conservatism. He was entirely at home with Nixon's "toughness" if not the dark self-doubt that stoked it, and often oblivious to Kissinger's strategic sophistication. It was an ideology of simple answers, and above all of secrecy, the right of the court to rule as it chose at the summit of both military and civil power. What Kissinger inferred from intellectual superiority and Nixon from political paranoia, Haig presumed from the bureaucratic ethic that war and politics are best left to professionals.

As his bureaucratic position grew more secure through 1969, he gradually expanded the customary role of military liaison to active lobbying for Pentagon budgets and the army in particular, whose chiefs of staff he kept discreetly informed of White House trends. He had been pleased "with the way the military got its message to [Nixon] in the past four years," he said in a 1973 interview. It was access for which he could take some credit, though often he used his court prerogatives merely to carry on old narrow interservice rivalries.

When Kissinger in the spring of 1971 moved toward recommending more money for the navy, Zumwalt recorded, it "roused the Army tiger in Al Haig," who was "not about to let that happen and mounted a sustained attack on the credibility" of the naval figures, which led to a budget "stalemate." Later in the same fiscal cycle, Zumwalt had been asked by the president, apparently without Haig's knowledge, to present naval priorities to Budget Director George Shultz. The admiral, walking through the White House to Shultz's office, passed Haig with no more than a casual greeting. While he was briefing Shultz, Zumwalt then reports, Haig anxiously called Shultz's secretary to ask why he was there, and when he discovered the reason, "hit the fan." Before Zumwalt could return to the Pentagon, Haig had called Laird to complain that the navy (though Zumwalt's visit in any other administration would have been a routine briefing) was taking "unfair advantage" of the army.

At the same time, Haig was not merely another bureaucratic claimant, and his insertion of a parochial army or Pentagon bias at Kissinger's elbow drew down similar anger from others. Early in 1969, he clipped one of his first cover notes onto a Sonnenfeldt memo on the issues of U.S. bases in Franco's Spain. The cover note put forth the standard Pentagon argument for keeping them at almost all costs. "I know something about that," he told Eagleburger. But Sonnenfeldt learned of the note, and the memo was swiftly leaked to the press, with minor but unwanted embarrassment. "That'll teach the sonofabitch," Sonnenfeldt told colleagues.

In fact, the leak only damaged Sonnenfeldt's own standing, and Haig went on writing tactical last-minute notes slid between Kissinger and his staff. Bases in particular he felt qualified to judge. "We ought to pay a little more blackmail," he told Zumwalt in September 1971 on the subject of renewing a British base in Malta—a deal later involving three times the rent of a former agreement, the United States paying nearly four million pounds a year. On other issues deemed of less strategic importance (issues the Pentagon commonly ignored), he could be cheerfully offhand, even derisive. When National Security Council meetings were still held at least *pro forma* in the first year, he often took notes for Kissinger, and solemnly did so at an early session concerning the Nigerian civil war and the U.S. relief policy toward starving Biafra, where Nixon decided on a "high profile" humanitarian effort. But when African relief came up at NSC staff meetings, Haig would smilingly beat the table like jungle drums, much to the amusement of Kissinger, who, astonishingly, shared the racial stereotypes and casual prejudice of both his military assistant and his president. Racist slurs peppered the telephone transcripts churned out in the West Basement. When Haig told and retold his Vietnam war story about the old man and the grenade, the moral, pressed home in the low tone and hooded look that later became familiar to reporters and questioning congressmen, was that "they" just did not value human life.

It was Vietnam that he staked out as his main policy concern. In part, his staff military role and past experience drew him there as a matter of course at the beginning. In part, too, among Kissinger's personal aides it was the one area early in 1969 that the cautious Eagleburger tried to shun as a burial ground of Foreign Service careers. Once established, Haig's involvement thickened not only as a result of his bureaucratic intimacy with Kissinger but also for the very good reason that he was so in agreement with the deepening secrecy and periodic ferocity of the White House war policy. His public statements years afterward hummed with the chauvinism he wore so easily at the side of Kissinger and Nixon.

"It was one of the most profound mistakes in the history of our country," he told the Senate Foreign Relations Committee during his confirmation, "not the war itself but the way in which it was fought." He had been more specific on NBC in 1978 when he said, "I think at any particular juncture the war could have been ended very rapidly had an American president been able to apply the full range of American power."

Beyond the half-million U.S. troops, the years of bombing, the B-52 carpet strikes, the mining and blockade that Haig by then had seen committed in the war, the "full range" of power seemed an unmistakable allusion to nuclear weapons or an all-out invasion of North Vietnam, "ends" to the conflict that later listeners to such remarks seemed reluctant to explore. Yet Haig's public rhetoric after the fact was wholly consistent with his position inside government from 1969 to 1973.

He began by fighting his own guerrilla action against National Security Study Memorandum number one, the "NSSM 1" later celebrated in a 1972 leak and, at the outset of the regime, a lengthy series of questions drafted by Halperin and others at the Pierre (among them a consultant named Daniel Ellsberg) to elicit a fresh appraisal of the war from every involved bureaucracy. When the answers about the political and military state of affairs produced an unusually candid and bleak picture—estimates of the time required for the pacification of South Vietnam ranging from "8.3 years" to "13.4 years"—Haig argued that the study had been produced by a "Democratic bureaucracy." The unpalatable NSSM had been "outdated and outdistanced" by events, he told a reporter in 1972, though in many ways the document in 1969 was the most thorough of its kind in more than a decade of U.S. embroilment in Southeast Asia. It was ignored not for being wrong or irrelevant, but because its awkward truths clashed with the emerging Nixon-Kissinger view of national interests and "manliness" in the conflict.

In the same vein, Haig joined Kissinger in urging Nixon to bomb North Korea after the April 1969 downing of a navy intelligence plane over the Sea of Japan, believing, as he later told a journalist, that as a result of their proposed "get tough" retaliation "the Indo-China war could be a whole new ball game." Sending a small flotilla to show the flag instead, Nixon began to be labeled in the West Basement as "weak," along with the other assorted descriptions.

By the summer of 1969, with Eagleburger gone and Lake come to the office with his own diplomatic experience as a consul and ambassadorial aide in Vietnam, Haig stepped up his memos, notes, and comments on the issue. Watching the growing frustration of the administration in the face of a negotiating deadlock in Paris and renewed Vietcong offensives on the ground—an impasse produced in large measure by Washington's failure to formulate a new policy and Hanoi's exploitation of the indecision— Haig pushed Kissinger to consider the old military nostrum, an unlimited attack on North Vietnam. Whether to dispose of the issue or genuinely appraise the option, Kissinger assembled a small, highly secret group of NSC staff planners in the fall, including Haig, to consider what he called a "savage punishing" blow. "I can't believe," he told the group, "that a fourth-rate power like North Vietnam doesn't have a breaking point."

It was the same logic Haig and other Pentagon officers had professed for years. When military plans were discreetly sent to the NSC as part of the study (without Defense Secretary Laird's knowledge, of course), they were no more than retyped versions of war plans drafted years before. Christened variously the "September" or "November Group" by its participants, the task force produced a "scenario" that contemplated the mining of the port of Haiphong and inland waterways, a naval blockade, carpet bombing of population centers, the destruction of the Red River dike system causing widespread loss of life and farmland in North Vietnam, and the closing of the main railroad pass into China by a nuclear explosion—all accompanied by a political-diplomatic campaign to neutralize domestic opposition, hold the Chinese and Russians at bay, and pressure Hanoi to a peace settlement.

When the plan was submitted to Nixon and finally to Laird and Rogers that October, it was narrowly defeated. As always, the military assurances of success were uncertain and wavering, and Laird and Rogers carried the argument for the moment with predictions of domestic uproar. But the very exercise gave the escalation a legitimacy it never had under Johnson, and paved the way psychologically and bureaucratically for the unleashing of many of the same actions in 1972. For Haig, the episode further vouchsafed his aura of "action." Unlike almost all his staff colleagues—unlike even the Joint Chiefs, who worried over weather or aircraft losses—the colonel in Kissinger's office (now brigadier general by November 1969) backed the attack without qualification.

Moreover, by his very presence at court—although at that point he was there largely by accident and due to a process of elimination on the NSC staff—Haig was once more a symbol. The two other men whose inner fears drove the Vietnam policy over the next four years were already visibly haunted by the reaction on the right to another "lost" war. The president—who after all had erected his own political career on the "loss" of China and the anguish of the Korean stalemate—talked ominously in his speeches that autumn of "remorse and divisive re-crimination" if the U.S. disengaged from Vietnam. Kissinger—with murmured allusions to "Weimar" and to his memories, as Nelson Rockefeller's adviser, of the howling Republican right that had so long and harshly denied his patron the White House—spoke to his staff in the same way of "fascism in the streets" as Pennsylvania Avenue filled with antiwar demonstrators for the 1969 fall moratorium. Whether the rightist specter was one more rationalization or a deeply felt presence, Haig, the soldier of stern opinion, was indeed, as the president said, "always down there," embodying in his banality much of the steely nationalism evoked in "the great silent majority." It was an intangible, emotional factor, but there is much evidence that in a Nixon and Kissinger somehow fearful of the consequences of peace, Haig determined that the war would go on.

Ironically, by the close of 1969, Haig's involvement in the September Group was almost incidental to a still more crucial role he had already begun to take on, and would continue to play, in the most furtive and in many ways most fateful part of the war policy—Cambodia. He had attended the first White House meetings in early February 1969 when the Saigon Command urged on the new administration its perennial request to bomb the Cambodian border areas, including the country near Ap Gu where Haig had fought, through which the North Vietnamese and Vietcong had marched and camped for years. The proposed bombing had never been approved in Washington, mainly because the military yield was uncertain as always, and Cambodia tolerated the sanctuary in return for Hanoi's ignoring the handful of local Communists, the Khmer Rouge. Under Prince Norodom Sihanouk, the small country existed as a neutral island of peace and relative prosperity while rebellion and suffering raged all around it.

Now, however, as Kissinger wrote later, the old recommendations to attack "fell on fertile ground." Nixon had contemplated a "very definite change of policy toward Cambodia" at the Pierre, and Goodpaster had obligingly supplied him the vague Pentagon intelligence about supplies pouring through the country and the need for "preemptive, operations." In late February 1969, when Vietcong attacks planned months earlier suddenly raised American casualties, Kissinger found Nixon "seething" with "all his instincts to respond violently" to what he saw as a challenge to his new authority. On February 23, while Nixon was on a European trip, Haig, Haldeman, Kissinger, and a Pentagon planning office charted the attacks in the presidential cabin of *Air Force One* at the Brussels airport. The bombing, they decided, would be strictly secret, and acknowledged only in the unlikely event Cambodia protested it. After some weeks of bureaucratic vacillation by Rogers and Laird (pushing Nixon still more toward Kissinger and Haig), the raids began on March 18. Though he felt there were "good foreign policy reasons" for the bombing, Kissinger later wrote of Nixon in the decision, "there was nothing he feared more than to be thought weak."

On March 19, Haig brought Kissinger the first ultra-secret damage assessment, which Halperin, there on other business, remembered Kissinger reading with a smile because the planes reported secondary explosions, seeming to confirm the logic of the strikes. "Menu," which Kissinger thought a "tasteless" cryptonym for the bombing, became one more in the war of code names. It issued in over 100,000 tons of explosives dropped secretly on a neutral country, with air-force records illegally falsified or burned; prompted "Salem House," clandestine ground raids into Cambodia by U.S. forces and mercenaries from among Mekong River pirates; squeezed the enemy sanctuaries deeper to the west, with (as the CIA found fourteen months later) "no appreciable effect" on the battle in South Vietnam; and through it all hurled the war inevitably into Cambodia. Later in 1970 and 1971, Haig watched silently as administration officials again and again lied to Congress, insisting that there had been *no* attacks against the sanctuaries before the May 1970 invasion. It had been one of those actions, as Haig recommended in his thesis, accomplished "without fanfare."

With the first sorties that March, Haig became the sole liaison between the White House and the Joint Chiefs on the Cambodian bombing. As such, he not only knew of the accompanying spread of the fighting but knew also of the shadowy Defense Intelligence Agency contacts with

Lon Nol and the officers who overthrew Sihanouk a year later. Spawned itself by the bombing and the inward wheel of the sanctuaries, the coup then shattered the country's traditional neutral bargain, provoked the Khmer Communists, and in turn set off Nixon again in manly retaliation—a serial of action and reaction that was to be Cambodia's brutal fate from then on.

As the White House coiled to invade in the spring of 1970, secrecy drew even tighter with Haig pulling over the cloak. At the end of March—as he and Kissinger and a few alarmed staff officers watched a flow of combative stream-of-consciousness memos on Cambodia spill down from the Oval Office—Haig repeatedly called Laird's office, ordering that "the State Department was to know nothing" of options being considered for Cambodia and that they were to "keep everything . . . on a very closely held basis." On Haig's orders, Laird later acknowledged, even the general's erstwhile fellow soldiers, Army Chief of Staff Westmoreland and the Joint Chiefs' long- and short-term-planning officers, were cut out of the decision until the end. When Westmoreland later in April unknowingly seemed to hint at an attack to reporters and one called to ask the White House, Haig told him to ignore the chief of staff since he was "inclined to push the panic button."

On the weekend of April 24–26, with Nixon lurching toward decision, Kissinger shifting with his mood, and Haig firmly in favor of an American ground attack into Cambodia, the train of events was expressive of the men and their rule. On Friday morning there was a rambling White House meeting with Nixon, ordered the previous midnight when the president telephoned Kissinger, who in turn called Watts to pull together needed documents, tell-

ing him, "Our peerless leader has flipped out." Friday evening, Kissinger met with three dissenting staff members
(including myself), who argued their opposition to the
invasion. Afterward, Haig told Kissinger to dismiss the
dissent as the views of the "Eastern Establishment," and
to disregard another staff member's critique of the plans
because he was not a military officer.

Meanwhile, having flown to Camp David with Bebe
Rebozo, Nixon called Kissinger frequently through Saturday, on one occasion with Watts listening in at Kissinger's
request as the president drunkenly taunted his adviser on
the invasion. "If this doesn't work, it'll be your ass, Henry,"
Nixon said thickly, adding in an aside at the other end of
the line, "Ain't that right, Bebe?" Saturday evening, Nixon
returned with Rebozo, was joined by Kissinger on the
presidential yacht *Sequoia*, watched the movie *Patton* for
the fourth or fifth time, and ordered the invasion. Back
in the West Basement on Sunday, an obviously gratified
Haig told Watts to coordinate a public-relations effort, but
the staff secretary refused, and said that he was resigning.
He could not quit, Haig said angrily to Watts. "You've
just had an order from your commander in chief." Watts
answered, "Fuck you, Al. I just did," and walked out.

Nixon announced the invasion April 30, and the aftermath amid the public furor reflected as well the tone of
the government. Nixon said he had bolstered a wavering
Kissinger, while Kissinger leaked that the president had
been "on the edge of a nervous breakdown." Haig pronounced three of his resigning staff colleagues "weak and
worn out"; said that Kissinger vacillated ("Henry tried to
talk him out of it but it had gone too far"); confided to a reporter that the "paranoia" was so bad that troops had been

brought to the White House basement to hold off potential
demonstrators; and outwardly supported the president
("He knew he was swimming against the tide," he later
told one author). But there was also a comeuppance, and
a reminder, for Haig. The next Sunday, May 3, he briefed
the larger White House staff on the progress of the invasion, another chance to make an impression. But Safire
records him cuttingly put down, almost humiliated in front
of the group for the dry detail and political irrelevance of
his presentation, by Haldeman, who showed "no concern
for Haig's feelings."

"We are all the president's men," Kissinger told his
assembled NSC staff the day the Cambodian invasion was
revealed. The remark was to prove profoundly ironic. No
policy, no series of events, had more divisive bitter issue
in both the inner politics of the administration and in
Southeast Asia. For Kissinger, the episode brought the
final eclipse of Rogers. He had been striving to demonstrate his outward loyalty and "it was the invasion of
Cambodia," wrote William Shawcross of the policy, "that
enabled him to do so." In the Oval Office, an already besieged president saw the demonstrations against his act
as new evidence of his many enemies, and of the need to
counter the extraordinary measures. "Kent State marked a
turning point for Nixon," Haldeman noted in his memoirs,
referring to the National Guard killing of protesting students following the invasion. "A beginning of his downhill
slide toward Watergate." Out of the turmoil triggered by
Cambodia came the infamous White House "Huston Plan"
with its proposals for criminal surveillance and repression
that one senator later labeled the product of "Gestapo
mentality." Approved by Nixon and rescinded only by a

jealous J. Edgar Hoover, the plan was the portent of more to come.

For Haig, the invasion was a triumph to equal Kissinger's. The "martinis that launched Cambodia," as journalists privately joked later about Nixon's drinking, now launched the general even more rapidly upward. When the smoke had cleared, his last potential rivals, Watts and Lake, had gone and the few remaining possibilities were tainted in one way or another in the litmus test of loyalty. Nixon and Kissinger were all the more isolated, cut off from an appalled academic world and a sullen, half-mutinous bureaucracy at State. The Cambodian decision in the abstract, if not in the reality of Nixon's caprice, was nearly another model of the decisionmaking he had recommended at Georgetown, a "politico-military" bold stroke informed by select expert advice (including Haig's) and which excluded until the last moment the muddled "vicarage" at the State Department.

Only weeks after the invasion, Haig was dispatched to Phnom Penh, his first important diplomatic assignment and the first of his several "stroking missions" to the feeble Lon Nol regime over the next three years. The State Department was initially kept in the dark about the trip, naturally, and when officials learned about it, one pleaded to Richardson, "We can't fight it but we can mitigate it . . . let's get one of our best men on Cambodia to go along," adding, in Foggy Bottom's worst indictment, "Haig does not have the substance." A State Department aide was added at the last moment, but Haig "paid little attention" to him. Cambodia was now his "special responsibility," as the *Washington Post* put it, and he moved with characteristic bureaucratic aggressiveness to make it a personal fiefdom. He would be, wrote British journalist William Shawcross in his study of the Cambodian War, "vital in defining the relationship between the White House and Lon Nol, between the White House and the United States Embassy, between the White House and reality."

As it was, he brought his own reality to Phnom Penh. Arriving in battle fatigues at then sleepy Pochentong airport, he took what witnesses remembered to be an instant dislike to the casual dress and manner of the current U.S. chargé d'affaires, who described himself as a "perfectly average" diplomat. The chargé, said one of his colleagues, "would seem a stuffed shirt to a man like Haig, who is into *machismo*." No command post for an embryonic war, the low-key U.S. mission in Phnom Penh was run out of a former servants' quarters with no air conditioning and few amenities, at which Haig also "made his distaste clear." Ignoring diplomatic courtesy (and the future effectiveness of the envoy with his hosts), he brusquely refused to take the State Department chief of mission with him to see Lon Nol, or to tell anyone in the embassy afterward what had been said. Pieced together by Shawcross and others, however, the encounter would be a rare glimpse of Haig the diplomat at work before he became secretary of state.

Lon Nol was visibly upset as their conversation began. The invasion had thrust the Communists away from the border and across Cambodia (as it was designed to do, after all), and his small army could only hold out with American troops. Haig told the Cambodian general that U.S. forces would be withdrawn from the border areas at the end of June and that Washington would then begin limited economic and military aid. At that, Lon Nol broke into tears and crossed the room to stand facing out of a window, his shoulders shaking. Haig went to him, put his arm around Lon Nol's shoulder, and said Nixon "supported him and would give him what help he could, despite the political constraints in Washington."

It was a fateful commitment. As Haig spoke, the Senate, as he well know, was drafting the Church-Cooper Amendment outlawing U.S. troops in Cambodia after June 30 and prohibiting even U.S. advisers or air support for the Cambodian army. Moreover, before he left Phnom Penh, Haig would learn firsthand that the Cambodian forces were pathetically weak and ill-led, that Lon Nol himself was involved in smuggling to the North Vietnamese, and not least that the Cambodian leader's "mind tended to take flight," in Shawcross's words, or as a CIA psychiatrist observed clinically in a later study, that he was "a vague and unstructured individual." In Phnom Penh, Haig had found a corrupt, decrepit regime with scant capacity for self-defense and no legal prospect of meaningful U.S. support. He returned to Washington with what he presumed Nixon wished to hear: Cambodia would be an American ally.

In the West Basement that summer, Haig presided over the expansion of the U.S. mission in Phnom Penh with a large military attaché's contingent and a new communications system, as well as the arming of Cambodian troops with light weapons. To circumvent the congressional restriction on military advisers, he recruited a retired army colonel and old friend from Almond's staff in Korea, Jonathan Ladd, former commander of the green berets in Vietnam, to run the aid program in Cambodia as a civilian. Ladd's cynical attitude toward the massive U.S. buildup in Vietnam having cost him promotion to general, he had gone off to set up a charter-boat business in Florida. But now he returned to work for Haig with assurances that "the lessons of Vietnam had been learned." Though Haig and Kissinger soon purged the casual chargé and had him replaced with a new ambassador trained in Communist affairs, Haig told Ladd that he, and through him Lon Nol, could bypass even the new embassy communications and communicate secretly and directly with the White House. Ladd might do this, Haig said, "through an American he would meet outside the embassy in Phnom Penh."

With the assurances and intrigue, Ladd advised the confused, unworldly Lon Nol over the next months and tried to tailor the millions in the new aid program to realistic local uses. But relentlessly the bloat and distortion he had seen in Vietnam overtook Cambodia, Washington's money and materiel leading only to debauchery of the local economy. As Cambodia's inflation rose and the Khmer Rouge forces gathered strength in the summer of 1971, Haig won approval from Nixon (the memorandum was his own and he signed it for Kissinger) to increase the Cambodian army to 220,000 men. As in South Vietnam, an alien regime spawned of American dollars and policy and ignorance had begun its lethal decay.

The Cambodian policy would have its further bloody sequel for Haig. But before that was played out, there was yet another consequence of that policy for the tortuous politics inside the White House. If the bombing had been devastating to Cambodia in a larger sense, its destructive impact had also been turned back on the administration. It was a May 1969 *New York Times* story on the secret Cambodian bombing, presumed to come from a leak, that started the notorious wiretaps of the Kissinger staff, other officials, and a number of journalists. On May 2, 1970, just after the invasion of Cambodia, Haig had telephoned the FBI to say that the latest leak had been "nailed down to a couple of people," and to ask for four more wiretaps. The request was almost routine; it was hardly the first time he had called on the subject.

The wiretaps were another feast in the bureaucratic cannibalism of the Nixon White House, and became an integral part of Haig's survival and rise in that setting. What began ostensibly as outrage over security breaches turned almost instantly into a sometimes intricate, sometime crude demonstration of fealty and interoffice political maneuver. Rights were trampled, the law skirted if not broken, loyalties betrayed, and public power abused in a cynical inquisition less to uncover heresy than to promote the priests conducting it.

When the taps were exposed almost by accident four years after they had been placed, the story trickled out only haltingly and in part. But one by one the rationalizations and pretexts crumbled away to reveal the base politics. They were after the news leaks mainly to one journalist, yet he was not tapped for a year after the hunt began. They were concerned about the divulgence of national security secrets, yet some of the taps continued months after the targets had left government, long after they had any access to secrets, and even after they had gone to work for an opposition candidate for the presidency. The eavesdropping was to be limited and precise, yet it lasted nearly two years and its scope was indiscriminate. Legally, the taps were supposed to be duly recorded, yet the logs were ordered removed from the FBI files and were eventually secreted in the White House. They said the taps were largely due to the undoubted dementia of J. Edgar Hoover, who had conveniently died in the meantime, yet the documentary record shows Haig and Kissinger obsequiously indulging Hoover, and Hoover deferring to their decisions. It was Hoover who supplied many of the names of those to be tapped, they remembered, yet there is no indication the FBI director had ever heard of most of the people, much less that he singled them out.

Safire, one of those recorded, observed that Kissinger's reaction to the whole episode was revealingly "un-Kissinger-like." "He gets visibly upset; he lies in an unstudied amateurish way that can be found out; he is not himself," thought the onetime speechwriter. "Kissinger tries to put the entire sordid story out of his mind, since it cannot be defended on any grounds. . . ."

Kissinger was not alone in dropping the subject. With Nixon's resignation—the taps having been prominent in one article of impeachment—the shrouded history receded still further. Fixed on their presidential prey, even the lucrative civil suits filed by the victims skimmed past questions of precise public responsibility to concentrate on money for damages. Yet if everyone seemed to recognize the bureaucratic politics at play, no role was left more obscure than that of the man who derived the most bureaucratically from the episode, whose involvement was so pivotal, whose loss and remorse were least in the aftermath, and whose responsibility was largely ignored—Alexander Haig.

Haig testified three times about his part in the wiretapping: to the Senate Foreign Relations Committee in

June 1974, in secret before a Watergate grand jury in June 1975, and the following July in a deposition in one of the civil suits. The facts about his actions were "straightforward," and none of those inquiries found "any culpability on my part," Haig said at his Senate confirmation hearing, adding that he had been dismissed as a defendant in the civil case because of his "inactive role and . . . lack of oversight authority." With that, the Foreign Relations Committee declined to ask anything more.

Yet there were those close to the Watergate investigation and the still-unreleased grand-jury evidence who believed Haig's role was far more serious than ever understood, and who had been overruled in trying to pursue the matter in 1975 when Haig was already NATO commander and the issue had grown cold. Moreover, both Kissinger and Nixon had testified further on the wiretaps in depositions in 1976, throwing fresh light on Haig's earlier sworn testimony. As Haig became secretary of state, the taps remained a story that had not yet been fully told.

Kissinger remembered later that "someone" had told him that spring the "wiretapping was necessary and the practices and procedures were well established," as if it were somehow new to him when it was used on his colleagues. In fact, wiretap information was a daily staple of the intelligence routed pro forma into the West Basement through Haig in the months prior to May 1969. Only the smallest, most inconsequential foreign missions in both Washington and New York went unmonitored, and Kissinger read some of the material avidly.

Nor was it novel for them to see FBI reports on the NSC staff or journalists. Hoover had objected at the Pierre to the hiring of Halperin and Sonnenfeldt, on the grounds that they had worked for the Democrats—a disability that would have also ruled out Haig, of course, along with most of the rest of the staff. As early as February 1969, Hoover had continued to send letters to Kissinger regarding Halperin, who was said to be suspiciously "of the opinion that the US leadership erred in Vietnam" and was one of what Hoover termed those "so-called arrogant Harvard-type Kennedy men." There were equally absurd reports, staff men would remember, about British journalist and Kissinger friend Henry Brandon being either a British secret agent, a colonel in Czech intelligence, or both simultaneously.

Not least, Hoover sent to Kissinger within weeks of the inauguration the same lascivious, Communist-crazed material on the Reverend King that he had been peddling through Washington's higher offices for years. Such material was vintage J. Edgar Hoover, the seventy-five-year-old director who had ruled the bureau for nearly a half-century with mounting personal corruption, blackmail, political impunity, incompetence, and senility. The FBI of 1969, said an assistant director and thirty-year veteran, lived in "dread" of its willful, reactionary despot. In one typical example of his unalloyed racism, Hoover had sent scurrilous information on Martin Luther King to the pope before King visited the Vatican. Another time, the assistant director remembered, an agent "was unable to get the promotion that was due him" because he failed to deliver rapidly enough to an eagerly awaiting Hoover photographs of civil-rights activists making love.

So ridiculous were some of the Hoover documents—including the early papers on Halperin, King, and Brandon—that Kissinger and Haig laughed openly about them,

showed them to Eagleburger, and spread the joke still
further by passing them to other staff members. But
whether embassy surveillance summaries or the director's
Mad Hatter memos, all the reports came routinely each
day to Haig, who from the outset was NSC liaison with
the FBI, just as Rostow's aide, Bromley Smith, had been
before him. Similarly, an FBI agent attached to the NSC
staff reported to Haig on internal security matters (such
as staff contacts with Soviet bloc diplomats) just as he had
reported to Smith.

Later, when everyone scrambled to avoid responsibility,
to present themselves as innocents caught in unseemly
circumstances, no investigating body understood—and
Haig never admitted—that from January 20, 1969, he was
the sole executor of the busy, ongoing NSC-FBI liaison,
the "staff man" for wiretaps as surely as another officer
handled Middle Eastern affairs, or another acted as the
contact with the Treasury or Commerce departments. It
was part of Haig's "account," as the official argot called
the staff assignment; and as with any other responsible
staff officers in their field, it was to Haig that Kissinger
would turn necessarily and routinely for internal-security
documents, recommendations, and further contact or liaison when the need arose.

The rough chronolgy of what happened in the spring of
1969 would become generally familiar, although the participants later disagreed about almost all the salient details. There had been a "continuing hemorrhaging of
highly classified information into the media," Haig testified in 1975, though the three and a half months of Nixon
rule prior to the taps saw at most five foreign-policy
stories remotely attributable to leaks. That was an almost

negligible number for Washington, and less than had occurred during the comparable periods under Johnson, or, for that matter, a decade later under Ronald Reagan.

Only one of those stories had appeared when Nixon met with Hoover, Mitchell and Kissinger on April 25 to discuss leaks, and discrepancies between versions of that meeting have never been resolved. Kissinger said under oath that while Hoover named Halperin, Sonnenfeldt, Davidson, and Brandon as old suspects, Nixon "authorized" the taps and "directed surveillance" against "specific individuals." Mitchell recalled no such detailed Nixon orders, and said he thought Kissinger was to come up with names. Earlier recorded on his own tapes telling John Dean that Kissinger "asked that it [the wiretapping] be done," Nixon swore in 1976 that he agreed with the wiretaps but that the names and duration of the eavesdropping were for Kissinger to decide—testimony that Kissinger later said he "couldn't believe" Nixon had given. As for Hoover, long dead when these *Rashomon* memories were assembled, he told his deputy at the time that "the taps were a White House operation," and "they would remain on until the White House requested they come off."

Kissinger immediately debriefed Haig, and Haig alone, on the April 25 meeting, while over the next week and a half there followed three more news stories that were thought to have been leaked. On May 5, duly briefed and scheduled by Haig, Kissinger met secretly with Hoover at FBI headquarters to discuss the leaks further, though there was, unusually for Hoover, no written record of what was said at their meeting.

Then on May 9, with Kissinger attending Nixon in Key

Biscayne and Haig overseeing the office at the White House, there appeared the famous *New York Times* story on the Cambodian bombing by Pentagon correspondent William Beecher. In a stream of screaming phone calls from Florida to Washington, Kissinger called Laird off a golf course to accuse him of the leak, repeatedly pressed Hoover to find the leaker with the promise to "destroy whoever did this," and talked with Haig several times about the problem. That day Hoover left records of his talks with Kissinger, but the Kissinger-Haig conversations, though said by aides to be routinely summarized by a listening secretary at both ends, would remain secret and never subpoenaed or questioned.

Meanwhile, between calls back from Hoover full of the director's gleeful but muddled accusations against Halperin and assorted other "McNamara people," Kissinger casually walked along the beach with, of all people, the same Morton Halperin (who was there as an aide), telling him he was suspected of leaking and should get no more sensitive materials for a while in order to establish his innocence in future stories. At 6:20 the evening of May 9, Halperin's tap was installed by Hoover with Kissinger's blessing, three days before it was legally approved by Mitchell.

In their calls on May 9 and again the morning of May 10, Kissinger and Haig talked at length about the next step. Later on the 10th Haig made his well-known appearance at the office of FBI assistant director William C. Sullivan. A dutiful career agent whom an associate described as "a Jimmy Cagney type with a New England accent thrown in" and far less anti-Communist mania than his boss, Sullivan gave a detailed account of the Haig meeting in an official memorandum of record at the time and in his later memoirs as well.

"Without mentioning any names," Sullivan noted, Haig told him he had come on "highest authority" to present a "White House request" on a "matter of most grave and serious consequences to our national security." With what Sullivan thought "honest concern in his voice," Haig described the leaks "plaguing" the administration and the need for the taps. By Haig's own account, he also discussed "trailing and surveillance and other investigations to accompany the overall assessment of a man's reliability." The wiretapping would be necessary, Haig remarked, for only "a few days to resolve the issue," and he would personally come over to the FBI to "review any information developed." "Because of sensitivity of the operation," as Sullivan recalled their talk, Haig ordered that "no written record of the program ever be made." Sullivan patiently explained to Haig that "no tap could be kept completely secret within the bureau," and that it was "impossible" not to have "some" records. But Sullivan promised "to keep the paperwork involved to a minimum," and noted that "Haig . . . a career army man, as familiar as I was with bureaucracy and red tape, . . . accepted what I said without argument." Haig then gave Sullivan the names of Halperin, Sonnenfeldt, Davidson, and Air Force Colonel Robert Pursley, Laird's principal military aide.

In subsequent testimony, Haig insisted that in the first Sullivan meeting he was only a "conduit." He was "absolutely confident" the taps were proper and had been duly authorized by Nixon, and said, "I never viewed myself as anything but an extension of Dr. Kissinger." He was only at the FBI, he explained, "confirming" a program that had already been approved at the "highest level."

Yet for all the presumed propriety, Sullivan was clearly impressed on May 10 by Haig's deliberate vagueness and careful denial of personal responsibility. He had pointedly avoided mentioning either Nixon or Kissinger as the "highest authority," and had obviously hoped, however impractically, to conduct the taps with no traceable written word. From the beginning of their meeting, Sullivan felt that Haig was "making sure that I understood that he was merely acting as a messenger in this affair."

Haig's wariness was not surprising in light of the questions that hung over the episode at the very outset. First, it was by no means certain that the taps were legal. Though federal law then excluded "national security" wiretaps from court warrants under certain conditions, Haig and Kissinger both knew that legal issues had been ignored at the April 25 meeting and that Hoover had frequently conducted dubious or outright criminal activities on similar pretext in the past.

Nor was the record so plain, or obscure, regarding the selection of the men to be tapped. Like Kissinger, Haig testified years afterward that the names came from Hoover and "represented his concerns regarding a number of people on Henry's staff" (presumably an echo of the Pierre and of the April 25 meeting at which the director was said to name names while Nixon ordered the taps accordingly). Yet if the origin was simply Hoover, why was Haig's May 10 mission to Sullivan even necessary after the numerous Kissinger-Hoover calls the day before? Sullivan knew nothing of the talks about leaks or taps before Haig told him, and Haig brought no written order that would have

distinguished his trip from oral instructions over the phone
to the same effect. The Haig-Sullivan meeting made sense
only if Hoover was waiting for the White House itself to
decide on the targets and to request the taps officially—
something that had not been done in the Kissinger-
Hoover conversations May 9, but only after Kissinger
spoke further with Haig on May 10.

Moreover, there would be no evidence in the FBI files
or later testimony (save Kissinger's) to show that Hoover
ever fingered Pursley, whose precise role and access to
relevant information as Laird's aide only Haig knew in
detail. If Hoover's April 25 references to Halperin, Davidson, Sonnenfeldt, and Brandon were the tapping blueprint
innocently followed in the West Basement May 10, where
was Brandon in Haig's request to Sullivan? "Pursley was
substituted," concluded one later analyst of the evidence,
"by Haig."

Not least, there was Haig's order on the taps "that no
written record of the program ever be made." He testified
that the extraordinary secrecy had been requested to avoid
any repetition of the way Hoover's reports on King had
been sent around Washington in the 1960s, which in one
case Haig witnessed "just about blew the Pentagon apart."
He said in a 1975 sworn deposition, "I think that is the
kind of concerns we had."

Yet that answer only deepened the contradictions in the
story. Though such lurid King reports were already in
Kissinger's files early in 1969, the sensation caused in the
Pentagon years ago could have been known in Kissinger's
office only by Haig. And he was also swearing that he was
making no decisions and offering no advice on these matters. He testified that he had "discussed" the taps with

Kissinger before going to see Sullivan May 10, but he was adamant that in those conversations he had been neither "an urger or an advocate or a disadvocate." That obviously belied the "honest concern" Sullivan had heard in his voice, and presented the farfetched image of Haig, the intelligence aide and Kissinger's sole staff confidante on the subject, saying nothing one way or another while Kissinger fumed and talked for hours on May 9 and 10. For his part, it all left Sullivan with his own "uneasy feeling" about the wiretaps from "the very first time Alexander Haig came to my office. . . ." Sullivan remembered that as Haig left that day, "I just knew they would cause trouble."

Haig later gave some flavor of those discussions he denied joining. Kissinger had been "very concerned," he told a Senate committee, "that he and we were suspect because of the character of the staff we had put together." They had gone along with the taps to exonerate their colleagues. "I feel quite frankly that part of Henry's own mental comfort with proceeding with this thing was an effort to vindicate these men and to assure those who had suspicion." In a later deposition he spoke even more bluntly about the Nixon court mistrust of Kissinger: "He was suspect to some individuals—I cannot say who—to some he may have been perceived to be part of the problem."

That explained why Halperin, Sonnenfeldt, and Davidson had been chosen to appease Hoover's obsessions—but not Pursley, whose home phone tap was clearly aimed at Laird, both to expose any leak and to spy on the secretary's policy positions. And it took nothing away from a cynical gambit in which their loyalty seemed assured in either outcome: If there were no leaks on the staff, they were clear; if leakers were flushed out, they had led the hunt. In any case, the taps now spun on with the momentum of any excess once enjoyed.

On May 13, Hoover met with Nixon and began to send his own tap reports to both Kissinger and Haldeman. ("Haig's plea for secrecy meant little to Hoover," said Sullivan; "he wasn't about to give any information to the president without getting the credit.") Two days later, Sullivan noted that "no information has been dedevolped," but on May 20 Kissinger and Haig went to Sullivan's office to read the transcripts. What they saw has never been published and no definite leaks were ever proved in the taps, but they now asked Sullivan to extend the original four taps a "little while longer" and to add the names of NSC staffers Richard Sneider and Richard Moose. "It is clear," Kissinger remarked to Sullivan, "that I don't have anybody in my office that I can trust except Colonel Haig here."

By May 29, Haig finally ordered a tap on Brandon, with Sullivan noting only that "Dr. Kissinger is aware of this request." In later testimony, Haig at the least dissembled about the Brandon tap, which he called "puzzling" and could not recall. Yet to another question he invoked what could only have been Brandon in the old Hoover-mongered rumor to justify the whole program. "In one instance, one of those people was a very, very prime suspect for espionage activity," he told a congressional hearing. "It was a person who was alleged to me informally to have been an agent of a foreign government."

Almost nothing about the statement was forthright.

Weeks before the taps, much to their skepticism and
mirth, Hoover had reported quite formally to Haig and
Kissinger that Brandon could be somebody else's "colonel." And again, if the tap sprang from Hoover's suspicions, why had Haig been necessary to order surveillance
for the director of the FBI? Now, at the end of May 1969,
Haig was ordering Brandon tapped not for those wild
charges but because the British journalist had been picked
up talking to a staff member on another earlier tap, and
this despite the fact that neither then nor later had
Brandon published any of the purported leaks.

On June 4, Hoover and Sullivan came to the West
Basement, ostensibly to review the phone surveillance,
but more, Sullivan thought, to show again the director's
zeal. Classified "Top Secret Sensitive," Haig's briefing
memo and talking points for Kissinger at that meeting
were eloquent of his own central role in the wiretapping.
"Express your appreciation to Mr. Hoover and Mr. Sullivan for their outstanding support in recent weeks in
uncovering security problems within the NSC staff," Haig
began his memo to Kissinger. "Inform Mr. Hoover that
you have discussed these problems in detail with the President (and with Messrs. Haldeman and Ehrlichman)."

Once more what had been "uncovered" was never disclosed. Davidson had resigned from the staff on May 29
"by mutual consent," but Kissinger afterward described
his wiretap information as only "ambiguous."

The rest of Haig's briefing was less cryptic, however.
"Ask Mr. Hoover for his views," he continued, "on how
we could proceed with Halperin, who has been involved
in indiscretions and who obviously has a reputation for
liberal views but who has yet to be firmly linked with a

security breach." At the same time, Haig cautioned Kissinger not to talk too openly. "I think it best that you seek Mr. Hoover's advice in this instance while avoiding any specific comments pro or con and especially avoiding opinions on this matter," the memo went on.

His final talking point for Kissinger continued the obeisance to Hoover, yet also revealed all the more clearly Haig's own decisive hand in the taps. "Ask Mr. Hoover if he has any additional information or guidance which he feels would be helpful in this very difficult situation," Haig wrote, adding parenthetically: "I think in the case of Halperin and Brandon that they [the taps] should be kept on for at least another two weeks so that a pattern of innocence can be firmly established."

Haig would later assure a congressional hearing that Hoover's wiretap reports had been "reflective of a sensibility we did not share." But that was hardly evident in the cloying June 4 memorandum. Nor was it a briefing by a man who was only a "conduit" with no views or responsibility in what was happening.

The Halperin and Brandon taps he recommended for "another two weeks" went on for another year and a half, as the number of targets rose steadily to seventeen with Mitchell adding his own sampling of dubious journalists and White House aides in domestic affairs. In June and again in July 1969, Sullivan reported that "nothing has come to light," and "suggested to Haig" that the taps be lifted. Those on Sneider and Moose were removed at the end of June as both men were on their way out of their NSC jobs for other reasons, but Sullivan's advice was generally ignored. Haig once told a hearing about the wiretap reports that he saw "an awful lot of garbage involved in it," yet he made at least eight visits to Sullivan's office to pore over the "garbage." He testified that he "urged Henry to disassociate the National Security Council staff, meaning me or anybody else, from what was essentially an internal security matter," to drop what he called "the murky business." He maintained that he "had growing personal reservations about it and our role in it and my role in it," but over the first year he read and passed to Kissinger some thirty-seven summary reports, wrote more briefing memos on the model of the June 4 talking points, and continued to accompany Kissinger to periodic stock-taking meetings with Hoover. On one such occasion he heard the director none-too-subtly warn Kissinger about the wiles of a woman agent loose in Washington, which Haig then joked about with others on the staff.

Meanwhile, by midsummer 1969, the wiretaps and their summary reports, kept in a small wired safe in the West Basement situation room, had become an open secret among the NSC staff. No one but Haig and Kissinger knew precisely who was targeted, but of the wiretapping in general there was little doubt. "Don't say anything you don't want Haldeman or Henry to read over breakfast," Eagleburger told at least two colleagues from his hospital bed that July. Lake, too, though he did not know his own conversations would soon be there, knew that there were shadowy FBI secrets in the little "sit-room" safe.

On September 15, Haig called off all the White House staff taps except for Halperin's (who by then had been gone from his job for several weeks), and it seemed for a time that what Sullivan called the "pileup" of specially hidden tap records had reached its peak. But with the

Cambodian invasion, Haig was back with four fresh requests, including, at last, Beecher, and a revival of Pursley. On May 13, 1970, though again he could not recall it when questioned later, he also ordered taps on Lake and Lord. (In their consecutive service as personal aides to Kissinger, they would be, of all the staff, the two men with whom Haig worked most closely.) Like Halperin's tap, Lake's wound on well after he had resigned and was working with Nixon's congressional opposition.

To later congressional questions about political abuse of the eavesdropping, Haig told a story about being summoned by an excited Sullivan to look at wiretap evidence of "a criminal matter." As recounted in Sullivan's memoirs, they "overheard Daniel Ellsberg . . . and Morton Halperin talking about effects of some drugs." But without telling the Senate committee what the "criminal matter" had been, Haig simply cited it ominously as a "very inviting thing," a "partisan exploitation" that had not been used as it might have been. With committee Democrats distracted, if not cowed, by his implication, he effectively dodged the issue of the continuing taps on Halperin and Lake. No report of a tap-discovered "crime" was ever made. "Just gobs and gobs . . . of gossip and bull shitting," Nixon eventually described the wiretap results to Dean.

Haig called Sullivan on February 8, 1971, to order the last of the taps discontinued, telling the FBI deputy they had "served their purpose." Sullivan then had the summary tap records held by Haig returned to him at his FBI office, where he continued to keep the entire archive of the program outside normal bureau files.

There was still one last act to be played out. That following summer, Sullivan himself broke with Hoover. But before leaving, lest the old man use the wiretap logs to "blackmail Nixon and Kissinger and hang on to his job forever," Sullivan turned the explosive records over to Assistant Attorney General Robert Mardian. Mardian in turn passed them back to the White House, where it was Haig and Kissinger who examined the logs to verify as best they could that none was missing. As they canvassed the records before further hiding in the White House, however, a federal court had already requested, in connection with the unfolding *Pentagon Papers* case, any and all government wiretap records on Daniel Ellsberg and all scheduled witnesses, including Morton Halperin. As Haig well knew, Ellsberg had been heard frequently on Halperin's tap. But he raised no question as the logs disappeared again, this time into Ehrlichman's safe, where they would be one more deposit waiting to be discovered among what Mitchell came to call the "White House horrors."

When the taps were revealed two years later, the furor descended primarily over the more famous Kissinger, who weathered it by invoking everything from national security to his resignation, and by pleading that he was only a novice and bystander next to lawyers Nixon and Mitchell and policeman Hoover, while Haig in tow contended that he only ran Kissinger's errands. They both denied the story baldly when it was first breaking, and came close to blaming one another before their accounts hardened into formal testimony in 1974. If Kissinger displayed unmistakable discomfort at mention of the subject, however, Haig's reaction was usually cool, sometimes remorseless. They "don't give me gas pains," he remarked on the taps to Safire, whose name he had given Sullivan and whose sense of personal and political betrayal over being tapped Haig ridiculed as "battin' gnats."

Though the Senate Foreign Relations Committee excused him along with Kissinger, and the court in Halperin's civil damage suit eventually dropped him as a defendant, Haig and the taps were judged more harshly by his former colleagues. The wiretap hearings clearing Kissinger and Haig had been a "joke" and a "whitewash," wrote Safire, and the general belonged "right with Nixon" in his responsibility. To Elliot Richardson, the whole episode was "the ugly glimpse of an incipient police state."

They were not alone. In 1974–75, though their dissent was never made public, there were those in the Watergate special prosecutor's office who argued privately that the grand jury should be told in more bureaucratic detail Haig's integral part in overseeing the taps, and that the general should be held accountable in some more tangible way for his part in the abuse of power.

From the contradictions and admissions in his own account, their summary of his improper acts was damning. By his story about the Hoover memo on King scandalizing the Pentagon, he had acknowledged, whatever his motives, his role in recommending special concealment of the wiretap logs, one of the counts of impeachment. Haig, or at least he and Kissinger together, had clearly fingered Pursley for reasons that had little to do with leaks or the "authority" of the April 25 meeting with Nixon. His June 4 briefing memo for Kissinger's meeting with Hoover documented his influence on the duration of the tapping, specifically his urging that the taps on Halperin and Brandon be prolonged, regardless of his

first assurances to the FBI that the program would take
only a "few days" and regardless of subsequent reports
that the surveillance was proving barren. (In 1976, a
federal court would find the disgraced Nixon, Mitchell,
and Haldeman all guilty of violating Halperin's Fourth
Amendment rights in that they made "no attempt" to
"minimize" the monitoring and that the taps were thus a
"dragnet which lacked temporal and spatial limitation.")

The record showed, too, that Haig gave misleading if
not perjured testimony under oath. He and Kissinger had
obviously indulged Hoover's phobias on the wiretaps, not
resisted or ignored them as he suggested. He trotted out
Hoover's suspicion of Brandon, then denied ordering
Brandon's tap. As executor and reader of the taps for the
NSC, he above all knew which men were still truly involved, or ever had been involved, in national security.
Yet he was party to the Halperin and Lake taps long after
that reason had vanished, and at a Senate hearing he
simply evaded and misrepresented the question of political abuse of the surveillance, another impeachment count.

All this, investigators and attorneys argued, should have
been made plain in a broader definition of responsibility.
If Nixon had authorized the taps, if Haldeman and Mitchell had exploited the political opportunity, if the now
dead Hoover had been mad at the time, if Kissinger was
as always a willing schemer, Haig nonetheless pulled the
strings as the sole responsible staff officer with the power
of recommendation to place, prolong, withdraw. But the
argument was overruled by Special Prosecutor Leon Jaworski, the last time in the summer of 1975, and there the
matter rested.

Meanwhile, as in so many disasters he attended, the

wiretap episode that damaged almost everyone else it touched had been a vertitable boon to Haig's influence and career. It was very much, after all, his Cambodian policy that was being protected by it all, and in the deepening distrust of the self-tapping White House, secrecy and policymaking narrowed still further around Haig. His role in the hunt for leakers gave him new power and leverage with Kissinger. His readiness to suspect his NSC colleagues further certified him with Haldeman. If Kissinger had it both ways, Haig did even more so: If a journalist's tap had discovered Henry in one of his frequent slurs on Nixon, there would have been only one man left to "trust" in the West Basement.

Ironically, among the ten NSC, State, and Defense officials tapped, there was no connecting link in terms of information known or press contacts. Perhaps the one thing the men shared was that they were all potential rivals or policy adversaries of Haig. When the taps and the Cambodian invasion were over, the NSC staff dissenters on Indochina—Davidson, Halperin, and Lake—were gone. Sonnenfeldt and Lord remained, but only under the wiretap cloud, and never so trusted or so influential as Haig. Senior aides in State and the Pentagon —men whose bosses might rival Kissinger and who themselves were Haig's counterparts in the shrinking circle of decisionmakers—were tainted as well simply for being once suspected. And the innuendo and snooping were doubly bitter when the supposed leakers were matched with the leaks. The offending newspaper stories early and late had but one element in common themselves: The only government officials who had known all those secrets beforehand were Kissinger and Haig.

In the end, there was an even more curious twist in unraveling the saga of the taps. For behind the scandal of the seventeen, there was the shadow of still more wiretaps never revealed. When Mardian had delivered those logs held by Sullivan for Kissinger and Haig to inventory, Kissinger had joked with him tastelessly, "Do you have what I said?" But he had also muttered afterward, an aide remembered, "What about the others?" When the seventeen taps were eventually acknowledged and handed back to the Justice Department in 1973, no "others" were with them, and the White House chief of staff who presided over the transfer of evidence would be Alexander Haig.

Of the Nixon administration policies in which his role was later questioned, none would be more charged for Haig than the covert U.S. intervention in Chile. Coming in the wake of the wiretaps and the Cambodian invasion, the Chilean episode in the autumn of 1970 possessed all the elements to excite its eventual 1975 senatorial investigation and revelation: corporate bribery and scheming; White House intrigues; military conspirators; CIA agents passing money and guns at some predawn rendezvous; and, in the end, assassination, torture, and tyranny. Echoing his testimony on the taps, Haig told both the congressional investigation on Chile and his confirmation committee that he "was not deeply involved," had "no responsibility," worked only as a "conduit" in such matters. But again he portrayed his own part in controversial events far too modestly, and his sworn statements clashed with the documentary record and the word of other officials. At issue in the Chile policy were not only his candor and historical role, but also a direct portent of Haig as secretary of state, when covert intervention in Latin America again became a burning issue in the Reagan administration's policy toward civil war in El Salvador.

One of the few Latin nations with a firm tradition of nonmilitary democratic rule, Chile also had a history of regular CIA intervention. The Eisenhower, Kennedy, and Johnson administrations all spent covert money to back pro-U.S. candidates, including $3 million in bribes and various secret subsidies in 1964 to ensure the defeat of Salvador Allende, the avowedly Marxist presidential candidate of a loose Socialist-Communist-moderate coalition. In the 1970 election, however, Allende's Christian Democratic and rightist opposition was splintered and leaderless, and his victory seemed likely.

Precisely what danger an Allende regime represented to Washington was one of the tragic puzzles left when it was all over. Unearthed by Congress years afterward, U.S. policy papers on the eve of Allende's accession indicated that the United States had "no vital interests" in Chile and that the tough-talking dentist, though his victory would be a "psychological disadvantage" to the U.S. and a "promotion of the Marxist idea," did not threaten the peace of Latin America or the world military balance. Allende pledged to maintain the Chilean constitution, and did. He contemplated expropriation of vast U.S. copper interests and land reform, though so too did his moderate opponents, and the land reform proceeded under a previous parliamentary statute voted by several deputies put in their seats by CIA campaign contributions. But then nothing about the Chilean episode was quite what it seemed.

Whether due to voter inertia, ignorance, or ideology, Allende's prospective triumph at the polls rang alarm bells throughout the administration's covert precincts early in 1970. The highly secret Forty Committee—the subcabinet body chaired by Kissinger, staffed by Haig, and responsible for overseeing clandestine operations— voted on March 25 to spend as much as $1 million on a "spoiling" operation against Allende in the September Chilean election. That sum was supplemented by $350,000 similarly spent by International Telephone and Telegraph to stave off nationalization of its lucrative holdings in Chile. Meeting again on June 27, the committee voted another $500,000 to bribe the Chilean Congress in its final presidential certifying vote in October should Allende win the popular election. "I don't see why we have to let a country go Marxist just because its people are irresponsible," Kissinger told the group in a memorable remark later stricken from a CIA memoir in a celebrated case of prepublication censorship. When Allende won in a free election on September 4, the committee launched still more covert actions prior to the October 24 congressional vote to prevent his assumption of power "either through political or military means."

With this intervention already in train, Nixon met on September 15, 1970, with Pepsi-Cola's Donald Kendall, an old supporter and corporate law client, who in turn had been lobbying the rest of Washington against Allende with a Chilean Pepsi distributor, "longtime ally of the CIA," and reactionary publisher named Augustín Edwards. Already harshly anti-Allende, Nixon emerged from the

Kendall meeting and summoned Helms, Mitchell, and Kissinger to order a new, wholly separate covert onslaught in Chile. In a policy typically to be kept secret from the Forty Committee, the secretaries of state and defense, and the U.S. ambassador to Chile, Nixon told Helms to go all out to mount a military coup to "save" Chile. ". . . Not concerned risks involved . . . best men we have . . . make economy scream," read some of Helms's handwritten notes on his instructions. "If I ever carried a marshal's baton in my knapsack out of the Oval Office," the CIA director later confessed to Congress, "it was that day."

Thus began "Track II," as it became known, the White House's last-minute intervention paralleling the somewhat less extreme "Track I" already laid out by the Forty Committee. Over the next five weeks, the two tracks snaked through Washington and Santiago while Allende went on to be confirmed by the Chilean Congress anyway. But before it ended, Track II had taken on the plot of a few Chilean fascist officers, and led to the murder of Chile's army commander, General Rene Schneider, who had spurned all coup conspiracies and was a bulwark of the country's constitutional process.

When all this was exposed in 1975, when Allende lay dead in a 1973 coup and Chile lay in the grip of a savage military dictatorship, Haig denied any knowledge of the conspiracy that killed Schneider. He had not even heard of Track II for that matter. "Well, again," he told a senator during his confirmation hearing, "I did not know there was a Track II specifically established." In his prepared statement on Chile to the Senate Foreign Relations Committee, he assured them that "I was not deeply involved in either overt or covert policies toward that country," and that "I had no responsibility to review or approve any CIA covert activities in Chile."

Yet by every other account in a remarkably documented record, including even Kissinger's exculpatory memoirs, Haig's role in the policy was unique. The Senate Intelligence Committee investigation concluded that he was the de facto "executive officer" of Track II as he had been for the wiretaps, "keeping tabs on it for the president," as the *Washington Post* described his role. Unlike Rogers, Laird, or most other responsible officials, he was one of less than a half-dozen men in the world who went to the meetings, heard the briefings, took the telephone reports, read the cables, and wrote the memos to Nixon—all on Track II.

Kissinger's memoir version of the Track II episode was sprinkled with references to his military assistant—"all the CIA reports to Haig and me," "neither Haig nor I"— because once more Haig was the only other person in the West Basement privy to the policy. It was another instance in which Kissinger did not trust even his own staff specialist; Viron Vaky, a quiet, able career diplomat who handled Western Hemisphere affairs for the NSC, was simply excluded from the beginning, leaving wisdom and nuance to the Latin expertise of Haig and Kissinger. Just as he had been with Sullivan at the FBI, the general was Kissinger's sole liaison with the CIA's Thomas Karamessines, Helms's deputy in charge of Track II. Haig would be there at every crucial juncture between Nixon's September 15 order and the October 22 murder of Schneider.

Whatever a congressional investigation later uncovered, there was at the time no doubt of Haig's role among the handful who knew along with him. Summoned back that fall from a post in Rio to the inner recesses of the CIA, where he would run the tiny Track II task force as a guarded secret even within the agency's already dense secrecy, agent David Atlee Phillips remembered his dismay at being briefed on the narrow authorship of the policy. "That was disturbing," he wrote in his memoirs, *The Night Watch*, "a covert action scheme to be launched directly by a President and his intimates—in this case Kissinger and Haig—without being on the agenda of the Forty Committee and at least being crafted by the Secretary of State and the Secretary of Defense."

"It was never more than a probe," Kissinger explained afterward, "an exploration of possibilities." Yet the mood was hardly so casual at the time. The high-level insistence on a coup was "as tough as I ever saw it in my time there," a veteran CIA agent testified to Congress. "I mean it was just constant, constant . . . just continual pressure . . . coming from the White House." The "pressure was constant and heavy," said Phillips, who slept on a sofa in his secret hideaway, recounting how Karamessines would regularly go to the White House to talk with Haig or Kissinger, or both, and "return with the word that we were to press on." He was under the "heaviest of pressure," Kissinger told the CIA, and they would feel the lash in turn.

In Haig's 1975 testimony about whether he was aware of a CIA-supported plot in all this to kidnap Schneider, the act that led to the commander's assassination, Haig told Congress, "I don't believe I was at all." Yet the conspiracy to remove Schneider was an integral part of the coup plans urged so heatedly that autumn from the West

Basement. Contacting twenty-one key military and police officials, the agency found and reported promptly to Haig that the "major obstacle" facing the would-be conspirators was "the strong opposition to a coup by . . . Schneider." With the CIA then "borrowing" the army attaché in Santiago to act as go-between because he knew the plotters better (a bureaucratic switch that involved a Defense Department cable kept secret from Laird but known to Haig), there ensued what Helms's biographer called generously "a succession of jerry-built schemes to kidnap General Schneider" to pave the way for some coup d'etat. "Schneider is the main barrier to all plans for the military to take over," the CIA station reported from Chile on October 8. The next day, under its "constant pressure from the White House," CIA headquarters replied, "This would make it more important than ever to remove him . . . anything we or station can do to effect removal of Schneider?"

The kidnapping supposedly got "no support, no endorsement, no assistance, and no approval," Kissinger has written. Yet CIA cables disclosed in the investigation showed that one Chilean general had been promised $20,000 plus $250,000 in life insurance by CIA agents on October 13, while another was pledged $50,000, all payments duly authorized in Washington. In the first two weeks of October, concluded the Senate investigative report, one of the generals planning Schneider's abduction "came to be regarded as the best hope for carrying out the CIA's Track II mandate."

Meanwhile, the same record documented the CIA's "constant consultation" on these matters with Haig and Kissinger. Karamessines's calendar showed him meeting with Haig five times and Kissinger six to ten times during the five weeks. From September 26 to October 5, when Kissinger and Nixon were abroad, Haig was the lone overseer of Track II. The CIA, said one analyst of the documents, "informed Kissinger and his aid, Alexander Haig, of the bleak picture on a regular basis."

Karamessines lunched with Haig on October 8, and on October 10 telephoned the general in a routine report on Track II and told him that the prospects were "negative." Asked by senators what "latitude" he had in passing on such reports, Haig answered that "at that time I would consider I had no degree of latitude, other than to convey to him what had been given to me." Yet for all the necessary precision in passing on such reports to Kissinger, Haig could never remember what he knew himself. "There was a specific program going underway [sic]," he told investigators, but he was only vaguely "aware" that the CIA was in touch with military plotters.

As it was, Track II and the kidnapping plot wound on. On October 13, having seen his half-informed ambassador to Chile about Track I, Nixon received Karamessines in Byzantine succession to discuss Track II. On the 14th— though all except Haig and Kissinger had no idea the United States was behind them—the Forty Committee heard among other things a scathing report from the ambassador on the kidnap- and murder-prone generals lurking about Santiago.

Then Karamessines met Haig and Kissinger on October 15 for a crucial report. By all versions, the coup prospects were dim, and they agreed ("It was decided by those present," said the CIA memorandum, again showing Haig a policymaker) to pull back from any "precipitate action" in the onrushing conspiracy of one of the original generals. "We had better not do anything rather than something that was not going to succeed," Haig remembered the conclusion.

With the October 15 meeting, Kissinger wrote in his memoirs, he now believed the plots and coup planning "ended." However, while the CIA cable to Chile after the meeting made it plain that one specific plot seemed fruitless, the telegram went on to tell the field that "it is firm and continuing policy that Allende be overthrown by a coup . . . we are to continue to generate maximum pressure toward this end utilizing every appropriate resource." Track II "never really ended," Karamessines testified. "What we were told to do was to continue our efforts."

In the later embarrassment over Schneider's murder and in the usual haste to shun responsibility, Kissinger and Haig would suggest that the CIA version of the October 15 meeting was simply a bureaucratic effort to "preserve the maximum degree of authority." Yet Haig had seen the telegram following the October 15 meeting as he routinely saw most of the agency's traffic on sensitive matters of special White House concern, of which Chile was obviously one. If it had so utterly misrepresented policy, he and Kissinger had done nothing at the time to correct it, or even to call the discrepancy to the CIA's attention.

Events now moved swiftly toward Schneider's murder. On the 17th, a CIA operative cautioned the generals to move "not too fast," but the coup plotting continued. Kissinger argued later that he and Haig had not known of one group of plotters "for the very good reason that they never did anything." Yet Haig's testimony referred in passing to "two" groups, and on October 19 and again on October 20, 1970, the same plotters attempted abortive abductions of Schneider. Later, Chilean courts quickly erased Kissinger's alibi in the distinction between plotters by finding the generals and their cohorts both guilty in the coup and kidnap-murder.

CIA records on the 19th showed headquarters badgering the field for news of the kidnapping and prospective coup because CIA officials "must respond during morning 20 October to queries from high levels." "High levels," of course, were by definition only Haig and Kissinger next to Nixon himself. CIA testimony confirmed that they not only knew of the plots but were eager for the news the next morning. Karamessines met with Haig on October 19, he testified, on an occasion when he "would have" given a complete report of the ongoing kidnap plans, but could not recall specifically if he had. "This is all very new to me," Haig said when questioned about the meeting. He had "no recollection" of plots, money, or kidnapping. At 2:00 A.M. on October 22, the machine guns were delivered to plotters in a remote section of Santiago. Six hours later, conspirators from the same group stopped Schneider's car with one of the guns, and when the general resisted, he was shot on the spot.

With Schneider's death, the Chilean army rallied to its new command and remained for a time apolitical. Track II, as Phillips described it, had "no more rails" and Washington's opposition settled into longer-run isolation of the Allende regime. Over the next three years, there would indeed be an effort to "make the economy scream" as aid, trade, and monetary relations, once a major portion of

U.S. help in the hemisphere, were slashed. Under a policy rechristened "destabilization," discreet liaison continued with the military, and encouragement was given the Chilean elements chafing under Allende's own financial mismanagement as well as the burden of long-overdue reforms and the external economic pressure from the United States.

No CIA "track," no direct U.S. connivance could be documented by congressional investigators looking into the 1973 military coup that eventually overthrew and murdered Allende midway in his term. But there were witnesses, including the former U.S. ambassador in Chile, who contended, too, that as many as nine assassination attempts were triggered by Track II, including one against Allende himself. Though the 1975 Senate inquiry found the evidence inconclusive, there were also investigators who believed Haig and Kissinger not only knew about but sanctioned an effort to kill the Chilean president.

In any case, the junta that took power was decidedly conservative and pro-U.S. It was also one of the world's most savage. Schneider's assassination had opened the way to a new breed of officer who did not share Schneider's devotion to constitutional liberties. But no Forty Committee meetings were called to mourn the extinction of human rights, political parties, or an independent press in Chile after 1973 as they had once met in alarm over Allende. No CIA operations were mounted to replace the unelected generals with their torture chambers, concentration camps, and mass murders, including the bombing of a former Chilean ambassador on the streets of Washington.

Was it Haig's policy as well as Kissinger's and Nixon's? Or was he, as he claimed so vaguely before congressional questioners, merely the neutral staff blotter? The CIA officers who worked closest with him, who took his calls and gave him their briefings, obviously felt, as Phillips said, that he, too, "launched" the policy. In February 1971, Zumwalt was called on the carpet for endorsing a visit to Chile, at Allende's invitation, by the carrier *Enterprise,* which might have strengthened moderate leadership in the Chilean navy. Being forced to turn down the invitation blew some of Kissinger's "cover" on the then outwardly "correct" Chile policy, Zumwalt recorded in his memoirs, and Henry was "in a black rage." But Zumwalt discovered as well that "Al Haig . . . had done some raging himself," though Haig at the same time "said to my face that he had sympathized with my recommendation and that the whole thing was just a difference of opinion."

While the responsible CIA officers spoke candidly about Track II and Schneider's murder in the later hearings, Haig would always shirk accountability. The assassination was "a profound and unacceptable mistake," he said once at his confirmation. But when he was asked at the same moment if the United States had done anything "at all improper" in trying to overthrow Allende in 1970, he replied, "I would not be the one to give you a blanket answer to that." It was not an answer he would give "blanket" or otherwise. Intervention was a "high-risk" policy, he told a senator at another point, and this effort in Chile not only did not work, it had been found out. Still, he lectured the committee, there were "vital interests" to be protected by unusual means. "There are many ways," he told the senators in a moral from his Chile experience, "to skin a cat."

However dramatic or portentous, grand strategy and clandestine maneuver were never far removed from the omnipresent politics of the court. Only weeks after the sequence in Chile, Zumwalt was casually discussing Mediterranean matters with Kissinger in the latter's West Basement office when the adviser's already deep voice suddenly "lowered conspiratorially." Zumwalt should come straight to him with any problem rather than going through Al Haig, Kissinger told the admiral. "He did not trust Haig, who was always trying to go behind his back directly to the President." Again on an official train to the Army-Navy game later that November, Kissinger repeated his concerns to Zumwalt, whose assistant he tried to recruit and whose notes of their talk read, "He says he can't trust Al Haig who is 'piping' around him to get to the President."

How much "piping" Haig was attempting at that stage is unclear, and the Kissinger encounter with Zumwalt could never be read (as the admiral himself shrewdly knew) without allowing for Kissinger's own playing on the navy's distrust of Haig the army general, and his typical ingratiation with Zumwalt. By the close of 1970, Haig's power was impressive. Since June he had been full-fledged deputy assistant to the president for national security affairs; and the accumulating secrets to be kept over the taps, Cambodia, and Chile only hardened his position. But his policy role was always to be curiously uneven. Although trusted and invoked as the staunch collaborator in dealing with raw issues of loyalty, invasion, and coup d'etat, he was often relegated to a more incidental role in other policies, and for the same random reasons of temperament and circumstance in the shifting Nixon-Kissinger dominion over foreign affairs.

Thus in the Jordan crisis of 1970, when Syrian tanks seemed about to ignite a Mid-East war and even a U.S.-Soviet confrontation, Haig's involvement was limited largely to arranging for the helicopter that brought Kissinger back from a Virginia retreat to a decisive White House meeting. In July 1971, he was among the inner circle who knew about Kissinger's China opening, the immaculate secrecy of which he much admired. "There are times when secrecy is not just better," he told the *New York Post* afterward, "it's essential." He was also Nixon's advance man to Peking in January 1972, leading the party of signal corpsmen and Haldeman aides that made logistics arrangements for the historic presidential trip the next month. His hosts then were the first mainland Chinese he had dealt with since watching Almond interrogate those ominous quilted prisoners in the hills above Hamhung two decades before.

Yet if Haig, like the rest of the White House, basked in the glory of the China diplomacy once it was done, he had been skeptical, almost viscerally opposed, in the earliest and most delicate stages of the secret gambit. He was a "constant brake" on the process, remembered one staff man who was also involved. The China opening was primarily Winston Lord's project on the personal staff, a subtle exercise in note-drafting and diplomatic tactics for which Haig had no gift, and, more plainly, no cachet with

Kissinger. Before the undeniable success of Kissinger's secret visit and the Chinese invitation to Nixon, Haig even fed the last-minute White House opposition to the policy by Haldeman, a small reactionary backfire that Nixon swiftly put out, only to face again after the trip in Vice President Agnew's thinly concealed sympathy for Taiwan. At that, Haig made no impact in his one passing diplomatic assignment in China. On the January advance trip, he carried to Chou En-lai a new U.S. proposal to resolve the sensitive Taiwan issue in the final presidential communiqué but left empty-handed. "The negotiation of a few sentences on Taiwan," Kissinger noted dryly, "was to take a great deal of time during the President's visit."

In the bloody repression of Bangladesh and the Indo-Pakistani war that followed in the autumn of 1971, Haig was once again a more enthusiastic adjutant, executing Nixon's snarling orders to "hit the Indians again on this," or calling in Soviet Ambassador Dobrynin's deputy (Haig's counterpart in the Kissinger-Dobrynin entente) to threaten fleet movements. One of the more callous and heedless of foreign policies ever practiced by a civilized state, Nixon's support of the military dictatorship in Pakistan in 1971 ignored the genocide and starvation of a million people, the agony of ten million refugees, the fervent dissent of State Department officers on the scene, and a long, unmistakable provocation of war in South Asia. Nixon personally despised the unruly Indians, preferred the oily manners of Pakistani colonels, and in any case thought the whole affair hostage to his heady China diplomacy, where Peking was Pakistan's ally and the Pakistanis helpfully arranged Kissinger's first secret flight to China over the Himalayas. But neither Haig nor Kissinger would moderate the mania, and, typically, they alone might have made a difference.

Kissinger recalls the three of them meeting in the Oval Office that December "in the solitude that envelops all crises," a *mise en scène* of their exclusivity and ingratiation when it seemed, incredibly, that the United States might actually join China and Pakistan in some conflict with Russia and India. It was a "lonely and brave decision," Kissinger wrote with unintended irony, particularly since the secretaries of state and defense were not present, Rogers being opposed to the policy and Nixon characteristically "prepared neither to confront his old friend nor overrule him." But in this case the crisis abates, the Chinese send a conciliatory note, and war is avoided, leaving only the wreckage of U.S. interests on the subcontinent for a generation, and a chilling passage in Kissinger's memoirs to footnote the vast, unquestioned power they once disposed.

On those issues in which he would claim some later authority as NATO commander—European politics and strategic-arms limitation—Haig made no real policy imprint during his NSC years. When Kissinger was ill with the flu, he sat in for him with Nixon during a December 28–29, 1971, visit to Washington by Germany's Willy Brandt. But among the episodes that agitated the administration's European policy in this era—the Mansfield amendment to reduce U.S. troops on the Continent, or the economic clashes over floating exchange rates and monetary policy—there was no hint of Haig. As he became America's chief military representative to the Atlantic Alliance in 1974, his experience with European

affairs was still largely limited to his German billet negotiations as a major in 1958–59. In the same vein, he was
a "note-taker" at one of the crucial bureaucratic auctions,
at which Kissinger traded weapons systems with the
Joint Chiefs in exchange for their agreement to deals he
had already privately negotiated anyway with Dobrynin
in SALT's legendary "back channel." With what Sonnenfeldt once described to a friend as "awe and anxiety,"
Haig watched Kissinger parley with the Russians over
arms increasingly after 1970, and duly kept the army informed, as indeed Kissinger, Zumwalt, and the rest of the
Pentagon expected him to do.

Through most of the SALT sequence, however, he was
an incidental figure with no visible aptitude or passion
for the complex issues of nuclear-arms control. When he
appears on stage, it is as Kissinger's enforcer in the jostling, often rude bureaucratic politics by which the rest
of the government was elbowed away from SALT.

The ostensible chief U.S. SALT negotiator, Gerard
Smith (whose memoir of his experience with Kissinger was
aptly titled *Doubletalk*), thus recorded Haig calling him
variously to repair a Nixon gaffe at a press conference,
tell Smith that Nixon would think him "underhanded" to
oppose a Kissinger position, warn that a negotiating point
"would be very poorly received" by the Russians (since
they had already turned it down in the Kissinger-Dobrynin
back channel), and snappishly instruct that only certain
members of the delegation could attend the signing ceremony, or that some sacrifice of basic tenets should be made
to purchase senatorial support. Often, as Smith wrote of
the congressional vote-buying, the crude byplay and Haig's
calls could be "hard to believe." Issues of enormity were

skirted, careers spitefully purged (including that of the ranking military officer on the preempted SALT delegation, who was accused of being "soft"), and rotten bargains struck with both the Kremlin and Capitol Hill—all in Kissinger's brilliant, blighted rush to the Moscow Agreements.

Sitting in the West Wing in 1969–73, Haig watched these SALT machinations in silence, discreetly playing bureaucratic bodyguard to the same settlements he later found it expedient to denounce.

There is no evidence that Haig took an interest in any of the several other foreign-policy problems breaking over Washington in the early 1970s, much less that he studied or negotiated them as experience for what lay ahead for him as secretary of state. The ignored issues would haunt the 1980s. Like Kissinger, he dismissed international economics, and with it the price of oil. While Chile was a periodic White House obsession, the rest of Latin America was left to the usual neglect, including the cankerous conditions in the Caribbean that were to plague Haig's State Department. In Africa, aside from an accommodation with corporate interests in white-ruled Rhodesia, the same inertia and indifference governed policy, while South Africa slipped further toward racial holocaust and Soviet exploitation. Bitterly excluded from the China diplomacy and buffeted by equally abrupt economic moves, the Japanese became in these years an increasingly alienated ally, squandering, ironically, the last of the MacArthur legacy. Not least, the uniquely powerful NSC adviser and his deputy dismissed almost completely the Middle East, leaving its deadly irredenta to be dealt with during Nixon's second term—and thus Haig to belated on-the-job training as Ronald Reagan's peacemaker among the Arabs and Israelis.

Whatever his grasp of world affairs, by the close of 1971 Haig had become more than simply Kissinger's deputy for foreign policy. As the wiretaps first certified him, he was as well the singularly "political" officer on the staff, increasingly absorbed in the internal-security and domestic trials of the beleaguered regime. That role also fueled his progress, of course, and two incidents during 1971—the exposure of the *Pentagon Papers* and the surfacing of alleged Pentagon "spying" on Kissinger— offer brief but clear glimpses of Haig at work in a White House sinking into Watergate.

"Ellsberg," one of the general's later interviewers found, "is a name Haig says through clenched teeth." When the former Pentagon official (and Kissinger consultant at the Pierre) gave the papers to *The New York Times* and the exposé appeared in the summer of 1971, Nixon was initially complacent, seeing the documents chiefly (and correctly) as a rebuke to previous Democratic administrations. But in what former White House aide Charles Colson remembered as "panic sessions," Haig and Kissinger inflamed Nixon with arguments that his own secrets were now in doubt, or at least his capacity to keep them —the detente with Peking, SALT, the secret Vietnam negotiations. The whole fragile structure of White House subterfuge, command, and success was threatened, they told a Nixon already deeply insecure about his reelection.

Haig "made matters worse," wrote one observer, "when he expressed the opinion at a White House meeting that hundreds of other top-secret documents might be floating around—and that they could find their way into print."

In part, their zeal was another demonstration of their loyalty. But the publication of the *Pentagon Papers* struck too at the old exclusivity and immunity of foreign policy, where such documents and decisionmakers were never so exposed. For Haig, it was also another anarchic act of defiance against the war policy he had so long supported. He had told an NSC staff colleague once that Senator William Fulbright was no better than a "traitor" for his antiwar stance, much as he complained to his brother, Frank, about the Berrigans and their unpriestly opposition to the war.

At any rate, the impact of their outrage was swift and far-reaching. On July 7, Haig sent out a memo to the rest of government requesting the names and security clearances of all persons authorized to see "top secret" materials (the classification of the *Pentagon Papers*), in an obvious open campaign to cow would-be leakers. Secretly and far more ominously, in a July helicopter ride with Kissinger, Haldeman, and Ehrlichman, Nixon hatched the "Plumbers." Soon afterward, the "Special Investigations Unit" quietly appeared in Room 16 in a remote basement corner of the EOB, complete with David Young, a former Kissinger appointments secretary and Haig's subordinate on the personal staff. Charged to plug leaks and help make Ellsberg an object lesson, the Plumbers promptly burgled the office of Ellsberg's psychiatrist that September, on their way to the Watergate Apartments, infamy, and jail. Meanwhile, Haig watched such Ellsberg developments attentively. In December 1971, he wrote Ehrlichman that he had received "information" that Ellsberg planned to use his trial on the *Papers* as a "political event." "Wouldn't it be the better part of wisdom," Haig asked, thinking ahead to the coming presidential election, "to seek to have the trial delayed until after November?"

That December, however, Haig had still other political worries. When columnist Jack Anderson published devastating revelations of Kissinger and Nixon during the Indo-Pakistani crisis, part of the leak was traced by chance to a young navy yeoman working for an admiral in the Joint Chiefs liaison office attached to the NSC staff. Prompted, ironically, by the admiral (an officer named Welander), the ensuing investigation not only pursued the Anderson leak but discovered that the yeoman had also pilfered sensitive NSC documents (in one instance from Haig's own briefcase during a "stroking" trip to Lon Nol in Cambodia) and passed them on to his then Pentagon superior (an Admiral Robinson) and eventually to the chairman of the Joint Chiefs, Admiral Thomas Moorer. The incident broke briefly in the press, and was quickly muffled as the participants were hurried off to new assignments.

Whether an overzealous yeoman (as the Pentagon maintained) or authentic interagency espionage (as Kissinger and Haig suspected, and anyway practiced themselves through the taps and myriad other sources), the "Admiral's spy ring" exposed with rare clarity the furtive, divisive, endlessly disingenuous manner of a government where other officials were treated like foreign enemies (and in some cases more suspiciously). Nixon's own first reaction to the episode was eloquent of what he thus expected of Kissinger. "Don't let K blame Haig," read Ehrlichman's notes from a meeting with the president on the Pentagon spying. Zumwalt, the unimplicated naval chief, found it all easy to understand "in the light of what I knew about what went on in the White House basement:"

> . . . Robinson believing that Kissinger expected him to keep us informed; Robinson/Welander, convinced that Haig was keeping Westmoreland fully informed, making a point of seeing to it that Moorer and I got everything Westy got; Kissinger telling me he distrusted Haig; Haig telling me and others he distrusted Kissinger; Haldeman/Ehrlichman trying to bushwhack Kissinger; Kissinger and the President using Moorer to help them make plans without Laird's knowledge and therefore pretending to keep Moorer fully informed while withholding some information from him too. . . .

"I am sure there were many more convolutions than that, but those are the ones that immediately come to mind," Zumwalt explained in his memoir. "Indeed, they created a system in which 'leaks' and 'spying' were everyday and essential elements."

As the Plumbers were revealed in the course of Watergate, leading to a skein of political crimes, Kissinger denied heatedly that he had ever known anything about such activities, though there was the apparent connection with Young and embarrassing shards of testimony linking Kissinger to the burglars. But the record left no question that Haig knew who and what were behind the door of

Room 16. When Admiral Welander first reported to Haig
the suspected Anderson leaks on the morning of December 14, 1971, Haig immediately summoned the Plumbers.
"He made a series of telephone calls and it was arranged
that I would meet with Mr. David Young in his EOB
office," Welander said in sworn congressional testimony,
and in a version borne out by Zumwalt as well. Haig told
Welander, the admiral went on, that Young "was going
to be running the investigation."

Informed of a leak, Haig had not called the FBI or
even the Pentagon's own security office, but rather the
vigilante administration group he already knew in December 1971 to be prying into Ellsberg and other matters.
He already knew, too, Safire recorded, about what the
speechwriter called "non-FBI clandestine operations,"
which Haig had almost casually dismissed. "There were
some dry runs made, but that was garbage," he said to
Safire, who later wrote: "This is a reference to the kind of
illegal espionage undertaken by White House agents."

Haig's familiarity with the Plumbers was hardly surprising. Just as he was the executive officer of the taps
and the Chile assassination plots, he was by all accounts,
for the same reasons of sensitivity and reliability, the Kissinger staff liaison with the growing extralegal apparatus
in the Nixon White House. The secrets to be kept, after
all, were mainly matters of national security. The Haig
connection was obscured in a sense by Young, on whom
Watergate investigators concentrated as the likely tie to
the NSC. Kissinger had never been close to Young and,
as he told Zumwalt in the fall of 1970, had "promoted"
him to the White House domestic staff to be "rid" of him.
Instead, it was Haig who dealt with the Plumbers directly

through Young's colleague, Egil Krogh, and through Ehrlichman himself—much as he now sent Welander to open
the leak investigation.

"Haig was involved in Watergate more than Kissinger,"
Zumwalt concluded reluctantly of his fellow officer in
June 1973. But by then, the general wore four stars, had
become the most powerful man in the White House, and
was already positioning himself once more to escape the
gathering debacle.

Part Three

REGENT

I was a pack horse in his great affairs,
A weeder-out of his proud adversaries,
A liberal rewarder of his friends;
To royalize his blood I spilt mine own.

Shakespeare, Richard III

It became a "malignant monument," wrote a historian of Teapot Dome, though its creatures were "less definably black and white than the legend." Like that other great political scandal of the century, Watergate was no less monumental, no less encrusted with legends. Most of its lore was ugly. White House courtiers plotted to savage their opponents and obstruct justice while a profane president strained to hide the outrage he had prompted, his vague, incoherent wandering toward impeachment traced on the spools of tape recordings whirring away in his own office. Surrounded by enemies, Richard Nixon had ended up bugging—and destroying—himself. Yet when all the muck and madness were gone, when Nixon had quit in the shadow of Senate conviction and flown to his California exile, there was the widespread view that the tragedy had at least one redeeming actor. White House chief of staff for the last fifteen fateful months, Alexander Haig was credited with not only avoiding the pervasive taint of scandal but discreetly steering an unstable, unwilling Nixon toward resignation.

Haig's role in the popular story was wrapped in mystery and paradox. "How Al Haig got Richard Nixon to decide that Richard Nixon must resign," concluded presidential lawyer Fred Buzhardt, "is . . . one of the most skillful, tactful, diplomatic, brilliant and sensitive feats in American history." The general's power, it was said, had been awesome. Watergate Special Prosecutor Leon Jaworski thought him "our 37½th president." Despite all that authority, however, his admirers set him apart from the obvious abuse of White House power taking place at the same time. Whatever had happened, they seemed to say in sheer gratitude for his feat, it might have been so much worse. "I could not help but believe that God's hand was in those final days," reflected Charles Colson, a contrite and convicted Watergate conspirator, "for the quirks of history might have positioned a man less honorable than General Haig to achieve far less noble results."

In the same vein, Haig was respected and rewarded for his staunch loyalty to the fallen president. Long afterward, he proudly refused to express remorse or apology for what he called "mistakes." ("I didn't make them," he assured a Senate Committee in any case.) Yet within weeks of his Watergate Gethsemane, he had also renounced his leader. "I am not a Nixonite," he told an interviewer in September 1974, and for that matter not even "a Republican."

Whatever his heroics or politics, Haig emerged from Watergate a formidable figure. Watching the new president, Gerald Ford, address a cheering joint session of Congress soon after the resignation, seasoned Washington journalist Jules Witcover looked up to see Haig in the VIP gallery of the House of Representatives, "standing erect and impassive . . . in the American version of the royal box, in a sense applauding his own deft achievement of presidential transition never contemplated in quite that way by the Founding Fathers." It had been "a bloodless presidential coup engineered by an army general, a man who had gravitated to the very right hand of one president and who, when that president fell, saw to a swift removal of the body and a ready replacement, maintaining at the same time his own proximity and influence," Witcover recorded. Haig's "presence and manner" there in the gallery, he thought, "suddenly were a bit unnerving if not frightening."

Beyond the drama of the moment, and the collective relief of friends and enemies alike at being rid of a corrupt president, Haig's regency was never so simple or so uncluttered. "There are probably some Democrats whom I could be comfortable with in this role," he told a reporter during those months. That, too, distorted the record. Once more, like his rise with Kissinger, Haig's historic progress and power as presidential chief of staff were unimaginable without Nixon, without the special esteem of that particular politician, and without the singular climate of the Nixon presidency both before and after Watergate broke the surface. So, too, he left his own peculiar stamp on the job. Set now against his earlier and later career, his record next to Nixon was in many ways vintage Haig. "The characteristics required wouldn't necessarily be better contributed by someone with a different background," he once said about his role. But how he came to be regent, and what he did or did not do beside the throne, remains one of the remarkable stories of American government, and no less dramatic than the black-and-white legend. For Haig the sequence began, like the

Watergate cover-up itself, more than a year before he succeeded Haldeman at a scandal-stricken White House.

He was discovered by *The New York Times* on the eve of his advance trip to China at New Year's 1972. "A button down Ivy League–style career army officer, who is above all loyal to the next man up in the chain of command," has a "passion for anonymity . . . thrives under pressure," and advances by "not disagreeing on issues," said a profile in terms that would fix his public image for years. Califano pronounced him the ultimate professional ". . . doing the job and doing it right." The man who kept "the machinery moving" while Kissinger dazzled with diplomacy, Haig was, thought the *Times*, "the next best thing" to his celebrated boss. The profile noted that after barely two years as brigadier general, he was again up for promotion. "Selection Boards pay attention to commendation letters from the White House . . . [and] recognize who a guy works for," offered a "senior Pentagon official."

In March, Haig was made a major general—at forty-seven, one of the youngest in the army and now far ahead of men in his West Point class who had ranked higher academically and had comparable or more impressive military experience. Looking at him that winter from the inside, Zumwalt drew a picture more candid than the *Times*'s. Haig "manages details and routine expertly," remarked the admiral, but also "is extremely ambitious," and "coveted daily contact with the President." As for Kissinger's relationship with his "next best" aide, "his dependence on Al was matched by his suspicion of Al,"

Zumwalt thought. And there was more than simply keeping "the machinery moving" when Kissinger was away at
secret statesmanship. "The decision about which one of
them would take a specific trip overseas," noted the naval
chief, "often depended on whether or not Kissinger's love
of high-pressure, highly visible diplomatic activity outweighed or was outweighed by his fear of leaving the
President alone with Haig for several days."

By the spring of 1972, Kissinger's "fear" seems to have
been justified if not fully realized. Haig—the clerk of the
taps and liaison with the plumbers, the envoy to Cambodia, deputy for a coup in Chile, and discreet ally of
Haldeman, the "man of action" who worked late and
self-effacingly while Kissinger courted both opponents
and personal celebrity—already stood out as the only
other foreign-policy adviser trusted or preferred by Nixon.
Had the relationship climaxed there, Haig almost certainly
would have gone on eventually, like other favored military aides to the president, to sure rewards of rank and
office in the bureaucracy. Vernon Walters, a less than
luminous colonel who happened to be Nixon's translator,
became a deputy director of the CIA (and later an
ambassador-at-large for Haig); Nixon's military adjutant
as vice-president, Robert Cushman, was named commandant of the Marine Corps. But Haig's influence and symbolic standing with the vulnerable leader were now
fortified by an extraordinary series of events, beginning
in the war in Vietnam. The conjunction of history and
personalities made his later succession to White House
chief of staff on Haldeman's fall almost wholly predictable.

With the long-forecast North Vietnamese offensive
across the Demilitarized Zone on March 30, 1972, the

administration began more than nine months of alternating negotiation and ferocity, which ended in the final
U.S. settlement with Hanoi, and in which Haig played
a central, sometimes decisive part. Hanoi's thrust that
spring threatened to collapse the ever-fragile structure of
South Vietnam. Launched just after Nixon's triumphal
visit to Peking and on the eve of the long-planned SALT
summit in Moscow, the attack also stood to make brutal
mockery of the most sensational White House diplomacy,
if not the president's prospects for a reelection that he
had deliberately tied to his foreign-policy finesse.

Through April, North Vietnamese troops took Quangtri
and swept south to occupy a major portion of the country
below the 17th Parallel. Kissinger meanwhile flew to Moscow and Paris in a desperate effort to stave off the advance and save his secret diplomacy on all fronts. His
concessions at that stage were historic. To both the Russians and North Vietnamese, he formally renounced the
old tenet of mutual withdrawal, a point he had been coyly
ignoring but never making explicit for some months.
Without bothering to consult his ally in Saigon, General
Thieu, he now agreed to the presence in the South of at
least 100,000 North Vietnamese troops. It was a surrender
that ever haunted his diplomacy, became an important
factor in Alexander Haig's rise, and would sooner or
later doom any postsettlement non-Communist regime in
Vietnam.

On the crest of its battlefield victories, however, Hanoi
for the moment ignored the capitulation and stalled the
talks. And while Kissinger negotiated vainly in a Paris
suburb, Nixon's diary of deliberations back in the White

House bore out vividly what Zumwalt and others saw as
the famous adviser's worst fears at court. "I had a long
talk with Haig, in which we concluded that we had to
have a two-day [bombing] strike . . ." Nixon wrote before
Kissinger left Paris. "Haig emphasized that even more important than how Vietnam comes out," the president went
on, in his memoirs *RN*, "is for us to handle these matters in
a way that I can survive in office." Nixon noted that Kissinger the diplomat was "understandably obsessed" with a
negotiated settlement; his deputy, the general, was obviously of sterner stuff. When Kissinger returned to Washington empty-handed late in the evening of May 2, he
found Haig together with a belligerent Nixon, a rump
government of two bent on a new onslaught of American
bombing.

Nixon's resort to escalation was instinctive and practiced. He proceeded to resurrect the three-year-old plans
of the September group to bomb the North intensively and
mine Haiphong Harbor. But now as then, Haig was an
unhesitating advocate of an all-out U.S. attack, and his
bellicosity secured his place with a chief executive
haunted by his own inner ghosts of weakness. As Nixon
then ordered the bombing and his blustery treasury secretary, John Connally, joined Haig's advocacy in the face
of the usual equivocations of Rogers and Laird and the
transparent public-relations straddling of Kissinger, the
moral the president drew was momentous. Haig and Connally clearly personified that private bravado, the mar-
riage of machismo and politics, that was the darker side,
the longing, of the man they served. "Only Al and John
understand," Nixon told Charles Colson that May, adding

"wistfully" that "you know, Chuck, those are the only two men around here qualified to fill this job when I step down."

Afterward the president was "totally sold on Al Haig," recorded Gulley, the director of the White House military office, who recalled as well the by-then-retired Nixon telling him early in the 1980 campaign that "he thought Haig was the next best qualified to John Connally to be president." When Gulley tactfully pointed out Haig was a patronage general with no "real" political experience, Nixon was "unmoved."

Vietnam was the arena of Haig's continuing rise and his crucial, somewhat serpentine policy influence through 1972. In the summer, the North Vietnamese offensive having petered out in front of Hue, he was twice in Saigon— believing Hanoi was "beginning to back down" because of the bombing, urging the reeling Thieu regime to invade the North, and bringing back to Nixon the usual "optimistic report." According to the account of a CIA operative then in Saigon and close to the August meetings with Thieu, Haig did not explicitly broach the issue of a continued North Vietnamese troop presence in the South, yet "said quite enough to convince Thieu that he was being stampeded," leaving the South Vietnamese "flabbergasted and enraged."

"I would see an improving situation for the South Vietnamese," Haig told *Parade* magazine when he returned in late August. At the same moment, however, he was complaining to Zumwalt that "he had to exercise considerable dexterity to stiffen the President's backbone when the President was in a bug-out mood." His chief vacillated between the urge to "get out of Vietnam as fast as possible at almost any price," explained Haig, "and an equally strong impulse 'to bomb North Vietnam back to the Stone Age.'"

Nixon, it seemed, was not always so strong as he had been in May, and Kissinger not the only fearful courtier. Haig "lived in dread," he told Zumwalt, "that some day the President would be with Henry instead of him when the bug-out mood came on and Henry would be unable to handle it." Having confided this to the navy over lunch at the Pentagon, Haig then returned to Kissinger, according to Zumwalt, and characteristically "gave Henry a version of our conversation that had so little relation to the facts that he might have been talking about a meeting on another day with somebody else."

At the same lunch, Haig had also asked Zumwalt what he should do next in his career. The admiral needled him about taking an obscure post in Panama to earn his way into high command, evoking a "totally untrue-to-life picture of Al Haig, chin in hand, thoughtfully watching the Gatun Locks slowly open and then close." But if the pre-Nixon Haig might have come to languish in the Canal Zone, it was by now only his navy rival's fantasy. On September 7, 1972, a grateful, admiring commander in chief lifted Haig to full general and, over the heads of some 240 senior officers, to vice-chief of staff of the army.

Gulley and others believed that Haig at this juncture already "saw what might be coming" with Watergate and "started making plans to get the hell away from the politicians." But that assumption seems largely hindsight. There were other reasons for his ostensible departure. He had wrung four stars from his White House patrons, after all, and may well have contemplated leaving the court intrigues, exposed or not, with some natural relief. In the summer and fall of 1972, despite the surge in Haig's stock from the May bombing, Kissinger still barred his formal rise in rank at the White House. Further Vietnam trials and further ingratiation with Nixon were still ahead, unseen. Not least, it was not his choice alone. Kissinger had persistently urged his appointment, in part to dispose of an obvious rival, but also, as he told Nixon, to have "one of your men" at the upper reaches of a recalcitrant Pentagon whose spies had been uncovered in the very bosom of the NSC. Intent on subduing the bureaucracy in his second term and replacing those who "stick the knife in" with proven loyalists, Nixon agreed to the transfer on the condition that Haig remain at the White House for what loomed as the final round of Vietnam negotiations. The irony was that the promotion and the waiting army sinecure only positioned Haig to rival Kissinger more overtly and powerfully than ever, opening his avenue back into the White House he was supposed to be leaving.

The promotion provoked the expected grumbling in the army officer corps and what the well-connected Gulley called "stiff resistance." But *Time* welcomed the "glamorous and politically sophisticated" Haig as "just what the Army needed," and the nomination sailed through the pliant Senate Armed Services Committee in early October with only perfunctory questions. Typically, the senators at the same hearing slapped Air Force General John Lavelle on the wrist by denying him one retirement rank for his involvement in falsified bombing reports in Southeast Asia, while passing over Haig, one of the three men ultimately responsible for American policy in the region, in willing obliviousness to his role. Not for the last time,

Haig enjoyed the genteel rubber stamp of Senator John Stennis of Mississippi, a former district judge from the rural South and the slightly distracted, seventy-one-year-old anachronism who chaired the committee. A model of congressional abdication, Stennis presided over promotions and Pentagon budgets alike content with what he was told by bureaucrats, and appeased too with the comparative exclusion of his lower-ranking colleagues. If abuse, excess, or evasion grew common in any administration, if unaccountable officials acquired unintended authority, it was only possible by such congressional irresponsibility.

Early in October, Kissinger was back in Paris, still hopeful of an agreement and yet to tell Thieu the bitter news of concession on the North Vietnamese troops in his country. For these first few days, Haig was silent and invisible. The unquestioning deputy, he accompanied Kissinger with Lord and others. On October 12, Kissinger flew home again to tell Nixon of a near-complete settlement. The president ordered steaks and Château Lafite-Rothschild while, he noticed, "Haig seemed rather subdued." He "honestly felt this was a good deal for Thieu," Haig told the president in Kissinger's presence, though he was "worried" about how Thieu himself would react. The next morning Haig, Kissinger, and Rogers were photographed smiling as they breakfasted with Nixon. The general repeated his support of the agreement, and Kissinger then flew off on a taut schedule for Paris, Saigon, and, finally, Hanoi for the dramatic conclusion of the settlement.

A week later, as the world soon learned, Kissinger's timetable came apart in Saigon as Thieu was asked to sign the *fait accompli* of a peace treaty he had never seen nor approved. The blunder was one of the worst among many in America's diplomacy in Asia. It derived in large measure from Kissinger's heedless momentum and more than a year of his calculated duplicity and avoidance with a temperamental client, whose culture and politics, the American should have known by now, required preparation and prolonged cajolery. Yet like most of the rest of their record since 1969, the notoriety of Kissinger's failure obscured how much of the tragedy traced as well to Haig—how he behaved in the crisis, how much his influence with Nixon affected the outcome.

Thieu balked from the first meeting on October 19. Kissinger argued then and in subsequent sessions that there would be, like the state under communism and with the same likelihood, "a withering away" of Hanoi's forces. At that, the South Vietnamese dictator only grew more adamant and bitter, frequently bursting into tears while an aide translated and "at the appropriate passages," Kissinger noted maddeningly, wept as well.

But if the scene in the Presidential Palace in Saigon was bizarre, Kissinger's cable traffic with the White House soon took on its own anguish. On October 20, Haig arranged for Nixon to see General Westmoreland, the former commander in Vietnam and on the verge of retirement as army chief of staff. As Kissinger described it later, Westmoreland now "suddenly surfaced objections" to the settlement all but concluded with Hanoi and being urged on Saigon—a turn Kissinger found "amazing" if only because the Joint Chiefs had all "endorsed" the main terms for the past two years. Without telling Kissinger about the Westmoreland conversation or the gravity of a potential Pentagon defection on the peace treaty, Nixon and Haig then sent him a cable stressing "solidarity" with Thieu and the necessity of Saigon's "wholehearted" acceptance.

When Kissinger reported to Washington what he saw as "the first hints" of Thieu's opposition, Haig cabled the American party in Saigon, on October 21, that in case of a "blow-up" the United States should "denounce" the political terms of the settlement entirely and attack Hanoi's previous concessions as perfidy. Determined to resist "proclivities in Washington to reverse course," Kissinger saw in Haig's cable "an inkling of those inclinations." Haig's recommendation, he thought, was "inconceivable." The United States had been considering less favorable terms for years, and the North Vietnamese "had just accepted our language on all major sections." The next day Kissinger replied to Washington that they should not "poormouth an agreement that we will not be able to improve significantly and which we should use instead as a tremendous success."

With Thieu's refusal the crucible, Kissinger and Haig now fought out a transpacific war of telegrams over the peace settlement. The mood came through in the careful yet revealing language of Kissinger's memoirs, where "tempers were further frayed" and "rose dangerously on both sides" in the "escalating misunderstanding." At one point the protocol and pretense of responsibility broke down altogether, and Kissinger noted almost casually in his memoirs "a flood of cables from Haig in Nixon's name." How often they had acted "in Nixon's name," from the taps to Chile to myriad other policies, in the same preemption Kissinger now disdained when the orders were aimed at him.

Nixon in his own memoirs later claimed authorship,

naturally, of all these October cables to Kissinger, but his diary makes too plain Haig's role. As Kissinger pressed Thieu, Haig brought the president a stream of intelligence about prospective communist terrorism after the cease-fire. "Haig was seriously concerned," Nixon recorded, adding in a diary entry his fear of a "murderous blood-bath." Watching from the Pentagon, the attentive Zum-walt described it more bluntly. "Haig thought that Kissinger was going too far and giving up too much—he talked the President into backing off his time schedule. . . ."

Shelled by Haig's telegrams, Kissinger meanwhile met with Thieu's foreign minister, who opened their session with a prayer and, with the "Amen," handed over twenty-three proposed changes in the agreement, many of them, Nixon wrote, "impossible demands." By October 23, Kissinger's mission was obviously at an end, hoisted on his own folly in Saigon and nakedly undercut at home. There was to be no more pressure on Thieu for the moment, and the final leg to Hanoi was canceled as Kissinger was called back to Washington. But before he returned, the Harvard professor who had hired Alexander Haig and helped him come so far sent the general an extraordinary cable that was an epitaph on the moment, and in some ways on Haig's undreamed-of future as secretary of state. "As for your characterization of the content of the agreement I would like to recall your view that it was a good agree-ment when we concluded it," Kissinger told him in a bitter reminder of the meeting on October 12 and their breakfast on the 13th. "It has since been greatly im-proved. . . ." And then the cutting point of intellect and station: "Many wars have been lost by untoward timidity.

But enormous tragedies have also been produced by the inability of military people to recognize when the time for a settlement had arrived."

There followed Kissinger's famous and all too premature pronouncement that "peace is at hand," the temporary collapse of negotiations as Nixon was distracted in the last days of the presidential campaign, and the continuation of the war while the president was reelected by an overwhelming margin. To those observing him most closely during these weeks, Haig's exact position and motives remained uncertain. There was evident conviction in his aversion to the peace treaty, a bureaucratic challenge to Kissinger in the manipulation of Nixon, no doubt some element of personal revenge on Kissinger, the man who had so often humiliated him, and the customary indulgence of Nixon's uncertainty and vacillation as well. Whatever the mixture, Haig and Thieu had set the stage for the final American flurry of diplomacy and violence.

Early in December, Kissinger was back in Paris, facing a new intransigence by Hanoi as well as Saigon. But this time, as a precaution, he had Haig at his side. Thought too powerful to be left in the White House, Haig had accepted Kissinger's assignment with alacrity, ironically because even his own feared access to the mercurial president had become sporadic. "Amateurs," Kissinger recorded later of Haldeman and other political or staff cronies, were "now Nixon's sole regular contacts in the strange mood that had settled over him since the election." (Bearing out Kissinger's suspicion, a typical Nixon diary entry on the negotiations during this period began, "As Haldeman and I add things up. . . .")

While other courtiers crowded around the throne, Haig's work in Paris was perfunctory, including what Kissinger acidly described as writing cables back to the White House "in his best Army prose" to shore up Haig's own staff substitute (a retired colonel) in dealing with what Haig's telegrams called those other "elements within the White House" who in Kissinger's and Haig's absence left Nixon "dominated by PR considerations."

On December 9, however, he was back in Washington as the talks sputtered, and he met Kissinger at Andrews Air Force Base on the night of the 13th when the adviser returned once more in diplomatic failure. As they drove back to the White House, Haig told him what had been implicit since the October fiasco: The general favored large-scale B-52 raids against the North Vietnamese. "There was another person not quite of the inner circle but getting ever closer to it," Kissinger wrote later about the 1972 Christmas terror bombing, "who played a significant role in the decision: my deputy Al Haig. . . ."

Deliberately disingenuous or not, Kissinger's memoir confession only acknowledged a power already firmly established. Coming back from Andrews that night, he knew once again that the decision to attack had been made essentially without him. So clear was Haig's influence in the president's anxious impulse to strike out that their meeting the next morning with Nixon was almost pro forma. Haig advocated a "massive shock," Nixon "accepted Haig's view," and "I went along with it," Kissinger wrote afterward.

Four days later, Nixon ordered "Linebacker II," the B-52s dropping their payloads on Hanoi and other targets in a saturation pattern measuring a mile by a half-mile, leaving untold civilian casualties (with neither side for its own reasons admitting the toll) and paying with the loss of twenty-six planes, ninety-three missing airmen, and thirty-one more U.S. prisoners. The diplomacy ended in twelve days of barbarism in the skies over North Vietnam, in part as the price of Kissinger deceiving Thieu. But Haig had watched the lethal course of that deception no less intimately than Kissinger, indeed had approved and abetted it until the failure overtook Kissinger in Saigon. And now the bombers flew again, not because the responsible cabinet officers urged it, or because Kissinger schemed at it, but because the president had accepted the view of his court general.

As the bombs fell and public outrage flailed against the reelected regime, Kissinger felt a "painful rift" with Nixon, while Haig was dispatched on another mission to Saigon. "Still the man to carry the message to Garcia," as Nixon described him at the moment, Haig this time took a virtual ultimatum to Thieu to prepare for the same agreement he had rejected in October or face a separate peace between Hanoi and Washington. In mid-December and again four weeks later as the North agreed once more to the old terms in Paris, he met Thieu with Nixon's threat to sign alone. And on January 21, the South Vietnamese relented, much as they would have been compelled to agree months earlier, before the Christmas bombing, had Kissinger—and Haig—practiced different politics and diplomacy.

The rest was almost Greek tragedy, the fate of their policy ordained in its flaws. Having promised Thieu massive future aid in the bargain, their savage bombing and furtive diplomacy only provoked a congressional back-

lash that eventually choked off the aid and left South Vietnam in the continuing war hostage to the cruel court
politics of October and December 1972 in the Nixon White
House. "There are at least two words no one can use to
characterize the outcome of that two-faced policy,"
thought Admiral Zumwalt, ironically echoing critics on
the left as well as in the Pentagon. "One is 'peace.' The
other is 'honor.' "

While the Vietnam negotiations were twisting to their
close, Haig was at last formally transferred back to the
army as vice chief of staff. In an Oval Office ceremony on
January 4, 1973, Nixon awarded him a Distinguished
Service Medal (known among career officers as the "generals' good-conduct ribbon") and lauded him as a "superb
military commander" and "a statesman and diplomat." He
was succeeded as deputy assistant for national security
affairs by the handpicked Brent Scowcroft, a better-
educated but diffident West Point classmate who had
made his climb by way of the air force, a Columbia Ph.D.,
contacts as an outer-office Pentagon assistant, and finally
promotion to brigadier general and White House military
aide, where Kissinger found him a relatively unthreatening successor to Haig.

With the change, there was "a lot less paranoia in the
office," chronicled one observer. "Kissinger feels a little
more secure with the President now that Haig has left."
Yet by March, with Nixon already distracted by Watergate, Zumwalt traced in his own diary notes the endless
bureaucratic maneuvering. Haig was now already in one
"tent" in a "polarization" of the Pentagon. Kissinger
threatened Elliot Richardson, the new secretary of defense, that he would be "treated the same as Rogers."

And they all jockeyed in a "surrealistic milieu of rumors flying, bureaucracy unraveling, leadership faltering. . . ."

Whatever Haig's new encampment and alliances at the Pentagon during what would be a four-month interval as the army's second in command, he was never to be far removed from his former role and patronage in the triumvirate with Nixon and Kissinger. In early February 1973, for example, a month after he had returned to the army, the president recorded in his diary a discussion with the general about wider diplomatic strategy for the second term and specifically Kissinger's need for "another great goal" after SALT, China, and Vietnam. "Haig feels strongly that it should be Europe," Nixon noted, adding that "I kept hammering, however, with Haig the necessity of doing something about the Mideast." It was hardly the stuff of army personnel or staff politics that customarily preoccupied vice chiefs. Nor did presidents commonly feel obliged to "hammer" the wisdom of grand strategy with officers beneath the Joint Chiefs, if them. In both Kissinger's visible relief at his departure and in Nixon's continuing reliance on him were the marks of Haig's extraordinary position.

Within the government, Haig's reassignment back to uniform was widely thought his stepping-stone to chief of staff or even chairman of the Joint Chiefs, posts to which Nixon might have named him directly had not the intrusion on entrenched service patronage promised such a storm. In the army's careerist politics, that succession would have usually required at least a relatively quiet, inoffensive tenure as vice chief as well as the continuing favor of the president. Even apart from his White House roles, however, he seemed fated at this point for controversy. Between the Christmas bombings and Watergate, in a little-known episode of his brief time at the Pentagon, Haig's only notable duty as vice chief of staff was to command the army's constitutionally dubious involvement in the siege of Wounded Knee.

At the end of February 1973, in symbolic defiance and protest of overall federal policy as well as local administration, some 200 Indians seized the tiny South Dakota Sioux village of Wounded Knee, site of the last great U.S. massacre of Indians in 1890. When the siege ended in a negotiated surrender of the protesters seventy days later, the dickering and sporadic gunfire left two Indians dead, one federal agent paralyzed, still bitter grievances, and what one onlooker called "a pervasive inconclusiveness about what had been accomplished . . . promises, bravado, debris—and no winners."

In the interim, Wounded Knee was invested by more than 340 marshals, FBI agents, and border police. Yet the army under Haig had also joined the siege and readied attack plans, in an encroachment on the civil sphere that would be challenged in the courts for a decade to come. Rooted deep in the Anglo-American abhorrence of military dictatorship and codified in an evolution of statutes dating from the Magna Carta, the doctrine and Act of *Posse Comitatus* made it illegal to use "any part of the Army" to enforce civil law unless violence and rebellion were clearly beyond the control of civil authorities, or the intervention was specifically empowered by an act of Congress. Though neither condition was met at Wounded Knee, and though the government ostensibly ruled out the use of troops, documents later unearthed by investigative journalism and lawsuits revealed in fact a major army involvement, with Haig at the center.

According to that record, the day after the seizure, Attorney General Richard Kleindienst asked the Army Department to send a "representative" to Wounded Knee to "evaluate" the situation. Haig took immediate command of the army role, becoming what legal documents later called "the supervisory employee" with "final approval." Whether as a result of his White House political standing, or in abdication by his weary chief of staff (and another former Vietnam commander), Creighton Abrams, or at his own initiative, the origin of Haig's role is not clear in the public record. Again it was scarcely a routine responsibility for a vice chief. In any case, what followed as a result is more plainly documented.

Haig's envoy, Colonel Volney Warner, arrived at Wounded Knee at dawn on March 3. He found a cordon of marshals, FBI, and border patrolmen ample for the siege, and Justice Department attorneys intent on peaceful negotiation. In the next few days, however, the army slowly established its bureaucratic and operational influence. Joined by other officers dispatched by Haig and in constant communication with the general back in the Pentagon, Colonel Warner began to function, in the words of his own report, as "a Military Assistance Advisory Group."

Accordingly, Wounded Knee soon took on the look as well as the nomenclature of Vietnam. A federal "free-fire zone" was charted. Relatively massive amounts of military equipment poured in on the small battlefield, outfitting the federal officers with 17 armored personnel carriers, 100 M-16 rifles, 200 flak vests, 9,000 parachute flares, and 123,000 rounds of ball and tracer ammunition —all arrayed against what soon became a guerrilla theater of squabbling and dwindling Indian factions that were far outnumbered and armed largely with hunting rifles and slogans. Like Vietnam, too, the record shows, Warner and Haig used the flow of equipment as leverage with the recipient Justice Department, giving the army a nearly equal voice in federal decisionmaking at the siege.

On March 12, according to a subsequent lawsuit, Haig received from Warner a detailed attack plan for Wounded Knee, including the use of army troops. With Haig's endorsement, the plan was first set in motion and then postponed in favor of further siege and negotiation. After five weeks of inconclusive talks, however, the attack was again scheduled. Through April and May, the Eighty-second Airborne and Fourth Infantry were placed on periodic alerts. Additional army officers flew in from Fort Carson, Colorado (Bernard Rogers's command), to assist with the attack. A situation report to Haig on May 1 set the assault for the morning of May 10. Following the original operational plan outlined in a memorandum from Warner to Haig, dated March 9, at dawn the Indians were to be warned briefly then gassed with fifty-five gallon barrels of CS riot gas (of the kind used in Vietnam) dropped from aircraft and fired from the armored personnel carriers. Troops would promptly move in to "neutralize" resistance, while Warner hovered overhead in a command-and-control helicopter. Only ninety-six hours remained in the army countdown when on May 8 the 120-odd remaining Indian holdouts surrendered themselves and a few rusty arms to federal agents.

It was a "whimperish ending," *Newsweek* said of the surrender, praising the government for its "loose rein." But at the time, only a handful of officials knew of the attack plans. Buried in secret Pentagon files, and exposed only by later court order, was another story of the army's calculated preemption of civil law enforcement, and the shadow of domestic political counterinsurgency beyond the Constitution, of Vietnam come home to an Indian reservation in South Dakota. Sixty of the documents in that archive carried the name of Alexander Haig. His role and that of other senior officers would be the subject of costly and lengthy litigation between the Indians and the federal government long afterward. Even had the attack gone off that morning of May 10, though, it seems likely Haig would have escaped the aftermath there, too. Six days before, he had been summoned back to that other battlefield in the West Wing for still more sensitive command, this time inside the narrowing cordon, as Nixon's chief of staff in the final siege of Watergate.

But while the countdown ticked away at Wounded Knee, there were two more episodes worth noting during Haig's interval as vice chief of staff, threads to the past that were significant both as part of his larger record and as the preface to his return to the White House. In January and again in April 1973, he was back in Cambodia for his final "stroking missions" with the addled Lon Nol. On the first visit, he assured the marshal "of our continuing support," read the reporting cable to Washington. In April, the Phnom Penh dictatorship having reached "an all time low," as "appalled" Senate investigators termed it, he offered Lon Nol medical care in the United States, urged him to "broaden" his government by bringing back collaborators from the 1970 coup he had since pushed out, and pledged again "maximal support" for the faltering regime.

Meanwhile, the war in Cambodia grew ever bloodier and the Khmer Rouge ever stronger despite the peace settlement in Vietnam. Haig now urged more aid. The shipments he had supervised since 1970 had made Cambodia's the fourth-largest air force in the world, but with little effect on Lon Nol's ebbing position. He also pressed for new and more intensive U.S. bombing, though that, too, was having scant effect on the war. "The enemy remained steadfast," concluded a secret history of one B-52 unit involved in Cambodian raids, "while Lon Nol's troops continued to decline in effectiveness."

Nonetheless, at Haig's urging a new onslaught of bombing began in February 1973, with targeting control secretly shifted to the U.S. Embassy in Phnom Penh. There, without the knowledge of the secretary of state, the mission chargé, named Thomas Enders, supervised the strikes. Tall, patrician, with a wealthy Italian wife, a background in Common Market economics, and an untested reputation, Enders had glided steadily up through the State Department's European Bureau, past colleagues of lesser veneer, until he ran afoul of a superior in the Belgrade Embassy. He was now struggling in Cambodia to retrieve laggard prospects by his zeal as an uncritical supporter of Lon Nol. In the process, as one observer wrote later, "he soon became Haig's favorite diplomat in the embassy."

Yet as the bombing now moved, with the Khmer Rouge, westward into populated areas of Cambodia, Enders was using maps that were only 1:50,000 in scale and several years out of date. Though U.S. pilots requested more recent, detailed maps to pinpoint military targets, they were not provided. The inevitable result was the mounting and indiscriminate slaughter of civilians from 30,000 feet. Inside the embassy, the political counselor "began to get reports of wholesale carnage," as he recalled afterward. But the strikes went on, Enders oblivious to the reports of mass casualties, and the embassy's targeting role concealed from inquiring senators, until an angered, too often deceived Congress halted the Cambodian bombing in August 1973.

By April 1975, after two more years of brutal fighting marked by widespread atrocities and starvation, the corrupt and U.S.-spawned Lon Nol government fell to the Khmer Rouge, who in their own savagery and fear emptied Cambodia's cities and plunged the once peaceful, relatively prosperous country into a prolonged nightmare of genocide, famine, and civil war. "It need not have happened," Kissinger wrote, blaming the Congress. "Cambodia was not a mistake," British journalist Shawcross concluded in a different view of the policy, "it was a crime." But not all the sequels were unhappy. Though in 1981 Cambodia still writhed in agony, part of the country occupied by Vietnamese while hundreds of thousands of desperate refugees huddled in camps abroad, the general who led the "stroking missions" to Lon Nol was secretary of state himself, and Enders, his "favorite," with new policies to explore in El Salvador and elsewhere, had been named Haig's assistant secretary for Latin American affairs.

"I had a good meeting with Haig and Henry," Nixon finished a diary entry for April 14, recording a session on Cambodia and Vietnam almost as if the general had never

left. Two weeks later, there was a similar echo as Haldeman told Nixon, according to a previously unpublished
transcript of the tape, "Haig did a great job out there."
Haldeman was not referring to Phnom Penh, however, but
to Los Angeles, where Haig had testified on April 25 for
the prosecution in the celebrated trial of Daniel Ellsberg
for leaking the *Pentagon Papers*. Another bit of ongoing
duty from his previous White House work, he appeared
as a rebuttal witness in the closing days of the trial to discredit witnesses for the defense and, as he told reporters,
"because I was asked to." One of many officers in the
case, he was the first to come to court in full uniform,
and the calculated effect was palpable. When he took
the stand, reported the *Washington Post*, "many of the
jurors seemed to stare at the four stars on each of his
shoulders and a nearly full chest of decorations." Ellsberg,
who knew him from the Pentagon staff in the Sixties, had
approached him when he entered with "Hi, how are you?
What brings you here?" Haig only shook hands in silence,
but in his testimony minutes later provided the answer
by deriding the credentials of both Halperin and University of Michigan professor Alan Whiting, who had
appeared for Ellsberg.

For those few who knew the inner workings of the NSC
staff, Haig's testimony on the two men amounted to virtual
perjury. Halperin, he told the court, was only one of ten
"senior staff officers" who served as a "transmission belt"
for the NSC. This misrepresented significantly Halperin's
role as architect at the Pierre and later coordinator of the
new decisionmaking system, or his early and feared potential as Kissinger's deputy months before the then

lower-ranking Haig himself became a candidate. So, too, he depreciated Whiting as just another member of "academia" who talked to Kissinger "on three or four occasions," though in fact, as Haig well knew, the scholar and former State Department intelligence analyst on China had been a key and frequent consultant to Kissinger in the latter's avid and careful secret homework before the clandestine 1971 flight to Peking. Beyond that, however, he "had no esoteric knowledge of what has happened here," Haig answered in cross-examination, and soon drove off with an army aide. "He got away again," remarked Anthony Russo, Ellsberg's codefendant.

What "esoteric knowledge" Haig had indeed taken away with him, however, would not be known for a while longer. In February 1973, *Time* magazine, in an account vehemently denied by the White House, reported the placing of the national-security wiretaps in 1969–71. The next month, L. Patrick Gray, nominated to be Hoover's successor at the FBI, was questioned in Senate hearings about such taps, but again officially denied the story. When Haig came to the trial in Los Angeles, the court had long since requested any government wiretaps on which Ellsberg had been heard, and been assured none existed. Of the tiny handful of men aware of the taps and their summaries, Haig was of course the only one, save perhaps Kissinger or Sullivan, who knew in such detail of Ellsberg's phone calls with Halperin. He had gone to Sullivan especially to discuss one of their conversations about drugs. Yet now, with the subject of the taps freshly headlined, and asked under oath about evidence he might have material to the trial albeit not about an Ellsberg-Halperin tap specifically, Haig said nothing. He had taken the stand, columnist Joe Kraft reflected when the taps became known, with "dirty hands."

On May 4, the same day Haig was named Nixon's new White House chief of staff, newly appointed acting FBI director William Ruckelshaus, having been tipped off by Bureau agents about the taps, began his own internal search for the records and informed the startled judge in the Ellsberg case that wiretap evidence on the defendant might exist after all.

"One of the first things that was brought to my attention," Haig said later in a sworn deposition about these first days in May 1973 back in the White House, ". . . was the fact that the Ellsberg trial was in a hung-up state because the judge out there had requested any electronic surveillance that may have taken place on Mr. Ellsberg." Haig went on in the same 1974 testimony to explain that he then told White House counsel Leonard Garment "that I knew there had been some such a [sic] wiretap and we should send it out to the judge." Haig said he warned Ruckelshaus and "instituted a search in the White House, and lo and behold, we found . . . them [the tap records] in Ehrlichman's files, in a cardboard box so big."

Yet Ruckelshaus's public statements at the time and FBI records indicate that it was Sullivan and Mardian, not Haig, who disclosed that the wiretap logs had been concealed in the White House. As for Garment, he "does not remember Haig's version" of the taps' resurrection, reported the *Washington Post* in an account of the episode and the Haig claim. Nor did the "lo and behold" tone of the general's deposition accord with his role in July 1971, when he and Kissinger specifically verified the tap logs being secreted in the White House after Sullivan had passed them to Mardian.

As so often in the regime's recklessness, the harsh remedy produced the ill at which it was aimed. Just as the secret and wanton bombing provoked congressional suspensions of aid and action that crippled foreign policy, so, too, the wiretaps, supposed to discourage leaks, became a count of government misconduct. The judge soon dismissed the charges against Ellsberg, by his own admission perhaps the only *real* leaker overheard on the taps. But then, did the story even end there, after the trail of Haig's half-true testimony? Calling the new White House chief of staff that spring to console him on the excavation of the tap logs, Eagleburger, now a Pentagon official and returning as Kissinger's executive assistant, found him almost relieved. "Just be thankful," Haig told his onetime fellow aide in a tone that invited no further question, "they only got the ones they did."

So tumultuous were the dying months of the Nixon presidency—the revelations of scandal and cover-up and the prospects of impeachment rumbling through the public consciousness like some interminable earthquake, each successive shock hitting more swiftly and jarringly than the one before—that Haig's period as White House chief of staff seemed to some afterward almost blurred, shaken out of focus. It was in many ways the single most important chapter of his public service, yet he appeared somehow both present and absent. "I wasn't there," he told an unchallenging Foreign Relations Committee during his confirmation as secretary of state, trying to draw a recognized border between himself and what he called only the "mistakes" of Watergate.

Yet if Haig's return to the White House at the beginning of May 1973 is indeed imagined as a sharp dividing line across that history which Gerald Ford called "our long national nightmare"—even with Ford's phrase narrowly construed to cover only the Watergate break-in and its aftermath rather than the whole range of presidential abuses predating the burglary, and even excluding the general's earlier roles in the wiretaps and as liaison with the plumbers—Haig's historical tenure amid the jumble of events in 1972–74 becomes clearer.

On the far side of that line, before he is chief of staff, lie the arrest of the Watergate burglars in June 1972; the preelection cover-up; the burglars' attempt at extortion and hush money; their harsh sentences by Judge John Sirica and resulting testimony implicating Nixon campaign officials; the gradual confession and plea bargains of those men, such as campaign director John Mitchell, aide Jeb Magruder, and various other campaign or White House figures; the April 1973 defection of White House counsel John Dean with his devastating testimony; the implication and resignations of Haldeman and Ehrlichman; Haig then becoming Nixon's most trusted and powerful aide.

Ahead, on the other side of the line, with Haig beside the Oval Office, from May 1973 to the autumn of 1974, lie the discovery of the seventeen wiretaps; the hearings of the Senate Watergate Committee; the disclosure of the existence of White House tapes, and their subpoena; the bribery conviction and resignation of Vice President Spiro Agnew for non-Watergate charges and his replacement by Congressman Gerald Ford; the hiring and then firing of special Watergate prosecutor Archibald Cox and the resulting resignations of Richardson and Ruckelshaus in what came to be known as the "Saturday Night Massacre"; the suspect alert of American military forces in October 1973; the discovery of an eighteen-and-a-half-minute gap in one of the subpoenaed presidential tapes; the White House release of tape transcripts with discrepancies later found between the official transcriptions and the actual recordings; the July 1974 Supreme Court order that the president release contested tapes; the hearings in the House Judiciary Committee and its voting of specific articles of impeachment; the surrender of the notorious tape of a conversation on June 23, 1972, implicating Nixon in the early cover-up; the rumors of a coup d'etat and Pentagon orders to ignore White House directives without other authority; the president's resignation in August 1974; and the subsequent pardon of Nixon by President Ford.

The line also separated destinies. On the far side, Nixon's chief White House aides went to trial and jail. On his side of the boundary, Haig of course went on to the NATO command, a candidacy for president, and the Reagan cabinet.

Haig was dining with fellow officers on a tour of Fort Benning when the call from Haldeman came on May 2. Credit for selecting Haig as the new staff chief was claimed in various quarters. Colson claimed to have written Nixon urging the appointment on May 1. Haldeman recalled that he came to meet with Nixon the next day (slipping into the White House "quietly" after his April 30 resignation) with General Haig at the top of his list of items to discuss—Haig's main qualification, he thought, being "diplomatic enough to have served under Henry Kissinger and survived."

Nixon remembered that *he* had chosen Haig. "We had the same man in mind to succeed him," he wrote of the meeting with Haldeman. Haig was "steady, intelligent and tough," knew how to "drive" and to "inspire" people. "Equally important to me," Nixon noted, "he understood Kissinger."

Gulley recounted that Scowcroft was the "first choice" to succeed Haldeman, and that Kissinger thought him too valuable to give up as his new deputy, but that seems at odds with everything else known about the character and history of all the actors. Kissinger would have readily preferred the pliable Scowcroft as regent, and by one account petulantly repeated his quotidian threat to resign when he learned of Haig's selection, only to be told by Nixon's longtime personal secretary, Rose Mary Woods, "For once, Henry, behave like a man."

Ehrlichman, too, apparently had misgivings. "I don't think Al's the right man for that job for all his qualities," he told a journalist months later. From a different vantage point, however, Herb Klein, another Nixon aide of long standing who had suffered harsh eclipse by Haldeman and Ehrlichman, saw Haig as "a breath of fresh air."

Reaction in the press generally followed Klein's sense of relief at the departure of perceived villains. White House reporter John Osborne wrote in *The New Republic* that "the chief significance of Haig's return to the White House is its evidence of the President's pathetic shortage of people whom he trusts and to whom he can turn in a time of extreme need." But the *Washington Post*, otherwise leading the Watergate hunt, pronounced the general to be of "great intelligence and integrity" in implicit comparison to his stained predecessors around Nixon; and Joseph Kraft wrote about the new chief's "interest" in a "short but drastic clean-up," Haig knowing "from observations at the headquarters of General MacArthur . . . how much damage an overzealous staff can do a reclusive leader." Deploring the "absolutely purposeless and useless crimes" of the old regime (presumably as distinct from purposeful or useful ones!), columnist Joseph Alsop hailed Haig's arrival as a "remarkable development" signaling "an end to drift" and lauded the general's "personal sacrifice."

There was a brief storm over the constitutional and political propriety of Haig's holding the top White House staff position while on duty as a military officer, and the issue threatened yet another congressional confrontation for the administration, but that subsided when Haig announced early in June that he would simply retire from the army. "Intellectually, it was not a tough decision," he said afterward. "But it was a problem of the heart. My wife almost decided independently and concurrently with me that it was best to step down . . . the President was in enough trouble already."

In retrospect, his readiness to leave the army after twenty-six years seems almost too casual, and probably taken with the expectation that he could be returned at some point by Nixon or his successor. At forty-nine, he might have calculated that the same patronage that had brought him such rank so rapidly, after all, could restore it, or at least replace it with comparable cabinet rank. The distinction between Haig the soldier and Haig the bureaucrat had long since disappeared for the general no less than for those watching him. It was, in any case, an impressive mark of Haig's commitment and loyalty, and perhaps in that sense its own insurance for the future. His decision was eased as well by maneuvered retirement at four-star rank. He would become a civilian, noted the admiring Alsop in June, "after a few further weeks in uniform that he needed to prepare for such a total change in way of life."

The reality was less noble. By waiting until August 1 to date his retirement, and with the White House pressing through special congressional legislation on a quiet Saturday morning that July, Haig received a yearly four-star pension of $25,764—nearly $4,000 more than two-star retirement benefits. Added to a White House salary of $42,500, his total annual pay would be $68,000 a year in 1973, making him one of the highest-paid federal employees.

In his confirmation hearing as secretary of state, Haig would claim that as Nixon's principal aide he spent "ninety percent of my time" on non-Watergate affairs. It was the same pretense made in the announcement of his appointment at the time by Press Secretary Ron Ziegler, who assured the public that Haig would be concentrating on "policy matters." But after a while on the job in 1973, Haig himself was more honest. He felt as if he had taken over "a battalion that has just been overrun," he said on one occasion then, with more experience on the subject than his listeners knew. White House logs from 1973 to 1974 obtained by the *Washington Post* showed, said the paper, "that Haig spent even more time defending the President than Nixon did himself," or as another writer described it, "more time on the subject even than Nixon, who ate, slept and drank his own defense."

One of his first acts was to try to shore up the sagging Nixon legal defense by bringing to the White House Pentagon counsel Fred Buzhardt, another wartime-class West Pointer. Buzhardt had resigned early to become a lawyer, had discreetly steered Haig's recent promotion through the obliging Stennis and his colleagues, and his reputation as a government attorney was for legal expediency if not brilliance. In the first weeks, Haig plunged as well into countering the new Ervin committee by the preparation of the May 22 presidential statement on Watergate, where his hand was evident in the rationale of national security that Nixon now drew over the record. The president had nothing to do with illegal campaign practices, the cover-up of Watergate, schemes of executive clemency for the burglars, or the break-in at the office of Ellsberg's psychiatrist, but he had justifiably tried to prevent exposure of "covert national security activities," and some of his aides "may have gone beyond my directives" in such patriotic efforts, to which he should have "given more heed." Still evasive, vague, and self-serving, the statement added up, said one observer, "to just another reassurance" that left a by now cynical Congress, public, and press unconvinced.

The very day after the statement was released, Haig was embroiled, too, in one of the more shadowy Watergate issues—the Nixon campaign contribution of $100,000 from millionaire eccentric Howard Hughes. He took "only one action of any significance," Haig told the Foreign Relations Committee about the Hughes affair, and that was to pass along from Nixon to the president's close

friend Charles R. (Bebe) Rebozo, who had received the
contribution, the name of a tax attorney for the imminent
Internal Revenue Service investigation of the matter. But
what Haig (and the committee) ignored was also of "significance." On May 23 he had called Treasury Secretary
William E. Simon to ask the status of the IRS investigation. Simon checked and told Haig later that the IRS was
indeed interested. Shortly afterward, according to Rebozo's own testimony to the Watergate Committee, Rebozo returned the same $100,000 in cash to Hughes. And
still later, in the account of Rebozo's lawyer, Haig leaked
to Rebozo the findings of a secret Federal Reserve study
that some of the hundred-dollar bills returned to Hughes
were issued after the date Rebozo testified that he had
received the $100,000.

Beneath the money-shuffling was the question of
whether shady campaign funds had been used for non-
political reasons, and even for Nixon's personal use without legally declaring it as taxable income. Watergate
Committee investigators came to suspect the Hughes-
Rebozo money had been so misused, but could not prove
it, in part because of White House protection of Rebozo
and a cover-up in which Haig had apparently played a
part beginning less than three weeks after he became
chief of staff.

By the end of May, such obvious political passion in
Nixon's defense had already taken some of the bloom
off Haig's initial reception in the press. When the general
called in reporters to smear quietly Halperin and other
former colleagues in an effort to rationalize the recently
exposed wiretaps, columnist Kraft angrily revised his
rosy opinion of less than three weeks earlier. "It was ex-

pected that Haig would do a rapid clean-up job," Kraft
wrote, surveying his own clips. "But Haig is not an officer
practiced in command. He is a bureaucratic general who
takes on the color of his surroundings. So he has been
spending quite a lot of time recently justifying to newsmen the wiretapping [and] . . . in the process he has been
blackening reputations and disclosing the contents of
wiretaps, itself a violation of the law. And all that in the
name of national security."

On Sunday morning, June 3, Nixon read the *Washington Post* with what he remembered as "a sudden sense of
dread." The story was that John Dean had told prosecutors and Senate investigators about his conversations
with Nixon on March 21 and earlier, in which the president had apparently taken part in the Watergate cover-up,
including the approval of paying blackmail money to
ensure the burglars' continued silence about White House
involvement. Feeling "discouraged, drained and pressured," as he recalled the moment in his memoirs, Nixon
asked Haig whether he should resign. The general's answer, wrote Nixon, was "a robust no," and Haig urged him
to listen to the actual tapes of the Dean meetings "to con-
struct an unassailable defense based on them." Haig would
"make the necessary arrangements" for the review.

The following day, Nixon listened to several of the
conversations, and late in the afternoon called in Haig
to discuss the tapes. Their conversation itself was recorded, and a transcript of portions of the recording
released over a year later. Read against the backdrop of
Haig's career, the dialogue provides not only a sense of
his early involvement in the Watergate crisis a month to
the day after his appointment, but also a rare glimpse of

Alexander Haig the successful aide, his substance and diction.

Their talk begins with Nixon saying he has another half-hour tape of the Dean meetings to hear, and "I don't know what the hell is on it." But Haig is intent on Dean's vulnerability. "You see it's so good because nobody in Congress likes him," he says of Dean. "You know, you don't know whether he's [unintelligible]."

"God damn it," Nixon then exclaims, followed by another "unintelligible." He is apparently listening to a damaging passage on the tape.

"Some kind of remark that the son-of-a-bitch could twist out of context," Haig promptly comments about the passage and Dean's potential use of it. "They know, they know, generally, whether, with, uh [unintelligible]." Haig then goes on haltingly about Dean: "The worst trouble he could do, even if, if he's reasonably accurate—now, if he's going into a full-fledged perjury job, uh, of the greatest magnitude, then we can take the son-of-a-bitch on." Apparently without knowing yet what Nixon has actually heard (he "never listened," he later testified), or even specifically what Dean will claim, Haig here at the beginning is bolstering, belligerent, profane, almost jaunty in filling his "action" role with the worried Nixon.

The transcript continues with an ominous note:

PRESIDENT: That's right. That's right. Well, as I told you, we do have one problem: it's that damn conversation of March 21st due to the fact that, uh, for the reasons (unintelligible). But I think we can handle that.

HAIG: I think we ca—, can. That's, that's the—

PRESIDENT: Bob can handle it. He'll get up there and say that—Bob will say, "I was there; the President said—."
HAIG: That's exactly right.

Nixon is concerned here about the March 21 discussion with Dean in which they broached clemency as part of the cover-up with the Watergate burglars. But he thinks he knows how to "handle" the "one problem." Again, though by his own later sworn testimony at various hearings Haig has never heard the March 21 tape nor at this point even seen a transcript, he is nonetheless quick to assure Nixon almost reflexively that he is right, that "we ca—, can" handle it. Haldeman will simply contradict Dean, says Nixon. And seeing the solution, Haig replies unhesitatingly, "That's exactly right." What he fails to say is as interesting as his words. He does not ask what precisely Haldeman will say, nor seem to care for that matter. Haldeman will "handle it," whatever needs to be said. That soothes Nixon for the moment. Clearly neither man is proposing, or even imagining, that the actual tape recording should ever be released to show what was really said between Nixon and Dean on March 21.

Nixon then turns back to the onerous task of listening to the Dean tapes:

PRESIDENT: So, we'll see what else is the god damned—
HAIG: [unintelligible] that's the thing for you to do, for your own, really for your own peace of mind right now.
PRESIDENT: Yeah.
HAIG: You just can't recall. It was in a meeting [unintelligible].

PRESIDENT: (sighs) As you know, we're up against ruthless people.

HAIG: Well, we're going to be in great shape now, 'cause we're going to prepare. We're going to [unintelligible].

To the Foreign Relations Committee at his confirmation hearing, Haig stated that he had "no independent recollection" of these controversial sentences, could not "reconstruct the precise June 4 conversation even with the transcript in front of me," but nonetheless knew "with complete certainty . . . that I never suggested then or on any other occasion that he [Nixon] should dissemble or pretend not to recall something."

Perhaps. But the passage is also unmistakably in the context of framing a defense against Dean's testimony. They are "going to be in great shape," Haig says in his helpful, confident tone, because armed with the secret weapon of the actual tapes they are "going to prepare" to fight what the president has just called these "ruthless people." In that setting, his words just before take on the cast of the "talking points" he wrote so often for Kissinger—"ask Mr. Hoover" . . . "express your appreciation." And here: "You just can't recall. It was in a meeting. . . ." Of course Nixon *can* recall by listening to the tapes. He *knows* it was in a meeting. Is General Haig telling the president of the United States vacantly what they both understand so well? Or is he drafting the dialogue, the cover story, for what Nixon should say *about* the conversation, just as they have talked a moment earlier about what Haldeman will say *about* the conversation? Whatever is actually on the tapes, after all, the president is to listen for his "peace of mind right now," not to reveal what he said to Dean. And the contents of the March 21 tape will not be released by the White House for another eleven months.

The ambiguous "you can't recall" passage became nearly the sole public focus in the June 4 tape, but whatever Haig meant by those words—whether he stage-whispered an obstruction of justice or simply talked idly in the Oval Office—the rest of the transcript left little doubt about Haig's common style and role.

After an "unintelligible" Nixon remark and a vague Haig response about work done at the White House late the night before, apparently on the Watergate defense, the president goes on:

PRESIDENT: You taking the issue here— Now take clemency, that's well handled, isn't it?

HAIG: That's bunk [unintelligible].

PRESIDENT: Yeah. And it's well handled in the March twenty-first thing. I put it in the context I said. "You couldn't even consider clemency until after the '74 election" is the way I put it. But, what the hell, in two years, poor bastards are in jail that long. I said—but I didn't—can't even consider it.

HAIG: Yeah, you see, it probably wouldn't hurt, uh, I mean it's conceivable now when, we get working with Buzhardt as we go down the line here. Oh, it may be that, uh, I can't, uh, mention that in front [unintelligible]. Well, that's you know, that's the judgment I wouldn't make now.

PRESIDENT: I won't. It's very important [unintelligible]. However, not even Buzhardt knows.

HAIG: Well, you know, Buzhardt knows this because you told me in your office.

PRESIDENT: [unintelligible]

HAIG: Uh, but he knew it also because when you were checking on wiretaps on the Johnson years, uh, with the Secret Service, it came out. Uh, those bellyaches who'd been handling it for Johnson, as a matter of fact [unintelligible]. So he knows it, but I tell you, he's the only one that knows it.

PRESIDENT: All right. No further. He shouldn't tell anyone. Uh, I don't want it put out that somebody is, uh been saying uh, they're going to get the, uh, the president's records and it's got—

HAIG: Oh.

PRESIDENT: Let's just assume we goofed. If you get back to Buzhardt you tell him you had national security stuff.

HAIG: That's right. That's right.

Translated, Nixon is once more telling Haig specifically that on the March 21 tape he discussed clemency to silence the Watergate burglars. The president wants assurance that it is "well handled" by what he said to Dean, and Haig once again answers categorically, without knowing the record, that the charge is simply "bunk." Nixon muses again about what he said to Dean, straining to recall that he uttered nothing incriminating. Haig then suggests they may not even want to tell Buzhardt, the president's lawyer and Haig's newly recruited colleague, about the specifics of the conversation. "Not even Buzhardt knows" about the tapes, Nixon says. Yet Haig reminds the president that his lawyer does know, though "he's the only one. . ." "No further," Nixon orders. There can't be people talking about the "records." If they "goofed" and let out the secret, if there are any questions, Haig is to apply the all-purpose stopper that the material involves "national security stuff." And the general once more reassures his commander in chief automatically, "That's right. That's right."

Nixon now goes back to complaining about the "hard work" entailed in listening to the tapes, but supposes "it's best for me to do it." Haig, who at future inquiries would always maintain his "arms-length" relationship with those explosive tapes, replies quickly, "Only you. Only you."

They can "put out that story," says Nixon, returning to Dean at the end of the talk, that "he [Dean] has telephone, uh, that he has mem-cons, chronologies, telephone recordings and all that sort of thing." Nixon is worried about what records his defecting counsel may have. Haig asks, "Why, do you honestly—!" "I wonder if that's— Huh?" Nixon answers in distraction. And Haig concludes, as he began, reassuring the wandering, worried president that Dean is not a threat, that there is no real evidence abroad, that it all can be handled. "He's an unstructured guy," Haig says of Dean. "I've had notes from him and he's just not that type. . . ." (Five months later, after the existence of the taping system had been revealed, Haig would also assure Republican senators in a Capitol Hill briefing that the tape of the critical March 21 meeting between Nixon and Dean was "exculpatory." He would maintain as well that before the congressional briefing he had no knowledge of the March 21 tape beyond what the president had told him in this June 4 conversation.)

While these conversations went on inside the Oval Office, other government observers of the regime's curdling culture saw Nixon all the more "withdrawn" into Watergate, and White House intrigues all the more Byzantine. "Haig puts a cover memo on each Kissinger memo," Admiral Zumwalt recorded attentively in his diary notes at the end of June. At that juncture Kissinger says "he will go unless they make him Secretary of State," and "Haig will stay on until they can make him chairman of the Joint Chiefs of Staff." Kissinger's resignation, Zumwalt chronicled, "is what Haig would like now . . . however, it's necessary for Haig to keep Kissinger in line because of Watergate problems." Inside the tortured White House, as he saw it from the Pentagon and through the ubiquitous inter-agency gossip, "there are five coups a day as various power centers try to take over."

By several accounts like this, access to the reclusive president narrowed still more during the summer of 1973, with the new "inner circle" consisting of Haig, Kissinger, and Ron Ziegler, a former Disneyland ride operator become press secretary, whom one writer perceptively called Nixon's "last link to a lost past" of Haldeman and Ehrlichman. Nor did the new government always run so efficiently on more prosaic matters in its sudden realignment. When Haig that summer blithely passed on from Nixon an all-considered order for an embargo on soybeans and cottonseed, the outcry in Europe and Japan was so furious and the blow to the battered dollar so punishing that the embargo was relaxed eight days after it was announced. Haig's knowledge of economics was "to say the least, limited," observed one columnist, and with the mismanaged embargo "the question of his capacity in such a wide-ranging domestic assignment remains."

Meanwhile, the shock waves of Watergate continued to strike. On Friday, July 13, Alexander Butterfield, now

head of the Federal Aviation Administration, revealed
the presence of the White House tape recorders under
questioning by Senate investigators. Their suspicions,
ironically, had been aroused by the unusually detailed
White House response to John Dean, which gave Nixon's
version of their conversations and which Haig had "coordinated" with such bellicosity. They had not even wanted
to tell Buzhardt about the tapes, but in Haig's zeal to
"take on the son-of-a-bitch," they had tipped their hand
fatally. "You can call Haig . . . just as well," Butterfield had
protested when Senators Sam Ervin and Howard Baker
of the Watergate Committee asked him to testify about
the taping system. But they insisted that Butterfield repeat openly what he had already honestly given to investigators, and he told the story to an astonished world on
July 16, 1973.

Two days later, Haig ordered the White House tape
recorders disconnected, though not before over 100 hours
of conversation between Nixon and Haig had been captured on spools in the period since May 4—hours that
the Foreign Relations Committee tried perfunctorily to
get and failed during the general's confirmation six and a
half years later. On July 23, the White House tapes of
Dean and others (though not Haig) were subpoenaed,
and the long, terminal battle of the Nixon presidency
began.

As the Watergate legal siege tightened in these months,
Gulley, watching it all from the White House military
office, recalled two episodes with the flavor of Haig's
response to the scandal. In the first, Haig summoned him
to discuss a "highly confidential project." Telling Gulley
"it was imperative the press not find out about it," Haig

ordered him to organize a "covert mission" to bring back
to the White House some thirty crates of Kissinger's telephone transcripts that had been stored for "safekeeping"
in a bomb shelter at Nelson Rockefeller's Pocantico Hills
estate. Gulley promptly arranged for "one of our unmarked planes" to fly to Westchester County Airport,
where a military office sergeant discreetly rented a truck
and rescued the crates, flying back in the unmarked plane
to Andrews. From there, Gulley recorded, the transcripts
were loaded into "an unmarked White House truck" and
driven back to be secreted, aptly, in an old bomb shelter
under the White House East Wing. To that presumably
safer cache, Kissinger would occasionally send aides to
pull selected transcripts, redolent of so much, including
Alexander Haig, all for "a little weeding and pruning," as
Gulley described it, "in anticipation of a possible
subpoena."

On another occasion, acording to Gulley, the General
Accounting Office threatened an audit of the long illegally
funded, opulent White House mess where the president's
men dined and drank at linen-covered tables and at prices
far below government cafeterias. Haig initially shrugged
off the prospect of an audit, saying, "We've got nothing
to hide." But when Gulley explained to him the illegal
bookkeeping and that they had "considerable to hide,"
Haig swiftly "changed his tune" and told Gulley to "see
what you can work out with Fred [Buzhardt]." Buzhardt,
however, would only suggest a "dummy audit board" (of
the sort he said he used before in the Pentagon in "that
big PX scandal over in Vietnam") to throw off the GAO.
Eventually, the military office director recalled, he simply
fended off the outside audit "as I did so often at the White

House," by claiming the subject was "classified information."

As the summer of 1973 wore on, Haldeman and Ehrlichman testified unimpressively before the Ervin committee, and tension mounted visibly in the beleaguered White House. On a trip to New Orleans that August, Nixon angrily shoved Ziegler toward waiting reporters he wanted to avoid. Ruckelshaus, now moved from his brief tenure as acting FBI director to be a deputy attorney general, recalled a "lecture" he received from Haig at this point. The chief of staff concentrated only on "the President's non-involvement in Watergate," Ruckelshaus said later, "rather than questions about my own opinions after running the FBI's investigation of Watergate."

For a time, the administration seemed to rally. Ten heads of state trooped to see Nixon in hastily arranged visits. Haig proudly announced eight cabinet meetings, twenty-seven presidential conferences with cabinet officers, and fourteen other "meetings," as if to prove the government still existed. Kissinger in his prestige was named secretary of state. By early autumn, the public appeared almost bored with the Watergate hearings, and it seemed that what Nixon had described to Mitchell as the "stonewall" would hold. But it was to be only a lull in the battle, of the sort Haig felt that night in the perimeter at Ap Gu. The registering round had already come in. On July 27, Elliot Richardson, now shifted to attorney general, had told Haig that Vice President Spiro Agnew was under active investigation for tax evasion, bribery, and extortion.

. . .

With its origins in petty suburban-boom corruption in Baltimore County, the Agnew case, of course, was never part of the generic beast of Watergate. But it obviously added to the political burdens Haig now carried in the crumbling regime, and offered yet another glimpse of how he worked. "Arranging that cop-out," Haig boasted later of Agnew's resignation and "no contest" plea which kept him out of jail, "was one of the greatest feats of bureaucratic skill in the history of the art." The record, however, was not always so edifying.

When Richardson first brought the "open-and-shut" case to Haig, his reaction was to pull back. "We couldn't accept that," Haig later told writer Theodore White, "we told him to go reassess." But after Richardson presented the same evidence to Nixon on August 6, the president sent Haig and aide Bryce Harlow to Agnew the same day to suggest the tainted vice president resign. In this first of what would be several meetings with Agnew, Haig spoke, according to Agnew's own memoirs, of "sustainable allegations," "uncontrollable circumstances," "points of no return," and "foreclosed options," finally asking Agnew outright to resign. He refused, and after "harsh words between an Agnew aide and the Nixon emissaries, Agnew, "seething with rage, frustration and despair," ushered them out of his office. Haig had "in effect brought the traditional suicide pistol into my office and laid it on my desk," Agnew remembered, adding in his not always serious memoirs that with Haig's request for resignation he was now "left with the bitter conclusion that I was definitely not part of the team."

The following day, the Agnew story broke, and for another month the combative vice president and favorite of Republican conservatives fought off his ouster. On September 10, Haig and this time Buzhardt had another "stormy" meeting with Agnew, during which they urged his resignation once more. According to Agnew's lawyer, who was also present, Haig told the vice president that Richardson had a "hard case" and that if Agnew took the issue to Congress for formal impeachment proceedings "you'll be playing high-risk ball." Still, Agnew refused to resign, and Haig and Buzhardt left "empty-handed."

By now Richardson was increasingly impatient to be rid of Agnew, openly worrying with aides about Nixon's "tremendous strain" and the prospect of Agnew's succession to the Oval Office. For his part, Agnew thought that Richardson, emerging as the only untarnished administration figure, "saw himself as my potential rival for the presidency." (It would be another irony that Agnew's ruin as a knight of the Republican right opened the way not to Richardson but rather eventually to Ronald Reagan, and to the other man who in 1973 pushed Agnew out—Alexander Haig.) At any rate, in mid-September, Haig's view was clear. "The SOB is lying," he said to Herb Klein, advising him to lend Agnew no support. "He's got to go for the country's sake," Haig said to Colson about the same time, and pressured him to ask a friendly industrialist and Agnew supporter not to contribute to the defense fund that Agnew was trying to raise.

At yet another meeting with Agnew, on the evening of September 12, Haig seemed at first to retreat. Nixon had ordered the case reviewed, Haig told Agnew. "The President wants to do what's right." But as Haig described the lack of support for Agnew on Capitol Hill and Nixon's Watergate-weakened authority, he became increasingly harsh, until Agnew's lawyer asked the vice president to leave the room: "I'll not have my client lacerated by you any longer," Agnew recorded the attorney telling Haig.

By the end of that meeting, however, Agnew had agreed to discuss a "deal," and events moved rapidly. On September 19, Haig told Agnew that "the President will call for your resignation," and though Agnew believed the policy might have been "dictated by Haig" rather than being Nixon's, he felt a sense of "terror." Agnew's lawyer told the Justice Department they would entertain a no-contest plea, but there must be no admission of bribery. Haig warned Richardson the next day that the prosecution could not be allowed to block Agnew's resignation, and that a jail sentence should be forgone if it were the price of Agnew's swift departure.

Also on the 20th, however, Agnew met Nixon to tell him the charges were false, and suddenly the momentum slowed. A week later, Agnew made a fighting speech to Republican women in Los Angeles, lashing out at the Justice Department. Another typically tough Agnew speech seemed in the offing at a Republican fund-raiser in Chicago on October 4. But "a funny thing happened to the Vice President on the way to Chicago," said one observer. "He finally realized there was no way out." October 4 was indeed to be the climax for Agnew, but in his own memoir the broken vice president told another, darker story.

Before he left for Chicago, wrote Agnew in his book, entitled *Go Quietly . . . or Else*, he "received an indirect threat from the White House that made me fear for my life." According to Agnew, the purveyor of the "threat" was Haig. At 11:45 that morning, Haig had called in

General Mike Dunn, Agnew's military aide, and as Dunn
reported the meeting to Agnew an hour and a half later,
including a written memorandum for the record, the vice
president thought it "a shocking story." In Dunn's memorandum, Haig said "the clock is running," that he knew
of "every phone call made" by Agnew, "conversations
were also not unknown," and that "further support from
Nixon [was] impossible." If Agnew admitted guilt on a
tax charge, "there would be no economic worry for debts
or for defense . . . no further trouble with the federal government and no jail sentence." In any event, Haig went on
by Dunn's account, once an indictment was handed down
"we are off to the races and cannot control the situation
any longer—anything may be in the offing. It can and
will get nasty and dirty." Dunn emphasized Haig's words:
"Don't think that the game cannot be played from here."
As Dunn rose to leave, Haig reportedly told his fellow
general, "The President has a lot of power—don't forget
that."

Agnew wrote later that he took this as an "open-ended
threat" from a Haig "who was the de facto president"
with "the power of the bureaucracy at his command" and
"direct connection with the CIA and the FBI." He had
"attended secret sessions" of the NSC, Agnew wrote. He
"knew something about the functioning of the intelligence community" and "missions that were very unhealthy
for people who were considered enemies." "I feared for
my life," he went on. "If a decision had been made to
eliminate me—through an automobile accident, a fake
suicide or whatever, the order would not have been
traced back to the White House any more than get-Castro
orders were ever traced to their source." Haig "already

knew enough about . . . the truth of Nixon's involvement
in the Watergate cover-up," thought Agnew, "and Haig
did not want me in the line of succession."

Asked by the *Washington Post* in 1980 about a veiled
threat of assassination, Dunn said he personally interpreted Haig's remarks only as a warning of a jail sentence
if Agnew did not cooperate, that a plot against Agnew was
farfetched, and that the vice president was "distraught
at the time." Yet Dunn also confirmed his memorandum
quoted in Agnew's book. (Recuperating at the time from
his 1980 heart surgery, Haig, said a spokesman, "laughed"
when told of Agnew's charge, saying "it was the most pre-
posterous thing he had ever heard of, and [he] would not
dignify it by discussing it any further.") Lost in the furor
over assassination would be Dunn's record of Haig otherwise offering Agnew a virtual bribe ("no economic
worry") and a plea bargain ("no further trouble") as
political coercion entirely apart from legal authority or
process.

On what happened next, however, there would be no
disagreement. Less than a week after Haig warned Dunn,
Agnew resigned the vice-presidency and appeared before
a Baltimore judge to plead no contest in return for a fine
of $110,000 and a sentence of three years' probation. His
"cop-out," as Haig called it, cleared the way for Gerald
Ford, a politician with greater appreciation of Alexander
Haig's talents.

Days after the Agnew resignation, Haig was to be embroiled in another, far more serious crisis. The office of
Watergate Special Prosecutor and its first incumbent, a

patrician Harvard law professor named Archibald Cox,
had appeared on the scene, along with Haig, in the spring
of 1973. From the outset there was a festering difference
of perception about the prosecutor's role. To Nixon, he
was to be a "supervising" official of vague and unthreatening function. To Richardson, who had pledged the prosecutor's independence as a condition of his Senate
confirmation as attorney general that May, Cox was to
have "full authority" to investigate Watergate. He could
be removed, Richardson had promised the Senate Judiciary in a May 21 written statement approved by Nixon
and Haig, only for "extraordinary improprieties on his
part." A dour New Englander as well as a distinguished
jurist, Cox took his charter seriously and plunged into the
Watergate legal investigation, which until then, in the
hands of hesitant U.S. attorneys, had been uneven and
often desultory at best.

Almost immediately the prosecutor clashed with the
general commanding the defense in the White House. On
June 19, less than a month after Cox's appointment, Haig
telephoned Richardson to complain about news-conference
remarks by Cox regarding a possible subpoena of the president. The "whole thing is blatantly partisan," Richardson remembered Haig saying then. From the president's
home in San Clemente, Haig angrily called Richardson
again on July 2, now to say that Nixon was "furious" about
a *Los Angeles Times* story that Cox was looking into the
president's real-estate transactions. That most sensitive
and least investigated of Watergate trails pointed back
toward tax evasion and Nixon's personal involvement, if
not Haig's own intercession for Rebozo. They might
"move on this to discharge Cox and . . . it could not be a

matter of Cox's charter to investigate the President," Haig told the attorney general, according to a later affadavit by Richardson. Though Cox was conducting no such inquiry into Nixon's houses and drafted a denial forthwith at Richardson's request, Haig and Nixon remained in high dudgeon. When Richardson called back with Cox's proposed denial, Haig replied testily that the statement was "inadequate," whereupon Nixon came on the line himself heatedly demanding stronger wording.

Soon again, on July 23, an agitated Haig telephoned the attorney general to protest a Cox questionnaire about wiretapping which had been sent to several government agencies. That subject obviously touched one more raw nerve for both the president and his chief of staff. Haig told Richardson on that occasion that "the boss was very uptight about Cox" and wanted "a tight line drawn with no further mistakes" by the prosecutor. "If Cox does not agree, we will get rid of Cox," Haig warned him imperiously. "If we have to have a confrontation, we will have it." The general, Richardson wrote in his memoirs, "constantly complained."

By mid-September, with Cox about to bring indictments in yet another area troubling to Haig as well as Nixon, the burglary of the office of Ellsberg's psychiatrist, Buzhardt suddenly protested that the resulting exposure of the plumbers would endanger "national security." At issue, Cox was told somberly, were other plumbers' operations involving a nuclear-targeting plan that Ellsberg was supposed to possess, a Soviet double agent who informed the CIA that the *Pentagon Papers* had been given to the Russian Embassy, a CIA agent high in the Indian government compromised by a leak the plumbers were plugging, and disclosure in a heretofore unpublished volume of the *Pentagon Papers* that the U.S. had been eavesdropping on the radio-telephone conversations of Kremlin leaders while in their limousines. It was heady stuff, and Cox—his own government experience limited to domestic affairs—postponed the indictments.

Whatever Buzhardt's sophistication in such subjects, of course, Haig of all people knew clearly from his NSC years the fraud of these obstructions: that the attack plan was by now obsolete and meaningless even if Ellsberg had it; the Soviet double agent an old invention; the CIA's man in New Delhi blown in 1971; and "Guppie," the intercepts of gossip, smut, and non-Marxist sex among Moscow's oligarchs, no longer a secret from the Russians and never much of an intelligence asset anyway. By autumn, however, the special prosecutor was anathema to the point where realities apparently did not matter. To the delight of other presidential aides, Haig was now referring to the prosecutor's staff as "the Cox-suckers."

Against this backdrop, October 1973 came as a month of turmoil and momentous events. During the second week alone, Agnew resigned; Ford was named vice president; the court of appeals ordered surrender of presidential tapes subpoenaed by Cox as well as the Ervin committee; and war raged in the Middle East, with Israel on the defensive, the Soviets posturing ominously, and U.S. military resupply to the Israelis ensnared in Kissinger's diplomatic and bureaucratic machinations. On the weekend of October 13–14, Nixon and Haig had wearily gone to Camp David to ponder the next step in Watergate, and from there Haig summoned Richardson to a White House meeting Monday morning October 15, hinting to the former undersecretary of state that the topic was the Middle East crisis.

When Richardson came to that session, Haig flattered him by showing a few cables on the war, but soon went to the real point. The president would not appeal the appeals court ruling on the tapes, he told the attorney general. Instead, Nixon would simply fire Cox, leaving no one to subpoena the tapes and thus "mooting the case." Richardson was now angry himself. He reminded Haig of the pledges to the Senate and said he would resign if he were ordered to fire Cox. At this, Haig apparently drew back and told Richardson he would call him on the subject that afternoon.

"I was, incidentally, against that approach," Haig later said of Cox's firing in an interview with the *Washington Post*. But looking back on the events later, Richardson had a different view. "From the beginning of the week," he wrote about the October 15 meeting with Haig, "the name of the game had been: get rid of Cox . . . the facts . . . are not susceptible to any other interpretation."

Minutes after noon that same day, Haig did call Richardson to say Cox would not be fired, and that the alternative was "his own" plan to have Senator John Stennis listen to the contested tapes and prepare a verified version for Cox and the court. Grasping at the compromise, Richardson said the idea should be "considered." Haig replied that he would "sell it" to the president. An hour later, Haig called back to say it had been "very bloody" but he had persuaded Nixon to accept the "Stennis plan," though the president had angrily insisted that "this is *it*" for Cox; that there would be no further access to presidential tapes or documents; and that if the special prosecutor did not agree to the compromise, he would be fired. Richardson then told Haig in a subsequent call that he would support the plan but still would not fire Cox.

That afternoon, Haig and Buzhardt visited the slightly deaf and ailing Stennis on Capitol Hill, securing the senator's agreement to the plan but leaving the impression, as Stennis recounted later, that the verified transcripts he was to prepare were for the Senate Watergate Committee rather than to satisfy a court subpoena. "There was never any mention of the court," Stennis said afterward. "I wouldn't have done it if there was. No, no, no. I was once a judge and the courts can ask for what they want." Nor did Haig inform Stennis, as Haig later admitted in testimony, that both he and Nixon already knew at this point that two of the subpoenaed tapes were missing altogether, and that Rose Mary Woods had obliterated an eighteen-and-a-half-minute portion of another tape. Armed with Stennis's half-knowing consent, however, he and Buzhardt returned to the White House for a 4:00 P.M. meeting with Richardson, who agreed again to recommend the Stennis plan to Cox. In apt symbolism of what was happening that week, Richardson and Haig smilingly attended a White House farewell dinner that Monday night for William Rogers, now formally supplanted at the State Department by Kissinger, and for the past four and a half years the butt of so many cruel jokes and deceptive maneuvers.

Over the next three days, Cox balked predictably at the Stennis plan, and especially at its restrictions on his further access to tapes. Haig called Richardson back to his office on Thursday evening, October 18. There was to be one more approach to Cox, said Haig, and failing that he would be fired. Richardson again prepared to resign.

But the next morning Haig, in characteristic seesaw tactics, seemed once more to pull back. Cox would not be fired after all, he told the attorney general. Stennis would give the transcripts to the court, and the court, not Cox, would be told there were no more tapes to be given up.

At this stage, on Friday the 19th, the already tangled story becomes still more entwined. Forestalling his resignation, and the clash with Cox, Richardson apparently believed—or at least wanted to believe—that a plausible compromise was still in the works, and that, from what Haig told him that Friday, Cox would not be specifically barred from requesting more tapes. For his part, Haig proceeded to sell the new, modified version to Stennis, Senators Ervin and Baker, and other White House aides, at once giving them the impression that Richardson was "on board" and pointedly avoiding the question of Cox's attitude.

In any event, at 7:00 P.M. on Friday night, October 19, the maneuvers were suddenly laid bare. It was then that Haig called Richardson telling him of a letter already sent to him from Nixon instructing the attorney general to order Cox to "make no further attempts" to obtain Watergate evidence from the White House. "Al, given the history of our relationship on this," replied an "angry and upset" Richardson, "I would have thought that you would have consulted me prior to sending any letter." Haig's exact reply went unrecorded. As Richardson should have recognized, there was in fact a larger "history" behind them, in which Richardson's State Department had been so often bullied, enticed, indulged, misled, then abruptly preempted in much the same manner. It was a method on which Richardson and Cox could have consulted General

Thieu in Saigon, William Rogers, Melvin Laird, or, for that matter, certain cadets from West Point.

There followed another call from Haig to Richardson at 10:00 that night, the general saying he was "sorry" Richardson felt badly treated. But the next day, Saturday, October 20, events took over. At 1:00 P.M., Cox held a defiant press conference. At 2:20, Haig ordered Richardson to fire Cox, and an hour later Richardson, at his own request, was ushered into the Oval Office with Haig to hand Nixon his resignation. "Brezhnev would never understand it if I let Cox defy my instructions," Nixon said to the attorney general as he entered the room.

Having resigned, Richardson returned to his Justice Department office only moments before Haig called Deputy Attorney General Ruckelshaus with an order to fire Cox. When Ruckelshaus refused as well, Haig snapped, as his listener remembered it, "Well, you know what it means when an order comes down from the commander in chief, and a member of the team can't execute it."

Haig told the *Washington Post* a month later that his remark was quoted "out of context." "I've been around this town. I'm not a virgin. I never used that kind of language," he said. But to some, the Ruckelshaus account was only a familiar echo of a similar moment three and a half years earlier, when Haig had confronted his dissenting NSC colleague William Watts in the West Basement. Haig then found the third man at Justice, Robert Bork, to execute the order to fire Cox, and the Saturday Night Massacre was done.

There remained one last sordid act that evening, and the general by his own admission was its author. At 8:25 P.M., a trembling Ziegler had announced the resignation of Richardson and the firing of Ruckelshaus as well as Cox, Haig having angrily refused the deputy attorney general the acknowledgment of a resignation after their brief discussion of the commander in chief. Scarcely a half-hour later, teams of FBI agents descended on the offices of Cox, Richardson, and Ruckelshaus to seal off the premises, barring employees who had gathered in the crisis from removing even personal items. Taking a framed copy of the Declaration of Independence from his office wall, Cox's press secretary told an FBI agent who stopped him, "Just stamp it 'void' and let me take it home." Cox himself issued a brief statement: "Whether we shall continue to be a government of laws and not of men is now for Congress and ultimately the American people." Haig had called the FBI to occupy the offices even before Ziegler made his statement.

On October 23, he faced a crowded press conference in the familiar confines of the West Basement. To a background of horns sounding outside on Pennsylvania Avenue in response to pickets' signs saying "Honk for Impeachment," Haig took a question about the FBI seizures. He stepped forward and thrust his face "out at them," and "for a second the urbane bureaucrat's mask gave way to the professional soldier's tight, combative smile," reported the *Washington Post*. "Guilty," Haig shot back, "almost joyously," thought one eyewitness. "We had reports that members of the staff were leaving rapidly with huge bundles under their arms," he said of the special prosecutor. It was "the responsible thing to do," he went on, "to ensure that the evidentiary material be retained. . . ." But there was no explanation for also sealing off the suites of the attorney general and his deputy, men who held no Watergate investigation files and whose main offense had been to defy Richard Nixon.

Cox's own staff thought the pretext of employees leaving with "huge bundles" that evening "demonstrably bogus," if only because, as two deputy special prosecutors later wrote, "copies of all potentially explosive documents had *already* been removed for safekeeping several days before." With a "strong enough sense of impending danger," Cox and his aides that week spirited away files to back closets, safety-deposit boxes, and grandmothers' basements. "The person with the greatest motive for doing away with the files," concluded one Cox assistant, "was the man in whose name the agents had been ordered to seize them."

Afterward, as an unprecedented barrage of public protest crashed over the White House, as Republicans deserted and Congress prepared several impeachment resolutions, Haig seemed to some outwardly subdued, almost fatalistic. They had "goofed" on the popular reaction, he said to a White House aide, and he was the first to use the memorable term "fire storm" to describe the political result of the episode. "Very few men who have occupied that chair"—he pointed toward his desk in one interview at the time—"have been able to escape political taint and smear."

His old patron Califano now thought Haig was "being eaten up . . . put through a moral shredder." A month after the massacre, he began to put Nixon at a distance. When Laurence Stern of the *Washington Post* asked him what might be the outcome of Watergate, Haig answered pointedly, "To restore a sense of confidence in the *office* of the presidency," and Stern observed that at that moment Haig's voice "lingers on that word" *office* "and the eyes seem to ask if you got it." "I'm not interested in politics," Haig told Stern, "but I might well be interested in continued public service."

Yet there was also the common belligerence and even malice. Talking to Republican senators after the Cox episode, he spoke derisively (as Agnew would later allege himself) of Richardson as acting in a political ploy aimed at winning the Massachusetts governorship or even higher office. In the same meeting and others, he said too that Richardson had been drinking heavily during the crisis, an echo of earlier West Basement stories in which Richardson was alleged to have a history of drunk driving. When Republican senators Edward Brooke and Charles Mathias later pressured Haig to take back the slander, the general wrote an apology to Richardson, but still privately disowned responsibility for the remarks. "He told me to," Haig said to one senator, motioning toward the Oval Office.

In the hours after Cox's firing, he had also "regaled" Bork, as aides later revealed, with the alleged "bias" of Cox's staff, and urged that all the key attorneys in the special prosecutor's office be fired as well—a step even Bork, who agreed with Nixon's authority to fire Cox, refused as "an outright obstruction of justice, an attempt to emasculate the entire investigation." Watching the FBI seizures, the order to Ruckelshaus, the attacks on Richardson, and the pressure on Bork, attorneys in the Watergate investigation joked blackly that autumn about the mentality in the White House. "We would know we were in real trouble," one of them remarked, "when General Haig began to wear his uniform to work."

It was the mark of that October that the joke about Haig was even less frivolous than the Cox investigators guessed. Only days after the firing of the special prosecutor, the general had a genuine opportunity to command —if not in uniform then under a questionable cloak of the ultimate presidential authority over war and peace—in one of the more ominous incidents in recent international relations.

Hardly seventy-two hours after the "massacre," and with a Middle East cease-fire already in effect, Israeli forces encircled Egypt's 20,000-man III Corps in the western Sinai, at once threatening annihilation of the cream of the Arab army and humiliation of its Soviet sponsor. On the afternoon of October 24, President Anwar Sadat and Brezhnev appealed for joint U.S.-Soviet supervision of the cease-fire, but Kissinger hesitated, shrewdly not wishing the Russians back in the region in such force, and calculating, too, that some hostage stalemate would be an asset in his own contemplated postwar diplomacy. But later that day (accounts vary the time from 7:30 P.M. to 10:40 P.M.) Brezhnev sent Nixon another, sharper message warning that without U.S. cooperation in the cease-fire, the Russians would "consider the question of taking appropriate steps unilaterally."

The meaning of that Soviet note has never been plain. Its tone of "consider" was never the ultimatum U.S. officials claimed later, nor were Russian actions so menacing. Soviet airborne units were reportedly placed on alert, but, as late as the evening of the 24th, secret Pentagon intelligence recorded "no Soviet flights" toward the Middle East. At any rate, what followed on the American side was historic. By official accounts at the time, an "alarmed" Kissinger called Nixon in the White House living quarters and recommended a firm response to Brezhnev's message. Nixon agreed but "left the details" to Kissinger.

At approximately 11:00 P.M., Haig, Kissinger, Defense Secretary James Schlesinger, Admiral Moorer as chairman of the Joint Chiefs, and Scowcroft, Kissinger's deputy, met in the West Basement situation room for what was to be described as an "abbreviated" NSC meeting, though only two of the council's statutory members were present and the president remained upstairs in the White House. At 12:25 A.M., according to Pentagon records, the orders went out for "Defense Condition 3," a worldwide alert of U.S. forces that sent U.S. vessels with amphibious troops steaming into the Mediterranean, placed the Eighty-second Airborne on wartime alert, put the commander of the Strategic Air Command in his underground command center, recalled B-52s from the Far East, alerted all U.S. forces in Europe, launched tanker planes to refuel strategic bombers, and brought to full readiness the North American Air Defense Command and all missile silos. Moorer warned that in a confrontation with the Soviet fleet "we would lose our ass in the eastern Med," Zumwalt noted in a later debriefing at the Pentagon, but the alert went forward.

At 3:00 A.M., Kissinger reportedly saw Nixon in the presidential bedroom and received his "ratification" of all the moves. (The group in the situation room "unanimously recommended" the alert, Nixon wrote about the foreign-policy crisis with unusual reticence in his memoirs, and "we flashed the word. . . .") Over the next few hours, U.S. forces moved to the uncertain edges of war. The

Sixth Fleet and Soviet Mediterranean squadron were "sitting on a pond in close proximity," said a sensitive Pentagon situation report for October 25, "and the stage for the hitherto unlikely 'war at sea' scenario was set." Watching from the Joint Chiefs "tank" in the Pentagon, Zumwalt doubted "that major units of the U.S. Navy were ever in a tenser situation since World War II ended. . . ."

Whether by intimidation or original intention, the Soviets promptly accepted a UN peacekeeping force and the crisis seemed to melt away as swiftly as it had loomed. There was widespread suspicion that the alert had been used by Nixon to deter not the Russians but the gathering domestic forces of impeachment, and both Kissinger and the president indignantly defended their actions in what Nixon called "the most difficult crisis we've had since the Cuban confrontation of 1962." Kissinger promised to release the "record," but it was never forthcoming, and was left, like the telephone transcripts Haig retrieved secretly from Rockefeller's estate, to the selective recollection of his memoirs.

Yet the most serious question left by the episode was not whether Nixon had in time-honored fashion exploited a foreign crisis for domestic salvation, or even whether the alert was more or less justified, but whether the president of the United States had commanded at all as the nation was plunged into a nuclear-armed confrontation with the Soviet Union. Eagleburger and other Kissinger aides later told a frightening story of Nixon upstairs drunk at the White House, slurring his words and barely roused when Haig and Kissinger tried to deal with him in the first moment of the crisis. As on so many other sodden nights, albeit of lesser moment, the general and his former boss decided, by that account, to call the Pentagon officials anyway and order the alert that Haig, then Kissinger, thought necessary.

If this was indeed another Cuban crisis, there were no meetings with the president at the head of the table. Schlesinger, Moorer, Scowcroft, and later CIA Director William Colby were never to see Nixon that night, never to know that he was unfit for decision. "I report no words or actions of the President," chronicled Zumwalt in the crisis, "because no such words or actions ever were reported to me." He had "wondered at the time whether Kissinger and Haig . . . had acted without him [Nixon]," the admiral wrote in his memoirs, and asked Deputy Defense Secretary William Clements. "I wondered the same thing and so I asked Jim [Schlesinger] if the President was in on this," Clements replied about the alert. "Jim said he was not."

It had been a expropriation of constitutional authority specifically reserved only for the elected commander in chief, or, in case of his incapacity, the elected officials in legal succession. In this instance, with Gerald Ford not yet confirmed as vice president, that meant the Speaker of the House and then the president *pro tempore* of the Senate before the secretary of state. It was also a foreshadow of another moment more than seven years later when Ronald Reagan lay wounded in a Washington hospital and Secretary Haig, with the habits of another regime, pronounced himself "in charge."

Deploring the lack of "stable domestic leadership" but believing the alert justified, the handful of officials like Zumwalt who knew the disturbing silhouette of the story served on for the moment in silence. To reveal the truth was not only to challenge an unpredictable president or point out to the Russians the depth of Washington's disarray, but also to engage Haig's immense power, visible during the alert. Returning to his State Department office in the predawn hours, Kissinger gave Eagleburger an account of the drunken Nixon and of Haig pressing to act militarily. He had no choice and the alert was "right," Kissinger repeated several times to Eagleburger. But the aide and onetime Haig rival later told friends that it had been an "appalling" night in the White House. . . .

With the Saturday Night Massacre and the October Alert, the Nixon presidency seems to settle even deeper into its own twilight world, in some ways reminiscent of the end of a doomed dynasty. What in retrospect now appears inevitable is still vague and by no means certain at the time. But the long imagined enemies have become real. Like the Romanovs or Hapsburgs, there is only a slowly dawning awareness of the ruler's predicament. Concessions are made reluctantly and generally too late. Supporters are rallied yet soon lost. Despite its efforts at composure, the regime continues to shudder at the spasms of its inner decay. At once the sovereign commands potentially awesome power, as in the alert, yet grows politically feeble and fearful. Constitutionally he remains in office, while losing the capacity, and the popular trust, to govern. The combination of power and impotence is volatile. Bravado, intrigue, and defiance alternate in policy with vacillation and compromise and an odd fecklessness.

Now the ruler's most ardent defender, now looking to his own fortunes, Haig becomes more and more the regent in these closing months. To most witnesses, he is either heroic or nefarious, but there is no doubt that he has become the dominant figure at court, acting for, through, in the name of, and in spite of, a numbed president. His record as chief of staff from the autumn of 1973 through the historic summer of 1974 charts the fitful, inexorable decline toward impeachment and resignation.

Having abolished the office of special prosecutor ostensibly for insisting on access to the tapes, Nixon within a week had reversed himself, handing over the tapes to the court and promising to name Cox's replacement, who would have "independence" and "total cooperation from the executive branch." Haig, who made the decision with Nixon, Garment, and Buzhardt on October 23, later called it "very painful and anguishing." It apparently came less in repentance, however, than out of political necessity. As impeachment bills poured into the House Judiciary Committee, Republican congressional leaders simply served notice on the White House that their continued defense of Nixon depended on his compliance in handing over the subpoenaed tapes and the advent of a credible new prosecutor. To succeed Cox, Haig urged and Nixon approved John Connally's old friend and recommendation for the position, a millionaire corporate lawyer and conservative Democrat from Houston named Leon Jaworski.

Haig telephoned Jaworski at the end of October in what would be the beginning of an interesting, ambivalent relationship between the president's closest aide and his legal predator. In Jaworski, an attorney for Sun Belt special interests and of no visible passion beyond his considerable fees, the White House clearly thought it was getting the fey, malleable prosecutor it had wanted from the outset. In their first call, Haig was insistent, talking

darkly about the "revolutionary" condition of the country
and telling the hesitant Jaworski "I'm going to put the
patriotic monkey on your back." Sending a White House
plane to bring the lawyer to Washington, Haig assured him
the next day that he was the "unanimous" choice for the
job, could sue the president for "any materials," and could
not be fired without "substantial concurrence" from a bipartisan array of congressional leaders. "It's no secret that
you're high on the list for appointment to the Supreme
Court," Haig mentioned as well.

It was transparent flattery, and under the circumstances
a crudely improper dangling of a future presidential appointment, "bait" at which the cynical and uninterested
Jaworski "suppressed a smile." Later the lawyer remembered it as "just part of Al's maneuver," and "just words
wasted," albeit "a little embarrassing to Al" in light of
Ehrlichman's similar offer of the FBI directorship to the
judge in the Ellsberg trial.

"Unlike Cox, Jaworski's a realist," Haig told Colson in
a "buoyant" voice after the prosecutor's appointment.
"He's got a great respect for the office of the president.
We have a good understanding; it will be a good working
relationship." Over the remaining months, in contrast to
his "constant" complaints to Richardson about Cox, Haig
carefully cultivated the new prosecutor, and would be
quick to argue his own innocence, apart from Nixon's, as
the latter became insupportable. More the "realist" perhaps than Haig intended, Jaworski on his side took up
Cox's staff and investigation virtually where the Harvard
nemesis left off, and saw himself and Haig as "adversaries"
with the general "trying to placate me while helping
Nixon frustrate me in my efforts to move forward in the

search for truth." At the same time, Jaworski plainly found Haig compatible, "recognized" his "loyalty" and "goal," and separated him from the president, a distinction another prosecutor might not have made and a crucial element in Haig's political survival of the scandal.

Haig would soon need the special prosecutor's dispensation in the controversies that continued that autumn. For a matter of days after the alert, the administration seemed to rally with the surrender of the tapes, the Jaworski appointment, and an intense political lobbying campaign christened by the press "Operation Candor." On October 31, Haig went to Capitol Hill personally to assure Republican leaders that the March 21, 1973, tape was "exculpatory" and that it showed the president learning of the Watergate cover-up for the first time on that date. Over six days in early November, he arranged for Nixon to meet nearly all the 236 congressional Republicans and 46 sympathetic Democrats in a series of breakfasts and cocktail parties that amounted to wooing the prospective jurors in an impeachment indictment and trial.

But awaiting this counteroffensive was yet another disaster with the tapes. At the end of September, Haig had arranged, too, for Rose Mary Woods to go to Camp David to begin transcribing the tapes subpoenaed by Cox, and there on October 1 (either at midday or late afternoon, by Haig's conflicting testimony on the subject), Miss Woods reported the famous eighteen-and-a-half-minute gap in a Nixon-Haldeman meeting of June 20, 1972. A static buzz obliterated precisely and solely that portion of the conversation which, according to Haldeman's notes later subpoenaed, dealt with the Watergate break-in days earlier.

Haig testified that the White House first believed the erased portion of the tape was outside the subpoena. But even when he finally learned from Buzhardt on November 14 that the eighteen and a half minutes were in fact included in the court order, Haig waited another twenty-four hours—an interval in which Nixon met with another seventy-eight congressmen and others to proclaim his innocence—to inform the president. Even after telling Nixon the bad news on November 15, Haig's talking points for a 4:00 P.M. meeting that day with Senate supporters advised the president to assure his guests that there would be "no more bombshells." And to questions about future embarrassment or worse, Nixon, whom Haig had told only hours before about the eighteen-and-a-half-minute erasure in a subpoenaed tape, duly answered there would be none: "No, absolutely not." Haig urged that they wait still another week to find the cause of the buzz before informing Watergate Judge Sirica. Only when Buzhardt told the general on November 20 that he found "no innocent explanation" for the gap, and that they could conceal the information no longer, was the confession made to a shocked courtroom the next day. In the new cascade of public outrage, "Operation Candor" was itself wiped out.

Called to Sirica's court to testify about the tape gap on December 5, Haig was characteristically truculent yet stricken. Jaworski's young deputy prosecutor, inherited from Cox, thought him "the toughest customer we had to deal with" and his answers "crisp." But Haig also "repeatedly blushed" under cross-examination, noted the Post, and at one point shot back almost plaintively, "It's easy for you to peck at me, but I'm not an expert."

The topic on which he might have testified most expertly—that he knew about the eighteen-and-a-half-minute gap and about two other subpoenaed tapes that could not be found *before* his "own" Stennis plan in late October, and whether the scheme to use Stennis was a deliberate cover-up of those discrepancies—was never explored. The judge "not inclined to have that can of worms opened," as the deputy prosecutor put it, Sirica sustained a White House objection to further questions about any relationship between missing tapes and the Stennis "compromise."

Before he was excused, however, Haig made, almost offhandedly, perhaps his most famous statement on Watergate. Asked to explain Miss Woods's first assumption that the gap was only five minutes (the time she had been on the telephone during the transcription and during which she supposedly erased the tape by accident) and the actual length of the gap, Haig described what he called a White House "devil theory." "Perhaps there had been one tone applied by Miss Woods in accordance with her description," he said, "and then perhaps some sinister force had come in and applied the other energy source and taken care of the information on that tape." Sirica then asked intently "who that sinister force might be," and Haig "helpfully" offered, as the prosecutor recalled it, that only Woods and White House aide Stephan Bull had access to the tapes. ("Sinister force," Sirica himself later reflected, was a term that "probably fitted the President of the United States as well as anyone.") Outside the courthouse, Haig told reporters in the same flippant tone that Miss Woods had probably underestimated the length of her telephone call. "I've known women," said the general, "that think they've talked for five minutes and have talked for an hour."

This White House effort to blame Nixon's old secretary, Sirica noticed, moved her personal lawyer to "curse under his breath" at Nixon's men in court, and to tell friends privately that "he could blow the roof off the White House with what he knew about the tapes mess." A month later, audio experts testified that the eighteen-and-a-half-minute gap was apparently caused by at least five and possibly as many as nine separate erasures on the kind of machine Woods operated on October 1.

But the mystery of the missing conversation—what Theodore White called "the last clue in the detective story 'who-dunnit' of Watergate"—remained unsolved. And in the headlines and the hunt for Nixon's hand in the erasures, Haig's own role with the tapes was itself obliterated. In addition to the president, Woods, and Bull, both Buzhardt and Haig's White House deputy, retired Major General John C. Bennett, had access to the tapes; Bennett had "immediate charge" of their security and Haig himself controlled the key to the vault where the recordings were held. Obscured, too, was the revelation in testimony that Haig had given Woods still more original tapes to transcribe even *after* Buzhardt told the general there was "no innocent explanation" for the gap.

Beyond Rose Mary Woods's apparent carelessness, much of the tape fiasco was blamed on Buzhardt, who had vacantly mistaken the gravity and legal import of the June 20 recording to begin with. But then, Buzhardt was also the crony attorney whom Alexander Haig had brought to the White House, and, to make matters worse, the counsel whom Haig and Nixon (in their recorded conversation on June 4) had decided, at first, to try to exclude anyway from the details and policy decisions on the tape issue. As autumn turned to winter in 1973, the Watergate siege had torn gaping holes in the White House defenses, but the commander whose generalship had allowed some of the major inroads somehow was not, would not be, held responsible.

Early in November, weeks before the new furor over the tapes, Buzhardt and Garment had flown to Nixon's retreat at Key Biscayne, Florida, to urge him to resign. There were not only the missing tapes or unrecorded conversations but even a Dictabelt that Nixon had claimed to have of a conversation with Dean, and which had disappeared under subpoena. "Why can't we make a new Dictabelt?" Nixon had replied when Buzhardt asked about the evidence, and the lawyers were now convinced the president should go. Outlining the history of concealed evidence and evasion to Haig, Buzhardt and Garment argued that "the cover-up was continuing and the President was dragging them all into it." But by several accounts of that episode, Haig "balked" at their approach and refused to let them see Nixon. Gerald Ford, still to be confirmed as the new vice president, was "not good enough to be President of the United States," Haig told them barely nine months before Ford became chief executive, and the effects of resignation on foreign policy would be "disastrous."

"We'll be happy to present the recommendation to resign to the President ourselves," Garment persisted. But the chief of staff, according to a typical description of the meeting, "would have none of that." Only on the next day did Haig see Nixon, carrying what the president himself called a "diluted report," which Nixon read "between the lines" to mean the "overworked" lawyers "had had it." He did not want his own position to be "misunderstood," Haig told the president. He was passing along "their judgment," referring to the lawyers. Faced with such "defections by our supporters," Nixon recorded in his memoirs, he and Haig agreed that the response to the attorneys' advice would be "that we look for another lawyer." Haig then went back to Buzhardt and Garment and told them simply, "The President doesn't want to see you." The two aides returned to Washington, their abortive mission leaving Haig stronger than ever, and Nixon all the more isolated from legal counsel.

With that extraordinary encounter in Key Biscayne and the public furor over the eighteen-and-a-half-minute gap later in November, White House Watergate tactics at the end of 1973 turned back abruptly from political lobbying to what one observer called a "tight-fisted, close-to-the-chest stance." Meeting with Republican congressmen during one of his fall parties, Nixon had promised to make public summaries of some of the disputed tape recordings, but by mid-December, with Haig arguing against further disclosures, Nixon canceled the planned release. At the same point, on the recommendation of Colson, the president hired James St. Clair, a prominent Boston trial lawyer who had been special counsel to the army in the Army–McCarthy hearings and whose reputation for effective "hired gun" litigation promised a protracted and hardened legal defense.

Zumwalt recorded the tenor of the new year-end pugnacity from a meeting of the president and the Joint

Chiefs on December 22. "The President is paranoid. Kissinger's paranoid. Haig is paranoid," Defense Secretary Schlesinger had warned the admiral beforehand, urging him "vehemently" not to give an unwanted briefing that might "drive them up the wall." At the breakfast meeting, Zumwalt said little, but heard Nixon deliver "a long, rambling monologue" on the virtues of presidential policies, the efforts of the "eastern liberal establishment . . . out to do us all in," and the "attacks on him . . . as part of a vast plot by intellectual snobs to destroy a president who was representative of the man in the street." Zumwalt thought it clear the president saw himself in Watergate "in mortal battle with the forces of evil."

Later that same day, Haig secretly visited Senate Minority Leader Hugh Scott at the Pennsylvania Republican's home in an effort to quell further congressional clamor for presidential tapes. In the inner White House deliberations over the release of further transcripts, Haig had finally read the notorious March 21 conversation between Nixon and Dean. "We're being blackmailed," Dean had told the president, and White House aides were perjuring themselves. "How much money do you need?" Nixon asked, and Dean replied that it might cost a million dollars. "We could get that," Nixon had said. ". . . I mean you could get the money . . . you could get a million dollars. And you could get it in cash." Later in the talk, as the White House lawyers had warned Haig well before he read the transcript, the president of the United States had endorsed payments of the burglars' demand for the "blackmail."

Now Scott was calling for disclosure of the tapes, and on December 22 Haig took him what proved to be a "selective, heavily edited" transcript of the March 21 recording. "This is the story," Scott remembered the general saying as he swore the senator to secrecy and assured him the transcript would prove Nixon's innocence of any cover-up. Before Scott had finished reading, however, Haig said suddenly that he must go to Camp David and take the transcripts with him. His reading unfinished, the evidence still vague, Scott reluctantly handed back the documents and Haig left.

The curt, foreshortened rendezvous with Scott was part of the prelude to an even stranger holiday season for the Nixon camp. The day after Christmas, Nixon and a small entourage stole away unannounced by commercial flight for California. There, the president alternated between long periods of seclusion, midnight bouts of insomnia and piano playing, and restless roving freeway drives with Bebe Rebozo, while Haig dealt with cabinet officers and other callers. Nixon was now walled off from all save the vestige Ziegler, Kissinger, who typically insisted on access at all costs, and the general.

Yet perhaps the most interesting twist in the December sequel had come earlier. Days after he had argued against the release of the tapes, and twenty-four hours before his impatient meeting with Senator Scott with the doctored transcript and the assurances of Nixon's vindication, Haig had called Jaworski to the White House Map Room for what the special prosecutor remembered as a talk "about the tapes." Jaworski said he had been listening to the subpoenaed recordings, the March 21 tape in particular, and Haig replied, in Jaworski's later account, that indeed "it was terrible beyond description." There was "no criminal offense involved," Haig went on. The White House lawyers had assured him. But Jaworski, shaking his head, answered, "I can't agree . . . I'm afraid the President engaged in criminal conduct." Get a good criminal lawyer and follow his advice, Jaworski told Haig. But the general "indicated he was satisfied," the prosecutor recalled, and Jaworski said only, "It's your problem, Al, and I hope you're right."

It is possible, in the charged circumstances of the moment, that Haig's remark to Jaworski about the Nixon-Dean talk being "terrible beyond description" might have been deliberate ingratiation to draw out the prosecutor on the subject. Yet in two separate versions of the incident—a 1976 memoir and a magazine interview three years later—Jaworski described a Map Room conversation with Haig in which the Texas lawyer apparently needed no prompting to give his dire opinion of the "unbelievable" March 21 tape dialogue. Nor were the two men coy in other encounters. What seems more likely is that Haig could now pronounce the tape "terrible," tell congressmen earlier and Scott the next day that it was "exculpatory," and boast to Nixon on June 4 that he was in "great shape," all without contradiction. It was much the same, after all, as he had once reassured yet ridiculed Kissinger; humored and afterward derided Nixon; allied himself both for and against Haldeman, the NSC staff, the Joint Chiefs; was fraternal with "Mr. T.," then gruff and virulent toward cadet Truscott.

In the ceaseless hypocrisy of power, in the constant positioning between shifting centers of authority and patronage, conviction clearly depended on the audience and tactics of the moment. By close of 1973, under dreary leaden skies in southern California and with Watergate abscessing back in Washington, the maneuver was beginning with new urgency.

In the winter of 1973–74, as the Nixon administration began its final descent, Haig was at the zenith of his power. The press found him in Haldeman's gold-carpeted West Wing office, a handsome, chain-smoking, rather self-conscious general in mufti, more "friendly" and "open" than his predecessor. In his first real exposure to journalists, interviewers thought him "affable" and "intense," yet toiling to be heard and taken seriously with an awkward technocrat's vocabulary of "confrontation," "fractionalization," the "essentiality of discipline," and the ever-present "caldron," "perceptions," and "vortex." "I have no pangs of self-consciousness or inadequacy," he told Nick Thimmesch of the *Los Angeles Times,* who concluded, to the general's later consternation, that "there will always be a military man in the civilian suits worn by Al Haig." "I maintain a degree of formality in our relationship which he expects and wants," Haig explained of his role with Nixon some months before the June 4 tape, with its camaraderie, toadyism, and easily uttered "son-of-a-bitch," became public.

Behind the general in these interviews for the first time was the public silhouette of his "lovely" family, his background, his personal views. There was the dutiful wife, Pat ("She is very understanding"), and the children— Alex, twenty-one, at Georgetown University; Brian, twenty, at West Point; and Barbara, seventeen, at Georgetown Visitation parochial school ("I have been a strong disciplinarian with them, something they will appreciate in later years"). There was also Father Frank, the Jesuit brother ("Al is really *my* mentor"), and a glimpse of Haig's religion, at least from Frank. "Al's right of center in religion," Frank explained. "He doesn't want to go back to the Latin mass, but he doesn't want any wild stuff in the church, either." "The Berrigan brothers bothered him," Frank Haig said of the chief of staff, adding, "Watergate is also a major concern to him. Al feels a man must work out his ethical norms before he takes a decision-maker's position." Thimmesch concluded his own profile of Haig with an observation from the general's mother: "I don't know how Alec can work so hard," said Regina Haig. "The strain has made him look so much older. He admires Nixon so much. I'll be glad when it's all over."

As usual, the view from the other side of the public facade had little to do with "ethical norms," the ecumenical spirit, or admiration, and would have baffled and alarmed the elder Mrs. Haig all the more, not to mention winsome journalists. Noting "almost complete disarray" at the White House in this "unbelievable period of history," Zumwalt that February of 1974 recorded that Nixon "castigates every ethnic group in the U.S. as against him— the Jews, the blacks, the Catholics, the wasps, etc," while "Haig works every day frequently to midnight or one o'clock and Sundays from nine to six . . . [and] Nixon has an almost paranoid resentment of any time Haig is not available. . . . Once in a while," Zumwalt continued, "Haig gets off to the tennis courts and the staff has to lie about where he is and get him to scramble back to answer the telephone call." The situation was often desperate, Zumwalt believed from everything he saw and heard. "When it was clear that the President was emotionally incapable of acting as President, Haig did so," wrote the admiral. "He [Haig] was conscious of the fact that he was well above his depth," and "was a frightened man but . . . desperately doing his best to hold it together."

Telephoning Haldeman that winter, Haig supplied yet another perspective on his work. After complaining briefly about Rose Mary Woods and Ziegler being "insecure" and about other ranking White House aides who "won't touch the Watergate business," Haig drew on his wartime lore and launched into an attack on what he called the "pussy fire group," referring, says Haldeman, "to groups of Vietnamese who shot from behind bushes and wouldn't stand and fight." In Haldeman's account of the call, "Haig said the pussy fires were a group of young White House aides who met every day—and gave Haig trouble every hour."

The general ended the call to Haldeman with an incidental, presumably unrelated warning. "They have an uncanny intelligence operation in the Jewish community that is out to get you—and the *Parade* [magazine] editor [whom Haig described earlier in the conversation as "a friend of his"] is a part of it," Haldeman recorded Haig telling him. "They're determined to do you in, and this ties back to your 'Nazi' atrocities and all that stuff, you know." The general "talked about the Jewish community as if it had a big sinister plot against me," wrote Haldeman, who told Haig at the time to "forget it" because the story was unbelievable.

By the end of 1973, longtime White House correspondents observed that despite the public imagery and talk of a newly open presidency, despite Haig's better press relations, the general's regime was in reality even more closed than that of his "Berlin Wall" predecessors. Nixon was "dealing now with fewer people than he did in the heyday of departed Bob Haldeman and John Ehrlichman," wrote John Osborne, conservative columnist in *The New Republic*. "I don't know that the system has been changed here," Haig admitted to Thimmesch in November. Reporters murmured over a later incident in April 1974 when, flying back on *Air Force One* from a presidential weekend in Florida, a military aide casually mentioned a call that weekend from Democratic Senate Leader Mike Mansfield to Nixon. "What did you say?" Haig demanded, standing up to berate the staff for not informing him of Mansfield's call. "I run this White House and don't you ever forget it. Don't ever let that happen again," Haig "growled" to assistants, who thought him "angry, serious, *formidable*." After a pause, Haig repeated, "I run this White House," and sat down in silence.

To help him "run" it, he chose (like Kissinger, at least at the outset) no comparable deputy but a loyal, unthreatening aide, Major George Joulwan, a thirty-four-year-old West Pointer with a master's degree in international affairs from Chicago's Loyola University and past army service on Haig's staff. An operations officer for Haig's battalion, Joulwan had conducted the press conference after the battle of Ap Gu that marked Haig's debut in the press. Another aide, Major General Bennett, came and went in a few months; while a third, a thirty-four-year-old former businessman and personnel specialist named Jerry Jones, completed Haig's immediate staff. But in contrast to his glowing reputation as a master staff man under Kissinger, Haig as White House chief soon came up against complaints, as Osborne noted, "that he wasn't taking hold," or that he was politically inept. Nixon "allowed Haig to hold the ultimate power as to what went on at the White House, who got hired and fired, and what to do when the crunch was on," Thimmesch wrote about Haig's dominant role in the Saturday Night Massacre to the exclusion of more seasoned politicians. "The result was a political disaster."

While the scandal worsened around the White House's iron fence, the bureaucratic bickering and burlesque inside became more pronounced, and often still more shocking. In January 1974, Colson listened to Haig threaten to quit "unless Nixon demoted Ziegler," a "bitter feud" that reminded Colson in his fresh rectitude of "Berlin in the last days when . . . haughty lieutenants, trapped, smelling death and defeat, turned bitterly on one another and indulged every hedonistic desire." Nor was the jockeying limited to current employees. "The President has an excessive desire to protect old friends," Haig said to a White House speechwriter that winter, complaining about continuing Nixon ties to the deposed Haldeman, Ehrlichman, and Colson, ties that both Haig and Kissinger not surprisingly urged Nixon to sever.

The effort to insulate Nixon from his former courtiers (while Haig offered office gossip and warnings of Jewish conspiracies in chatty calls to Haldeman) illustrated another trait of Haig's White House governance—that the old habits and practices of bureaucratic realpolitik went on regardless of the national crisis gathering in the Congress and the courts. Having succeeded to unchallenged authority with the president, Kissinger and Haig would of course have naturally moved to cut Nixon off from his old aides whether Haldeman and Ehrlichman had retired in honor or resigned in scandal. In the same vein, Colson chronicles that neither Haig nor Ziegler came to the White House staff Christmas party in 1973 because each refused to appear where the other had been invited, a petty slight in the obsessive office rivalries that had nothing to do with Watergate.

Some of Haig's scarce time was similarly occupied by simply covering his bureaucratic flank, shielding his own history and future contacts whatever the course of impeachment. And given the peculiar character and malodorous past of the regime, those duties might take a bizarre turn. Thus only weeks after becoming chief of staff, he received a blackmail letter from a ranking Defense Department official who threatened to expose details of the Pentagon investigation into the NSC military "spy ring" unless Nixon named him FBI director. According to *The New York Times,* to whom Haig "confirmed" the story, the general "subsequently" told the official "to go to hell," although the dismissal of the blackmail was apparently less than total. "The extortionist had not been fired from his Pentagon job," a later Watergate Committee chronology summarized the incident, "for fear he would make his information public."

Other incidents were still more shadowy. Colson recorded reading that winter at the White House two six-inch-thick folders stamped "top secret" in "bold blue" and filled with evidence of expressly illegal CIA operations inside the United States on the murky edges of the Watergate burglary. The damning material was never fully revealed even after a congressional inquiry, said Colson, because "other voices, principally General Haig, convinced him [Nixon] he should do nothing to injure the intelligence establishment."

It was the stuff of old White House staff neuroses, and pulp novels, but the scope and depth of CIA domestic spying and manipulation were also the great unexplored story of Watergate. And however the revelations might have drawn the wolves away from a weakening president for the moment in 1974, Haig's protection of the CIA stored valuable bureaucratic capital for the future (when he would enjoy cozy relations with the agency as NATO commander, and still later when, as secretary of state, CIA estimates and forged documents would underwrite his policies in Central America).

In the *sauve qui peut* climate descending on the West Wing, no precaution was ignored. An old acquaintance of Haig's in the Defense Intelligence Agency, the Pentagon's smaller equivalent but rival to the CIA, remembered a call from the general early in 1974 asking, of all things, for any DIA files on Nixon's connections with the Mafia. If such records were not already available, Haig told the intelligence officer, a totally discreet handpicked DIA team should investigate the possible ties between the president and the organized-crime faction.

Whether to protect Nixon against some expected blow or to arm Haig with his own Hooveresque dossier on the commander in chief, the purpose of the DIA's mafia inquiry was never clear to the officer, and in any case the "investigation" soon petered out after two preliminary and insubstantial reports to Haig. Later the shocked intelligence official quietly told his story to a *New York Times* journalist and to Senate Foreign Relations Com-

mittee staff when Haig was named secretary of state. But
there was no further inquiry, the sordid episode falling
like so many others down the comforting memory hole.

Meanwhile, the Watergate battle grew in ferocity, and
Haig continued his tactical maneuvers with Jaworski, the
sole adversary who could prosecute the president's men as
well as Nixon. Late in February 1974, with rumors of
imminent indictments, Haig called Jaworski to ask if any
"present White House aides" were to be named by the
Watergate grand jury, and when the special prosecutor
assured him there was none, Haig answered, "You're a
great American, Leon." Meeting regularly with Jaworski
(having excluded even St. Clair, the president's new lawyer, from this key liaison with the prosecutors), Haig also
told Jaworski that he was never a part of the obvious
White House campaign to smear John Dean. "He assured
me he was personally not involved in those efforts,"
Jaworski once told Dean about a conversation with Haig.
It was, as the June 4 tape of Nixon and Haig would show,
a blatant lie, but part of the general's calculated pose with
Jaworski. The guise was not always convincing. "Jaworski
used to rant and rave aplenty about Al Haig," a former
staff attorney told *Time* when it was all over and memories had softened. By March, even Haig was reporting
back from his meetings with the prosecutor that Jaworski,
"once sympathetic, was souring."

Nonetheless, the general's approach was not necessarily
so warm or subtle. Haig "said some things I interpreted
as threats," Jaworski told his staff about an unusual April
28 meeting at the White House to which he had been
spirited from his Texas ranch in an air force plane sent
by Haig. The "threats," a Jaworski aide wrote later in

striking parallel to Agnew, were "more Haig's tone than
anything specific." Over an hour and a half, the general's
"wrath" was vented against Jaworski's staff for what Haig
saw as "manipulating the grand jury" and working from
baseless evidence. When Jaworski, by an aide's account,
replied heatedly that the staff had behaved "professionally," that its charges were "documented," and that they
were now ready to "lower the barriers" if the White House
wished, Haig only warned Jaworski in kind that St. Clair
would be "tough."

All this posturing, courtesy of a special plane and at
considerable taxpayers' expense, apparently climaxed
when Haig suddenly changed his "tone" and, as Jaworski
related the story, "the real purpose of the meeting
emerged." Haig wanted Jaworski to read the fifty-page
"summary" of tape transcripts that the White House was
about to release in a dramatic Nixon television speech,
some of them drawn from recordings Jaworski had been
seeking by subpoena. The document "proved the President was innocent," Haig told him, and the chief of staff
now wanted Jaworski to "comment" on the disclosure.

At this, both Jaworski and his staff, whom he told later,
were incredulous. "Why Haig or Nixon believed the special prosecutor might fall for such a ploy beggars the
imagination," wrote Jaworski's astonished deputy. "Haig
was suggesting no less than that Jaworski join the President in an exculpatory public judgment on the transcripts without even reading them—on the basis of the
President's own 'summary'!" Haig had flown Jaworski in
from Texas, thought the prosecutor's staff, "to supply the
ultimate blurb for Nixon's 'blue book.'" When Jaworski
then agreed to read the summaries but refused to com-

ment, Haig became very "nervous," the prosecutor noted, guessing that "Milhous must be waiting for him up at Camp David on pins and needles." The talk at an end, Jaworski flew back to Texas on his special plane.

On April 29, without Jaworski's blurb, the White House released an overall summary and hours later the edited, partial transcripts of forty-six tapes. It was the president's last major effort to fend off Watergate, and, like the firing of Cox, it was a public-relations disaster, with Haig's exact role never quite clear at the time. Facing simultaneous subpoenas from both Jaworski and the House Judiciary Committee in its impeachment inquiry, Nixon was inclined by mid-April to again soften the winter's unyielding policy and preempt the subpoenas by volunteering selected versions of some of the requested tapes as well as others that supported the presidential case. Haig now argued for disclosure as well, though witnesses remembered him for the most part "standing back" while Nixon and Ziegler decided on publication.

Carefully edited and released in a well-delivered and -staged presidential speech, the transcripts for a time evoked the desired effect. Senator Scott, whom Haig had left unable to finish a reading of the March 21 dialogue, was now moved to call John Dean, Nixon's main accuser, a liar and perjurer. But the conniving, shabby, often vulgar tenor of the conversations, which no editing could mask, soon brought down public indignation of the kind and magnitude provoked by the Saturday Night Massacre six months before.

More damning than the vernacular of the tapes was their obviously tendentious editing. Moth-eaten with more than 1,800 gaps ranging from "inaudible" to "unrelated," the transcripts carried blanks most often in conversations with Haldeman and Ehrlichman, least frequently or intrusively in the mostly vague talks with Dean, and registered twice as many "inaudibles" in Nixon's lines as in all other speakers together. When the Judiciary Committee compared the actual tapes it already had with the White House transcriptions, there were stunning contrasts. In the White House versions, for example, Nixon is saying "in order to get off the cover-up line" and that the burglars "are covered on their situation"—while the committee's audio experts, including a blind listener with sharpened hearing, heard the same passages as "in order to get on with the cover-up plan" and "our cover there." The committee also found large portions of the recordings missing altogether from the transcripts with no indication of deletion, including Nixon's infamous March 1973 order to Mitchell: "I don't give a shit what happens. I want you all to stonewall it, let them plead the Fifth Amendment, cover-up, or anything else, if it'll save it—save the plan." The White House later justified the omission on grounds that the passage was of "dubious relevance" to the president's responsibility.

To the renewed chorus of criticism over the transcripts, including the charge of tampering or rerecording, Haig told the *Washington Post* it would be "blasphemous speculation" and a "gross intrusion on grand jury proceedings" to imply any doctoring of the tapes. Yet at the same time he confided to Jaworski that "I haven't the slightest doubt that the tapes were screwed with."

Once again, the question of Haig's own role in the tainted release of the tapes was skirted. Haig had been in charge of the team of White House stenographers who

for weeks that spring had transcribed the tapes under the
heaviest security in the office recently vacated by Haig's
former deputy, Major General Bennett. With Buzhardt
and Nixon, he had reviewed the transcripts. With Ziegler,
he argued in favor of retaining the famous deleted
expletives. He had previewed the president's speech text
for congressmen and cabinet officers, even playing for the
latter a selected scratchy fragment of tape to prove the
authenticity of the "inaudibles." Scarely the "arm's length"
relationship to the tapes he later claimed before the Foreign Relations Committee, his role was decisive and central at every stage in what one analyst and former White
House staffer called afterward "a deliberate effort to hide
Nixon's involvement in a criminal obstruction of justice . . .
itself an act of obstruction of justice by those who knew
it was a distorted version."

Nor were the tape transcripts the only discrepancies
staining Haig's record. When the Senate Watergate Committee sought about the same time a White House memo
on political espionage—a memo that in the original named
Haig to draft a "preliminary scheme" to combat a prospective *Life* magazine article discovered through the Halperin
wiretap—the version finally surrendered to the committee
by the White House "had been doctored," as one writer
put it, "so as to exclude any reference" to Haig.

The president had now released "all the relevant information on the Watergate story," Haig said soberly after
the transcript publication. But as the White House refused again further disclosures and the Judiciary Committee and Jaworski persisted, the inner war went on at all
its levels. The same day Nixon spoke on the transcripts
that would "tell it all," Haig had telephoned Deputy At-

REGENT   283

torney General Lawrence Silberman trying to limit
Jaworski's grand jury investigation, and soliciting the Justice Department as well to obtain "internal memoranda
from the special prosecutor's files" that might suggest that
the long-gone Cox had improperly influenced John Dean's
damaging testimony. Such a "demand," Silberman told
Haig (and later the *Washington Post*), was "unprecedented" and could only be refused.

The following week, "obviously rankled," his deputy
thought, by Haig's "threats," Jaworski took his own initiative. At a discreet White House meeting on Sunday afternoon, May 5, while Joulwan tried to entertain Jaworski's
young attorneys in the Map Room with wartime tales of
service with Haig, Jaworski told the chief of staff that a
grand jury had months earlier secretly named Nixon an
"unindicted coconspirator" in the Watergate cover-up.

While St. Clair "flushed with color" at the news, one of
the prosecutors recorded, "Haig, on the other hand,
seemed calmer." Ever the bureaucrat, the general "ap-
preciated the fact that we had been able to keep this
totally unexpected development secret for months. . . ."
Jaworski offered to keep the grand jury action secret even
longer and drop his own subpoena in return for a minimal
number of White House tapes essential to the forthcoming
Watergate trials. Haig "asked for time" for the president
to consider, and as Nixon began listening to the requested
tapes for the next two days, the compromise seemed possible. But by late Tuesday, May 7, the White House
abruptly announced it would not comply with any parts of
the subpoena. With this, the final battle was joined that
would lead to the Supreme Court decision two and a half
months later, and then to the president's resignation.

Over the next several weeks, the tape issue was shunted to the courts and the House impeachment hearings began only haltingly, while Haig continued his defense of Nixon. On May 10, rampant Washington rumors of Nixon's resignation were fed by an Associated Press interview in which Haig spoke of the President stepping down "if he thought that served the best interests of the American people." Though Haig had added that "at this juncture, I don't see anything on the horizon which would meet that criterion," he was forced by an angry Ziegler and Nixon into a subsequent "clarification" that his words were not a "softening" of Nixon's position. The next day Haig emphasized that Nixon would not be "pressured out of office" and that "we just can't succumb to the fire storm of public opinion."

By May 15, the general was in executive session of the Ervin Committee expressing what one staff lawyer called "resentment and concern" at committee leaks of his earlier testimony. Some stories about the Rebozo case, Haig told the senators sternly, "suggested to the reader that I had knowledge that I don't believe I had, which is bothersome to me personally." He would "expect" the committee to abide by its own "rules," Haig admonished them; and as the cowed senators drew back, he had won a precedent for future appearances before other committees on other issues.

In private with Jaworski, he was still arguing for the cloak of national security over the production of evidence in the trial of conspirators in the burglary of Ellsberg's psychiatrist. "The national security matters he described didn't appear to be very grave to me," thought the special prosecutor. Still later, with Haig a prospective presidential candidate, Jaworski's view of the general's position in the summer of 1974 visibly mellowed. "I don't know how much of that he fully understood," he said to an interviewer about Haig's national-security argument on the burglary. "The one thing you must remember is that we have to make allowance for Al being terribly sensitive to ideas of national security, because of his background, his work with Kissinger, and so on."

But by the end of May, Haig and Nixon seemed to understand very well that foreign policy and national security would be the last political defense against the scandal. On the twenty-third, Haig assembled in the old Indian Treaty Room of the EOB a special closed meeting of some 250 sub-Cabinet officials of the now demoralized administration. The president was wholly in command and performing effectively and in detail in all the major trouble areas, Haig told the quiet audience in a thirty-minute speech, predicting smilingly that Watergate "will be a very long footnote" in the history of the Nixon presidency. To some who heard him, his lengthy praise of Nixon's diplomacy amounted to a "denigration, a subordination" of Kissinger that the secretary's admirers found in "bad taste." The regime's foreign policy was not the result of "wizardry," Haig had said pointedly, but rather a carefully considered presidential "design."

The swipe at Kissinger was ill-advised. The surviving prestige of the secretary of state was now the last legitimate personal coin of the regime, and it was thrown onto the scales in the summer of 1974 in an almost desperate effort to fight Watergate with extravagant diplomacy. Beginning June 10, Nixon, Kissinger, and Haig left for a nine-day swing through five Middle East countries, fol-

lowed almost immediately by a third annual summit meeting with Brezhnev in Moscow. The trip produced a
memorable Kissinger press conference in Salzburg in which
he petulantly threatened to resign over questions about
the wiretaps (which were to prove all too justifiable),
and a frightened Senate promptly expressed its confidence
in the secretary. Haig and Kissinger characteristically
squabbled over whose quarters were closer to Nixon's.
Exuberant crowds greeted the president in Cairo and even
at Caribou, Maine, where Haig staged a prime-time home-
coming speech for the president in front of an uncritical
audience of air-force-base dependents. But when it was
over, the diplomacy had been wholly empty and ceremonial, the Russians had plainly begun to separate themselves from Nixon, and back in Washington the nightmare
remained.

The Russian trip left one unsettled footnote involving
Haig and an issue of vast consequence. Though Nixon
badly needed a more tangible treaty triumph, and though
he remembered Kissinger in the negotiations fighting
"brilliantly and valiantly," the Americans and Soviets
could not reach agreement on a limit to offensive nuclear
weapons, specifically future production of multiple-
warhead missiles, or MIRVs, in which the U.S. lead was
significant. The failure haunted peace and fueled the arms
race for years to come, while back in Washington the
Joint Chiefs, ever intent on budgets and paper superiority, feared an agreement like "defendants waiting for a
jury to bring in a verdict." Zumwalt recorded before the
summit that Schlesinger "had gotten his 'ass chewed out
by Kissinger and Haig'" for the Pentagon's "disloyalty" on

the issue, and that Nixon now regarded the Chiefs as "all 'a bunch of shits.' "

As it was, Nixon signed nothing on MIRV ("We won," the admiral noted), an impasse the president in his memoirs rather cryptically ascribed to the "military establishments of both countries." But in the relieved Pentagon, some credit went to the White House general. He had "no way of knowing" what produced Nixon's "unexpected firmness in the talks," wrote Zumwalt, but wondered "whether Al Haig found, in a moment of national crisis, his professional conscience. . . ." Whatever his role in the negotiations in Russia that summer—and Nixon, never loath elsewhere in his memoirs to detail Haig's influence, does not mention him at all—Haig's last diplomatic foray with Kissinger and the president was to be cast in the suspicions and shadows of a collapsing regime, setting the aide apart once again from his tarnished patrons, and winning him ironic, probably undeserved credit from his old military constituency.

The last seventeen days of the Nixon presidency: No interval in recent American politics bore more drama and anticipation at the time; none excited more scrutiny and speculation afterward. Newspapers and television networks rushed to retrace what could be learned in days or even overnight about the final chronology of resignation. Books on the fall appeared within a few months carrying glib narrations and colorful quotations, their authority almost entirely derived (ironically like so many of the worst products of the Nixon regime) from secrecy, in this

case the "national security" and literary "executive privilege" of unnamed sources. Yet when that first orthodoxy
had been assembled, Alexander Haig's part in the history
was still clouded. Had he cunningly and patriotically
orchestrated the resignation, as the popular albeit anonymous accounts suggested? And apart from his credited
removal of Nixon, had he then secured the ex-president's
controversial pardon in some last-minute deal with the
incoming Gerald Ford?

Stalking both questions was the continuing paradox of
Haig's more general public image as the dutiful, loyal,
yet unaccountable aide. If Nixon and Kissinger had been
the sole villains or heros of the West Wing and Haig only
their adjutant, he was now suddenly in the final two weeks
an independent force, "the acting President of the United
States," as Theodore White called him, who "knew that
he must act." Responsible personally for none of the regime's previous abuses, he was now to critics and disillusioned supporters alike the engineer of perhaps its
most significant and laudable act, its abdication—and to
some, also of its parting affront, the Nixon pardon.

If the first excavations had followed more closely the
contours of Haig's earlier career, and more realistically
his efforts to preserve both the Nixon presidency and his
own newfound prominence in the fifteen and a half
months before the resignation crisis, his role at the climax
would have been more decipherable. Between the self-
injuring extremes of deserting the president and going
down with him, Haig navigated a characteristically careful course. If the slowly emerging reality did him much
less credit than the early mythology, he salvaged what
mattered in the bureaucratic and political world in any

case—survival in the short run, and the chance to wield power again.

First, there was the countdown to resignation, in many ways separable from the twisting record of the pardon decision. Said to be "absolutely resistant" to quoting his talks with Nixon, Haig reportedly told inquiring authors to await the presidential memoirs on the last days. "It's his story," Theodore White has him saying of Nixon's exit, "he'll write it his way when he gets round to it." Yet when Nixon and others published those stories, the chief of staff was often a more banal, less noble figure than White's "acting President." On July 23, 1974, the day before the Supreme Court decision on the surrender of the tapes, Nixon recorded Haig "not ready to give up" despite their vain calls from San Clemente to retrieve defecting southern democrats on the Judiciary Committee. Over the past weeks, Nixon noted, Haig had stood consistently against the president's contemplation of resignation, arguing that "it would not only look like an admission of guilt, but . . . would mean a dangerously easy victory for the radicals—not just over me but over the system."

The next morning came the news of the unanimous court decision that the president must hand over the tapes. As Haig in California called Buzhardt back at the White House to discuss the decision, Nixon took the phone and told the lawyer, "There may be some problems with the June twenty-third tape, Fred," asking him to listen to the recording. First heard by Nixon in early May as part of his review of tapes for Jaworski's suggested compromise, the June 23 conversation was to be the symbolic "smoking gun" of presidential guilt long sought by the Watergate investigations. The tape revealed the president and Haldeman discussing use of the CIA to obstruct the initial FBI Watergate investigation, the probable complicity of Mitchell, and the tactics of the cover-up, all with obvious prior knowledge and conversation on the subject only six days after the break-in. That recording was now included in the Supreme Court enforcement of previous subpoenas.

When Buzhardt had heard the tape, he called Haig to say the evidence was "conclusive" and that the question was not whether Nixon would leave office but only "how." Yet Haig, who "often remarked" to Nixon that Buzhardt was an "alarmist," now found him "too gloomy" and asked the attorney to listen again. Even after that second hearing and an equally dire appraisal, however, Haig would tell the president, "I think we can cope with it."

When the Judiciary Committee (as yet without knowledge of the June 23 tape) voted the first article of impeachment three days later, Haig was apparently still urging the beleaguered president not to "run out." "Al and Ziegler have been splendid in this period," Nixon marked in a diary entry following the vote. Then, despite repeated warnings from Buzhardt about the June 23 incriminating evidence, Haig made a series of extraordinary public statements. A few hours after the committee action, he told CBS's "60 Minutes" in Los Angeles that the charges against Nixon were "a grab bag of generalities" and that "the case for impeachment is not there." "At this juncture, Haig told Mike Wallace in somewhat strained syntax, "I see no value served in the interests of the people to have presidents driven out of office." Returning to Washington aboard *Air Force One* on July 28, the general conceded to accompanying reporters that the president had sustained "very severe losses," but maintained he would be "vindicated."

Over the next two days, the Judiciary Committee voted its Articles II and III of impeachment, St. Clair turned over to Sirica twenty of the subpoenaed tapes with admission of still another five-minute gap, and Nixon by his own account as well as others began to spend sleepless nights pondering his plight. By then, having reviewed the June 23 conversation still further, both Buzhardt and St. Clair were convinced Nixon should resign. But Haig remained the pivotal figure, just as he had been for more than a year, by virtue of the sheer power of his regency. Commanding the rest of the White House staff besides the lawyers, dispensing power and policy to the government beyond, he had been singulary privy (witness the June 4 conversation) and singularly decisive. His advocacy or neutrality or opposition had shaped the alternating advance and retreat in White House strategy on Watergate from the May 22 statement, with its national-security rationale, to the fitful give-and-pull-back on the tapes through the spring of 1974. "I would need Haig to rally whatever loyal staff was left and to keep the White House running if I choose not to resign but to face a Senate trial," Nixon admitted unabashedly in his memoirs. Now by all accounts, on Wednesday July 31, the general read for himself for the first time the June 23 transcript which he had learned a week before was so damning.

It is at this crucial point that the versions of Haig's role part ways significantly. In the fashionable unattributed accounts of the moment, he begins to act "largely on his own," as one writer summarized the descriptions, edging Nixon toward a resignation he would not have chosen otherwise. But with little to gain from stark falsities that could be shown up in other memoirs, the later documented accounts of major participants, including Nixon, throw a different light. "I'm afraid that I have to agree with Fred and Jim St. Clair. I just don't know how we can survive this one," Nixon records Haig reacting to the June 23 transcript that Wednesday. "I knew what was really happening there, and I know how you feel about it, but I think that we have to face the facts, and the facts are that the staff won't hold and that public opinion won't hold either, once this tape gets out."

The quoted advice was no more nor less than Haig would say repeatedly in public and private over the ensuing years—that Nixon faced resignation not because he had wrongly covered up, withheld evidence, or misled his supporters, including Haig, but that in any case his political support was gone. Later that day, while Ziegler met with Nixon and gave him much the same judgment about the tape, Haig warned Kissinger about the June 23 evidence and told his old boss that the senior White House staff was now nearly unanimous in urging resignation. As the secretary afterward related to his staff, Kissinger advised Haig that they should all "stay clear of the wreckage" (as indeed Kissinger had done for the entire Watergate debacle) and let what's left of "our friend's instincts" draw him out of office.

At nine the next morning, a cloudy hot August 1 in Washington, Haig telephoned Vice President Ford and asked to come over to his office immediately. Their meeting was to be widely ascribed later to Haig's initiative, part of his orchestration, though Nixon recounts it as one

of a series of steps he ordered Haig to take that morning
when the president told his chief of staff "I had decided
to resign." Clearly, seeing Ford without Nixon's knowledge
would have been an uncharacteristic risk and bureaucratic
mistake had Haig alone been constructing a veritable
coup. Knowledge of his unusual meeting with the vice
president in the latter's second-floor EOB office that morning might easily have leaked through, and out of, the
taut White House, suggesting cabal and pushing the
ever-suspicious Nixon in precisely the opposite direction.
Moreover, the likelihood that Haig was following presidential orders was underscored by what he now told Ford
and the circumstances of their meeting.

Haig was "surprised" and visibly uneasy, Ford noticed,
at finding with the vice president the latter's chief of
staff, Robert Hartmann. His disquiet was natural enough;
he did not know Hartmann well and had sensitive information to impart. Yet it seems altogether unlikely that
Haig would have then said *anything* in Hartmann's presence if Nixon did *not* know about the approach to Ford.
It would have been too easy for the brusque general, the
keeper of "national security" secrets, to ask Hartmann to
leave or to arrange another meeting. Ford's unknown
chief of staff was precisely the sort of potential leak Haig
would have feared had he been conspiring behind Nixon's
back. But the general now informed the vice president
that "things are deteriorating" with the discovery of a new
"smoking gun" tape, and that "you'd better start thinking
about a change in your life." He lied to Ford that "he
hadn't seen the evidence," probably to exclude Hartmann
for the moment. In this forty-five-minute meeting, Haig
also stressed, as he would to Jaworski and others, that

he "hadn't even suspected the existence of this new evidence."

At noon, Haig called Ford again to schedule another talk for 3:30, and "this time," Ford wrote later, "he didn't want Hartmann there." It was to be a momentous meeting in the history of the pardon, and the details belong to that story traced below. But the conversation left Ford's aides, who learned of it later, all the more convinced that Haig had not approached the vice president "without Nixon's knowing about it." Looking to Ford "more beaten and harassed" than he had earlier, Haig now described the June 23 tape and asked the vice president if he was ready "to assume the presidency in a short period of time." Saying "I just don't know what the President is going to do," Haig outlined as coming from "knowledgeable people" on the White House staff a number of Nixon's "options," including resignation and subsequent pardon. Not telling Ford about Nixon's decision to resign that morning, Haig asked the vice president if he had any recommendations on Nixon's course. According to his own memoirs, Ford replied that he did not think it "proper" to make any, but stressed that "pressure couldn't be applied directly" to force Nixon's resignation. They then talked briefly about pardon power, and parted warmly, promising, as Haig said, to "keep in contact."

At 7:30 that Thursday evening, back at the White House, Haig asked to see Raymond Price, longtime Nixon speechwriter. "We need a resignation speech," Haig told him by Price's own account. The president, Haig explained, planned to announce his decision the following Monday night. In resignation lore, this Haig request for a speech was "a thought of his own." Still, the Price, Ford,

and Nixon memoirs as well as other sources all make plain
from different vantage points that the order to the speechwriter came from the president himself, however tortured. And once again, for Haig the practiced bureaucrat
to have asked Price for such a speech, and risked his telling an unknowing, unstable Nixon inadvertently or deliberately, would have been a remarkable lapse—and
folly in any serious scheme to manipulate Nixon.

At this stage, with the epiphany of the June 23 transcript, Haig was obviously anxious for Nixon to go. The
president recalled him urging resignation the *next night*
when Nixon told him of the decision that morning, August
1. The June 23 tape was to be surrendered to the court
Friday morning, August 2, Haig told him, and he should
be gone before it "surfaced publicly." But Nixon had
decided on a later date at Ziegler's urging during the
afternoon of the first.

The White House, remembered Price, "was now a
rumor factory, with many of the staff scurrying around
trying to pry out what was really happening and the other
half frantically gossiping about what they imagined might
be happening—and many apparently babbling their
imaginings to the press." Keeping secrets in that sort of
atmosphere, he went on, "requires not only the will to
do so but also, frequently, considerable skill and practice."
With no unusual order from Haig *not* to discuss the speech
with Nixon, Price began drafting it the evening of August
1, maintaining "an elaborate facade of normality" only
for the rest of the staff. Working for Nixon since 1967,
Price recognized, too, that the decisionmaking process,
particularly "on this most final, most personal decision of
his presidency," would be fitful, with Nixon typically

"going to keep reassessing, keep reexamining, and possibly reverse himself." That evening Nixon dined aboard the *Sequoia* with Rebozo, telling him of the decision to resign and thinking "how helpless and hopeless it was."

The next evening, Friday, August 2, Price went again to Haig's office, after working through the day on the resignation address. This time he read the June 23 transcript. Along with Haig, Buzhardt, fellow speechwriter Pat Buchanan, and Joulwan, they "all agreed that resignation was the only course." So, too, Haig told them, did Congressman Charles Wiggins, a California Republican and Nixon stalwart on the Judiciary Committee to whom, as Price related, "the President had had Haig and St. Clair show . . . the transcript that afternoon." Like much else in those days, showing Wiggins the damaging dialogue would be described later as Haig's "bold move—worthy of Richard Nixon himself." The less dramatic reality was that it *was* indeed Nixon, who promptly heard Haig's report that Wiggins thought after hearing the tapes that "impeachment in the House and conviction in the Senate were no longer in doubt."

The same day—with or without Nixon's knowledge is not wholly clear—Haig had called other loyalists like Michigan Senator Robert Griffin and Cabinet Secretary Casper Weinberger (his future rival in the Reagan cabinet) to tell them about the June 23 tape and not least to assure them, as he said to Weinberger, that "I think we're going to be able to persuade the President [to] step aside." Coming on that Friday, with Nixon showing no wavering in his decision to leave, those calls take on in retrospect a deliberate gloss for Haig. It would be "very difficult" for a staff member to suggest resignation, Wig-

gins was told that afternoon by Haig, who had told Nixon
in effect to resign July 31 and again August 1. The pose of
the realistic, struggling general saddled with a volatile,
quixotic chief executive now ironically made a virtue of
the presidential vice Haig and others had so long concealed. What was consistent in concealment before and
weary confession now was solely the aide's self-interest.

Nixon sat up again much of the night of August 2–3.
Before leaving for Camp David the following Saturday
afternoon, he called Haig to say that Price should shift
from the resignation announcement to an aggressive
speech of defense and explanation to accompany the public release of the June 23 tape the next Monday. Nixon
would resume the "countdown" if the reaction to the tape
was "as bad as I expected."

If the purported Haig orchestration of resignation up
to this point had produced anything, it was fresh hesitation and intransigence in Nixon. The subsequent stories
of Haig's heroics would have this as a "crisis" in the effort
to push out the seeming felon in the Oval Office. Yet when
Price came once more to Haig's office at noon on Saturday
to learn of the change, he found an extraordinary and
very different scene. Strongly in favor of resignation the
night before, St. Clair now argued that they should go
through a Senate trial for the "constitutional precedent."
Haig, too, suddenly adopted a different tone. The general "stressed," Price wrote afterward, "that over the past
several days he had kept changing his own mind on
whether the President should resign, leaning first one
way and then the other." Price thought he was "watching
a familiar process at work" in White House politics.
"When the President changed his mind," he reflected,

"his chief of staff changed with him." Some uncertainty of position was "natural" in the strain and enormity of the moment, Price allowed. "But when I saw minds changing in unison, I was afraid the President was getting echoes of his own shifting moods, not independent advice." Price asked Haig at the Saturday meeting to convey to Nixon the speechwriter's own counsel that the president should "leave now, rather than fight it out and be clawed to shreds."

On Sunday, Haig, Price, and other staff assembled at Camp David, Price having drafted, as well as the requested speech, an "option B" announcing resignation. After spending time with Nixon alone, Haig returned to the group to tell them the president had now decided on a "two-track" strategy of publicly disclosing the tapes with a simple statement rather than a formal speech, and appearing to fight on while privately assessing the damage and readying to resign. "He was not foreclosing resignation," a "relieved" Price noted. "He was simply preserving his options."

They then set to work on a statement to accompany the release of the explosive June 23 transcript. With Haig and Ziegler "constantly calling Nixon and being called by him" as they worked, Price and the others were struck by the fact that the president had heard the fatal recording on May 6 and said nothing until the Supreme Court upheld the subpoena, what Price called "that damning sequence" however Nixon explained it. (Already in the files of the special prosecutor were the telltale White House tape logs showing the check-out of the June 23 tape and that on May 5 "P listened.") Accordingly, they drafted a statement emphasizing Nixon's failure to inform *them* of the tape's existence more than the contents of the recording or an apologia for it.

When Haig later took the president the draft, Nixon was unsatisfied and handed him his own notes to incorporate a further explanation that he had not, in fact, obstructed the FBI investigation, regardless of the dialogue with Haldeman. Incredibly, however, the general now found his own reason to disobey an order from the commander in chief. "It's no use, Mr. President, we've been working all afternoon on this thing, and this is the best we can come up with," Nixon remembers Haig telling him that last Sunday evening at Camp David. "If I do, St. Clair and the other lawyers are going to jump ship, because they claim they weren't told about this beforehand and they based their case before the House Judiciary Committee on a premise that proved to be false." Haig was again blaming the defection of others, and casting the argument in naked political terms.

"The hell with it. It doesn't really matter," Nixon replied bitterly in his own account. "Let them put out anything they want. My decision has already been made." Three months before, Barry Goldwater, Nixon's crusty bulwark in the Senate, had reflected on such a moment: "When the time comes to resign," Goldwater had said, "he'll know it."

Sunday night, Haig telephoned House Minority Leader John Rhodes to warn him to postpone a scheduled news conference the next morning on Rhodes's position regarding impeachment. On Monday morning, August 5, House members began listening to the tapes already surrendered ("There are a lot of low-class people in that White House," pronounced New York congressman Edward Koch), while

Price put final touches on the June 23 transcript release and Griffin called for resignation based on his warning from Haig. Meanwhile, "very much upset," the general and St. Clair telephoned Jaworski in Houston to say they had "just learned" of the June 23 tape (twelve days after Buzhardt had first alerted them) and planned to turn it over to Sirica. "We didn't know about it, Leon. He didn't tell us about it. . . . I'm particularly anxious that you believe me, Leon. I didn't know what was in those conversations . . . he wasn't letting us listen. . . . He had these recordings under his own control," Haig implored Jaworski. "I wouldn't let any grass grow under my feet," the special prosecutor replied tersely.

Just before the four o'clock release of the transcript, Haig gathered a meeting of some 150 White House staff members. In the same old Treaty Room where he had assured subcabinet officials of Nixon's innocence in May, he now read his colleagues the statement about the June 23 tape. "You may feel depressed or outraged about this but we must all keep going for the good of the nation," he told them, ending in a lower voice, "And I also hope you would do it for the President too." As he turned to leave, many of the staff rose to their feet and cheered him. Others simply left in tears, their heads bowed at the final betrayal of their loyalty and trust.

Yet along with this, there was also now a curious ambivalence about Haig's actions toward the toppling president. As the release detonated across Washington that evening, Nixon left the White House for another escape cruise on the *Sequoia*, and as he walked to his car was himself cheered and applauded by almost a hundred staff members waiting along the driveway and calling out, as

Nixon remembered vividly, "Hang in there," "We're still with you." Encouraged by Haig, it was a demonstration that did nothing to speed Nixon's decision to resign. If anything, it seemed, to the general's credit, that he had rallied new sympathy for his leader by the tearful staff briefing that afternoon. When Rose Mary Woods later that night asked Haig on behalf of the president for a report on the first reactions to the release, his response was amazingly perfunctory, considering the wave of public revulsion and Republican dissatisfaction already visible. "Just tell him that this thing is coming about the way we expected," read Woods's notes of her talk with the chief of staff. Imagining the city "whipped into a frenzy" but with Haig's report vague and equivocal, Nixon spent another wakeful night, still awaiting the reaction that would seal his fate.

August 6 came with a sense of climax now felt in various quarters of government. For Haig and the staff, as Price recalled, it was a day of "watching as the avalanche cascaded down the hillside." Reading the transcriptions, Minority Leader Rhodes announced he would vote for impeachment. By noon, all ten Republicans who had opposed the articles in the Judiciary Committee announced their reversal, Wiggins having called for the president's exit the night before in an emotional statement. "Nixon should get his ass out of the White House—today!" Goldwater remarked with typical bluntness to a Senate luncheon of Republicans, and when Haig called him during the meeting to count senatorial votes, the Arizonian estimated no more than seven, already several less than another reading tallied only that morning and far short of the thirty-four votes necessary to avoid conviction.

The congressional leaders of his party decided that Goldwater, the former candidate and strong Nixon supporter, should convey to the president in person the depth of the disaster. When the White House congressional liaison told Nixon this, he agreed to see Goldwater the following afternoon. (Goldwater's visit to the White House would be another step attributed to Haig when its actual origins were less conspiratorial and very different.) By afternoon, the clamor was massive. Deathwatch crowds gathered outside the White House. In California, Governor Ronald Reagan joined the politicians' chorus for resignation.

Meanwhile Nixon, too, "recognized the inevitability of resignation," but went through with customary bravado a somewhat bizarre cabinet meeting he had asked Haig to schedule the night before. "Determined not to appear to have resigned . . . because of consensus of staff or cabinet opinion," he "would play the role of President right to the hilt and right to the end." Yet, as so often in his tragic stormy career, his anxious intentions produced almost the opposite result. When he postured against resignation to draw out his own cabinet, insisting on talking about inflation or the agriculture-appropriations bill as impeachment loomed as a certainty, the intimate observers Kissinger and Haig passed it off. But those less subtle and experienced, like party chairman George Bush, saw for perhaps the first time the wandering, surreal Nixon—the Nixon that Haldeman had long ago told the staff prudently to ignore, the Nixon that Haig and Kissinger had so often exploited and feared—and emerged from the cabinet meeting to leak stories of presidential irrationality and intransigence that would, ironically, paint Haig as a savior.

Yet as the cabinet session broke up late Tuesday morning, the issue seemed to have been decided. Kissinger stayed behind briefly to warn Nixon of the harsh consequences of a prolonged Senate trial for foreign policy, but the president offered no argument, and told the secretary of state he "totally agreed." He then paused to take stock of the bleak outlook on Capitol Hill, and to ask Haig to schedule Goldwater. In the midst of all this, Haig told Nixon as well that Haldeman had telephoned, "strongly opposed" to resignation but, if the president had decided to go, urging a sweeping presidential amnesty for Watergate defendants and Vietnam draft evaders before Nixon left office. Given Nixon's continuing ties with his longtime aide and Haldeman's obvious influence with the man (an influence that had brought him in many respects to this disaster), that, too, was scarcely the sort of message Haig would have transmitted had he now been a selfless conspirator for resignation rather than the cautious, uncertain, self-preservative aide so much of the record suggests.

Alone by midafternoon, Nixon sketched out "resignation speech" notes on several pages of a yellow legal pad and then summoned Haig and Ziegler to his EOB office. "Things are moving very fast now," he remembered telling them. He handed over the notes to Haig while both "wrote diligently" as he dictated further thoughts for the nationwide television speech to be given Thursday night. Walking back to the White House, Nixon looked at Haig's face and was struck by "how tired he was, how much all the political stress had taken out of this superb military man."

Putting his arm around the general's shoulder, Nixon told him, "Buck up."

Soon afterward, Haig called Price, who found the chief of staff at 4:30 in his office absorbed in reading Nixon's yellow-pad notes. "We'll need a thousand words," he said simply to Price when he looked up. Haig then rehearsed for the speechwriter the tenor of the "healing speech" Nixon wanted, "healing" but not, he told Price, to satisfy those "who crucified him and are now trying to get him to say they were justified." As they spoke, Haig himself ate a "late lunch" and his aide Joulwan came in asking "if we were back on the other track," as Price remembered the moment. "We were never really off it," Haig replied. His words, of course, could have applied as easily to the consistency of Nixon's actions over the past days as to any campaign of his own. In either case, they expressed the inevitability of Nixon's removal, which had become so plain with the June 23 tape.

Onto this tense ritual, however, now broke a still more extraordinary development, and it reflected the larger atmosphere of the regime and the moment beyond the hour-to-hour sequence at the White House. "If impeachment is inevitable," Haig had said to Colson back in January, "then better we go peaceably. We must not take the whole government down with us." He seemed to mean that they should not paralyze policy further by a lengthy trial and process. But hanging over his remark was the portent of the unpredictable, belligerent Nixon, what Safire saw as the "hater, the impugner of motives" layered within the calculating politician.

It was that shadow Nixon threw and the cabinet saw Tuesday morning, and Defense Secretary James Schlesinger reacted dramatically. That afternoon he gave secret orders that no military unit was to accept a command from "the White House" without Schlesinger's countersignature. Unmistakably, it was a precaution against some desperate move somewhere in the world to divert attention from the domestic crisis, to block a coup d'etat. At the same moment, General David Jones, chief of staff of the air force, the service most sympathetic to Nixon for his past policies in Indochina, made a pointed speech—and the only address by one of the chiefs during this period—reminding the military that its duty, as one report put it, was to "stand apart from politics."

Days after the event, Schlesinger typically leaked the story in a Pentagon "backgrounder," part of a government-wide effort of senior officials to separate themselves in every way possible from the disgraced, deposed president. But if the public revelation certified Schlesinger, it only drew the ire of the ranking officers of Schlesinger's Pentagon constituency, who were, as the *Baltimore Sun* described them, "insulted and shocked by the inference that elements of the military might be responsive to unauthorized or illegal orders reaching them through some circumvention of the chain of command." It was tortuous logic. Orders from Nixon would not have been "unauthorized" or "illegal," and many of the fateful decisions of the war, particularly with the air force and its falsified records and secret bombing, had been part of a habitual "circumvention of the chain of command." But the same officers who gladly executed those other orders now bristled indignantly at the "inference" of a putsch.

So, too, did a "furious" Gerald Ford, who pulled Schlesinger aside at a cabinet meeting August 27 to ask

about the incident. "I had a meeting today with the secretary of defense," the new president said in a remarkable
statement afterward. "We discussed the matter. And I
have been assured that no measures of this nature were
actually undertaken." But in his memoirs Ford would
reveal that he had been "assured" to begin with by Haig,
that it was Haig who told him that the story of the precautions "had been leaked deliberately from the highest
level of the Pentagon," and that Haig was there when
he dressed down Schlesinger in the Oval Office after the
cabinet meeting.

It was all characteristically Byzantine. Colson, Haig's
admirer and sometime confidant, credited the general
with "asking the Pentagon to disregard any order from its
constitutionally designated commander." Haig himself
was at pains to keep the mystery alive. *The New Republic*
found that he "hinted darkly" of "dangers to the country
deeper than Watergate." To the *Los Angeles Times* he
once spoke cryptically of the threat of "extra-
constitutional" measures in the last days. "There were considerations of the moment that haven't yet come out," he
said in an *Atlantic* interview in 1979. "The whole thing
was a constitutional crisis and a lot of people haven't
looked at what kinds of alternatives were possible during
that process." The general, concluded the interviewer on
that note, "refuses to explain further."

New evidence on the putative threat of a coup appeared
briefly during the Senate Foreign Relations Committee
confirmation of Haig as secretary of state, but in that
largely ersatz inquiry it was soon dismissed. Senate staff
aides received a call before the hearing from a former
Secret Service agent who had worked at the White House

in August 1974 and was now living in retirement in the East. There had been serious consideration of using troops on "national-security grounds" to protect the president from being "driven from office," the ex-agent told the aides. The committee should know Haig had been involved. The Pentagon precaution was justified.

"Aghast," as one assistant remembered himself and a colleague upon hearing the story, the staff members repeated it to at least one Democratic senator. But the retired Secret Service agent steadfastly refused to testify in person or even to divulge his name in a signed statement. "He said he wasn't crazy," one aide remembered the agent's response. With only that lead, however authoritative, and with Schlesinger himself refusing to say more, the issue then demanded a thorough investigation for which the Foreign Relations Committee obviously had neither the personnel nor the stomach. The subject was never pursued in the hearing, and the "dark hints" and "considerations" remained a mystery.

Had Schlesinger ordered the precaution on the basis of his own frequent and harsh appraisals to Zumwalt of "paranoia" in the White House, and in the aftermath of his midnight experience with the October alert? Did Haig pass along to the defense secretary his own warning through discreet army channels, much as Colson reported and the general implied, as part of his own rescue of the country from Nixon? And did he then, when the story broke and the new president was embarrassed and angry, blame it on Schlesinger, with whom he and Kissinger had often clashed and whose eventual removal by Ford was only in Haig's interest? Had he sown the same "considerations" with the Secret Service as part of the image—or had he indeed contemplated with Nixon one more bold stroke?

What was clear was the backdrop of carprice, venom, and arbitrary power that made any or all of this sadly plausible. It was a regime in which the FBI could be sent to seal the offices of the special prosecutor and even of its own superior, the attorney general; where B-52s were sent furtively over neutral countries or to carpet-bomb Hanoi in the midst of negotiations, with Haig and Nixon deciding alone; where the best and worst of policy was conducted in grim, self-righteous secrecy, from wiretaps in Washington's suburbs to assassination in Santiago; where Congress and the public might be handled, as the thesis read there in the Georgetown archives, "with little fanfare."

That June of 1974, Zumwalt, who was retiring, paid a farewell call on Schlesinger. The defense secretary told him of "threats from the White House" if he publicized his opposition to SALT policy. "The White House had further stated that they would destroy me (organizing retired Navy community, and all others to ensure that I had no future)," Zumwalt recorded in his notes. Haig "had become paranoid," Schlesinger repeated to the admiral, who observed that "Al always had been but that he was cleverer than the other two [Nixon and Kissinger] at concealing it." As Zumwalt rose to leave, the secretary of defense said, "Take care," and then, following him to the door, added that his advice "was not said lightly."

It was the echo of so much else, so many others in widely different times and circumstances—they would "destroy" the leakers of the Cambodian bombing story, the "threats" Agnew and Richardson and Jaworski and

others heard. Through it all ran the common thread, and
the common presence of Alexander Haig. In the angry,
fearful, half-lunatic world he exploited and helped foster,
the real or imagined or contrived shape of coup d'etat in
the Nixon sunset was perhaps to be expected.

Awake again late into the night Tuesday, Nixon found
a note on his bed from his daughter Julie urging him to
"go through the fire just a little bit longer." But he packed
it away for the "massive move" and noted later, "My mind
was made up past changing."

Wednesday morning, August 7, he sent Haig again to
Ford to tell the vice president that resignation was imminent. Meanwhile, Nixon and Price "worked back and
forth" on the resignation speech, the president inserting
a passage on the bleak congressional briefing hours *before* he met with Goldwater, Scott, and Rhodes. "He
knew what their reports would be," Price wrote.

When the legislators arrived that afternoon, Haig reportedly told them in private, "The president is up and
down on this thing. Please give him a straight story—if
his situation is hopeless, say so. I just hope you won't
confront him with your demands. He's almost on the edge
of resignation, and if you support it he may take umbrage
and reverse." The general's briefing entered the lore as
another of his skillful tactical maneuvers, while in fact
Goldwater and his colleagues were delivering their dooms-
day head count to a president already polishing his resignation address, including a description of what they were
about to tell him.

That night there were Nixon's famous and emotional

meeting with Kissinger, a stream of phone calls, and more consultations with Price. At five in the morning, in the last of several calls to the speechwriter, Nixon told him, "I just wanted to say—on this one—don't run it by the NSC or Haig or anyone. Just send it to me . . . I want this to be my speech."

On Thursday morning, while Nixon formally notified Ford, Haig informed other senior White House aides and quietly arranged a lunch with Jaworski at the general's Virginia home. Haig told the prosecutor that Nixon was resigning, and would not pardon himself or other Watergate defendants before leaving office. Haldeman and Ehrlichman had "been around" asking for pardons, he told Jaworski—but as Jaworski told the story to aides afterward, "Haig intimated that on Haig's initiative these entreaties had not been permitted to reach the President's ears." Jaworski's deputies thought it the "final irony" that the old "Berlin Wall" was prevented from reaching Nixon "by his new gatekeeper." Yet that assurance to Jaworski was a lie. Haig had told Nixon about a call from Haldeman on Tuesday, and, as Haig knew, the president telephoned his old aide himself on Wednesday. Indeed, while Haig was lunching with Jaworski, Buzhardt, at Haig's suggestion, was showing Nixon a letter from Haldeman's attorney outlining the pardon idea again.

For his part, Jaworski told Haig at the outset that he could make "no commitments" regarding Nixon's future prosecution, but later asked if Haig expected Congress after the resignation "to press a resolution that would, in effect, tell me not to move against him (i.e. Nixon)." Haig replied, "Oh, yes! I think it will be passed within a day or two. With no difficulty."

Returning directly to the White House from the luncheon, the general immediately went to the president. Jaworski thought he had made the "right decision" to resign, Nixon recalled Haig's debriefing on the lunch meeting, and "from their conversation he got the impression that I had nothing further to fear from the Special Prosecutor." Jaworski had said nothing to suggest such a conclusion, and Nixon seemed to sense Haig's slant. Considering the past record, he reflected, "I had little reason to feel assured." Moreover, he had told Haig before the meeting with Jaworski that he wanted no "special deals," and would not be "cajoled into resigning in exchange for leniency." Some of the best writing in history had been done from prison, he said to Haig in a remark widely quoted in the press. "Think of Lenin and Gandhi."

After Nixon's tearful farewell to congressional supporters, Haig came to check on whether he would be able to "get through" the evening's resignation speech. "Al, I'm sorry I cracked up a bit in there," Nixon told his "man of action," explaining that "it just gets to me" when others cry. "I'll be all right now, so there's nothing to worry about."

Early the next morning, Haig quickly brought him the formal resignation letter to sign, and some time later Nixon called him from a staff meeting for a "final goodbye." "The hell with the staff meeting," Haig said to him, "I would rather spend these last minutes with you." Nixon wished him the "very best," telling Haig that "words could not express my gratitude for everything he had done for me over the years." There was the last, emotional appearance before the cabinet and White House staff, the walk to the helicopter with Ford and his wife, and

Richard Nixon was gone. Protocol reserved an ultimate irony with the two great survivors of Watergate. At 11:35 A.M., as the presidential plane was over central Missouri, Alexander Haig delivered the letter of resignation to Secretary of State Henry Kissinger.

The "bananas thing" Safire called the rampant post-resignation speculation about Nixon's madness, and the former ghost-writer-become-columnist wondered about the "sources" who benefited most from such stories. "If you circumstance Haig—if you circumstance anybody as Haig found himself in those days," Jaworski reflected years later, "I don't see how he could have done any differently." Yet there remained somber questions over Haig's reputed heroics as well as the supposed limits of his duty. The record would show him a bystander at the crucial moments of the final days. Nixon, not Haig, ordered the June 23 tape read and analyzed. Clearly it was Nixon, too, who ordered Price to draft the resignation speech, Haig to tell Ford, and the congressional leaders to be shown the new evidence, then polled and summoned to give the formal verdict. In the Haig that emerges from the accounts of Nixon, Price, Ford, and others would be an authentic reflection of what the general would show so plainly later in public—a partisanship, a self-promotion, a bellicosity and moral insensibility about the worst political scandal in modern American history.

When Haig voted for resignation, the evidence was overwhelming, the popular tide wholly turned. Even then, the record shows, he acted because St. Clair and Buzhardt had made it clear that they, including Haig, were vulnerable as well. The trail of Jaworski's tightly bounded "circumstance" had opened in fact onto several alternatives. How different that fateful, sordid history might have been if Haig had not so reflexively conspired with Nixon to exclude Buzhardt from the first inklings of evidence about the tapes. If the general had acted as he was credited with acting later, uttering the truth of misgovernment and marshaling congressional and public opposition, after the scandal of the October alert. If he had supported Buzhardt and Garment in their November 1973 plea for resignation. If he had moved candidly and forthrightly when he acknowledged to Jaworski in December the "terrible" March 21 tape, and Jaworski told him Nixon was "criminally" liable.

The price of his long-practiced aide's ethic was a period of further national political agony and drift at home and abroad. The Arab oil embargo began its gasoline plunder of an unprepared West, inflation continued unchecked, arms control languished amid bureaucratic conflict and presidential weakness, Indochina sank further toward nightmare—all while Nixon brooded over his historic evasion. Haig would win justifiable praise and gratitude for forestalling utter collapse during the period, for keeping the paper flowing and the government sitting in a semblance of rule. But in the end, his means had again undercut his ostensible ends. Rationalizing his defense of Nixon as preservation of the presidency, he left an office stained by dishonesty and disillusion, and true national security visibly weakened.

As Nixon flew away in bitter retirement and Haig handed the resignation letter to Kissinger, there remained one last great event of the regency—the presidential pardon. At the climax of an era of suspicion and controversy, it was in some ways the most suspect and controversial episode. Justified by President Ford as an act of compassion and unity, the pardon seemed to much of America the consummate political cynicism, an incriminated ex-president waved beyond the law after all by his hand-picked, unelected successor. It reeked of a political deal, or at least of some private manipulation of the new president. Yet for all the public dismay, the background to the decision—beginning in late July and spanning the resignation to Ford's announcement on September 8—remained murky, blurring still more as it receded. And at its center was Haig.

A year and a half after the resignation and before he died, Buzhardt revealed that "serious discussions" of Watergate pardons took place among the "White House staff" during the early months of 1974. On the day of the Supreme Court decision on the tapes, July 24, Buzhardt had raised the issue specifically in one of his calls to California, with Nixon, Haig, and St. Clair on the line. The whole matter might be "mooted," he told them, if the president pardoned all the Watergate defendants as well as himself, and then resigned. Buzhardt said he had researched the subject and believed the presidential pardon power could be applied "prospectively" to those not yet indicted, meaning in the first instance Nixon himself. As the lawyer remembered the Washington–California conversation that day, Nixon said he would take the pardon option "under advisement," while Haig and St. Clair agreed with Buzhardt that it was a "drastic" alternative.

On August 1, by the accounts of both Nixon and Buzhardt, the president told Haig to "bring the Vice

President up to date." Before he met with Ford that morning, however, Haig had a session with Buzhardt. There the lawyer and the general discussed the breaking storm on Capitol Hill, and Nixon's remaining options. Buzhardt mentioned again to Haig his opinion that a president might pardon others and himself even before indictment. Buzhardt also spoke in passing, he later told reporters, of a "sixth option," in which Nixon could resign and "hope" for a pardon from his successor. But that option, he stressed pointedly, was one that neither he nor the White House staff "originated and then proposed." His staff had "carefully limited itself only to exploring actions that could be taken by the President [Nixon]" and had deliberately avoided discussing "any action by the Vice President."

When Haig first met Ford on the morning of August 1, with Hartmann present, the general made plain the bleak situation, and that Ford's succession was likely. It was not until their second meeting that afternoon—alone, at Haig's request—that he recited to Ford the "options" discussed a few hours before with Buzhardt. The president could "ride it out," resign, step aside under the Twenty-fifth Amendment on presidential incapacity, settle for a censure vote, or pardon himself and everyone else involved and then resign, Haig told Ford. These were the options being considered by "knowledgeable people" on the White House staff. The last alternative, as the vice president and former House minority leader well knew, would be disastrous political anathema for both the Republican party and the new Ford administration. And, Haig added, there was another course. "According to some on Nixon's staff," as Ford recorded the description in his memoirs, "Nixon could agree to leave in return for an agreement that the new president—Gerald Ford—would pardon him." Haig emphasized, wrote Ford, that "these weren't *his* suggestions," though "he didn't identify the staff members and he made it very clear that he wasn't recommending any one option over another."

If Ford's version is accurate, however, it leaves Haig entwined in misrepresentation. Just as he had lied that morning to Ford that he had not seen the June 23 evidence, he now disavowed his own earlier recommendation to Nixon (recorded by Nixon and others) that the president resign as St. Clair and Buzhardt had both concluded. Moreover, if these were not *Haig's* suggestions, Buzhardt's passing allusion to a sixth option, the resignation "hope" for a pardon, was now dramatically altered in Haig's mouth to an option in which Nixon "could agree" to resign "in return for" Ford's "agreement" to pardon—all of it, as the vice president heard, quite specific and in terms of an implicit bargain. Finally, Haig's disclaimer of any position on the options seems less than subtle— only one of the options, the last, involved any action by Ford, or any conceivable recommendation by Haig to the vice president.

Though Ford then declined to respond to Haig's invitation for "recommendations," the vice president did ask, "because of [Haig's] references to pardon authority," about the presidential pardon power. "It is my understanding from a White House lawyer," Ford recalled Haig saying, "that a President does have authority to grant a pardon even before a criminal action has been taken against an individual." Again, Haig "didn't name the lawyer," and Ford regarded it as "simply a general inter-pretation."

When Haig had gone, Hartmann went in to see Ford, finding him looking "as if a two-hundred-pound blocker had just hit him in the stomach." Ford told his aide about the "devastating" new evidence and they talked casually about the first five options. But when Ford mentioned the sixth, Hartmann let out an audible "*Jesus*," thinking, "So that's the pitch Haig wouldn't make with me present." Hartmann asked him quickly, "What did you tell him?" "I didn't tell him anything," Ford answered, "I told him I needed time to think about it." And at that the aide fairly shouted, "You what?"

By Ford's version, the last option set off "warning bells" in Hartmann, who told him plainly, "I don't like it." Though the vice president insisted that Haig had broached the pardon as "just one of the ideas . . . being kicked around," Hartmann was unconvinced. "I know. I know," he replied. "But Haig didn't come over here to go away empty-handed. And he didn't discuss this delicate matter without Nixon's knowing about it. And he mentioned the pardon option. And you sat there listening to him. Well, silence implies assent. He probably went back to the White House and told Nixon that he'd mentioned the idea and that you weren't uncomfortable with it. It was ex-tremely improper for him to bring the subject up."

In Hartmann's own memoirs, his statements and views were even stronger. The general had committed a "mon-strous impropriety," reflected the aide and former news-paper man. Ford's reply had been "the worst answer Haig could have taken back to the White House." Ford had told the general that he was "at least willing to enter-tain the idea" of a pardon, and that was "probably all Haig and Nixon wanted to know." "I think you should have taken Haig by the scruff of the neck and the seat of the pants and thrown him the hell out of your office," Hartmann "stormed" at Ford. "And then you should have called an immediate press conference and told the world why." As Ford then left, promising to discuss the issue further the next day, another aide thought Hartmann himself now "looked like death warmed over."

There is no doubt the vice president's men sensed the gravity of Haig's remarks to Ford, and even the shape of their amiable chief's coming debacle. The next day, August 2, Hartmann was joined by another aide and ex-congressman, John Marsh, as well as former Nixon assist-ant and now Ford confidant Bryce Harlow, to caution the vice president further. Before they could meet, however, there was another extraordinary encounter between Haig and Ford. At 1:30 A.M. that night of August 1–2, Ford telephoned Haig. As the vice president told his aides the following morning, he had "talked it over" with his wife and concluded "we were ready . . . this just has to stop, it's tearing the country to pieces." He "decided to get it over with," Hartmann remembered Ford describing the nighttime conversation, "so I called Al Haig and told him they should do whatever they decided to do; it was all right with me."

For his part, Hartmann "couldn't believe [his] ears," when Ford related this. "God knows," he thought, "what they'd said to make matters worse." Nor could he later believe Ford's version of the call in his memoirs, which had Haig initiating the call at 1:30 A.M. simply to report,

"Nothing has changed. The situation is as fluid as ever."
By Ford's account, he then told Haig that "we can't be
involved in the White House decision-making process."
But if that had been what happened, Hartmann asked
afterward, "why would Haig telephone the Vice President
at 1:30 A.M. just to say nothing had changed?"

Ford's version of the call became even more dubious
the next day when the vice president met with St. Clair,
who confirmed Haig's appraisal of Nixon's plight, but who
also pointed out, in response to Ford's rehearsal of the
six options, that as Ford later testified, "he [St. Clair] had
not been the source of any opinion about presidential
pardon power." Hartmann saw the Boston attorney "instantly sensitive to the impropriety of such a discussion,"
and St. Clair "quickly took himself professionally out of
being a party to it." Why had Haig the day before vouchsafed to Ford "the most dire secret of the Nixon
White House," Hartmann wondered, yet failed to
identify his legal source by name? That Haig and St.
Clair were acting without Nixon was, he was convinced,
"unthinkable."

When St. Clair had departed, Ford discussed the situation with Hartmann, Marsh, and then Harlow. Marsh told
Ford that "the mere mention of the pardon option con-
stituted a potential time bomb." He could "not for a
moment believe that all this was Al Haig's own idea,"
Hartmann repeated. It was "inconceivable" that the general was not "carrying out a mission for the president, with
precise instructions . . . to test your reaction." Harlow
echoed the other two advisers, saying, "There must not
be any cause for anyone to cry 'deal' if you have to make
that decision." Ford should "tell Al Haig, straight out and

unequivocally," Harlow urged the vice president, "that whatever discussions you and he had yesterday and last night were purely hypothetical and conversational, that you will in no manner, affirmatively or negatively, advise him or the President as to his future course, and nothing you may have said is to be represented to the President, or to anyone else, to the contrary." Harlow's "soliloquy" (as Hartmann remembered it later), coming from a veteran of the Nixon White House and of dealings with Haig and Kissinger, seems expressive both in emphasis and precision of the problem Ford and his advisers now faced.

Listening intently to all this, Ford agreed to call Haig to make the point, and even wrote out in longhand what he would say. "I want you to understand," Ford told Haig, "that I have no intention of recommending what the President should do about resigning. . . ." Ford then hung up and told his men simply, "Al agrees." But if the vice president had indeed told Haig the night before that "we can't get involved," Hartmann asked later, why did he "go through it all over again" in this afternoon call to Haig? With this conversation, however, the pardon issue seemed deceptively irrelevant for the next month. "We thought that was the end of it," Hartmann recorded for August 2.

Following the resignation, as Haig acknowledged to the *Chicago Daily News* later in September, the general "had been in telephone contact" with Nixon, who stuttered and seemed "plainly under strain." Nixon, said Haig from the White House, was obviously "not the same President I knew here."

On August 9, Ford's first day in office, his press secretary, Jerry terHorst, had been asked about a pardon, had referred reporters to a previous Ford statement that the public would never stand for it, and had even elicited a "that's okay" when he asked Ford about continued use of the statement the next day. But when terHorst left the Oval Office, he was stopped by an angry Haig who had just witnessed the simple exchange with Ford and who asked the new press spokesman, as one account later described it, "what right he had to try to commit Ford on the possibility of a pardon." There was "never any doubt . . ." said reporter Richard Reeves retelling the story, "where Haig and the other old Nixon assistants stood on clemency. . . ."

Over the ensuing weeks, Haig's staff prepared memoranda on Nixon's retirement appropriation, and recommended to Ford a congressional bill for $850,000, which was $300,000 more than the sum received for former president Johnson. On the day Ford approved that recommendation (later to be more than halved by Congress), Haig sent him as well a memo from former Nixon counsel Leonard Garment. The three-page document, later leaked to the *Washington Post*, indicated that Nixon's "mental and physical condition could not withstand the continued threat of criminal prosecution." The memo implied, too, that unless he were pardoned, Nixon might take his own life. Haig also reportedly included with Garment's "impassioned" plea a two-and-a-half-page statement Ford might use in announcing the pardon. At that point, reported the *Post*, Ford had given Haig "a private assurance" that the pardon would be granted. (In December 1975, though he would later refuse comment on interviews with

Buzhardt and others, Haig confirmed from his NATO headquarters, *after* the White House acknowledged the fact, that these August 28 conversations had taken place.)

"Haig was for it although he never flatly said as much," Ford later wrote of the general and his pardon decision. "He laid out the pros and cons, then stepped back and said, 'It's your decision, Sir'."

Meanwhile, inside the White House, as in the later *Post* reports, there was the sense of a decision already made. "Perhaps it would be better if I excused myself on this," Haig said when Ford summoned his closest advisers on August 30 to tell them about the pardon. Hartmann remembered that the general "wiggled nervously in his chair." But when Haig later ducked out, "his fine sense of honor left me cold," Hartmann went on. Haig "had been alone with the new President no less than two or three hours a day ever since he took office." It was "taken for granted," wrote Reeves, "that Ford would take care of Nixon."

After August 30, Ford counsel Phillip Buchen met secretly with Jaworski, who told him Nixon was under investigation in ten separate areas, and gave Buchen a memo from the prosecutor's staff saying there was nonetheless "a strong argument for leniency" and that Ford should do it "early rather than late." Haig had glibly assured Jaworski before the resignation that Congress would bar further prosecution, but that had not happened and Ford was the only escape. On Sunday morning, September 8, Ford announced to a stunned nation that he had pardoned his predecessor. The statement was taped in advance, and while it was broadcast, the new chief executive was playing golf in suburban Maryland with his old friend Melvin Laird. In the public outrage that came afterward, "hope was painfully shattered," wrote one observer of Ford, and "the great storehouse of good will that had been his for the taking was emptied as rapidly as it had been filled."

A House committee later probed the pardon with Ford himself testifying, but, incredibly, as Hartmann noted from the White House, the congressmen never really asked if there had been a "deal," or why Haig had been so insistent on seeing Ford alone at their second meeting August 1. In the subsequent books and articles praising Haig for the final days, Hartmann found "a curious consistency to a strange assumption: that Gerald Ford, the certified honest man, must have had ulterior motives but that Alexander Haig, Nixon's closest collaborator, acted only from purest patriotism." The confessional Colson, now in jail but still well connected at the White House, concluded without pause that Haig had "negotiated" with Ford over the pardon. Even Hartmann, who believed Ford honest and the pardon right, thought it altogether possible that Haig reported back the talks of August 1–2 in his own way for his own reasons, and "Nixon believed he had a deal."

Over it all hovered the question of Nixon's tortured personality—the darting, impulsive, enshrouded mind that sought refuge in gin and generals from his own frailties; the mind which Haig had so long manipulated, which was so volatile, and which could only have seemed now to Ford (with Haig's knowing reminders) the breeding ground of some ultimate national, personal, and political tragedy. In the end, the shadows of the corrupt regime had grown so long they engulfed everyone in their path, including the next president of the United States.

When it was all over and Ford had been tainted and eventually defeated for reelection, his acerbic aide Hartmann was "puzzled" at why Haig was "at such pains to deny any and all involvement" in the pardon, as the general would continue to do through his confirmation as secretary of state. It was "normal and natural" for Haig to seek clemency for his boss, Hartmann thought, adding with unelaborated emphasis that it would have been improper to solicit the pardon only *"in order to prevent one's own prosecution."* In the uproar over Ford's action and the continued animus toward the rescued Nixon, it was often forgotten that the pardon not only delivered a president from the law but also effectively closed the Watergate books at the departure of Haldeman and Ehrlichman. Without Nixon to pursue, the prosecution stopped at May 1973 as at some great unbridged precipice. Across the chasm, unexplored, was the continuing cover-up, from the falsified statements and attempts to obstruct Cox and Jaworski to the destroyed evidence, the doctored transcripts, and the lying to Congress. There, too, lay still more unsavory White House tapes, including some 100 crucial hours between Haig and Nixon at the height of the cover-up in May–June 1973.

The sheer chronology of obstruction of justice was stark. "By April 1973 the news system had the story in raw outline, by May in detail, and by midsummer the Ervin committee had put face, flesh and voice to the drama in public, yet Nixon persisted in concealment," Theodore White summed it up. "From mid-April of 1973 to his end in 1974," White described Haig's regency, "the President lied; lied again; continued to lie; and his lying not only fueled the anger of those who were on his trail, but slowly, irreversibly, corroded the faith of Americans in that President's honor."

To pardon the president was never to know the further abuses, excesses, crimes committed in and by his court. In the Nixon testimony, memoranda, staff witnesses, and other evidence never gathered would be the unfinished, unpunished last half of the Watergate scandal that made the conviction and jail sentences of its first perpetrators a cruel discrimination. An earnest and pressured Gerald Ford had let off not only Nixon but also the persistent solicitor of clemency. In a sense, he had pardoned Alexander Haig as well.

Part Four

PRETENDER

God bless the King, I mean the Faith's Defender,
God bless—no harm in blessing—the Pretender,
But who Pretender is, or who is King,
God bless us all—that's quite another thing.
                    John Byrom, *Miscellaneous Poems*

"There is nobody in the White House who has suffered more from walking close to Richard Nixon than me," Haig told *Newsweek* following the resignation. It was a remarkable lament. There were not only the promotions and immunity of the past, but the launching of a future no one could have contemplated for a colonel who joined the NSC staff as an intelligence briefer in 1969. Five years after Nixon's exit, Haig would be a candidate for president. In little more than six, his candidacy postponed, he was to be named secretary of state, the "vicar" whose writ he once deplored but whose potential power he came to covet most next to the presidency. In the interim, he became supreme allied commander in Europe, the army's coveted SACEUR, with glittering perquisites and protocol that moved one visiting senator to call it "the nearest thing to God on earth," and later a corporate president of a huge Pentagon contractor with an income in six figures. In the sum of power, money, and enduring political promise, and especially the last, he eventually surpassed even his fellow survivor of the debacle, Henry Kissinger. The ultimate aide-made-good, he would pretend to the throne he had served so profitably. And he owed it all to "walking close to Richard Nixon."

Haig's self-pity in the faded summer of 1974 was plainly political, reflecting his new ambition against the wider wreckage of Watergate and the sense of profound public disillusion with its identifiable villains. Like other great disasters of his era—the loss of China, defeat in Korea, the Bay of Pigs, the shock of the Tet offensive—it seemed a time of political reckoning, and of self-justification. "Nothing on the battlefield was as tough as this," Haig said then of his White House tenure. "I had to do things I would not have done under normal circumstances. You cannot avoid responsibility." Yet he was, as always, personally remorseless about his difficult duty. Were there times when Nixon had been irrational? he was asked. "If there were, I wouldn't tell anybody," he quickly replied. "I am at peace with myself." On September 14, less than a week after the pardon, he told a wire service, "I have no regrets. I have no sense of apology." He had not had the "luxury of playing it safe."

Yet three days later, in an extraordinary interview with Peter Lisagor of the *Chicago Daily News*, he blandly renounced Nixon, and even the party whose presidential candidate and secretary of state he would later maneuver to become. "I never was a Nixonite," Haig told Lisagor. The general "scoffed" at such reports, the *Daily News* quoted Haig, "saying that he was not a Republican, that he had worked for two Democratic presidents, John F. Kennedy and Lyndon B. Johnson, and that when Nixon beckoned in the Watergate upheaval, he felt a duty to respond." No one "on the outside" could "imagine what it was like in here," Haig said in that interview. He "deserved better" than criticism.

It was his most disingenuous public statement, yet went

almost unnoticed save for John Osborne, *The New Republic*'s chronicler of White House minutia who repeated the remarks and observed that "the pressures [had] affected Haig in unpleasant ways." The effort "to dissociate himself from his sometime patron and benefactor . . . didn't make pretty talk," Osborne thought, especially coming from a soldier so well and swiftly promoted and who "in his final year of civilian service was a fierce and willing advocate of the Nixon cause."

What Osborne could not foresee (and what Haig with similar artlessness later denied convincingly to the credulous and ailing reporter) was how much at that same moment in the autumn of 1974 the unattributed accounts of the Nixon abdication being murmured to writers like White and the *Post*'s Robert Woodward and Carl Bernstein would rescue, almost immunize, Haig's reputation. Though the various Watergate authors rightfully honored their major source's anonymity and that of his intermediaries and spokesmen (some of them known and some planted), Haig's lips in the self-absolving versions of the regime's last moments often moved too noticeably, particularly when the possible witnesses were so limited in conversations of two or three. As Hartmann noted wryly about an account in Woodward's and Bernstein's *The Final Days* of Haig's initial August 1 meeting with Ford and his aide, neither Hartmann nor the vice president were likely leakers since the story was "hardly flattering to either of us," while the authors were "extremely generous to the General." In disgraced exile as in office, Nixon was one more commander to be publicly respected (albeit with occasional disavowals of personal or party affiliation) and privately pitied or vilified, exorcising from

Haig the ghost of the spent patron with all his detractions.

As this hoary political ritual was conducted, Haig remained White House chief of staff through the weeks following the resignation, and the brief interlude with Ford was another revealing perspective on his bureaucratic power and politics. His relations with the new president offered a rare glimpse of the hold, real and imagined, of the practiced bureaucrat over even the long-termed yet usually shallow and comparatively unsophisticated electoral politicians come to executive office.

Haig took the symbolic upper hand from the first moment of Ford's vice-presidency. When Nixon called the Michigan congressman in October 1973 to tell him he was the choice to succeed Agnew, the president began by saying, "Jerry, General Haig has some good news to tell you." Haig then came on the telephone and it was he who informed Ford. It was an apt beginning. Haig moved to place his own men in key places on the new vice-presidential staff, what Hartmann called an "*ad hoc* committee to control Ford's settling in," and made quiet bureaucratic alliances with the newly important and competing men around the heir.

At the same time, he might use Ford as a foil for his own protection. When Nixon fumed at Senator Griffin's call to resign during the last week, the Michigan Republican's public statement and letter to the president having been prompted in large part by Haig's portrayal to him of the June 23 tape, Haig had blamed Ford for his colleague's stridor. Similarly, when the White House released the June 23 transcript, Haig deliberately provided Ford with only the Nixon statement and not the transcriptions, in effect censoring any independent statement on the evidence, a maneuver Ford aides thought "deliberate sabotage."

For his part, however, Ford himself viewed the general with a characteristic mixture of equanimity, naïveté, and occasional awe that would mark their relationship throughout. The vice president told a reporter in the spring of 1974 that he thought Haig a "great manager," and Ford noted in his memoirs that later as president he believed the general was "100 percent loyal to me."

Loyal or not, there was little doubt that Haig and his staff were taking their own precautions in the collapse of the Nixon regime and the threat of further legal envelopment. "People have been hauling suitcases and boxes out of here all this week," one Ford aide, on August 8, told another about the exodus of documents, albeit worrying less about criminal evidence than administrative continuity. "If we don't have any records, how can we carry on the government?" he asked. On hearing this, Hartmann promptly tried to enlist the White House police to stop the removal, ordering assistants not to "let anyone . . . burn or shred anything that we may need." But when Ford's then-senior aide returned from the new president's swearing-in and entered the small suite recently used by both Rose Mary Woods and on occasion by Haig adjacent to the Oval Office, he found the room "was heavy with the acrid smell of paper recently burned in the fireplace."

That evening, by different accounts, Haig's own office down the corridor was stacked with large "burn bags," already sealed and waiting to be removed by security officers for shredding and then incineration. While an exceptionally busy office like Haig's might fill one or two such sacks in a day, one witness remembered that night a half-dozen or more bulging bags in Haig's suite. So obvious was the purge that one apprehensive Ford aide warned the new president, only to be waved off with a frown and a muttered reply to let Haig "get 'em out of this house." What Haig did not destroy, recorded Hartmann, the chief of staff simply evacuated and "had successfully removed all of his own files from the White House even earlier." When Haig's removal of documents was "discovered," Hartmann noted tersely, the general "agreed to bring them back" and the incident was "never disclosed."

Again it was an extraordinary glimpse that was lost in the maw of Nixon stories. The beribboned general who had testified for the government at Ellsberg's criminal trial for theft of the *Pentagon Papers,* who had conducted the wiretap hunt for leakers, now spirited out of the White House his own papers, returning them—all or only some, no one could say—when he was caught. Nor was it the first time such liberties had been taken with sensitive government documents, as Gulley testified later about the Kissinger files shuffled between Rockefeller and White House bomb shelters. Why were so many documents destroyed as Nixon left? Why did the general appropriate his own files without authorization? As Kissinger and Haig (or Laird and Zumwalt and others) might have explained to Hartmann and his appalled colleagues as they entered the inner recesses of the regime's animal farm, some purloining, some "national security," is more equal than others.

At any rate, on the day Nixon left, Haig had already begun writing the archives of the new administration.

Less than an hour after Ford was sworn in as the thirty-eighth president—at a ceremony where Haig saved the choice East Room seats for Nixon loyalists to the back-row exclusion of Ford staff and friends—the new chief executive was sent an anonymous briefing memorandum for a crucial 1:00 P.M. meeting with the White House staff. Ford's own transition team had earlier recommended a "thorough housecleaning" of the presidential staff, with the sole and temporary exception of the general, who "has done yeoman service for his country" and who, they wrote Ford, should be asked to stay on for a time "to help you and your transition team." The advisers made clear as well, however, that Haig "should not be expected, asked, or given the option to become *your* chief of staff," a recommendation with which the new president nominally agreed.

Yet when Ford went to the staff meeting that afternoon, he carried quite another set of talking points, which, unsigned, he assumed to be prepared by the transition advisers. That memo told him to "reassure the staff of your respect, your need for their help, and your regard for President Nixon." It instructed him, under a capitalized "DO NOT," not to commit himself to "dealing directly with anyone but Al Haig," and, under "DO," to ask staff members to alert Haig to problems or suggestions. The staff should remain "intact," said the talking points, and they praised "the special and heroic role of Al Haig." For the official files, and history, Hartmann noted, Haig initialed what bureaucrats would call a "sanitized" copy of this memorandum without the reference to his "special and heroic role," but "it was the anonymous first memo the president carried in his coat pocket to the meeting."

As Ford's advisers stood around the back of the room

"aghast," the president proceeded to plead for everyone to stay on. Haig, "in full command," as Hartmann saw it ruefully, agreed "unselfishly" to continue, pledging the entire staff "in our hour of common cause" to the same dedication and loyalty given Nixon. Haig and his aides then rose, applauded, and escorted Ford out the door, leaving the "interlopers," as Hartmann called Ford's out-maneuvered advisers, "standing there." When terHorst, the new press secretary, tried to get Ford to visit the press room as the transition team had planned—a gesture meant to symbolize the new president's openness and a refreshing contrast to Nixon—Haig brushed him aside with "There's no time for that." Later, Ford asked his old assistant Hartmann how the staff meeting had gone. When the aide explained that the transition team was "a little unhappy," a surprised Ford pulled the Haig talking points from his pocket and exclaimed, "Why . . . here's what they gave me," obviously believing "they" to be his own closest advisers. Hartmann thought it "wasn't the right time to dissect the deception" and the incident passed.

At 5:30 P.M. that first day of the new presidency, Ford met again with Haig and the transition advisers, going down a checklist of schedule items and after each one uncertainly asking, "Al, what do you think of that?" As the Ford men remained silent, Haig reeled off his recommendations, ending with "if you think best, Mr. President" and invariably getting Ford's agreement. Only Kissinger, holding his certifying prestige and the mystique of foreign policy over the cowed former congressman, matched such influence in the first weeks. "We had to keep Haig, he had all the clout in the government," terHorst said later. "There was business in the pipelines . . . but we didn't even know where the pipelines were, and Haig made it clear that he'd been running the government for the last eight or ten months of the Nixon presidency."

Once more, and not for the last time, Haig benefited incalculably from the mediocrity and ignorance of the men around him at the higher levels. Here the consequences of weakness were momentous. Had Ford and his advisers, after watching the monthly decay of the regime for nearly a year, been genuinely ready for their responsibilities—had Haig then been politely and promptly reassigned, had the new president not been hostage at the beginning to his power, advice, or influence—the outcome of the Ford administration, the pardon, Haig's subsequent career, the Red scare in NATO, the resurgence of military budgets and the arms race, the disarray in Jimmy Carter's European diplomacy, the chauvinist tenor of the 1980 presidential campaign, the course of American history and foreign policy in particular over the next decade, all might have been rather different. Haig obviously did not alone determine that destiny, but his role and authority after 1974 were crucial conditions of events happening as they did. And for now in the opening moments of the new administration, "while President Ford happily posed for happy photographers," as reporter Richard Reeves marked the occasion even more bluntly than terHorst, "Alexander Haig and Henry Kissinger ran the country."

It was "unfair," and "mythology," Haig complained to reporters in mid-September when a rush of Ford staff leaks portrayed him as the continuing autocrat of the White House, though the press clips of the time would resemble closely the picture of Haig's power, albeit painted more sympathetically, in later books about the resignation. As holdover staff chief, he had been doing "essentially what I've always done in directing the flow of paper work to and from the President," he told the Associated Press.

The statement was accurate enough in a sense. Reeves and Hartmann, from different vantage points, later described Haig's style in dealing with former Pennsylvania governor, State Department envoy, and Ford adviser William Scranton when the president asked Scranton, not Haig, to brief him on White House operations. The general "volunteered to help" and offered to schedule a meeting with Scranton and Ford at 9:30 A.M. on August 10. But when Scranton arrived the next morning, he found Haig already closeted with Ford, having begun at 8:30 with orders not to be disturbed. "The fight had gone out of Scranton" and, never having told Ford of the incident, he went back to Pennsylvania "discouraged," recorded Hartmann.

At the same meeting, Haig used a "fat black briefing book" describing the White House in administrative detail down to assignments and pay, a system, said one newcomer, "nobody could possibly understand except Haig." Yet when Ford asked for a copy, Haig refused. "Incredibly," Hartmann remembered, "the General in mufti told the President of the United States he couldn't have it. It was Haig's only working copy!" Though Ford then "blandly" asked Haig to have copies made, neither he nor Hartmann ever received one.

"Quiet but rather imperious" as Osborne described his manner in the Ford White House, Haig could be still more aggressive with lesser officials than the commander in chief. When Buzhardt misled Ford on the issue of the tapes becoming Nixon's personal property, and when terHorst, after an embarrassing misrepresentation in turn to the press, announced Buzhardt's resignation August 15, Haig angrily confronted not Ford, who had fired the lawyer, but the press secretary, calling him "the little executioner." "Do you feel good executing a sick man?" Haig shouted at terHorst in allusion to Buzhardt's earlier heart attacks.

His bitterest rival, however, was Hartmann, who unleashed a steady barrage of critical leaks, matched, as one of the receiving journalists remarked, only by Haig-inspired columns about Hartmann's "incompetence and slipping status." "You've got to get this guy under control. Otherwise I can't serve you," Ford notes Haig telling him about Hartmann "on more than one occasion during my first month as president." Concluding it was Hartmann who "stirred the pot," Ford resolved to talk to his aide and implored the general, with his exclusive briefing book and knowledge of the "pipelines," to stay "at least a while longer."

Ron Nessen, an NBC reporter who succeeded as press secretary when terHorst resigned over the pardon, found Haig amid the court politics that autumn looking "cool and thoughtful but weary." To Nessen he defended himself as emerging with his "integrity intact" after Watergate, deplored the "bad-mouthing" by a Ford staff he doubted was "good enough" to run the White House, assured him Ziegler "never told a lie," and, pointing to his own head, called himself "a great computer," taking in and analyzing everything in the White House. Nessen was visibly impressed, and Hartmann thought him, unlike terHorst, a Haig "recruit to the Praetorian Guard."

Weeks after Ford's accession, in any case, only Nessen and three other Ford advisers had offices in the prestigious West Wing, the Nixon staff remained lodged in place, and the general's power seemed to some nearly total. With Ford's schedule and all memoranda in and out of the Oval Office controlled by Haig, Reeves wrote, "the Ford transition team couldn't even find out what decisions the President was being asked to make," an exclusion he saw as "the business of locking the new man into Nixon Administration policies." Hartmann and others saw Haig enter the Oval Office with "stacks" of memos on actions that "constitutionally only the president can direct," emerging later with the documents initialed "H" instead of the "southpaw GRF" Ford aides knew so well. Whether through "combat fatigue" or "force of habit," Hartmann noted, Haig had "neglected" to tell the president that his own initials were supposed to be on the decisions. Several federal officials explained to him, Reeves noted, that there was not much difference, after all, when presidents changed.

With all his apparent power in these first weeks, however, Haig remained, as it were, in hostile territory in the new Ford regime, and the battle took its toll. TerHorst described him as the "hardest hit" by Ford's comparative openness and candor with both the public and his associates. Occasionally, even Ford was moved to challenge the old style. When Haig assured the nervous new president there were no more bugs in the Oval Office, and after ten days in the room a staff informant furtively told Ford's assistants there were still microphones in the desk and walls, apparently unconnected but easily activated, Ford exploded, called Haig for a private dressing down, and ordered the apparatus removed by the next morning. Hartmann, too, had his revenge when he casually mentioned to Ford in early September the appointment of Nixon speechwriter Pat Buchanan as ambassador to South Africa, one of the decisions Haig had swept by the new president.

The Buchanan nomination was erased and memos eventually began coming out of the Oval Office with "GRF." Ford seems to have recognized Haig's differing policies as well, even if he was not always willing to confront the general administratively. Readying to announce in August his controversial amnesty for Vietnam draft evaders, the president deliberately bypassed Haig, who, when he finally read the speech on the plane to the VFW convention in Chicago, turned "white" in "anger and astonishment" and warned Ford, "They'll boo you." As the convention gave Ford a standing ovation, Hartmann recalled, Haig with the presidential party only "scowled."

By mid-September, Senators Griffin and Charles Goodell of New York as well as others were urging Ford to remove Haig. And as the staff infighting became more savage and public, the president finally moved. "I began to look at the broader picture," Ford said of Haig's departure in his memoirs. "[Haig] did possess a 'Nixon image.'" Typically, the exit was eased by more bureaucratic jockeying as well as issues of general politics or policy. Eager to replace Haig, succeed to the cabinet, and ultimately run for president, Don Rumsfeld, a former congressman and Nixon official who was Ford's friend as well, was now ready to return from a NATO ambassadorship to become the new chief of staff. His own grasp for power put his rising influence behind the general's swift, happy departure and thus Haig's request for a suitable job.

Hartmann observed that "contemporaries in the Army whom Nixon had jumped over in elevating Haig to Vice Chief of Staff didn't want him back at the Pentagon." Ford and his aides, and not least Haig himself, preferred to avoid a bruising Senate confirmation that might only rekindle Watergate. After discussing appointments as army chief of staff or secretary of the army, both requiring the feared confirmation, "we concluded that the best alternative was for Haig to take the NATO job," Ford wrote later. Hartmann noted similarly that "the NATO command was decided upon."

What neither admitted, and perhaps never knew, was that the prospect of Haig as SACEUR, a potentially important foreign-policy proconsul in Europe, had initially enraged the other indispensable figure of the infant administration, Secretary Kissinger. When Kissinger threatened to veto the posting with his own enormous cachet despite the advantage of avoiding a confirmation probe and despite the consensus of Ford, Rumsfeld, and Haig, the appointment hung in what one high-ranking State Department aide remembered as a "twenty-four-hour limbo." According to Kissinger assistants, Haig then "stormed into Henry's office and had a little talk about what could come out" in a Senate hearing or a series of leaks. Looming over that conversation with his old boss were all the shadows they had cast together, yet so far publicly escaped—the truth of the wiretaps; Kissinger's (and Haig's) liaison with the plumbers, which the secretary had solemnly denied to the Foreign Relations Committee under oath; the long trail of sordid policies not yet exposed. "It took about a half an hour," said one Kissinger confidante of the talk that September, "and Henry saw what a great NATO supreme commander Al would make."

Leaked and then formally announced in late September 1974, Haig's appointment drew a flurry of criticism that centered on his Watergate role more than his military qualifications for the command. The mercurial Joseph Kraft thought the general was connected with a "mountain of dirty work." The *Washington Post* editorialized that he was Nixon's "principal aide in the later cover-up years," adding that "few people seriously argue . . . that General Haig . . . is uniquely qualified for the job," and asking pointedly why Haig was more fit for NATO than Buchanan for South Africa. A handful of Democratic senators called for an Armed Services Committee inquiry, but Haig was rescued from even that feeble opposition by old liaisons. Committee Chairman Stennis called Jaworski to solicit a letter from the prosecutor saying he "knew of nothing that . . . rendered Haig culpable." With Jaworski's testimonial in hand, Stennis then overrode his colleagues, although the prosecutor's investigation had concentrated on the pre-Haig era at the White House, leaving the foreign-policy connections and the post–April 1973 period untouched after the pardon.

Hartmann recorded amid all this that the reward "involved a rather brutal eviction" of the incumbent SACEUR, General Goodpaster. Abroad, the London *Economist* called Goodpaster "one of the most distinguished . . . NATO commanders" who was "only 59 and has given no sign that he wants to retire yet." It was strange, thought the magazine, that Ford should "force out a popular and effective commander in favor of a controversial officer who lacks the most valuable credential of all—command experience." But the publicity soon faded, and the transfer was secure.

Meanwhile, back in the White House, Nessen saw staff conditions "close to anarchy" as Haig's grip fell away from the Oval Office. Indeed, before he left on November 1 for his old posting at Stuttgart, where he would first be U.S. European commander, and then to Brussels as SACEUR on December 15, Haig himself seemed to drift. "Poor Al just wandered around here for a week," a White House aide told Reeves, "he didn't know what to do with himself."

As Haig left for NATO at the close of 1974, the *Washington Post* grumbled in an editorial about Nixon's "spent men being packed off to comfortable government jobs." It was another case of underestimating the man and what he might make of his opportunity. At fifty, restored to four-star rank and a bureaucratic power base, Haig was hardly "spent." Nor was the job necessarily "comfortable." Across the jagged cold-war frontier arbitrarily dividing Europe, a million and a half men faced each other in a state of permanent mobilization, engaging the partisan fears, politics, budgets, and survival of the wealthiest and most powerful societies on earth. An intensely political command, the NATO posting was no less important militarily. In the sophistication, economy, and generalship of the Allied force was at least part of the arsenal that both kept the peace and risked war for the Continent and al-

most certainly for the world beyond. The importance of
the front had not saved it from the postwar atrophy of
the American officer corps. A succession of less ambitious
and astute soldiers had come and gone from the command
of that ominous frontier over the past quarter-century
with little fanfare, except for Dwight Eisenhower (whose
fame derived mainly from the earlier war), and with
scarce individual impact, leaving the alliances on both
sides to strain and creak as they settled into imperial
stalemate. But for Haig, the role of SACEUR was less
sinecure or even sentinel than a vehicle back to the
more sweeping power of Washington, and he would
use the substantial potential in the mission. How he conducted the job thus became both an epitaph on his military career and a preview of his style and substance as
secretary of state.

His appointment as a "political general" and "Watergate refugee" drew quiet yet sharp criticism among Europeans. NATO delegations muted their official opposition
only in deference to the new president in Washington, and
at that the Dutch foreign minister openly pronounced
Haig's promotion "a public relations disaster." Dismay
was still worse in the American forces, whose 300,000
army, air force, and navy personnel Haig would now lead.
To "many command officers," the *Washington Post* found
that September, Haig's transfer "is clearly a bitter pill"
and "sentiment . . . is overwhelmingly hostile" about the
general's obviously political promotions and slim command experience.

Returning to Stuttgart amid that resentment, little
more than fifteen years after he left it as a major whose
main European defense experience was in billet negotia-

tions, Haig encountered the perhaps inevitable bureaucratic backlash. When his dog, Duncan, was chauffeured
130 miles by two enlisted men in an army staff car, the
privilege of rank was promptly leaked, moving a congressman to complain and the embarrassed new commander
to pay for Duncan's trip, order "counseling of the individuals concerned," and promise an "investigation of related possible abuses." Less than a month later, a similar
leak revealed that the general had brought along cases of
vodka and wine incorrectly labeled "glassware," a violation of army rules which a spokesman said was committed
"innocently and inadvertently," and again Haig anted up
to repay the government.

Along with Duncan and the contraband liquor, Kissinger and Watergate ghosts also came indiscreetly in his
baggage. Early in his tenure, congressional committees
began to expose parts of the Chile story, while in the
spring of 1975 special prosecutors readied to recall both
Haig and Buzhardt to testify before a federal grand jury
about the controversial and often dubious transcription
of the presidential tapes released by Nixon the previous
spring.

At the end of March 1975, Haig even quietly flew home
for a weekend visit with Nixon in San Clemente to discuss
the possible further testimony and the ex-president's plans
for memoirs. On the way back he saw Ford, and again
there was a moment of the old dash. Hanoi's final spring
offensive had broken over Vietnam. The northern troops
left by Kissinger's peace treaty were plunging south, pre-
ceded by the flight of the corrupt and crippled ARVN,
pitiful hordes of refugees, and the small army of the
Saigon regime's American-bred profiteers, honking their

way through the exodus in Mercedeses. The South was
now at last cut off from further U.S. intervention, the cost
of the dishonest, often illegal war policy. And now in the
face of the worst retreat since Hungnam, the general gave
Gerald Ford some advice.

"I told the President what he should do," Haig recalled
it later for *Esquire*. "Go on TV. Take it to the public. Roll
up his sleeves and *put the monkey where it belonged*, in
the Congress. Say, okay, this is what's happening, and
it's the Congress' fault. We've got legislative anarchy in
this country, and I need the support of the *American people*. He didn't do that, and that's . . . [here *Esquire* recorded the SACEUR stabbing his finger in the air in the
1978 interview] . . . that's where he lost the presidency. . . .
Right there. It would've worked, and he would have been
the most popular president of our time." The general's
eyes "twinkled," noted the interviewer, as he came to a
conclusion. "It would have been," Haig told him in a
strange parallel, "a real Truman number."

As Vietnam fell and Watergate dimmed, however, he
found his own fresh controversies. He wanted "to be
judged on my performance, not on how I got here," Haig
told reporters when he took over NATO headquarters in
Belgium in December 1974. But the new start seemed
largely inauspicious. The general announced almost casually in an early 1975 interview that a U.S. Army brigade
would be stationed for the first time in northern Germany,
and did not bother to inform the Germans in advance.
The move "smacked of American insensitivity," said one
account, and clearly angered German defense officials
around whom NATO's delicate military diplomacy now
centered. When similarly unannounced Haig visits to

German military maneuvers in the same period annoyed Bonn still more, Haig received a bitter censure for his lack of tact from his old antagonist, Defense Secretary Schlesinger, during the latter's swing through Europe.

By the autumn of 1975, Schlesinger was gone, another enemy survived, a casualty of his own mismanagement, Ford's dislike, and the Pentagon and congressional under-cutting of well-placed officer corps enemies like Haig. But by then, too, the new SACEUR was in more diplomatic difficulty. Taking his cue from Kissinger's strong public stance against Eurocommunism in the winter of 1975–76, and especially against Communist participation in French or Italian governments after elections later in 1976, Haig issued a series of dire warnings about the danger of Communist regimes in NATO. The remarks provoked ringing nationalist rebukes from both Rome and Paris, the French foreign minister reminding Haig (rather belatedly) that "it is not up to a military leader to take a position on political questions. . . ." He was chided also by *The New York Times* for "hectoring allies" and "admonitions" that "can only play into the hands of the Communists and make it more difficult to keep them out."

As a Communist-Socialist alliance registered important gains in France's local elections in March, it was plain the U.S. pressure had backfired. By early summer, after the exposé of $6 million in CIA subsidies to Italian politicians, Kissinger himself retreated, though only to find his former aide once more conducting his own diplomacy and not easily controlled. When Haig remarked that Communist participation in the Italian government would be "unacceptable," the State Department gingerly termed the statement "volunteered" and "not authorized." If Kissinger ruefully shared the observation in the *Nation* that the general was indeed "making policy instead of applying the directives he gets from his civilian superiors," he did not care to acknowledge it.

Though the Eurocommunism alarm faded in turn, there now seemed a visible difference in Haig's position at NATO. Often shrill and diplomatically inept if not insubordinate, he had won by his very stridency approval and support among his allied military constituency, or at least was thought to have won it by a press whose views of the general now noticeably mellowed from the harshness of Watergate or the Ford staff leaks. After a train of dour, meek commanders, Haig cut a dashing figure. From the otherwise drab headquarters near Mons, forty miles from Brussels with road signs pointing to shrines of battle—Waterloo, Dunkirk, and Bastogne—he emerged in tailor-made combat fatigues and what one impressed reporter called "a spiffy raised-eagle belt buckle that no GI would be permitted to wear." The outspoken manner and the carefully pressed fatigues were modern variants on the Dai Ichi style, but the effect seemed undiminished.

By May 1977, the once critical *Washington Post* reported that "most of the NATO hierarchy" had made a virtue of Haig's "political" credentials. He was thought "bright, attractive and obviously well connected," said the paper, with a photo of Haig captioned simply ". . . articulate, competent." "Ironically," the *Post* went on, "some of the growing respect for the General . . . has also come from an unexpected source," a new book called *The Final Days*. Portrayed by Woodward and Bernstein as "tireless, unflappable and eventually as the skillful stage-manager of the resignation of a battered president," as the *Post* explained it, Haig was now seen in a wholly new light by appreciative allies.

Before the *Post* dispatch, the *Frankfurter Allgemeine* had called the Haig portrait in the book "of special significance for Europeans." Haig, said a column in the influential German paper, was "a mixture of a brilliant modern general staff officer and a far-sighted Machiavelli . . . a living computer who, in the final days of the Nixon administration, may have established for himself the basis for a political career that may lead to his moving into the White House someday."

Commenting more modestly, Haig told the *Post*, "I don't see myself as unique. I've been in a position that's been unique by happenstance. I'm a trained soldier, public servant, and that's the limit of my aspirations."

But there were "new strategic currents stirring these days" at NATO, the paper noted, including talk of the alliance reaching out to combat Soviet gains in Africa or elsewhere beyond its "established geographical charter." Haig talked ominously about political "evolution" in Portugal and Spain, Greece and Turkey, but he was also newly circumspect. "I'm only one-fifteenth American in this job," he reassured the *Post* and its anxious State Department readers. But if things were already better, he added in recognizable style, "it doesn't mean we don't have a plethora of meaty difficulties to deal with."

If the general now acquired a fresh image and better press notices, he had also found the issue that would fire his revival. The great task for the West, Haig said in a Canadian Broadcasting Corporation interview duly given to *The New York Times* early in 1976, "is managing global Soviet power." Detente "can never be a substitute" for strength, he said in an open reproof to Kissinger and an echo of MacArthur. Debates over negotiation with Moscow were "far less relevant" than understanding that the West is "confronted" with "a global Soviet military capability" that "must be managed. . . ." The theme was at odds with much of the Nixon-Kissinger posture toward the Russians, and represented a land-army version of the naval alarms Zumwalt had sounded for the first four years of the decade only to be muffled by Haig as chamberlain or regent. But now as field marshal and pretender, he discovered the Red menace and the perils of detente, as it were, with a vengeance.

Through the autumn of 1976, as Ford fought for his political life in the presidential campaign and Haig's own prospects seemed uncertain with his two-year tour as U.S. European commander ending in November, he continued a drum roll of warnings. In September he called in *The New York Times's* venerable and obliging military correspondent, Drew Middleton, to deplore NATO's "reduced warning time" and "the relentless improvement of the Warsaw Pact capability." In October he was in Washington addressing the Army Association on the "relentless growth in sheer Soviet military power" and his own urgent effort "to break the grip of the long-standing complacency" about NATO, another speech more resembling an opposition candidate's than that of a Ford administration appointee. The speech again brushed both his history and a portent of the future. Haig condemned what he called "a garrison mentality" among NATO troops, almost an evocation of his own garrison life long ago in Japan when slackness proved so costly. At the same time, he cautioned against any "hasty change" in doctrine, a defense of his own plans for improving readiness in the face of even more harsh critics of NATO unpreparedness, Georgia Democratic Senator Sam Nunn who would be a later Haig ally, and Lieutenant General James Hollingsworth, his old commander at Ap Gu and now a former commander in South Korea who had derided the European force in a recent secret report to the army staff. The rhetoric should not be excessive, he implied, to the point where Haig's own record and exploitation of the issue were threatened. Days after Ford's defeat by Jimmy Carter, the general was at New York's Economic Club to talk about the Russians' "dynamic progress" in weaponry, their "global threat to Western lifelines," and their new "imperialistic phase."

Ford extended Haig's U.S. European Command by two more years on November 12, technically for the moment still a lame-duck appointment. While both the U.S. and the NATO posts were customarily held by the same officer, SACEUR was of indefinite term at the president's pleasure and Carter could replace him at Mons after January 20. In Paris later in November, however, Haig was jaunty about his continued tenure amid the Republican defeat. "My friend Henry Kissinger is like the earth," he joked with a society reporter about the election "a sphere . . . flattened at the polls." And to a question about the effects of the election of a new Democratic president on his command, he gave a reply that, considering his career, seems somewhat incredible: "I'm not aware that they do or should have any. There is a traditional exclusion of the military from political affairs," said Alexander Haig, "and I hope it will continue."

He spoke more from a bureaucrat's calculated confidence than any profound irony. In carefully placed interviews ten days before and three days after Carter's inauguration, he warned of the "global dimensions" of the Soviet threat, the prospect that the Western deterrent "could ultimately collapse," and his frontier soldier's certainty that Moscow had not "rejected the possibility of a nuclear conflict." Backed by Senator Nunn, Carter's fellow Georgian, and other conservative southern congressmen uneasy about the new president's military resolve, he now represented to the incoming regime less a relic of the Kissinger-Nixon-Watergate past than a litmus test of its own toughness. Moreover, in the ceaseless incest of the foreign-policy establishment, he had powerful allies and patrons in the "new" administration: Carter's secretary of state, Cyrus Vance, his old superior at the Pentagon; Califano as the secretary of health, education and welfare; and, not least, Harold Brown, a Pentagon house scientist whom Haig had quietly favored when Brown was a member of the Nixon SALT delegation. Brown, as an erstwhile Johnson air-force secretary, had approved Haig's zeal for bombing in Indochina, and now, as the new secretary of defense, shared Haig's passion for higher military budgets and saw the general as a convenient counterweight to the warring factions he would encounter among the Joint Chiefs and Carter's NSC staff.

When the politics of foreign policy were understood in that light, when it was grasped that past party records and alliances meant far less than the expedients and myths of the moment, that bureaucratic ties meant far more than political or ideological loyalties in any case, that vacillating presidents remained hostage to the clubmen they hired to govern, Haig's continuation as NATO commander under Jimmy Carter was not surprising. It was his removal that would have been truly unusual. After all, Haig had explained, he was not a "Nixonite."

Not that his presence under the new regime was without its incongruities. Anthony Lake, the old colleague he had wiretapped, returned now as Vance's director of policy planning; and Richard Moose, whose ties to the "traitor" Senator Fulbright he had once denounced, came back to State in administration, then African affairs. (As Moose's friend, Eagleburger, like Haig, survived the presidential change, quietly moving from his position as Kissinger's key aide to become ambassador to Yugoslavia.) But for the moment, the uncertain men of the Democratic restoration needed Haig as he needed them, and there was no genuine opposition to his retention.

By June 1977, *The New York Times*'s James Reston certified Haig's position in a column aptly entitled "The Lone Survivor." Watergate was now history. "All that, he seemed to be saying," Reston recorded from a carefully answered interview at Mons, "was in the past." Now the general was concentrating on the Soviet problem. In sharp contrast to his later position as secretary of state, but now with his new commander in chief in mind, he told Reston there was undoubted virtue in the Carter emphasis on human rights, which had "clarified the philosophical conflict between East and West" and moved the alliance members to improve their defenses. But then, many of the issues facing NATO were "political," Haig demurred, and "therefore beyond his authority."

In the early autumn of 1977, another awkward ghost broke in briefly from the dismissed past. A House investigation revealed that as early as the winter of 1971–72 Haig and Kissinger had received three different memos from Hoover outlining "criminal activities" by South Korean intelligence agents in Washington, including bribery of both congressmen and congressional staff to the tune of more than $400,000. The top-secret "eyes only" documents were opened only by Haig and Kissinger, and no others on the NSC staff "had ever been consulted with regard to these matters," the investigators found. But the crucial information, the early silhouette of what came to be known as the "Koreagate" scandal of lobbying corruption, was never acted upon by the powerful men in the West Basement. Haig testified simply that he had "no recollection" of the memos, which in any case he would have left to the FBI. As it was, the scandal was not exposed until more than three years afterward when State Department officials, inundated with reports of bribery, finally brought in the Justice Department.

Behind the corruption and its neglect was the shadow of an old Haig-Kissinger squabble with Laird, who advocated the reduction of U.S. troops in Korea, and Haig's opposition to any similar reduction of Pentagon aid to the Seoul dictatorship of General Park Chung Hee. Left to flourish, the Korean CIA bribery after 1972 had held off congressional pressures to reduce the troops and the aid. At the least, the seamy record uncovered by the House showed once more that the same Haig who read the wiretap transcripts so diligently and testified at the Ellsberg trial was not always so stern, or so ready to take the initiative, when informed of subversion. But the investigation halted, stymied by what a final House study deplored as the absence of any "institutional memory" of the NSC as a governmental body. If Haig's or Kissinger's telephone transcripts shed any light on the issue, they, of course, were not available. There were no memoranda or other documents in the files, all of them having been destroyed or shipped out with Nixon's and Kissinger's papers, and perhaps with what Hartmann discovered Haig to have evacuated of his own files. Less than two weeks after the Korean story broke, Haig was back with the *Times*'s Middleton assuring Americans and their allies that the warning time for a Soviet attack on Western Europe was not so short after all, that "Russian readiness to attack . . . might not be as high as some past estimates had held." And SACEUR's porous memory about Korean payoffs on Capitol Hill disappeared into an unread 1978 congressional report. The subject did not arise during his confirmation to be secretary of state.

While Haig's prestige seemed to grow, the popularity of the new president fell steadily after his first year in office. From stalled SALT talks to equivocations on human rights to heated controversy on the Panama Canal, Carter's foreign-policy leadership in particular came under mounting criticism from both left and right in Congress and the media. It was against that backdrop in the spring of 1978 that Haig skillfully turned his own bureaucratic fire on the floundering regime, and began to clear a political path back to Washington.

The issue at hand was the neutron bomb, in some respects the perfect instrument for a clash between an aggressive frontline general and a temporizing White House. Part of a second generation of more sophisticated nuclear arms, the neutron weapon was not a "bomb" in the usual sense, but rather a small warhead producing significantly more radiation and less explosive blast than earlier atomic charges. It was designed to fit the same short-range lance missiles and howitzers then armed by the 7,000 older U.S. tactical nuclear warheads in NATO. Because it might kill an enemy army on the battlefield without necessarily destroying or contaminating surrounding areas, it was supposed at SACEUR headquarters to be a more politically acceptable and thus strategically credible deterrent in populous Central Europe. Moreover, Haig and a faction of Pentagon, State Department, congressional, and NATO officials all ardently championed the neutron device as a ready response to the old bugbear of the alliance, the Russians' 50,000–17,000 superiority in tanks.

Development of the weapon began under Nixon and Ford, but when Carter requested funds for actual production in 1977, the warheads became public and set off popular protests in Western Europe among Communists and non-Communists alike. The furor pushed Carter to defer production or deployment until controversy subsided, especially in West Germany where the weapons would be based, where the protests were loudest, and where the Bonn government quietly favored the weapon as a cheap answer to military modernization yet was typically loath to make public its approval before the Americans announced production and absorbed the political clamor. After a first flurry of publicity in mid-1977, the issue did fade from the news. Haig and European bureaucrats continued to fence on the subject over the following winter, and the Germans eventually gave their discreet approval for deployment, the NATO military constituency apparently taking for granted that Carter's decision in favor of the bomb would follow.

On March 1, 1978, Haig warmly endorsed the new weapon in testimony before the Senate Armed Services Committee, telling Nunn and other approving members that his NATO colleagues "are of one mind" in wanting the neutron bomb. He returned to the theme again at a March 21 Pentagon news conference, claiming that "we are experiencing a problem of a rather dramatic shift in the nuclear balance" and that the neutron warhead "raises, not lowers, the nuclear threshold." Under questioning, he admitted that the Soviets had not yet deployed tactical nuclear weapons to match or overtake NATO's clear superiority, but praised the neutron warhead for "its usability, its credibility . . . a system more discriminating." Although deployment was a "political question," he told the reporters, "from a purely military point of view we feel it is a most desirable modernization step."

By late March, however, it became clear at both the Pentagon and Mons that the already weakened Carter was backing away from the decision to produce and deploy. The White House had canceled a NATO meeting scheduled at that point to discuss the issue. Cables to SACEUR outlined Carter's misgivings about the effect of the neutron bomb on the larger arms race, the ambivalence in West Germany, and technological and production timetable questions that made a decision "not quite as urgent as it seems."

As the commander in chief pondered his order, however, he now came under what one newspaper column later called with no intended irony "a firestorm of criticism." On April 1, *The New York Times* reported from Brussels allied "uneasiness and bewilderment" over the "wavering and dissension" in Washington. Based on leaks from "a representative number of senior alliance officials" who "as usual did not want to be identified," the *Times* dispatch made plain the danger in Carter's indecision for the "military balance" in Europe, and quoted no other officials or views. An accompanying *Times* "news analysis" by Richard Burt, the paper's political-military affairs correspondent and an admirer of Haig's, stressed the view of certain highly placed and authoritative U.S. officials that the president's "deferral" was "a huge mistake," had been "as badly handled as any question in recent history," left "a deep scar in alliance relations," and added to troublesome "doubts" about Jimmy Carter as a leader.

The NATO leak now triggered a week of scathing press attacks on Carter's policy, chiefly from the *Times* and the *Washington Post* and drawn overwhelmingly from anonymous sources on both sides of the Atlantic. Depicted as bungling and irresolute, his regime in disarray, European allies "vexed" in a climate of "disorder, disillusionment and incredulity," the American military suffering "shock waves of dismay and anxiety," President Carter, concluded the *Times*, had been "made to look foolish." Few episodes "have been more disturbing." Though Carter then announced under the barrage that "development" of the weapon would continue and that deployment was only being conditioned on responses from the Russians, the critics—journalists as well as powerful and ubiquitous leakers—were unappeased. NATO reaction, the *Times* reported on April 8, was still "tart and scathing."

In a companion story that day, the *Times*'s Washington bureau reported fleetingly that certain unnamed "officials" had been moving "along a track Mr. Carter had not approved and was shocked to discover" in the diplomacy of the neutron bomb. Flashing by and then gone was the shape of Haig's backroom politicking and unauthorized commitments with the Germans and his campaign with both the press and Congress. But the more dramatic, the more embedded theme was Carter's ineptness. The neutron episode was seemingly another part of that growing image, and the tangled bureaucratic politics of the event went unexplored.

Were there reasons to doubt the Germans, to bargain with the Soviets for arms-control concessions, to suspect bureaucratic insubordination or political motives? Was the weapon what Haig and others claimed? Only three months after the April agitation, the *Los Angeles Times* would report from London the scientific findings that the "deadliest" conventional weapons were "now more powerful than the smallest nuclear warheads," a development that had "made obsolete a key argument over whether or not to deploy the neutron bomb." And if the controversy left such a "deep scar" on alliance relations, why had the subject disappeared so completely from the corridors of the NATO ministerial meeting late that May in Washington, where both officials and reporters were absorbed in Haig's dire briefings about atrocities in Zaire and Soviet mischief in Africa?

All these questions and more were continually ignored in a shallow journalism that found more titillation in official backbiting and the cliché of Carter's incompetence. Nor was the West's commanding general likely to volunteer the answers or point up the complexity of the issue.

On April 25, both the *Post* and the *Times* ran reports from anonymous "government sources" that General Haig had threatened to quit over the administration's "handling

of several defense issues, including the . . . neutron bomb."
"Upset," said the *Times*, that "a small group in State and
the Pentagon and the White House was making decisions
in isolation," the fifty-three-year-old commander was dis-
suaded only by new promises of support and extended
tenure from a beleaguered administration "aware of General Haig's popularity among West European political
and military leaders [and aware] that the abrupt departure
of General Haig could weaken the alliance."

The next day, SACEUR duly denied threatening to
resign but confirmed that he was asked "to stay on" for
another two years when his European command (and
nominally the NATO post) expired again in October
1978. "I won't judge the value judgments of Pentagon
speculation and gossip," Haig told reporters asking about
his politically charged gesture of resignation. He simply
wanted to remain at NATO "as long as I can make a contribution." It had all been, concluded the *Christian Century* magazine some weeks later, "a classic case . . . a
friendly journalist passes along supportive phrases from
unnamed sources to build up a general who appears to
have attacked his Commander-in-Chief from behind pro-
tective anonymity."

The formal renewal of his appointment by Carter
would be announced in October 1978, and meanwhile he
continued to campaign, sometimes publicly, sometimes
privately, on issues that burnished his image of toughness
vis-à-vis the Soviet Union, and marked often subtle but
real differences with his Democratic civilian superiors.
In May 1978, fresh from his political triumph on the neutron bomb, he denounced Moscow's "gluttony" in aiding
African guerrilla groups, and called for a concentration of

the West's "vast political, economic and military resources" in the third world. Though nominally part of
wider administration policy that summer to lift the congressional arms embargo imposed on Turkey in 1974 after
its invasion of Cyprus, he took a notably harder line than
Vance or Brown, flatly denying to the Armed Services
Committee $30 million in shady NATO sales to Turkey
that technically contravened the embargo and that Vance
had admitted in testimony hours before. Resuming the
arms flow to Turkey, he told *The New York Times*, was
his most "grievous concern," and the continuing embargo
had "incalculable" consequences.

In September he complained openly to reporters about
a "decade of neglect" at NATO, encompassing all three
of his presidential employers—Nixon, Ford and Carter—
in the indictment, but adding that he felt "cautious op-
timism" on the basis of the changes he had made in the
Alliance's military posture. A month later, he was calling
the current reduction in shipbuilding an "unacceptable
risk" (a statement Admiral Zumwalt at least would have
found ironic in retrospect). And though "Haig did not
directly criticize Carter Administration policy on the matter," noted the Associated Press, his view seemed indis-
tinguishable from Carter's "critics."

As if to underscore the protean nature of such politics,
the general went to Paris at the end of November to visit
an old friend who found the Democrats wanting as well.
For ninety minutes at the Ritz Hotel he met with Richard
Nixon, now a private citizen touring the Continent. "We
did some reminiscing and exchanged views about the
situation in Europe," Haig told waiting reporters. Later,

Nixon told aides that he had advised the general "to run, and to run hard."

Reporters and other visitors now found him more than ever the confident, attractive, vigorous commander, visiting troops in the field more than any predecessor, imparting enthusiasm to subordinate officers, but at home, too, in the $65,000 Mercedes limousine, the personal DC-9 jet, and the eighteenth-century château that were SACEUR's luxurious perquisites. There was also the displayed power of being privy to ominous secrets about Soviet forces that he could reveal only in the urgency of his policy warnings. It was the old mystique of national security. "I'd only say that if you knew everything I know, you'd agree with everything I'm about to say," he told a visiting group from the Council on Foreign Relations late in 1978. There were also quotable one-liners for such audiences: "The arms race is the only game in town." "The next war could be a come-as-you-are party." "Did you see Hal Brown's statement last week where he said we'd left an essentially stable situation in Southeast Asia?" he asked one reporter, smiling in what the writer saw as "world weariness" with the folly of his superiors.

Not all guests accepted his style easily. Hearing Haig lecture on the failings and ignorance of Congress, a recurrent theme, Republican Senator William Scott of Virginia once slammed his hand down on SACEUR's conference table, shaking the microphones that recorded the commander's every word for posterity and protection, and said sternly, "General Haig, I hear arrogance coming out of your mouth." More often, however, the general's manner, and especially his history, were unquestioned in the prevailing cynicism or indifference of press and politicians. *Esquire* portrayed him and his cowed guests laughing heartily when he was asked about the tape-recorded meetings. "Oh, I never think of not taping," Haig responded, to more laughter. One of those reportedly enjoying the joke was Laurence Silberman, lately Ford's ambassador to Yugoslavia but in the spring of 1974 the deputy attorney general who recorded in a memorandum Haig's improper effort from the White House to curtail Jaworski's investigation. Later, the same *Esquire* writer described Haig in an apparently routine protocol occasion with U.S. Ambassador to Luxembourg James Lowenstein; amid the official smiles, it was forgotten that Lowenstein has been one of the Foreign Relations Committee investigators deliberately misled by the general about the U.S. Embassy's secret direction of B-52 targeting in Cambodia in 1973.

He was "not bashful" about claiming credit for NATO improvements, noted another reporter. "Let us review the situation as I found it four years ago," Haig began a typical press conference in the fall of 1978. There followed an oft-repeated recital of Soviet arms spending and what Haig commonly termed his "core accomplishment," an agreement by NATO countries to counter the Russians by increasing military spending by 3 percent a year. NATO had added great numbers of new antitank weapons and ninety-six sophisticated F-15 fighter aircraft. Under Haig's "three Rs," he had introduced a program to overcome the garrison mentality and improve combat readiness, to rationalize plans of the separate forces, and to speed the arrival of reinforcements. He had also expanded the size and sophistication of NATO maneuvers—all to the applause of other allied officers and approving journalists on military affairs who found good stories both in the improvements and maneuvers as well as Haig's evident "comeback" in popularity.

Yet there was another side of the lauded NATO record that was seldom seen. The actual proposal for the 3-percent spending increase had come from Carter, with the credit falling to Haig in the Continent's growing disillusionment with the president. "Only in answer to a later question," *The New Republic* reported from a Haig press conference on the subject in 1978, "did he allow that 'I do not feel exclusively responsible for the progress we've made.'"

The maneuvers involving hundreds of thousands and colorful dispatches were also criticized sharply in European parliaments for being provocative, expensive, and, as one reporter put it, "advertisements for General Haig." Within NATO there remained lethal weakness beyond the outward glitter of the new SACEUR. Ammunition, radios, spare parts, and even fuel were not yet interchangeable among the fourteen member forces. Deployment policies and strategic plans were chronic problems unaffected by Haig's claims. The Alliance was "such a mess," declared one German officer reviewing its problems for a visiting writer in 1978, "the only thing that will save it in a war is the responsibility of the soldiers to disobey their orders."

Finally, there was the root question of the enemy's strength, the staple on which Haig traded as a political general at NATO. With its 177 divisions to the Allied 71, with 3,000 tactical aircraft to NATO's 1,600, a three-to-one advantage in tanks, and four-to-one in artillery, the

Soviet forces loomed in SACEUR's speeches like a colossus over the West, exercising its spell on behalf of bigger budgets and more resolute presidents. But there was another Russian opponent as well. Backed by uncertain allies and with restive Poland in its strategic rear, that force would attack down the three primary and perhaps six secondary routes into the West, heralded by electronic intelligence and soon to face a fully mobilized German army almost the size of its own, as well as the world's most sophisticated, effective antitank weapons. The power of a prepared defense against the massive tank assault that was and is the orthodoxy of the Warsaw Pact would be shown in the Arab-Israeli war of 1973. While Haig had been intent on Watergate prosecutors and a sodden chief executive unable to order an alert, the Israelis had destroyed nearly 900 Syrian tanks in four days with a force half the Syrian size. Between them, Israel and the Arabs had also lost in two weeks of fighting more than the equivalent of two years of tank production in both the U.S. and USSR.

Yet locked in the glamour and convention of the massed tank battle, Haig at NATO five years later earnestly prepared to fight the last war. Ignored were both the vulnerability of Soviet forces to economic defense and the gathering obsolescence and exorbitant cost of the tank and even of tactical aircraft, all in an era of surging technology when a $10,000 missile can destroy a $2-million tank or $20-million fighter. But then, such ambiguous realities were not the stuff of dramatic press conferences and congressional testimony, or the raiment of a fighting commander.

By 1978, in any case, Haig was clearly looking beyond

NATO proper, and beyond his present command. "More aroused by actual Communist advances in South Yemen than by potential ones into Schleswig-Holstein," one journalist described him that autumn. He saw a pattern of subversion from the Soviet take-over of guerrilla movements to aid from satellites to eventual open Soviet intervention. "There should be greater concertion [sic] to insure that the collective political, economic and security strengths [of the West] are displayed in ways to show the Soviets that these third-world intrusions are just as unacceptable as aggressive activity here," he told a reporter interviewing him in Germany. But when pressed for specific policies, he remained vague. "I am not suggesting interventionism. Far from it. We've all experienced what unfortunate results that can lead to," he said in the same interview. It must be done "by hard policies—interface policies, resource policies, security policies . . . by the application of will in areas where we are vastly superior." And what about the Carter administration? he would be asked frequently. And back came the polite answer: "I never indulge in value judgments of the American administration."

By the close of 1978, he was ready to leave NATO. The battle lines were already drawn with a weary Carter regime that had begun belatedly to fight back bureaucratically. He learned of the provisions of SALT II only at the same time as the European allies, the White House deliberately excluding him in anticipation of his opposition to the restrictions on deployment of the cruise missile and the controversial MX mobile missiles until the end of 1981. In a stream of telegrams to Washington, he had recommended that the U.S. actively encourage the Iranian military to take control of the country from the tottering shah. But when Carter finally dispatched Haig's aide, General Robert Huyser, to Teheran in the last days of the dynasty, it was with vague orders and a neutrality SACEUR deplored. Carter's timidity in Iran, he told one journalist, made him "wistful for the Eisenhower years."

At a New Year's press conference billed as an update on the East-West military balance, he startled reporters with the announcement that he had sent his resignation to Carter only hours before, depriving the White House of the timing and description of his departure. There would be no humiliating orders like those delivered from Truman to the Dai Ichi nearly three decades before. He was not resigning in "protest," as he later claimed. He refused to be drawn into a discussion of SALT II, saying he would make "a value assessment" later. Otherwise, he repeated his stock warnings about Soviet aggression, and referred twice in passing to "my friend Dr. Henry Kissinger." But his intentions seemed plain. Routinely provided to reporters and others, his autobiographical sketch after his resignation would read that "he has built a reputation as being the finest NATO commander since Dwight D. Eisenhower." One journalist at the resignation press conference described him afterward as "the most politically oriented, if not politically ambitious, American military man to hold the allied command in the last 36 years."

A senior British officer on Haig's staff remarked to a reporter, "You know, when I talk to Al Haig just conversationally I always get the feeling that in everything he says he is thinking about someplace else—the White House."

Before he was gone, however, there was one last act of battlefield drama to climax his army career. At about 8:30 A.M. five days before his departure, halfway between his home and headquarters on a secondary road Haig traveled only occasionally, his Mercedes was crossing a small fifty-foot bridge over a culvert when a deafening explosion shattered the road in a crater three feet deep and ten feet wide. Haig's limousine was thrown to the side but remained upright, Haig, his driver and adjutant unhurt, while the trailing security car was damaged and the three Belgian and American bodyguards injured. His car had missed the mine detonation by what he called in a press conference later at headquarters "a fraction of a second." A length of detonating wire and a walkie-talkie were discovered near the scene, but the would-be assassins were never traced further and no group, unusual for European terrorists, claimed responsibility. For his part, Haig joked about his narrow escape in light of his rumored presidential candidacy. "I don't think I have quite enough support in the United States at the moment to justify such drastic action," he told reporters. But he called the attack more somberly a "strong reminder" of the terrorist threat.

The attack obviously still affected him when he gave a final news conference at the transfer of the NATO Command on June 30. Unleashing a verbal attack on the Soviet Union, he charged the Russians with "a large measure of responsibility for this international disease" of terrorism "with which we are all plagued today." He went on about the "virulent forces" at work in the world and "Soviet paranoia" over the Chinese—remarks that went, said the *Washington Post*," "far beyond those tra-

ditionally expected of military officers and undoubtedly
. . . a preview of the line he will espouse as he enters
civilian life and a possible shot at high political office."
On that subject, Haig spoke in characteristic terms: "As
of now I have no political plans," he said. "When I return
home I intend to speak out publicly on the concerns that I
depart [sic] here within the security area. I will assess
the productivity of such public statements and continue
them or terminate them depending on the contribution
they do or do not make."

The news conference, thought the *Post*, was also "emotional and combative," the general's voice "rising sharply
and falling to emphasize points." At one point, angrily
answering a reporter about the effects of U.S. support for
fallen dictators in Iran and Nicaragua, Haig snapped,
"If that doesn't answer your question, then think about it
for a while."

Handing over command to an unsmiling General Bernard Rogers, his former commander at West Point and
the official historian of Ap Gu, he went through the customary troop ceremony and staff farewells. Then, thirty-
five years after he had first entered the academy in that
expectant wartime class, he took off his uniform for the
last time, and was gone from the army. He had been "at
the center of political-military power in the United States
longer than anyone serving today," reflected the *Post*. "As
an old soldier," added the *Los Angeles Times*, "General
Haig does not intend to fade away."

"Al's gonna run," Joe Califano casually remarked to an
aide after a transatlantic phone conversation with Haig
that spring of 1979. In Washington there was little ques-

tion that the general would be a Republican candidate
for the presidency, but more doubt about his relatively
late start and what the *Post* called his "slim chances."
About Haig's own confidence in his qualifications, reporters thought him assured by his own experience at the
highest levels. With the neutron bomb and other Carter
episodes, wrote one of them later, "Haig must have added
to his list another clay-footed American president about
whom he could tell himself: I could do better." It was
"understandable," said a sharp critic, that "having seen
with what little wisdom the world is governed," the General "should have formed an excessive opinion of his
own."

Less clear was Haig's tactical road to the nomination.
Without a political base in the party, Congress, or a state-
house, he could only hope to stage a surprise sweep of
some early primary where the constituency was favorable
—such as Florida with its retired military, Cuban, and
conservative Jewish communities responsive to his anti-
Soviet rhetoric. Otherwise, his hope was to scavenge a
convention or primary deadlock of the other candidates,
among them Ronald Reagan and George Bush, whose
government he would join. His 49-percent name recogni-
tion in national polls was higher than Carter's at a comparable stage four years earlier and pointed to a
potentially formidable run against the president, yet it
was the nomination of the Republicans, the party he had
renounced less than five years earlier, that now stood in
his way. "He felt electable but not nominatable," wrote
one observer of Haig's 1979 dilemma.

Still, he began aggressively, and by again exorcising
the past. "It is sort of ludicrous that a decade later ques-

tions are still being asked about something that has been examined in minute detail with respect to my personal role," he said of Watergate on television's "Meet the Press" in mid-1979. "I have absolutely no qualms of conscience about it in the context of what was done." The response ended the questioning, and the press did not often raise the subject afterward. "We've got to shed the sackcloth and ashes of our Southeast Asia involvement," he said at the same time; and Vietnam, if it was discussed at all in his public appearances in 1979, came to be synonymous with a crippling "self-paralyzing . . . attitude" in American policy rather than a part of Haig's own history. Repeatedly he called for "a new kind of post-Vietnam leadership," his listeners apparently unstruck by the paradox that the speaker had belonged to the "Vietnam leadership" as well.

The campaign began symbolically if not formally at his long-awaited appearance before a congenial Senate Armed Services Committee to testify on SALT II in the summer of 1979. His presence propelling the usually dull committee into the Senate caucus room with live television coverage, the performance was a predictable yet modulated attack on Carter. "Americans want to be number one," said the Haig in mufti. SALT II was unwise and defenses had been allowed to weaken. A "demonstration of renewed U.S. strength and ability to lead is overdue," he testified, and was duly praised by senators for his "statesmanship."

From the klieg lights of the caucus room, he launched a nationwide speaking tour, booked through a New York lecture agent at a reported fee of $10,000 for each speech and taking him through more than a hundred addresses in thirty-five states over the next six months. Meanwhile, he established offices from temporary academic sinecures at two familiar bases, the Foreign Policy Research Center at the University of Pennsylvania in Philadelphia not far from Bala-Cynwyd, and Georgetown's newly endowed and conservative Center for Strategic and International Studies. At Penn he planned a seminar on presidential decisionmaking and projected two studies on NATO defense needs and the organization of the presidency.

His speaking campaign drew mixed reactions. "He was simply the most impressive man I saw that year, Republican, or Democrat," one listener told a reporter later. But another observer noted that "on the road Haig did not always sparkle." Sometimes "awkward" in small groups or "overshadowed" by other speakers sharing a platform, he was "at his very best," thought the *Atlantic*, talking alone about grand strategy and delivering a "direct and chilling" message of Soviet threat that "played into the angry, frightened mood of the American people."

His themes were familiar echos of NATO statements. Categorical about the Russian menace, he remained vague about the solution. "It is time for us to pull up our socks and rethink this issue and put the Soviet Union on notice," he told the Foreign Relations Committee in August, but his recommendations then trailed off in ambiguous, often wandering talk of "integrating assets" and a "global strategic framework." On policy toward China, he seemed to reverse both his earlier secret opposition to the Kissinger opening and some of his more recent remarks about the Soviets. The United States should not provoke the USSR over its hostility with China—"poking sticks

into the polar bear's cage," he once called it—yet the
new "increasingly pragmatic China" should see the United
States as more "reliable," and he seemed to favor arms
aid. He was scarcely more specific or original about the
Middle East. Addressing the Zionist Organization of
America in Miami in October, Haig "spoke warmly" of
Israel, as the *Washington Post* later reported, and dismissed any necessity to recognize the Palestinians, while
cultivating Arab states like Saudi-Arabia as "highly important to U.S. security."

Often his most effective line as a putative campaigner
was his critique of an "America . . . no longer the America
it was," a condition his audiences seemed to feel more
easily than the nuances of diplomacy, and which Haig
commonly attributed to Vietnam, "the mistakes of Vietnam." Had more "vigorous and direct" steps been taken
before intervening, "including mobilization," one magazine quoted him, "we never would have had to intervene."
But from the folly of partial action in Indochina, he
traced the "overdose of dialectic" that destroyed the old
bipartisan foreign policy, that ridiculously portrayed
those in power as "immoral, irrational and incompetent,"
and produced everywhere "a nagging concern that we
are a nation less and less able to preserve our vital interests abroad." Thus Carter had "unnecessarily cornered
himself" and failed to apply "a host of additional levers"
in the episode of a Soviet brigade discovered in Cuba in
1979. And there were other crises in Afghanistan, and
perhaps Poland. "He comes off as a man of action who
understands how the world really works and would not
turn sentimental notions such as human rights into pre-
cepts of foreign policy," noted one interviewer.

Haig was clearly "the antithesis of the people who worked in Carter's State Department" (some of whom, the writer neglected to mention, were Haig's ex-colleagues, patrons, and future employees). At the end of August, an "unauthorized" draft-Haig committee was formed in Washington, and he was at the threshold of formal candidacy. "It's safe to say he is considering all options," said a spokesman for the general, to whom the draft movement "didn't come as a great surprise."

The speeches continued routinely through September and October, and at that point, with the seizure of American hostages in Iran at the beginning of November, Haig made the most controversia' statement of his brief campaign. On the morning of November 8, four days after the taking of the hostages and two days after the Carter White House had publicly renounced the use of military force in the crisis, Haig, accompanied by a retinue of aides, spoke to 150 public-relations executives at Washington's Shoreham Hotel. Described by a reporter as dancing "up and down on the balls of his feet like a boxer preparing to make his way to ringside" before the speech, he delivered a brisk, well-received criticism of current U.S. policy. When the assassination attempt against him was bungled in Belgium, he joked, he had told a Carter appointee, "I immediately thought of you people." He recalled his close relations with German Chancellor Helmut Schmidt, and a time earlier "when I spent four hours talking with Chou En-lai." The speech ended with the customary call for new leadership to stand up to the Russians.

In the question period that followed, he was asked about the hostage seizure, and his response was described by

David Nyhan, a syndicated columnist from the *Boston Globe* who was the lone reporter covering the 10:00 A.M. speech. Haig replied quickly that it had been "a mistake" for Carter to rule out the use of force so early. Though Americans should "rally round" Carter, "the president under such circumstances should strive to maintain as many options as possible, 'Even,' and here Haig lowered his voice after a pause, 'the unthinkable.'" Nyhan went on to record that "nobody asked whether that meant nuclear weapons, or precisely what he meant. . . ."

Nyhan's account of the remark was carried in the *Globe* on December 2, 1979, and in the *Los Angeles Times* on December 26, 1980, after Haig's appointment by Reagan. Asked about the report by Democratic Senator Claiborne Pell at his confirmation, Haig simply replied, "I don't recall that . . . I don't even recall the incident. It does not sound like my language—'unthinkable.' I would have been more precise if I had felt it was justified." When Pell said an aide had just given him a copy of the report, Haig bristled. "I'm glad. He probably gave you the question, too," he shot back at the diffident senator. "So he's probably the expert on it."

"Well, good, I'm delighted," Pell had said to Haig's answer, "and I trust the story is inaccurate, and I'm glad to assume it was." The general's taut failure to "recall" prompted Nyhan to repeat and reaffirm his account in the *Globe* on January 15, 1981, and there the issue rested.

Yet Nyhan's was not the only eyewitness version of Haig's remark. One of the general's campaign aides later reportedly told Senate staff that the story was "essentially true." "He said it. I suppose for effect," confirmed the aide, "but he said it and we were worried at the time that it sounded a little like [General Curtis] LeMay." But like the retired Secret Service agent who refused to come forward with testimony about the last days of the Nixon regime, the aide refused to be named, and the further evidence of Haig's rhetorical recklessness and dissimulation before Pell was never used.

Ironically, Nyhan's account of the Haig remarks on Iran were consistent as well with other, albeit less momentous, speeches and interviews on the record. Six days after the disputed utterance of "the unthinkable," he told a Republican fund-raising dinner in Fort Worth that Americans should "rally behind our president," in words similar to Nyhan's quotation. Again on November 22, at a breakfast with Washington reporters, he sharply criticized Carter for "impulsively" ruling out force in the hostage crisis. "The worst thing we can do in one of these situations where there is lawlessness is to suggest at the outset that we reject the option of force." There were "limits on the use of force," the *Washington Post* described him arguing, but he plainly retained "his air of command [and] periodically stabbed the air with his finger and fixed his listeners with a steely blue-eyed gaze and raised his voice aggressively."

At the same breakfast press conference, Haig curtly rejected the prospect that he might be running for the Senate: "I'm not a committee man," he snapped. But at the same time, his presidential hopes seemed to be dwindling. "I think I am as promising a national candidate as there is in the field," he told the reporters, "and the least nominable [sic]." It was an opinion shared, he said, by knowledgeable "erstwhile colleagues" like Henry Kissinger, Richard Nixon, and Gerald Ford.

In December he was back at Penn, where an *Atlantic* interviewer found him in a Gucci belt, "flashy" gold ID bracelet, impeccably tailored clothes, and neat, unmoving "gun-metal" hair, smoking "almost without polluting the air" and wearing "a veneer of elegance like a diving suit." He didn't mean to sound "arrogant or megalomanic," he told the reporter, but he had "seen the office" of the presidency and had a career "of extensive breadth." He had been "fairly close to the highest levels of policy." A few days later, however, Haig had a discouraging meeting with his campaign staff, and began to conclude there was neither the money nor the votes for a serious run in Florida or elsewhere.

On the Saturday before Christmas 1979, less than six months after he left NATO, he called journalists and sup-porters of the Draft Haig Committee to tell them it "wouldn't be a constructive thing" for him to run. In a formal statement on December 23, he said the decision not to run came after "anguished assessment," and he cited his "very late start and doubts about the organiza-tional framework available to me. . . . You might say I tested the water," he said, "and it wasn't hot enough." He had called Nixon at the same time, it was reported later, and the former president had "congratulated" Haig on the "wise decisions" he had made. It was a lucrative if disappointing effort. One source at Haig's lecture agency told a reporter the general had made "a bundle" on his speeches, perhaps as much as a million dollars. It had also been a remarkable campaign, expressive of the man and his perspective. For six months and more, as the nation writhed in both inflation and recession, Haig had run seriously for president of the United States without one substantive discussion of domestic affairs or policy.

He had seen the defeat coming and, like a good officer limbering his guns to fight again, he prepared to retreat. Weeks earlier, Haig's name had gone quietly to the board of United Technologies Corporation, a huge defense contractor and the largest single employer in Connecticut. On December 26, 1979, as he basked in the sun in a familiar setting at Key Biscayne, he was voted the corporation's chief executive. For the next few months, with salary and perquisites amounting to more than a half-million dollars a year and a nineteenth-century Federal era house in nearby Farmington, Connecticut, he presided over United Technologies in Hartford with what one writer called "his cold, hard-driving manner" and "his ability to make others feel vaguely uncomfortable in his presence."

By all accounts, he left no executive impact on the corporation and brought no notable new business to its already large portfolio of Pentagon contracts. The presidency was to last only ten months, however, and would be interrupted for six weeks by his open-heart surgery. At fifty-six, his regimen of tension, chain-smoking, hastily eaten cheeseburgers, and legendary long hours duly recorded by the press, Haig had developed symptoms of atherosclerosis, a blockage of coronary arteries threatening a major heart attack. In April 1980, he flew to Houston, where surgeons performed a triple bypass, taking unclogged arteries from his leg to implant in his chest. The operation was successful and he reportedly recovered without incident, though continuing to smoke despite doctor's warnings.

Even before his surgery, Haig had actively sought to be a Republican delegate at the 1980 nominating convention that summer in Detroit. During his convalescence, he also maneuvered for a chance to address the convention, and, with help from both Ford and Kissinger, was scheduled to speak. Though he addressed a convention that was still distracted by Reagan's abortive effort to enlist Ford as a running mate, his speech certified his physical recovery, the continuing Haig orthodoxy of American weakness and Communist peril, and not least his open if belated support of Reagan. "The Soviet threat," he told sober and convinced delegates, "has now become a threat to the very nexus of Western vitality—political, economic and military." As for a return to public office under a new Republican regime, however, he was now unassuming. "Haig said he had heard speculation that he would be nominated for Secretary of State if Ronald Reagan were elected in November," the *Chicago Tribune* reported an interview with him in August, "but he wasn't interested in the position."

His selection by president-elect Reagan would remain murky, awaiting the memoirs of the participants for the sifting of details. He was said to be a third or fourth choice after other figures from the Ford and Nixon years— chiefly former Treasury secretaries George Shultz and William Simon—who had declined or been rejected for lack of experience. What seemed clear by most accounts, however, was Richard Nixon's strong support for Haig, added, ironically, to the approval of Nixon's old nemeses, the moderate Rockefeller Republicans of the East. Haig, who had scoffed bitterly a year before at being a "com-

mittee man," had come to sit on the corporate boards of
Chase Manhattan and Crown Cork as well as United
Technologies, and his cachet now came from a powerful
faction of the business community of New York. But,
said the *Post*, it was Nixon who "campaigned avidly" for
his former regent, telling several party leaders as well as
Reagan that the general was "the meanest, toughest, most
ambitious s.o.b. I ever knew, but he'll be a helluva Secretary of State." It was final anointing praise from the
president who had motioned him long ago to sit down
with Safire and Kissinger to work on the speech they were
drafting, the "man of action" joined to the "man of
thought."

In early December, already alerted to the appointment
while Reagan waited for congressional soundings before
an announcement, Haig was in Washington when the
opposition began. "Haig Chance for Cabinet in Jeopardy,"
headlined the December 6 *Post* over a story of Watergate
doubts and the prospect of a heated confirmation fight.
But in the same paper, columnist Joseph Kraft, who had
once pronounced Haig "damaged goods," now heralded
him as "of high caliber," a figure who "personifies authority" and is "highly articulate." Haig had been involved in
"several ugly operations" and "did some ignominious
things," Kraft noted, "but Watergate ought not to stand
in the way" of his nomination. The columnist found it
"hard to believe" any wrongdoing would have escaped
the "scrutiny" of the Watergate prosecutor. "As top aide
to a crooked president," Kraft concluded of Haig, "he
was in an impossible position."

By December 11, Haig's appointment seemed still more

certain when conservative Senate leader Jesse Helms of North Carolina revealed that Nixon himself had cleared Haig of any incriminating material on the still unreleased White House tapes. Was there anything there "that could discredit Al Haig?" Helms asked Nixon. "Absolutely not," the ex-president was said to reply. "And I know more about those tapes than anyone else." Meanwhile, there were reports of favorable reaction among Europeans to the prospect of Haig at the State Department, and a column by Evans and Novak admonishing Reagan that he could not be "bullied" by Senate Democrats opposed to Haig.

In the convoluted politics of cabinet appointment, his nomination was then formally announced on December 17, though even the new president's public commitment did not still the continuing rumble of controversy to come. "Why General Haig?" asked the *Washington Post*, calling him a "somewhat soiled figure on the Washington scene, a man of more ambition than talent, someone whose political scars, if they were campaign ribbons, would match the collection already pinned to his tunic." Otherwise, though, Haig's reviews were more positive. *Time* praised him for "a quick mind," a "forceful speaking style," and apparently with no intended irony, "a prodigious memory."

As the probability of his confirmation became plain despite the early opposition, however, there was another warning alarm about what would happen still later, inside the fresh administration. "He's an enormously competent man," the *Post* quoted an anonymous "top Reagan aide" saying the day after the general was appointed. "Yet he produces a feeling of uneasiness, something that's hard to put your finger on." Back in government again for only hours, there was a registering round to signal that Haig's battles were starting once more.

For three weeks between the announcement of his nomination and the opening of his confirmation hearings, much of the press seemed to relish the prospective inquiry of the Senate Foreign Relations Committee into Haig's past. Prompting the putative congressional critics, the *Washington Post* supplied at the end of December a lengthy series summarizing some of the high points of the general's record in Watergate, the wiretap episode, the pardon, the Chile policy, the Cambodian bombing, and his views on various diplomatic issues. At the same time, there were editorial warnings that the confirmation hearings should not fail to examine Haig's intellectual qualifications for the highest cabinet post as well as his history. There was "scant evidence" of Haig's larger grasp of the substance of foreign policy in the 1980s, editorialized the *Post*. He was "without visible strengths on the economic side," his views on the third world were "largely a blank," and his public statements were "in the limited vein of a summons to ramparts." Judging him "a technician, an able one, without his own large view of the world," the paper thought that "a Senate confirmation inquiry that fixes on Watergate and slides over these crucial matters of perception and policy will not do."

But in the event, the hearings slid without fixing. Expecting lush, perhaps gruesome dramas, the audience to Haig's confirmation as secretary of state was largely treated instead to farce.

Behind the public imagery, the protagonists provided a vivid illustration of the politics of foreign policy, in

which presidents and bureaucracies, whatever the quality
of their men, had long maintained a lopsided, sometimes
dangerous dominance over America's relations with the
rest of the world. At the zenith of his career, Haig now
faced one of Washington's classic unequal struggles of the
executive versus the legislative branch.

Like all congressional bodies, the Senate Foreign Relations Committee was hostage to its professional staff.
Since the heyday of William Fulbright's first questioning
of the Vietnam War in the mid-1960s, however, that staff
had been an ironic paradox to the committee's nominal
prestige and prominence, its ranks with few exceptions
filled with derelicts or aspirants of the same bureaucracy
it was expected to check and balance. Added to its un-
gifted personnel was Foreign Relations' tradition of genteel irresponsibility, Fulbright's publicized dissent apart.
No oversight committee of the Congress was more excluded or shielded by official secrecy from the business
it was overseeing, none more timid in challenging the
nominees of either political or career nepotism, none more
loath to question policy lest it be saddled with the consequences of authority. The abdication had been sweeping
in the commanding and ingratiating presence of Kissinger,
who vouchsafed to selected members selected morsels of
his dramatic policies in intimate White House briefings.
The committee had held hearings on the wiretap issue
only at Kissinger's angry behest when the press accounts
in 1974 became too damaging, and then the summoned
vindication had been to order, the senators sheepishly
hearing the secretary of state and Haig with no independent investigation worth the name.

At root, the committee was as effective as its members were knowledgeable, sophisticated, and independent. In January 1981, the array was not impressive. In the chair, beneficiary of the Republican capture of the Senate majority the previous November, sat Charles Percy, a former camera-company executive from Illinois whose long years on the committee had typically given him far more seniority than substance. When the Haig hearings were finished, Percy would not even know the constitutional procedure by which the nomination entered and exited the committee, and his motion to approve Haig would have to be amended to accord to the law.

On the majority side, however, the chairman suffered little embarrassment by comparison. Tennessee's Howard Baker, the new majority leader and disappointed presidential contender, was the mouthpiece for the administration. Below Baker were S. I. Hayakawa, a conservative California school administrator; former Indianapolis mayor Richard Lugar; Maryland's Charles Mathias, a bruised and thus cautious Republican moderate; and three junior members: Senators Kassebaum of Kansas, the granddaughter of onetime presidential candidate Alf Landon; Minnesota salesman Rudy Boschwitz; and Pressler of South Dakota, a younger man with the majority's only agile mind. More politically formidable than all was Jesse Helms, an ultraconservative radio announcer from North Carolina who was titular leader of the party's vocal right, but whose shallow nostrums crippled even his own ideology's potentially powerful critique of bureaucratic foreign policy.

On the other side of the dais resided the newly humbled Democratic minority, led by Claiborne Pell, a cadaverous Rhode Island patrician who had spent his seniority, like

Percy, in diffidence. Then there were Delaware's Biden, privately ridiculed by his colleagues for his often vacant love of his own voice; former military astronaut and now Ohio senator John Glenn, a would-be presidential candidate whose views reflected his earlier Pentagon constituency; Zorinsky of Nebraska, an earnest but uninformed midwesterner; and Alan Cranston, a former foreign correspondent and now the minority's assistant leader by way of California state politics, an aging liberal with the mind and experience but no longer the stamina nor boldness to become a major voice on the committee. Rounding out the Democrats were three younger members: Christopher Dodd, scion of a Connecticut machine and hostage to Haig's United Technology employment rolls, the largest in his state; Maryland's Sarbanes, a hardworking Baltimore lawyer facing a harsh reelection challenge and early besieged by hate mail for his announced skepticism about Haig; and Paul Tsongas, a young Massachusetts Democrat in the shadow of Edward Kennedy, new to foreign policy and already steering fashionably rightward in domestic affairs. Saddled with the worn committee staff, neither Sarbanes nor Tsongas possessed their own personal staff expertise in international affairs.

In all, the committee was of roughly the same quality as its predecessors since World War II, the scrutiny of Haig, with the exceptions of Sarbanes and Tsongas, no better nor worse than that of a Democratic or another Republican nominee, and, as usual, it was to be a constitutional mismatch.

For his part, Haig retained his old patron and friend Califano as legal counsel for the hearings, the latter having been sacked from the Carter cabinet in midpassage and returned to a lucrative law practice in Washington representing corporations and other special interests. It was shrewd if ironic politics, Califano the prominent Democrat at once certifying Haig's bipartisan background and drawing on his own establishment credentials with the minority. But Califano's presence was also symbolic of the stigma Haig carried into the confirmations, the first time in history a nominee for secretary of state was appearing with a hired lawyer in anticipation of serious questions about illegal or improper actions during previous service at the highest levels of government.

Along with Califano came a series of the ritual and obligatory letters from senior figures in past regimes recommending the new nominee. In this case, too, there was ample irony between the lines. Some of the letters came from men Haig had bureaucratically savaged, like former Ambassador to Vietnam Ellsworth Bunker or State Department Undersecretary Joseph Sisco; from Winston Lord, whom he had fought in Kissinger's retinue; from Gerald Ford, whose letter bore the strange and glaring error that Haig had been on the NSC staff during Ford's tenure as vice president; and a terse plea for a crisp hearing (no "spectacle which could cripple the office of Secretary of State") from Dean Rusk, a preceding vicar whose influence Major Haig had so bemoaned twenty years before.

Meanwhile, the State Department supplied the nominee with detailed briefings, including the bland, noncommittal answers to written questions from other congressmen or senators or public organizations, while Califano's legal assistants helped the general prepare the financial and other forms required by the ethics law and answers to written questions from Congress about his personal holdings and interests. The latter revealed that he had enjoyed only relatively modest officers' rewards before leaving NATO. Château, Mercedes, and full general's pension plus White House salary notwithstanding, he had few assets from government service. But the months speaking and then at United Technologies had earned him well over a million dollars, and the position he was giving up in Hartford entailed eight or nine million over a four-year period, he testified, impressive evidence of Haig's sacrifice, his passion to be secretary of state, and presumably his conviction that comparable rewards lay beyond.

He began on January 9 with a carefully prepared statement reciting his previous appearances to testify on the wiretaps, Watergate, and Chile. "None of these investigations have [sic] found any culpability on my part," he said three times in both oral and written statements. He had "no personal responsibility" and was not aware of any "subsequent inaccurate statements" given the Congress in the Cambodian bombing. "Dr. Kissinger and I" advocated the Christmas bombing of North Vietnam, but there was no "indiscriminate 'carpet bombing' of civilian areas." He took "only one action of any significance" in the Hughes $100,000 campaign contribution, suggesting a tax lawyer to Rebozo. As for tapes, he "never personally listened to a tape . . . never participated in reviewing any transcript for accuracy or in deciding the relevancy to Watergate . . . never physically had any tape in my possession." He could not "reconstruct the precise June 4 conversation even with the transcript in front of me." He met with Ford on August 1 only to "emphasize" that he had to be prepared for the presidency, and to review "courses of action . . . developed by the White House lawyers" and "a number of transition matters."

Lost in the sworn statement were the history of the Cambodian policy from MENU to the orders to Enders, the undercutting of Kissinger in Saigon, the leaks of investigative data to Rebozo and his lawyer, the whole tape story from the hurried approach to Scott through the promotion (and bewailing) of the transcripts with Jaworski to the fact that he kept the keys and his aide was responsible for security. Gone, too, was the whole campaign against Dean that was the prologue, aftermath, and context of the June 4 conversation with Nixon, the exclusion of Buzhardt and St. Clair, the after-midnight call to Ford and the vice president's worried call back the next day, the postresignation pressure on Ford and his men—and a host of other related matters, from his removal of his files to his withholding of evidence in the Ellsberg trial. But if the committee saw any of the discrepancies, all to be had in the public record, it did not seem to care.

Much of the dissembling was brash, apparently based on the correct assumption that neither committee nor staff read very widely. As Nixon's chief of staff, he spent "90 percent of my time" on "other business" than Watergate—a patent absurdity by every account and not least the versions that made Haig the hero of the resignation. He had a "limited involvement" and no "special responsibility" in covert policies toward Chile, and "I did not know there was a Track II specifically established." It was an evasion belied not only by the abundant history of the NSC staff but also by detailed congressional testimony of CIA officials, Kissinger's repeated statements, still other CIA memoirs, and various other published accounts, such as Helms's biography.

To Pell, he pointedly denied that nuclear weapons had ever been considered in Indochina or that he had ever recommended any such action in Vietnam, though had the committee bothered to look into the November Group, by then public knowledge, there would have been disturbing testimony of another sort. "I certainly hope, Senator," he berated Pell in what would be commonplace, "that your question doesn't suggest or intend to suggest that you have evidence that I did," to which the ranking minority member quickly assured the general, "It does not," and went on to other matters. Later would come his similar umbrage with Pell taken at the *Boston Globe* report of his Shoreham remarks on the "unthinkable."

The first day's hearing ended with Haig telling the committee he simply would not "interpose" himself in President Nixon's legal affairs and therefore would not request documents and the some 100 hours of Haig-Nixon tapes sought by the Democratic senators. Swiftly resigned to Nixon's evocation of presidential privilege, the committee for the remainder of the hearings seemed to agree with Baker that in the absence of the documentary record or other witnesses, the "best evidence" was the general himself.

By the third day of hearings, the committee was almost apologetic, responding more to the press's expectations of its ardor than to its wanderings in the event. "Do you think we have been extreme?" asked Senator Dodd anxiously on January 12. "No," answered the general, "I have been delighted with the questions that have been asked here."

The next day was perhaps the most heated, though more interesting for what was *not* said. "There were tracks in Mr. Kennedy's administration on the Cuban problem" outside the normal intelligence channels, Haig admitted at one point. It was an inviting shadow of his own distant Pentagon past and his penchant for clandestine operations in Latin America, but the senators passed over it. And as for anyone excluding the secretary of state from any action in the Reagan administration, the general replied, "It had better not happen on my watch." When Sarbanes asked what he thought of William P. Rogers being cut out of Track II, Haig simply assured him that "frankly, it wasn't an issue that I focused on."

Did he think the wiretaps of his colleagues and newsmen right or wrong? Sarbanes asked. "It is really a question that I can't answer for you, Senator, because I just wasn't in the vortex of the pressures. . . ." Had he thought the resignations of Richardson and Cox "honorable"? "I don't think you would ever have found me to say otherwise," he testified, adding, in a rare show of unease, "unless you have some information that I am not privy to." But there was no discussion of the malicious rumors about Richardson's drinking, or the public apology afterward, or the "Coxsuckers," and Haig was even able to claim that he had resigned himself from NATO over principle.

"Now what do you expect me to say?" he flashed at Sarbanes, who was far more intent on philosophical contrition over Watergate than the facts. "What is it you

are after, something that you want me to say that you
have been unable to get from somebody else with respect
to that tragic period in our history?" Yes, "mistakes were
made," but "I didn't make them." In fact, "I never made
a move without checking with White House counsel." At
the close of this line of questioning, he glared at Sarbanes
and said, "Nobody had a monopoly on virtue, not even
you, Senator." It was, ironically, a variation on Kissinger's
familiar quip to war protesters that no one had a monopoly on anguish. But Sarbanes, frustrated by the predictable dead end of his own moral tactic and not knowledgeable enough to dispute the record, wearily acknowledged
for Haig and his uncertain Maryland constituency that
he did not believe in such "monopolies" either, and that
"we have probably gotten as much from you as we are
going to."

The Watergate break-in itself had been "wrong, of
course," Haig told Percy, who thought that "answers it
forthrightly"—"it" presumably being the larger political
and ethical question of the cover-up as well as its relatively small precipitating crime—and the issue was nearly
gone. Later, when Tsongas pressed him again for at least
a judgment on the political scandal of the epoch, he replied that "the kinds of 'mea culpa's' that I sense in your
question you want I just can't give because I don't feel
them."

On Tuesday afternoon, Senator Lowell Weicker, a
member of the Ervin Watergate Committee, gave scathing if somewhat vague testimony against Haig on the
basis of the cover-up record and Haig's own repeated
misleading of Republican congressional supporters of
Nixon. The office of secretary of state "is an honor to be

bestowed upon the courageous, the forthright, the ideal-
istic," said Weicker. "No such nominee is before your
committee."

There followed an embarrassing exchange between
Helms and Weicker, with the latter producing minutes
of a meeting of Republican senators late in 1973 when
the general had concealed the explosions he knew to be
coming on the tapes and other issues. Helms sputtered
ineffectually, and for a moment the tide seemed unclear.
When Haig returned after a short recess, Califano had
extracted from him a statement to stem the shift. "I cannot bring myself to render judgment on Richard Nixon
or, for that matter, Henry Kissinger," said Haig. "I worked
intimately for both men. It is not for me, it is not in me, to
render moral judgments on them. I must leave that to
others, to history and to God." It was to be the high-water
mark of the general's regret about the past. When Biden
asked him later the same day if he had ever been "confronted with a request to abuse power," he answered,
somewhat incredibly: "I can think of a number [of re-
quests] over the years," but to discuss them in open session would "take unnecessary and unwarranted advantage
of others who may have been participants in something
you challenged."

On January 14, his confirmation in no doubt, he told
Dodd that he had no personal records from his White
House service, ignoring with confidence the telephone
transcripts and other documents he had spirited in and
out of the executive mansion for himself and Kissinger.
The committee seemed most gratified that, as a "military
man," he assured them that he would be, in Pell's phrase,
"a secretary of peace." At the same time, when he spoke

in his closing statement of his common objectives with the committee—"a strong America, working with honor and grace to fulfill its global responsibilities"—the word "peace" did not appear once. "Your experience at the White House, particularly with respect to the National Security Council, should be invaluable in helping you operate as the policymaking Secretary of State you clearly intend to be," Cranston told him with no intended irony. Just before, Tsongas had publicly and sheepishly expressed the hope that he had not evoked any "rancor" from the general, his Jesuit brother, or his wife.

For six days the committee had spoken far more than Haig—its ardor spent on his "attitude," his most easily hidden secret, rather than his rich record—and learned almost nothing from its political narcissism. The Chile policy, let alone Cuba, remained a mystery, a specter of unwanted history over the volatile events coming in Central America. The Cambodian bombing and policy remained interred with much of that nation. Having nipped at the general to admit the moral infamy of the wiretaps and the Watergate cover-up, the committee left neither themselves nor history no more clear idea of how, why, or by whom it had been done. Of some salient parts of the story, the collective senatorial ignorance and fecklessness simply found no trace at all: the October alert, the Ellsberg episodes and Haig's liaison with the Plumbers, the Vietnam diplomacy, his Russophobia and real or imagined accomplishments at NATO, the question of a coup in the final days—all that and more.

In the end, some observers could salvage only a fey cynicism. "Of course the man's treacherous," one writer summed up the attitude in "knowledgeable" circles, "but he's familiar with the issues and besides, there's nobody else." In an age accustomed to outrage and its mutant standards, Haig had been deemed qualified to be secretary of state in the absence of a proven felony, open admission that he would overthrow a government, or visible inclination to start a war.

The committee vote was 15–2, with Sarbanes and Tsongas dissenting. On January 21, the day after Ronald Reagan was sworn in, the Senate formally confirmed him by 93–6, yet aptly the Congress was already behind the game. The day before, almost twelve years to the hour after Kissinger and Nixon consummated their coup by reorganizing the machinery of foreign policy through presidential edict, their protégé had attempted the same. The Reagan government returned from its inaugural to find what should have been an unsurprising proposal from the new vicar in Foggy Bottom—that its crucial foreign-policy power be vested in Secretary of State Alexander Haig.

EPILOGUE

Long since we were resolved of your truth,
Your faithful service and your toil in war,
Yet never have you tasted our reward,
Or been compensated with so much as thanks,
Because till now we never saw your face.
                              Shakespeare, *Henry VI*

He is expected to be the most powerful figure in the new administration, the natural result of his legendary bureaucratic skills and his presumed mastery in the field. But in barely two months he is reported angry, brooding, near resignation over a series of poisonous bureaucratic struggles with the White House, whose power in such matters he knows so well, or should. He has entered yet another court, though as a minister, not chamberlain or regent, and he does not seem to understand the distinction.

He offends the president's men with his self-enthroning charter of foreign-policy control while some of them are

still in morning coats and striped pants at the inauguration. He leaks unseemly complaints when Reagan's budget
director cuts foreign aid at the president's sweeping order
to reduce spending. He refers publicly to presidential
appointments at the State Department as "my nominees".
He pressures Reagan to keep a grain embargo on the
Russians, boasts of his influence, and is then reversed by
domestic political considerations. Ironically, he harshly
opposes new plans to revive the neutron bomb—but then,
this time the proposal comes from his rival, Defense
Secretary Casper Weinberger, an old Reagan friend, and
the issue is not weapons strategy or arms control but
Haig's authority. He trumpets the Soviet threat in Central
America while Reagan strives to gather support and attention for his domestic economic program. He brashly
upstages other presidential advisers in sensitive trade negotiations with the Japanese. He begins to quarrel savagely
with the new national security adviser, Richard Allen, an
old Nixon campaign aide and early casualty of Kissinger's
NSC staff. And when Reagan's men, knowing nothing of
foreign policy but being practiced courtiers, strike back
with public humiliation by making Vice President Bush
chairman of a White House crisis group, seeming to dimin-
ish Haig's power and prestige, he is stunned and petulantly
threatens to resign, much as he saw Kissinger do so often.

In the midst of this early virulence, Reagan is shot at
a Washington hotel on March 30, 1981, and as confusion
reigns at the White House and Bush is away, Haig comes
before microphones and cameras in the presidential press
room, as he has so often before, and announces, "I'm in
charge here." Visibly shaken he also misstates the constitutional order of succession, placing himself ahead of

the Speaker of the House and president *pro tem* of the Senate. He has managed, says one reporter, "by his quavery, Queeg-like demeanor, to suggest that he was far from in charge—even of himself."

Unseen, there is genuine pathos as well as nervous ignorance in his pronouncements. How many times indeed has he been left "in charge" (without microphones or cameras) during the sodden nights of the Nixon era. But never understanding his past, the media are all the more shocked at his blunder in the present. In his reach for foreign-policy power, so imitative of Kissinger without the political or intellectual sophistication, he seems to columnists inexplicably a "bush leaguer," who "should have learned long ago". Not grasping the rituals and politics of Haig's rise, they are now puzzled by his performance at the top.

As usual, the damage to the country from such bureaucratic strife and obsession with prerogative is far greater than the press's superficial absorption in who is up and who is down at court. Haig's very failure to be a strong, sophisticated secretary of state, or his inability in turn to share intelligently the authority he cannot dominate, to know any other tactic than the old backstabbing, leaves the new regime without a coherent diplomacy in almost every crucial issue facing it. The Pentagon unilaterally sells military aircraft to Saudi Arabia, and creates a new Persian Gulf command, including a rapid-deployment force, without consulting Haig, while Washington's Mideast mediation is mortgaged and confused as Israel drifts toward war over Lebanon. Arms-control talks with the Soviet Union are at a standstill, while negotiations to reduce nuclear forces in Europe, long promised the NATO allies, are undercut by the Pentagon-State Department rivalry.

Meanwhile, the secretary of state struggles against leaks, vicious rumors, his own vocabulary. His remarks in secret staff meetings appear in the next morning's newspapers. There are now jokes and rumors about Haig squalidly reminiscent of the barracks smut in the West Basement about William Rogers. Yet at one point Haig summons past secretaries of state and senior officials to bolster his Central American policy with a ceremonial briefing, and it is Rogers who stands in the lobby of the State Department, supporting the policy and Haig, oblivious to history far and near.

For every defender, however, there are powerful critics. The regime is scarcely a year old when Kissinger himself turns on his protégé in a scathing attack in *The New York Times* on the disarray in American diplomacy. Where Haig has spoken, the contrast has been painful. "And so I caveat it that way." "To exacerbate this kind of mutual restraint." "I'm talking about in functional priority areas." One writer calls it cuttingly "a compensatory stress on semilearned formulations . . . the Agnew Syndrome." CBS television news does a montage of Haigisms, and the effect is sad.

Yet it is clearly too early to count him out. He has stocked the State Department with Haig's Haigs, though that, too, seems an imitation of Kissinger. Eagleburger is his undersecretary for political affairs, the third man in the department, while Richard Kennedy, his first recruit to the NSC staff in 1969, is undersecretary for management with control over personnel and appointments. Richard Burt, the journalist who wrote the useful articles embarrassing Carter on the neutron-bomb episode, first named the director of the political-military office and then made assistant secretary for European affairs. Closer to the bureaucracy, the key assistant secretaries of state are also his: John Holdridge from West Point and the Kissinger staff now running the Far Eastern bureau; Africa under Chester Crocker, who worked for Richard Kennedy; and not least, Thomas Enders, once the general's young man in Phnom Penh for targeting and other policies, now an older, puffier retainer entrusted with Latin America, from guerilla clashes in the Caribbean to the war in the Falkland Islands.

Moreover, by the end of the first year, Haig's venomous NSC rival, Allen, is gone himself, casualty of a small but persistent scandal in which he received money and gifts from Japanese interests for arranging an interview with Mrs. Reagan. Haig has eased along his detractor's demise by helping to bring out the tarnishing information and then pointing up the damage to the regime's credibility abroad of this "whiff of Watergate." To Allen's place comes William Clark, an affable Reagan crony made California judge who has been for a time Haig's under-secretary, and who cannot in his confirmation even identify the names of major foreign leaders.

Retreating from his earlier confrontation with the White House, Haig is once more by early 1982 the loyal aide, and, for better or worse, he begins to leave his stamp on policy more lastingly. Left to formulate administration strategy in the Polish crisis, he and Eagleburger (then assistant secretary for European affairs) are unprepared for the martial-law repression of that tormented country late in 1981, and the West again meets the extinction of

Polish liberty in confusion and inaction.

In Central America, he launches with Enders covert CIA campaigns against the left-wing government in Nicaragua, props up juntas in Guatemala and Honduras, and pours more military aid, advisers, and clandestine support into El Salvador, where a right-wing oligarchy fights a growing and radical guerrilla army at the climax of decades of social neglect and brutal oppression and over the political corpse of the moderate center. Defending the U.S. intervention in El Salvador before a House committee, the secretary of state tells Congress that three American nuns and a missionary murdered by government forces near San Salvador were provocative. "I would like to suggest to you that perhaps the vehicles the nuns were driving in may have tried to run a roadblock," he says. The church women were found twenty miles away from the roadblock in question, individual bullets fired one by one into the backs of their heads, with no underwear, one nude from the waist down, and all of them sexually molested before being executed. Haig does not explain why nuns should remove their panties before running a roadblock.

With similar taste the administration supports the Pol Pot regime in Cambodia, the Communist successor to Lon Nol and author of mass genocide, simply because it opposes a Soviet- and Vietnamese-backed government in the country.

Asked why the United States should favor as well a repressive military regime in Argentina, Haig answers that the Argentinian generals share with Americans a "belief in God." Through 1981 the Reagan administration quietly draws closer to Argentina in obvious courtship of its support in Central America. When in blatant violation of international law Argentina later invades the Falkland Islands, British possessions in the South Atlantic, Haig conducts a dramatic Kissinger-like shuttle to mediate between London and Buenos Aires. At NATO he has said that it is left-wing "totalitarian" governments with their "doctrinal conviction" that aggress on others and cause international tension, while "authoritarian" rightist governments do not have such dangerous "pretensions." But as the Falkland crisis slides toward open war, Haig is in still another battle, arguing with James Baker, his successor as chief of staff at the White House, over the comforts and appointments of the official plane he is using in his shuttle.

Then, with apparent suddenness, he shocks the world on June 25, 1982 by resigning as Secretary of State. That afternoon a perspiring Reagan walks unexpectedly into the White House press room to announce the resignation "with great regret" (repeating the phrase twice), names George Shultz (Nixon's former Treasury Secretary) as the successor, and strides out quickly for Camp David without further comment. More than an hour later, Haig appears before a thousand reporters and employees in the State Department auditorium, reads a resignation letter denouncing the administration for "shifting from the careful course" of "consistency, clarity and steadiness of purpose," courteously thanks the assembled journalists and bureaucrats for their cooperation, and leaves the stage just as abruptly without taking questions. Later, Reagan answers Haig's sharp but vague letter on policy failures with a punctilious presidential reply about the General's "standard of excellence and achievement seldom equaled in our history" and Haig's "quality of wisdom which has been critical to the resolution of the most anguishing problems we face." It is all vintage Washington hypocrisy and subterfuge.

Behind the public facade has been yet another rancorous round of inter-office bickering over Haig's authority and prerogatives, what one anonymous White House aide calls "500,000 little offenses," another terms "18 months of tension," and a reporter sums up as the "dazzling mismatch" of Haig's personality and style with the rest of the regime. "Prickly" becomes the cliche to describe Haig as the Reagan courtiers eagerly tell reporters how often the secretary has threatened to resign. "No one tried to talk Al out of resigning this time," they say. "No one wanted to." Haig is said to have gone to Reagan with a list of complaints and another virtual ultimatum at mid-week. And on Friday—half to his surprise, if only because Henry's similar offers were never quite taken up—Reagan under pressure from his court decided Haig should go.

But deeper still than the predictable press leaks and gossip are other, more shadowy Washington rumors about this strangely strong and weak figure whose contentious presence so dominated the government. Weeks before, Haig is alleged to have asked an old Pentagon associate to come over to the State Department to schedule speaking engagements and other contacts for a possible 1984 campaign against Vice President George Bush for the Republican presidential nomination if Reagan declines to try for another term. The General has sniffed the coming battle and Bush's maneuvers. "I told him time after time," he says of Reagan to Safire at lunch

the day before his resignation, "that he has to stop telling
those guys around him that he's not going to run again."
But there are also hints of even more sinister ambition.
From the White House to Capitol Hill, for example, there
are newly-whispered tales of Nixon's final days, of the old
mystery of some planned coup d'etat, of Haig as the
bureaucrat-on-horseback. Fittingly, the General departs
government this time in much the same climate of
bureaucratic savagery and political squalor, of innuendo,
slur, suspicion and malice, in which he operated so long
and so successfully under Richard Nixon.

Alexander Haig's stormy exit from the Reagan cabinet
is rich in ironic echoes of his rise to power. He is
supposed to have quarreled with Reagan over the
President penalizing European allies for cooperation in a
gas pipeline with the Soviet Union, and over Haig's
ardent support for Israel in the invasion of the Lebanon.
Yet this is the same Haig who has built his career on
toughness toward the Russians, advocated a grain
embargo on Moscow, dutifully abided Richard Nixon's
anti-semitism, and left the Mid East to drift into a war
that has weakened Israel abroad and riven the nation at
home. Haig is reported to be furious at the White House's
"backchannel" contacts with the Arabs and the apparent
"two tracks" of Middle Eastern policy—he who with
Kissinger elevated furtive White House diplomacy in the
back channel to the sole instrument of foreign policy, and
who casually laid out fateful separate "tracks" in Chile,
Cambodia and elsewhere.

He has ascended to the heights of power through the
weakness and insecurity of a succession of presidents,
and now his vicarage over foreign policy fails because his

latest president is too weak to manage the old, inevitably conflicting baronies of bureaucracy, and too insecure to trust Haig's own aggressive management of power. Haig had been Kissinger's deputy and eventually a cutting rival. And now it is Clark, Haig's onetime deputy and supporter at State, who moves close to Reagan as national security adviser and becomes a decisive voice for Haig's ouster. Fearing Allen will drive him out, Haig helps engineer Clark as Allen's replacement, and it is Clark who does what Allen could not. And then there is perhaps the last irony—that the Haig who erected a stunning career on stamina and perseverance is now visibly fatigued. "Schooled in taking shit," one aide has called his long experience. Now, on top at last, vainly trying to emulate Kissinger's mastery and avoid the humiliation he helped inflict on Secretary of State William Rogers—the two main lessons of his climb—he is simply in part too proud and too tired to wage the old demeaning war.

At the same time, everywhere in the story of his fall with Reagan are the marks of his past, like relics of some ancient battlefield. Much of his argument with the administration is over where he sits in state dinners, which helicopter or which apartment he occupies on a foreign trip, the measures of military rank, the coin of Kissinger's prestige, the certificates of the lack-luster office from Bala-Cynwyd who made it despite the odds. There is also still the aide's habitual exaggeration and sycophancy. "Our entire foreign policy depends" on Reagan attending the funeral of Egyptian President Anwar Sadat, he tells White House aides at one point. And when the other officials say they believe Reagan should not go, Haig later tells them "our entire foreign policy depends" on the President *not* going. The aides, according to the *Washington Post*, then "looked at the ceiling." On other occasions, the Secretary of State would unnerve the President and his advisers by obsequiously calling a simple presentation or trivial event "a big victory" for Reagan's foreign policy. "It stands out," says one White House assistant of Haig's pandering. "Unlike others, I don't believe in flying off the handle," says Weinberger, looking pointedly at Haig.

Still, his very falling out with an unpopular, often doctrinaire regime leaves him once again in almost heroic imagery, much like his public persona after Watergate. Now he is a "moderate" among right-wingers, says the *Washington Post*, while *The New York Times* praises him for representing "experience against faith, realism against doctrine." "Haig had the voice of a hawk but his heart was approaching that of a dove," observes Senator Pell. "I'd trade Haig for the rest of them in a moment's notice," adds his old confirmation adversary Senator Tsongas. Columnist Gary Wills sees him sarcastically as "a dangerous leftist" in the regime, and another journalist calls Haig "the lone protector of professionalism in the diplomatic corps." "He knew more about foreign and military affairs than the President," writes James Reston "... and had the bad judgment to make this known." Again, they are writing about the same Haig who launches a new American intervention in El Salvador, who at one NSC meeting so parrots the conservative Pentagon position that Weinberger jokes that he would now "turn to foreign policy," and who staffs the State Department with retainers from the Kissinger years.

"History will show that I am the hardliner in this administration," he proudly tells Safire in a conversation he never expects to be quoted. But again, as so often in the past, he has benefitted politically, been spared the consequences of his policies and actions, by the relatively greater disrepute of the men around him.

All the old supporters are on hand for his going, and for the imagery. Columnist Joseph Kraft assures the public that Haig resigned "on principle" rather than personality. Patrick Buchanan, whom Haig once pushed as ambassador to South Africa before Ford "discovered" the appointment and now a columnist, chastises the regime for placing "collegiality above conservatism; experience and temperament over brilliance and talent." To make the public relations complete, there is even a front page account by the *Washington Post*'s Bob Woodward, summoning old anonymous sources to say that the General was "set up," "entrapped," and "sand-bagged" by a hostile White House staff executing a "master plot" to get Haig. By this account, full of Washington ghosts, the vicar has been deposed by White House aide James Baker who was once Eliot Richardson's assistant, by another Reagan staffer who once worked for Richardson, and not least by Henry Kissinger, who is close to the far more pliable successor, George Shultz. When the Haig version of the resignation has been purveyed to the press, the plot has widened to include almost all the old actors, all the old scores to settle.

He leaves behind a battered administration, eddies of gossip, a State Department weakly staffed, a successor of little substance whose only politics is administrative blandness, and no real accomplishment in foreign affairs.

The bureaucratic disarray in Washington is mirrored in relations abroad. There is the mistaken notion that somehow Haig has been Reagan's managerial problem, when he is much more. As he resigns, he positions himself to run for the presidency again. "Al Haig will be back," headlines the *Christian Science Monitor*, while his aides coyly tell reporters the General will "play a prominent role in American politics in the future." And it is plainly foolish to mark his progress, his ambition, done. He has survived the Yalu debacle, Vietnam, West Point scandal, Henry Kissinger, Watergate and Nixon, Ford's resentful court, Carter's opposition, an abortive presidential campaign, and major heart surgery. His tempest with Reagan leaves him more prominent, more formidable, more than ever convinced of his superiority to the men he has served. A week after Haig's resignation, President Reagan tells the press "the case is closed." In light of the General's history, it is a remarkably premature pronouncement.

His press critics ridicule him for his diction, style, and policies, all lacking grace. But there is a nagging sense that they are uneasy with him not only for his lack of veneer but also because of what he represents, and what they share with him. If in Haig ambition and anger now flash too nakedly, he is still more ordinary than unique in the organizational careerism that dominates much of American life. A bureaucratic everyman, he has given his fealty and risen regardless of talent or substance. He has done for each master—Almond, Califano, Vance, McNamara, Westmoreland, Rogers, Kissinger, Nixon, Ford, Carter, Reagan—what they expected of him without cavil or pause, his ethic theirs across all the differences of men and moment because it was simply the disembodied ethic of advance. That he scorns them as they are discarded, or even before, is not surprising; fealty is not loyalty, or admiration. And it is rarely responsibility. He can claim to be at the "vortex," yet have done nothing. He can have "seen" the presidency, yet be blind to its use. Like knowledgeable, scarred bureaucrats everywhere, his career is laced with opportunities to open the process, to expose and thus reduce its toll on people. But he has remained ensnared in the parochial ambition of his profession, half feared, half admired, a creature of others, and a disquieting reflection of the successors and pretenders in corporate suites, faculties, governments, and newsrooms throughout the world.

What singles him out is that he has missed the responsibility and the opportunity in such a fateful field—America's relations with the world. He has been near or at the top of foreign policy for fourteen of the last eighteen years, and it is remarkable how much the world has changed in that period, how litle U.S. diplomacy has changed with it. He is harried by self-defeat. What he struggles to defend and preserve—the army, Cambodia, Vietnam, the presidency—has been weakened if not destroyed for the toil. And in his narrow, reflexive fear of change in Central America, in the name of national security, he now threatens to bequeath to his country a new hostility of its neighbors, and a still deeper insecurity.

In the end, the failure of "thought" in Nixon's "man of action" has not been only the lying, evasions, and ethical suspension of the West Basement or the later Watergate, but also the failure to understand the complex world in which he was given to act. His career seems an epitaph on American power, seeing itself through Haig and others as benign despite its excesses and folly, an America, like Haig himself, sanctioned by something deeper than the acts and words by which other nations, other men are measured.

Tragically he came to govern in a time where even the virtues and values of his West Point youth, the qualities of war and "action," have been abandoned to the coup d'etat, conspiracy, guerrilla attack, atrocity. "They merely substituted slyness for courage, treason for comradeship, massacre for combat, and subversion for loyalty," wrote a Canadian officer of those phenomena of the postwar years. "The transition from Bastogne to My Lai marks a falling off that is steeper and far more tragic than the decline between Marathon and Chaeronea."

Haig is a man of that century, not the American century but rather of its frustration. It has been an epoch of dashed hopes for the United States, of coming to world power in the glow of victory and finding only the uncertain, sometimes maddening shadows of stalemate and danger in the postwar era. Requiring subtlety and tolerance, the challenge provoked belligerence and fear. And its symbols, his symbols, are of defeat and disillusion—Ned Almond looking out over the Yalu, the command post at Ben Suc, the rancor and pettiness and scandal of the Nixon White House, the folly of Ronald Reagan's secretary of state. It is a world Alexander Haig, like many of his countrymen, cannot control, yet angrily does not accept. The question he poses at the uncertain peak of his career is whether his nation will find a new vision or choose again to be led so cynically by the same dark and dangerous disappointment.

NOTES

(To simplify citations, the traditional *ibid* is used below to denote the same magazine article or exact page number of a book cited immediately before. Otherwise, the note is given in full. I have similarly dispensed with the use of *op. cit.* for the same reasons of clarity and speed of reference.)

Prologue

Page   Identification——Source

XVIX   "seems to have just floated away": Drew, 416.
XX   "guards rolled up": Ford, 40.
XXI   "none of MacArthur's men": quoted Manchester, 19.
XXII   "the facts of Alexander Haig's rise": *The New York Times* Biographical Service, May 1981.
XXIV   "we'll be back": author's background interview.

PART ONE: *Apprentice*

3   "the expression": O'Hara, 130.
4   Bala Golf Club directory: author's interview with Philip Nolan.
4   "a matter of pride": O'Hara, 119.
5   "lace curtain Philadelphia Irish": quoted Thimmesch.

Page   Identification——Source

5   snapshot: reproduced in Duggan.
6   "one Jewish family": Nolan interview.
6   "he was a breadwinner," "minimum estate": quoted
           Thimmesch.
6   "ours was a typical childhood": quoted Duggan.
7   "the leader," "a houseful of boys": quoted Timmesch.
7   "working always": *ibid.*
7   "I had to pretty much fend," "I had to be self-reliant":
           quoted Shearer and Thimmesch.
7   "whatever hopes": quoted *Wall Street Journal*, Decem-
           ber 17, 1980.
7   "I even worked as a floorwalker": quoted Shearer.
7   "whatever it is that a mother is supposed to do": quoted
           Duggan.
8   Neeson career: *The New York Times*, September 2,
           1945.
9   "our uncle": quoted Duggan.
9   mother's ambition: Thimmesch.
9   "Al knew": *ibid.*
10   "athletic, vigorous," "Al is definitely not": quoted Duggan.
10   "the closest he ever came": quoted Thimmesch.
10   "adolescent to a man," "coming home": *ibid.*
11   "financial necessity": Shearer.
11   "pulled strings": *Wall Street Journal*, December 17, 1980.
11   "if he had followed": quoted Thimmesch.
12   West Point in old mold: Ellis and Moore, 51.
12   horses auctioned: Lovell, 48.
13   "unless the pictures": Grady, 34.
13   "fit to fight" course: Flemming, 322–23.
14   "I'm not here to answer questions": quoted Mylander.
14   "over the dead bodies": quoted Flemming, 322.
14   narrow curriculum: Mylander, 44ff., Flemming, 352.
14   "here at West Point": Flemming, 345.
15   "crowning glory": quoted Mylander, 44.
15   "rife," "for years": Galloway and Johnson, 116–17.
15   "catholic . . . interests": quoted Flemming, 345.
15   "designed for the mediocre student": Ewell Board Re-
           port, quoted Flemming, 352.
15   nearly failed to graduate: Mylander, 198.
15   "rough times": quoted Thimmesch.
15   "he was the last": quoted Mylander, 198.
16   "strong convictions": reproduced *The New York Times*
           Biographical Service, May 1981.

Page   *Identification——Source*

16   "an ideology," "anointed access": Galloway and Johnson, 32.

17   "blissful obliviousness": Ellis and Moore, 197.

18   "she was playing Chopin": quoted Shearer.

19   "Mother, I'm going to get married," "Is she Japanese?": quoted Duggan.

19   "on the very definite decline": *The New York Times*, April 3, 1950.

20   Fox in line for Leavenworth command: *The New York Times*, June 23, 1950.

21   "inner sanctum": quoted Thimmesch.

21   "last of the great colonial overlords," "our authority is supreme": Manchester, 550, 551.

21   "and why, as a sovereign, should I?": Sebald, 119.

21   "head of government": Sebald, 107.

22   "there to be used": Manchester, 578.

22   "I was always interested in politics": quoted Thimmesch.

23   "more appropriate": Manchester, 466.

23   "poured it on": quoted Manchester, 439.

23   "not reassuring": Manchester, 620.

23   "the greatest man alive": quoted Manchester, 584.

23   Almond career: *Current Biography*, March 1951.

24   descriptions of Almond: Heinl, 44, 54, 58; Sebald, 196; *Time*, October 23, 1950; Manchester, 684.

24   "hates correspondents": Rees, 72. "unholy nuisance": Sebald, 116; "chief's characteristics": Leckie, 147.

24   "riding the political horse": Sebald, 106.

25   "fat and happy" and "all conceivable advantages": quoted Leckie, *Wars*, 866. See also William F. Dean, *General Dean's Story*, New York, Viking, 1954, p. 24.

26   "steamed and stank," Leckie, *Wars*, 866.

26   "I could watch": quoted Thimmesch.

26   "harsh and inept": Leckie, *Wars*, 847.

26   "why are you alive": quoted Alter.

27   "I had to go to Taiwan": quoted Shearer.

27   political embassy to Chiang: Manchester, 668ff. Also *The New York Times*, August 6, 1950.

27   "handpicked" staff: Fehrenbach, 241. "act of military nepotism": Heinl, 261–62, called it "jury-rigging X Corps."

28   "not interested": quoted Heinl, 45.

28   "the first of several near misses": Duggan.

Page *Identification——Source*

29   Almond's personal van "rigged" and other "amenities":
      Heinl, 189. The General's van is also described in
      Time, October 23, 1950.

29   "twentieth-century Cannae": Collins, 122ff.

30   "or at least the announcement": Leckie, *Conflict*, 128.

30   "political undertone": Heinl, 212.

30   "holocaust": Leckie, *Conflict*, 129.

30   "outstanding heroism": official citation, Department of
      the Army.

30   "Resistence was negligible": Heinl, 220.

31   "surprised . . . lightly manned": Appleman, 530.

31   another noted incident: see pp. 34–35 and note.

31   "poor record . . . faulty map coordinates": Heinl, 260–61.

32   "victory fever": Leckie, *Wars*, 886.

32   "tension": Rees, 127. "snarling": Fehrenbach, 296.

33   "run out of targets": Leckie, *Wars*, 888.

33   "might" have crossed: see Appleman, 750ff.

34   "If . . . these people turn out to be Chinese": Fehren-
      bach, 296.

34   "heartiest congratulations": quoted Leckie, *Conflict*, 169.

34   "gibbous" moon: Fehrenbach, 360.

34–35 Almond's visit to task force: Fehrenbach, 361; also
      described in Gugeler, 61.

35   "consolidate": Fehrenbach, 362.

35   "ever-sanguine": Rees, 160.

35   "confident": Collins, 229ff.

36   "But we're saying goodbye to them all": Fehrenbach,
      372. For accounts of the retreat, see Fehrenbach,
      362ff.; Leckie, *Wars*, 894ff.; Rees, 130ff.

36   "everyone was wrong": Collins, 175.

36   "so no stinking Chinese general": quoted Morris, 144.

37   "dispirited command . . . a gloomy foreboding": Collins,
      241.

37   "repeated flights . . . exposure": official citation, Depart-
      ment of the Army.

37   "in a light unarmed aircraft": *ibid.*

38   "the happiest group": quoted Manchester, 780.

38   "sickening": Rees, 221.

39   "I learned a lot": quoted Thimmesch.

39   "penchant for round-tabling": *Washington Post*, Sep-
      tember 30, 1973.

39–40 "He was one of the dying breed," "gave me gas pains":
      quoted Thimmesch.

Page   *Identification——Source*

      Wilson, *The US and the Trujillo Regime* (Rutgers, 1972), 139ff.

63   Martin's account is in his *Overtaken by Events* (Doubleday, 1966).

64   "bureaucrats and functionaries": Bosch, 76.

64   "we wound up": quoted Thimmesch.

64   "at McNamara's right hand": *ibid*. One of McNamara's deputies later described the secretary, a former Ford executive, as having "a very thin background in foreign affairs." See Hoopes, 18.

65   "officials exaggerated the facts": Eugene Windchy, *Tonkin Gulf* (Doubleday, 1971).

66   "so little of him": *Pentagon Papers*, 415.

66   Haig's "tough" memorandum: described by Loory, 106–7.

66   "ultimate professional": quoted *The New York Times*, December 31, 1971.

67   "I've served in many administrations": quoted Thimmesch.

68   "almost always high-school level": author's interview.

68   "justified": *ibid*. See also Confirmation Hearings, Part 2, 86.

69   "had discovered the military answer": *ibid*.

69–70 "in an exposed position": official citation, Department of the Army, 13 September 1966.

70   "scroff this fellow up": quoted Buckley.

71   "armed like a dagger": Leckie, *Wars*, 981.

71   "a dozen times before": David Ross in Al Samboli's *Everything We Had: An Oral History of the Vietnam War* . . . (Random House, 1979), 45.

71   "Fortified supply and political center": Rogers, 31.

71   "swift, decisive strike": Rogers, 34.

72   "destroy first and search later": Schell, 24.

72   Grimsley's briefing and the camp description: Schell, 25–27.

72   "a fantastic mess": Rogers, 36.

73   Hollingsworth's attack: *Stars and Stripes*, January 12, 1967.

73   captured weapons: Schell, 61–62.

73   "no friendly casualties": Schell, 44–45.

73   conflicting Army account: Rogers, 37.

73   "what do you mean": Schell, 62.

73   "concentration camp": Santoli, 45.

PART TWO: *Chamberlain*

113   "not smart": quoted Blumenfeld, et al., 176.

113   "he pounds": Safire, 389. "Only someone schooled": quoted Woodward and Bernstein, 194.

113   "personable . . . likeable": *ibid.*

113   "loners": Safire, 272.

114   "He gets the diamonds": author's personal experience.

117   "He never would have got anything read": quoted Blumenfeld, et al., 207.

118   Safire's accounts: 391, 404. "The most sensitive": Safire, 389.

119   "I'm going to call the Pentagon," "There's no point": quoted Shawcross, 101.

119   "I don't need," "only kidding": quoted Safire, 389–90.

119   could not "have gone to the bathroom": quoted Alter.

119   "dumb, stupid animals": Woodward and Bernstein, 194.

120   "generals who can win": Woodward and Bernstein, 195.

120   "Al, if you're a good boy": quoted and described by Alter.

120   "fits . . . mind in his pants": Morris, 143–44.

121   "found a way to make use of Bob Haldeman," *et seq.*: Gulley, 144.

121   "Kissinger's man . . . Haldeman's man": quoted Alter.

121   "basically unsure of themselves": Richard Whalen quoted Rather and Gates, 227.

122   Kissinger's threat to resign and subsequent funk: author's personal experience and background interviews.

122   "stop smiling . . . race between a second star and a cardiac": quoted Safire, 279. Haig's comment seems less a joke in light of his later heart disease.

123   "that criminal": quoted Woodward and Bernstein, 411.

123–4   "thought and action": quoted Safire, 165.

124   "the President—unknown to Kissinger": *ibid.*

125   "Haig's always down there": Morris, 142. "When you see the lights": quoted Duggan.

125   Haig's memos to Nixon: Blumenfeld et al., 176.

126   "So Haig gave . . . a tilt": Gulley, 143.

126   "intermediary": Zumwalt, 398–99.

127   "delicately": Woodward and Bernstein, 196.

127   "those shits," "our drunk," "limp wrist": Woodward and Bernstein, 191, 195, 197.

128   Butterfieldgrams: see Szulc, 180; Morris, 146.

128–9   "no crazier than most": Morris, 144. "I've got to get out of here": Woodward and Bernstein, 196.

Page Identification——Source

129 EC-121 incident: see Hersh on Nixon's drinking during the incident.

129 "god damn": Morris, 144.

129 "He moved me up": Blumenfeld, et al., 177.

129 "He was always perfectly comfortable": quoted Duggan.

131 "with the way": quoted Thimmesch.

131–2 "aroused the Army tiger," "hit the fan": Zumwalt, 341, 347.

132 "I know something": author's personal experience.

132–3 "We ought to pay": Zumwalt, 355.

133 jungle drums, war story: author's personal experience. See also Morris, 131–32.

134 "It was one of the most profound": *Confirmation*, Part 1, 371.

134 "I think at any particular juncture": quoted *Washington Post*, December 23, 1980.

134–5 NSSM 1 findings, "outdated and outdistanced": Kalbs, 152. It was, of course, the same "Democratic bureaucracy" of which Haig was a key member.

135 "a whole new ball game": quoted Thimmesch.

136 "I can't believe": Morris, 164. For an account of the plans, see also Szulc, 150–57.

138 "fell on fertile ground": Kissinger, 241.

138 "very definite change," "preemptive operations": *ibid.*

138 "seething" with "all his instincts": Kissinger, 243.

139 "nothing he feared more": Kissinger, 247.

139 Haig brings assessment: Shawcross, 26.

139 "tasteless": Kissinger, 247. "no appreciable effect": Morris, 156.

139 repeated lying to Congress: Shawcross, 94, 410.

140 "to know nothing": Shawcross, 130. Westmoreland excluded: Szulc, 253. "push the panic button": Szulc, 256.

141 "Our peerless leader has flipped out": quoted Szulc, 257.

141 "eastern establishment," disregard critique: *ibid.*

141 "If this doesn't work": quoted Shawcross, 142 and Morris, 147. See also David Wise, *The American Police State* (Random House, 1976), 92.

141 "You've just had an order": quoted Shawcross, 145.

141 "on the edge": see Shawcross, 154.

141 "Henry tried": quoted Morris, 194.

141–2 troops in White House: Shawcross, 153.

142 "He knew he was swimming": quoted Kalbs, 195.

155   "making sure that I understood": Sullivan, 219.

155   "represented his concerns": quoted Pincus.

156   "Pursley was substituted": Pincus.

156   "no written record": Sullivan, 219

156   "just about blew," "I think that is the kind": quoted *Washington Post*, July 10, 1975.

157   "an urger or an advocate": quoted *Washington Post*, July 10, 1975.

157   "uneasy feeling . . . I just knew": Sullivan, 227–28.

157   "very concerned": quoted *Washington Post*, December 20, 1980.

157   "I feel quite frankly": quoted Lukas, 50.

157   "He was suspect": quoted *Washington Post*, July 10, 1975. See also Szulc, 185.

158   "Haig's plea . . . meant little": Sullivan, 221.

158   "no information": quoted Szulc, 186.

158   May 20 visit to FBI: *ibid.*

158   "Dr. Kissinger is aware": quoted Szulc, 187.

158   "puzzling": quoted Pincus. "In one instance": quoted Alter.

159–60   Haig's briefing memo: *Washington Post*, December 20, 1980.

160   "reflective of a sensibility": quoted Sullivan, 222.

160   "nothing has come to light," "suggested to Haig": quoted Szulc, 187.

160–1   "an awful lot of garbage": quoted *Washington Post*, December 20, 1980.

161   "urged Henry," "personal reservations": quoted Lukas, 57.

161   wiles of a woman: Lukas, 56–57.

161   "Don't say anything": author's personal experience.

162   "overheard Daniel Ellsberg": Sullivan, 222.

162   "very inviting": quoted Pincus.

162   "Just gobs and gobs": quoted Morris, 159.

162   "served their purpose": quoted Lukas, 60.

163   "blackmail Nixon and Kissinger": Sullivan, 223.

163   came close to blaming: John Osborne, "Tapping for Henry," *The New Republic*, February 4, 1976.

163–4   "don't give me gas pains," "battin' gnats": quoted Safire, 168.

164   "joke . . . whitewash": *The New York Times*, January 15, 1976.

Page   *Identification——Source*

164   "right" with Nixon: Safire, 657.
164   "ugly glimpse": Richardson, 18.
165   "no attempt . . . dragnet": quoted Shawcross, 108.
167   "Do you have what I said": quoted Lukas, 61.
167   "what about the others": author's background interview.
167   "was not deeply involved": *Confirmation*, Part 1, 25.
168   "no vital interests": quoted Morris, 239.
169   "I don't see why": quoted Morris, 241. June 27 meeting: Powers, 227.
169   "either through political or military": quoted *Washington Post*, December 22, 1980.
169   "longtime ally": Powers, 228.
170   Helms meeting with Nixon: Powers, 234–35.
170   "I did not know there was a Track II": *Confirmation*, Part 1, 374.
171   "Executive officer," "keeping tabs": quoted *Washington Post*, December 22, 1980.
171   "to Haig and me": Kissinger, 674–76.
172   "that was disturbing": Phillips, 221.
172   "never more than a probe": Kissinger, 674.
172   "as tough as I ever saw . . . constant, constant": *Confirmation*, Part 1, 126 (excerpts from Congressional investigation of "Covert Activities in Chile").
172   "pressure was constant and heavy": Phillips, 223.
172   "heaviest of pressure": *Confirmation*, Part 1, 126.
172   "I don't believe I was": quoted *Confirmation*, Part 1, 139.
173   "major obstacle": quoted *Washington Post*, December 22, 1980.
173   army attache's role: *Confirmation*, Part 1, 128ff. and Powers, 236.
173   "succession of jerry-built schemes": Powers, 236.
173   "Schneider main barrier," "more important than ever": quoted *Confirmation*, Part 1, 130.
173   "no support": Kissinger, 677.
173   promises of money: Powers, 237, 363. "came to be regarded": *Confirmation*, Part 1, 130.
173   "consultation": *Confirmation*, Part 1, 135.
174   "informed Kissinger and . . . Haig": Powers, 236.
174   Karamessines' "negative" call, "no degree of latitude": *Confirmation*, Part 1, 137.
174   "It was decided": *Confirmation*, Part 1, 137–38.
175   "we had better not": *Confirmation*, Part 1, 138.

PART THREE: *Regent*

Page   Identification——Source

193   "malignant monument . . . the legend": Francis Russell, *The Shadow of Blooming Grove: Warren G. Harding and Times* (New York, 1968), 488.

193   "How Al Haig got Richard Nixon to decide": quoted Buckley.

194   *"our* 37½th president": quoted *Armed Forces Journal*, reproduced *Confirmation*, Part 2, 81.

194   "I could not help": Colson, 295.

194   "mistakes . . . I didn't make them": *Confirmation*, Part 1, 319.

194   "I am not a Nixonite" nor "a Republican": *Chicago Daily News*, September 18, 1974.

194–5   "standing erect . . . frightening": Jules Witcover, *Marathon: The Pursuit of the Presidency, 1972–76* (New York, 1977), 42.

195   "there are probably some," "the characteristics": quoted Thimmesch.

196   "a button-down . . . officer": *The New York Times*, December 31, 1971.

196–7   "manages details," "fear of leaving": Zumwalt, 398.

199   "I had a long talk": Nixon, 600.

199–200   "only Al and John": quoted Colson, 71.

200   "totally sold": Gulley, 146.

200   "optimistic report": Szulc, 606.

200   "said quite enough": Frank Snepp, *Decent Interval* (New York, 1978), 24.

200   "I would see an improving situation": quoted Shearer.

200–1   "had to exercise considerable dexterity," "gave Henry a version": Zumwalt, 399.

201   obscure post in Panama: Zumwalt, 398.

201   "saw what might be coming": Gulley, 144.

202   "one of your men": author's background interview.

202   "stiff resistence": Gulley, 145.

202   "glamorous and politically sophisticated": *Time*, September 18, 1972. Senate Armed Services Committee actions: *The New York Times* and *Washington Post*, October 7, 1972.

203   "Haig seemed rather subdued": Nixon, 693. For the final Vietnam sequel, see also Szulc, 610ff.

204   "a withering away": Kissinger, 1391.

Page   Identification——Source

Ken Tilson, Esquire, attorney for the Wounded Knee defense. In *Lamott v. Haig* and other action the defendants uncovered official army memoranda, logs of the Pentagon's Directorate for Military Support coordinating army plans at Wounded Knee, and other documents. See also *Garden Plot and SWAT: US Police as New Action Army*, special supplement to *Counterspy* magazine (Fifth Estate Publications, Washington, D.C., 1979).

213   "representative" to "evaluate": *Garden Plot*, 51.

213   "supervisory": author's background interview with Tilson.

213   "a Military Assistance Advisory Group": Volney Warner, "After Action Report," August 28, 1973, Department of the Army. Noted *Garden Plot*, 59.

213–14   munitions: *Garden Plot*, 52–53, and Warner.

214   leverage: *ibid.* Warner had the final recommendation on military equipment requested by the Justice Department.

214   attack plan: Warner to Haig memorandum dated March 9, 1973. Legal file.

214   situation report: Directorate of Military Support to Haig, May 1, 1973. Legal file.

215   "whimperish ending": *Newsweek*, May 21, 1973.

215   Sixty of the documents: author's background interview with Tilson.

215   "our continuing support": quoted Shawcross, 262.

215   "an all time low": quoted Shawcross, 275.

216   "maximal support": Szulc, 684.

216   "the enemy remained steadfast": quoted Shawcross, 273.

216   "Haig's favorite diplomat": Shawcross, 270.

217   "began to get reports": quoted Shawcross, 272.

217   "need not have happened": Kissinger, 1384. "Cambodia was . . . a crime": Shawcross, 396.

217   "I had a good meeting": Nixon, 823–24.

218   "Haig did a great job": quoted *Washington Post*, December 19, 1980. "because I was asked to," "jurors seemed to stare": quoted *Washington Post*, April 26, 1973.

218–19   Haig's testimony: *ibid.*

220   "dirty hands": *Washington Post*, May 15, 1973.

220   "one of the first things . . . a cardboard box so big": quoted *Washington Post*, December 20, 1980.

220   Garment "does not remember": *ibid.*

Page   Identification——Source

221   "just be thankful": author's background interview. See
       also Hersh in *The Atlantic*, May 1982 and his
       forthcoming book on Kissinger.

224   "diplomatic enough": Haldeman, 299.

224   "we had the same man": Nixon, 856.

224   Scowcroft "first choice": Gulley, 145.

224   "For once, Henry": Woodward and Bernstein, 32.

224   "I don't think Al's the right man": quoted *Washington
       Post*, September 30, 1973.

224   "a breath of fresh air": Klein, 393.

224   "the chief significance": *The New Republic*, June 9, 1973.

225   "great intelligence and integrity": *Washington Post*,
       June 3, 1973. "short but drastic clean-up": *Wash-
       ington Post*, May 8, 1973. "absolutely purpose-
       less": *Washington Post*, June 8, 1973.

225   "intellectually, it was not a tough decision": quoted
       Thimmesch.

226   Haig's pay and pension: *The Nation*, September 24,
       1973.

226   "ninety percent": *Confirmation*, Part 1, 13.

226   "a battalion . . . just overrun": quoted Lukas, 439.

226   "spent even more time": *Washington Post*, December
       19, 1980. "more time . . . than Nixon": Alter.

227   May 22 statement, "just another reassurance": Lukas,
       340–41.

227   "only one action": *Confirmation*, Part 1, 26.

228   Rebozo-Hughes sequence: *Washington Post*, December
       19, 1980.

228–9 "It was expected": *Washington Post*, May 29, 1973.

229   "sense of dread": Nixon, 873.

229   "discouraged, drained . . . a robust no": Nixon, 874.

320–5 June 4, 1973 tape transcript: *Washington Post*, July
       21, 1974.

232   "no independent recollection": *Confirmation*, Part 1, 27.

235   "exculpatory": quoted *Washington Post*, December 19,
       1980.

236   "Haig puts a cover memo . . . five coups a day": Zum-
       walt, 420.

236   Ziegler "last link": Lukas, 393.

236   Haig's knowledge of economics "to say the least lim-
       ited": *Washington Post*, July 10, 1973.

237   "You can call Haig": Dash, 181.

237–8 moving Kissinger telephone transcripts: Gulley, 208–9.

Page   Identification——Source

263   "no innocent explanation": quoted Lukas, 460.
263   "the toughest customer": Ben-Veniste and Frampton,
        181. "repeatedly blushed," "it's easy for you":
        quoted *Washington Post*, December 6, 1973.
264   judge "not inclined": Ben-Veniste and Frampton, 181.
264   "sinister force" testimony: quoted Sirica, 198.
264-5 "I've known women": quoted Ben-Veniste and Framp-
        ton, 182.
265   "curse under his breath": Sirica, 197.
265   "immediate charge" and Haig controlled key: Pincus.
266   "Why can't we make a new Dictabelt?": quoted *Wash-
        ington Post*, December 19, 1980.
266-7 Buzhardt and Garment approach: *Washington Post*,
        December 19, 1980; Woodward and Bernstein,
        21–30; "defections": Nixon, 946.
267   "tight-fisted": Lukas, 465.
268   "the President is paranoid" *et seq.*: Zumwalt, 459.
268   March 21 conversation: *Washington Post*, December
        19, 1980.
269   "selective, heavily edited": *ibid.*
269-70 "terrible beyond description" *et seq.*: Jaworski, 60–62.
        See also Ben-Veniste and Frampton, 210, and
        Confirmation, Part 2, 85.
271   technocrat's vocabularly and "there will always be a
        military man": Thimmesch, whose interview was
        tape-recorded. "I maintain": *ibid.*
271   "very understanding," "strong disciplinarian": *ibid.*
272   "Al's right of center": *ibid.*
272   "almost complete disarray" *et seq.*: Zumwalt, 478–79.
273   Haig's call to Haldeman: Haldeman, 308–9.
274   "dealing with fewer people": *The New Republic*, October
        27, 1973.
274   "I don't know that the system": quoted Thimmesch.
274   "what did you say," incident on *Air Force One*: *The New
        Republic*, May 4, 1974.
274-5 "wasn't taking hold": *ibid.* "allowed Haig . . . political
        disaster": Thimmesch.
275   Haig's threat over Ziegler, "Berlin in the last days":
        Colson, 205.
275   "the President has an excessive": quoted *Washington
        Post*, February 1, 1974.
276   Christmas party: Colson, 205.
276   blackmail episode, "go to hell . . . for fear he would

Page   Identification——Source

make . . . public": *The New York Times*, January
25, 1974. See also *Chronology*, II, 158.

276–7   "other voices" and CIA in Watergate: Colson, 229–30.

277   unexplored story of CIA: for an interesting "reflection"
on Watergate and the Agency, see Price, 360–74.

277–8   call on Mafia and Nixon: author's background interviews.

278   "You're a great American, Leon": quoted Jaworski, 119.

278   "He assured me": quoted Dean, 346.

278   "rant and rave aplenty": quoted *Time*, December 29,
1980. "once sympathetic . . . souring": Colson,
229.

279–80   "the real purpose of the meeting," *et seq.*: quoted Ben-
Veniste and Frampton, 276.

280   "standing back": author's background interview.

281   contrasts in transcripts and tapes: see Lukas, 489.
Nixon to Mitchell, "dubious relevance": quoted
Lukas, 490.

281   "blasphemous speculation": *Washington Post*, February
17, 1974. "I haven't the slightest doubt the tapes
were screwed with": quoted *Time*, December 29,
1980.

282   "a deliberate effort": Mollenhoff, *Man Who*, 173.

282   memo "had been doctored": Pincus. See also Truscott
in *The Nation*, November 2, 1974.

282   "all the relevant information": quoted Lukas, 494.

283   call to Silberman, "demand . . . unprecedented": quoted
Washington Post, December 19, 1980.

283   "obviously rankled" by Haig's threats and May 5 meeting: Ben-Veniste and Frampton, 276–78.

284   "if he thought": quoted *Associated Press* dispatch, May
10, 1974. "softening . . . pressured out of office":
quoted *The New York Times*, May 12, 1974.

284   "resentment and concern" before Ervin Committee:
quoted James Hamilton, *The Power to Probe* (New
York, 1976), 282–83.

284   "the national security matters": Jaworski, 27–28. "I
don't know how much": *Confirmation*, Part 2, 84.

285   "a very long footnote" and May 23 meeting: *Chronology*,
II, May–June 1974, 154. "denigration . . . bad
taste . . . design": quoted *Washington Post*, May
25, 1974.

286   "brilliantly and valiantly": Nixon, 1032.

Page	Identification——Source

299   "when the time comes": quoted *Washington Post*, May 11, 1974.

299   "there are a lot of low-class": quoted Lukas, 551.

300   "very much upset," call to Jaworski: quoted Jaworski, 248–49, 258; *Confirmation*, Part 2, 83; quoted Lukas, 555.

300   "you may feel depressed": quoted *Washington Post*, September 29, 1974.

301   "just tell him that . . . we expected": Nixon, 1064.

301   "whipped into a frenzy": Nixon, 1063–64.

301   "watching at the avalanche": Price, 337.

301   "Nixon should get his ass out": quoted Lukas, 559.

302   "recognized the inevitability" *et seq.*: Nixon, 1064.

303   "totally agreed" with Kissinger: Nixon, 1066.

303   Haldeman "strongly opposed": Nixon, 1067–68.

303–4   Nixon's notes, "how tired he was": Nixon, 1067–68.

304   "We'll need a thousand words" *et seq.*: Price 339.

304   "If impeachment is inevitable": quoted Colson, 294.

305   Schlesinger's order: James W. Canan, *The Super Warriors* (New York, 1979), 340–41; White, 22–23; Lukas, 559.

305   "stand apart from politics," "insulted and shocked": Canan, 340.

305   Ford's statement: *ibid.*

306   "assured" by Haig, "leaked deliberately": Ford, 136.

306   "asking the Pentagon": Colson, 294. "hinted darkly": *The New Republic*, December 8, 1979. "there were considerations": quoted Unger.

306–7   ex-agent's call: author's background interviews.

308   "destroy me . . . take care": quoted Zumwalt, 510.

309   "go through the fire . . . my mind was made up": Nixon, 1068–69.

309   "he knew what the reports would be": Price, 340.

309   "The President is up and down": quoted Lukas, 563.

310   "on this one—don't run it by": quoted Price, 344.

310   luncheon with Jaworski: Ben-Veniste and Frampton, 296.

310   "to pass a resolution . . . Oh yes!": Jaworski, 261–64.

311   Haig on Jaworski, "right decision," "no special deals": quoted and described Nixon, 1080.

311   "Al, I'm sorry": Nixon, 1082.

311   "the hell with the staff meeting": quoted Nixon, 1086.

312   "bananas thing": *The New York Times*, May 8, 1975.

PART FOUR: *Pretender*

Page   Identification——Source

329   "there is nobody": quoted *Newsweek*, December 29,
           1980.

330   "nothing on the battlefield," "I am at peace": quoted
           Reeves, 124.

330   "I have no regrets": *Washington Post*, September 15,
           1974.

330   "I never was a Nixonite": *Chicago Daily News*, Septem-
           18, 1974. See also, *The New Republic*, October 5,
           1974 for another account of what he told Lisagor.
           "pressures had affected": *ibid.*

331   "hardly flattering": Hartmann, 127.

332   "Gerry, General Haig has some good news": Hartmann,
           26. "*ad hoc* committee to control": Hartmann, 91.

332–33 Griffin and transcript episodes: Hartmann, 141 and
           145–46.

333   "great manager": quoted Hartmann, 116.

333   "100 percent loyal": Ford, 185.

333   removal of files: quoted and described Hartmann, 161.

333   "acrid smell of paper": Hartmann, 173.

333–4   burn bags: author's background interviews.

334   "had successfully removed": Hartmann, 245.

335–6   briefing memo for Ford: Hartmann, 173–74.

336   "there's no time for that": quoted Reeves, 64.

336   "Al, what do you think": quoted Reeves, 65.

336–7   "we had to keep Haig": quoted Reeves, 73.

337   "ran the country": Reeves, 71.

338   "essentially what I've always done": *Washington Post*,
           September 16, 1974.

338   Scranton encounter: Hartmann, 203–4. See also Reeves,
           74.

338   briefing book denied Ford: *ibid.*

338   "Quiet but rather imperious": *The New Republic*,
           October 5, 1974.

339   "do you feel good executing": quoted Reeves, 76–77.

339   matching leaks: Reeves, 122.

339   "you've got to get this guy": Ford, 185.

339–40 "cool and thoughtful," *et seq.*: Nessen, 16–17.

340   "a recruit": Hartman, 290.

340   "the Ford transition . . . couldn't even find out": Reeves,
           77.

Page   *Identification———Source*

340   "stacks" of memos: Hartmann, 205. not much difference: Reeves, 80.

340   Haig "hardest hit": *Washington Post*, September 15, 1974.

340–41   microphones still in Oval Office: Hartmann, 199.

341   abortive Buchanan appointment: Hartmann, 205.

341   "white" in "anger," "they'll boo you": Hartmann, 213–14.

341   Griffin and Goodell urge removal: Reeves, 123. "I began to look at the broader picture": Ford, 185.

342   "contemporaries in the Army," "decided upon": Hartmann, 206. "best alternative": Ford, 185–86.

342–3   Kissinger opposition and meeting: author's background interviews.

343   "few people seriously argue": *Washington Post*, September 20, 1974.

343   Jaworski "knew something": *Confirmation*, Part 2, 82.

343–4   "brutal eviction": Hartmann, 206. "one of the most distinguished": quoted *Commonweal*, October 4, 1974.

344   "close to anarchy": Nessen, 74. "poor Al": quoted Reeves, 129.

344   "spent men": quoted *Commonweal*, October 4, 1974.

345   "public relations disaster," "bitter pill": quoted *Washington Post*, September 23, 1974.

346   Duncan and "glassware": *Washington Post*, January 22 and 30, 1975.

346   flight home: *The New York Times*, March 27, 1975.

347   "I told the President": quoted Buckley.

347   "to be judged": quoted *Washington Post*, May 17, 1976.

347–8   "smacked of American insensitivity," Schlesinger censure: *ibid.*

348   "it is not up to a military leader": quoted *Washington Post*, March 6, 1976.

348   "hectoring allies": *The New York Times*, March 23, 1976.

348   "volunteered," "not authorized": *The New York Times*, June 13, 1976. "making policy": *The Nation*, March 20, 1976.

349   "a spiffy raised-eagle belt": *The New Republic*, October 7, 1978.

349–50   "most of the NATO hierarchy," *et seq.*: *Washington Post*, May 15, 1976.

350–1   "managing global Soviet power": *The New York Times*, March 6, 1976.

Page   Identification——Source

351   "relentless improvement": *The New York Times*, September 26, 1976.

351   Army Association speech: *The New York Times*, October 14, 1976.

352   "dynamic progress": *Washington Post*, November 9, 1976.

352   "my friend Henry Kissinger," "I'm not aware": *The New York Times*, November 25, 1976.

353   interviews around Carter inauguration: *The New York Times*, January 10 and 23, 1977.

354   "The lone survivor": *The New York Times*, June 12, 1977.

355–6 Korean investigation: *Korean-American Relations*, 141.

356   "might not be as high": quoted *The New York Times*, September 15, 1977.

358   "are of one mind": quoted *The New York Times*, March 2, 1978. "a ratner dramatic shift": *Washington Post*, March 22, 1978.

358–60 reporting of neutron bomb "crisis": Roger Morris, "Eight Days in April," *Columbia Journalism Review*, Nov.–Dec. 1978.

361   "I won't judge the value judgments": quoted *Washington Post*, April 26, 1978.

361   "a classic case": *Christian Century*, May 10, 1978.

362   "vast political, economic, and military," "grievous concern," "incalculable": quoted *The New York Times*, May 23, 1978.

362   "decade of neglect": *The New York Times*, September 26, 1978.

362   "unacceptable risk": Associated Press dispatch, October 4, 1978.

362–3 Nixon meeting: *The New York Times*, November 27, 1978.

363   "I'd only say," *et seq.*: quoted Buckley.

364   "Oh, I never think of not taping": *ibid.*

364   "not bashful": *The New Republic*, October 7, 1978.

365   "such a mess": quoted *ibid.*

366   missiles vs. expensive craft: a point made dramatically by the war in the Falkland Islands.

367   "more aroused," "greater concertion [sic]": *ibid.*

368   "wistful for the Eisenhower years": John Judis "Why Not the Worst?" *The Progressive*, February 24, 1981.

Page   Identification——Source

392   "I just can't give": Part 1, 338.
392–3   "no such nominee": Part 1, 342.
393   "I cannot bring myself": Part 1, 359.
393   "I can think of a number": Part 1, 373.
394   no personal records: Part 2, 38.
394   Haig's closing statement: Part 2, 93. "your experience
        . . . should be invaluable": Part 2, 76.
394   hope no "rancor": Part 2, 63–64.
394–5   "of course the man's treacherous": Lewis Lapham,
        "Haig—No," *Washington Post*, January 13, 1981,
        reprinted, Part 1, 336.

Epilogue

400   "by his quavery, Queeg-like": Duggan.
401   "a bush leaguer": Jack Germond and Jules Witcover,
        "Haig's Defeat," *The New Mexican* (Santa Fe),
        April 6, 1981.
402   "And so I caveat it," *et seq.*: quoted Gary Wills, "What
        Did He Say?", *Albuquerque Journal*, May 1, 1981.
404   Haig's testimony on nuns murder: See T. D. Allman,
        "The Haig Doctrine," *Harper's*, June 1981.
406   "merely substituted slyness for courage": D. J. Good-
        speed, *The German Wars* (Boston, 1977), 518–19.

BIBLIOGRAPHY

A truly comprehensive bibliography would embrace America's postwar army and foreign policy as well as Watergate and the Nixon, Ford, and Carter administrations, a literature much too large to list here. I have confined this selection to those sources bearing most directly on Haig's career, and of these, some are especially outstanding and worth a careful reading in their entirety: Zumwalt and Hartmann for their extraordinary candor and insight into the bureaucratic culture; Nixon and Kissinger as rich and revealing memoirs when read critically; Cincinnatus on Vietnam and the Army; Shawcross and Szulc as valuable portraits of foreign policy; and Lukas as still the best book in general on Watergate. Among the biographical articles on Haig, Thimmesch's tape-recorded interview remains the most interesting for the general's own words and I have drawn gratefully on it, while Alter and Ungar are perceptive portrayals in their own right.

The following includes the principal books and magazine articles cited in the Notes. Incidental references are cited in full as they appear in the Notes. Newspapers are carried *only* in the Notes in their specific citations.

Agnew, Spiro. *Go Quietly . . . Or Else.* New York, Morrow, 1980.
Alter, Jonathan. "Tinker, Tailor, Soldier, Bureaucrat." *The Washington Monthly*, March 1981.

Appleman, Roy E. *South to the Naktong, North to the Yalu.* Washington, Department of the Army, 1961.

Ben-Veniste, Richard and Frampton, George Jr. *Stonewall.* New York, Simon and Schuster, 1978.

Blumenfeld, Ralph, and the staff and editors of *The New York Post. Henry Kissinger: The Private and Public Story.* New York, New American Library, 1974.

Bosch, Juan. *Pentagonism.* New York, Grove Press, 1968.

Buckley, Christopher. "Saving the West with General Haig." *Esquire*, September 26, 1978.

Casserly, John J. *The Ford White House.* New York, Colo. Assoc., 1977.

Cincinnatus. *Self-Destruction: The Disintegration and Decay of the United States Army During the Vietnam Era.* New York, Norton, 1981.

Collins, J. Lawton. *War in Peacetime.* Boston, Houghton Mifflin, 1969.

Colson, Charles. *Born Again.* New York, Bantam Books, 1978.

Committee on Armed Services, US Senate, 93rd Congress, 2nd Session. *Transmittal of Documents from the National Security Council to the Chairman of the Joint Chiefs of Staff.* Hearings, Parts 1 and 2, Feb. 6, 20, 21, 1974. Washington, US Gov. Printing Office, 1974.

——. 92nd Congress, 2nd Session. *Nomination of Major General Alexander Meigs Haig, Jr. to the Rank of General, US Army.* Hearing, October 6, 1972. Washington, US Gov. Printing Office, 1972.

Committee on Foreign Relations, US Senate, 93rd Congress, 2nd Session. *Dr. Kissinger's Role in Wiretapping* (Executive hearings made public September 29, 1974). Washington, US Gov. Printing Office, 1974.

——. 97th Congress, 1st Session. *Nomination of Alexander M. Haig, Jr.* Hearings, Parts 1 and 2, January 9, 10, 12, 13, 14, 15, 1981. Washington, US Gov. Printing Office, 1981.

Committee on International Relations, US House of Representatives, 95th Congress, 2nd Session. *Investigation of Korean-American Relations.* Hearings Report, Parts 4 and 5 and Appendix Vol. 1, October 31, 1978. Washington, US Gov. Printing Office, 1978.

Select Committee on Presidential Campaign Activities, US Senate,

93rd Congress, 2nd Session. *Watergate and Related Activities*. Washington, US Gov. Printing Office, 1974.

Congressional Quarterly Staff. *Complete Watergate: Chronology of a Crisis*. 2 Vols., Washington, 1975.

Current Biography. "Alexander Meigs Haig, Jr." January 1973, Vol. 34, No. 1.

Dash, Samuel. *Chief Counsel*. New York, Random House, 1976.

Dean, John. *Blind Ambition*. New York, Simon and Schuster, 1976.

Department of State. Citations of Alexander M. Haig, Jr. January 27, 1982.

——. "Alexander M. Haig, Jr. Sworn In," Press Release, February 1, 1981.

Drew, Elizabeth. *Washington Journal: The Events of 1973–74*. New York, Random House, 1974.

Duggan, Ervin S. "The Little Engine of Alexander Haig." *The Washingtonian Magazine*, November 1981.

Ellis, Joseph and Moore, Robert. *School for Soldiers: West Point and the Profession of Arms*. New York, Oxford University Press, 1974.

Fallows, James. "A Military Without Mind or Soul." *The Washington Monthly*, April 1981.

Fehrenbach, T. R. *This Kind of War*. New York, Macmillan, 1963.

Flemming, Thomas J. *West Point*. New York, Morrow, 1969.

Ford, Gerald R. *A Time To Heal*. New York, Harper & Row, 1979.

Gabriel, Richard A. and Savage, Paul L. *Crisis in Command: Mismanagement in the Army*. New York, Hill and Wang, 1978.

Galloway, K. Bruce and Johnson, Robert Bowie, Jr. *West Point: America's Power Fraternity*. New York, Simon and Schuster, 1973.

Gelb, Leslie. "How Haig is Recasting His Image." New York Times Biographical Service, May 1981.

Grady, Roman C. *Collected Works of Ducrot Pepys*. New York, Moore, 1943.

Gugeler, Russell A. *Combat Actions in Korea*. Washington, Office of the Chief of Military History, 1970.

Gulley, Bill, with Reese, Mary Ellen. *Breaking Cover*. New York, Simon and Schuster, 1980.

Halberstam, David. *The Best and the Brightest*. New York, Fawcett Crest, 1972.

Haldeman, Robert, with Dimona, Joseph. *The Ends of Power*. New York, Times Books, 1978.

Hartmann, Robert T. *Palace Politics: An Inside Account of the Ford Years*. New York, McGraw-Hill, 1980.

Hauser, Lt. Col. William. *America's Army in Crisis*. Baltimore, Johns Hopkins, 1973.

Heinl, Robert Debs Jr. *Victory at High Tide: The Inchon-Seoul Campaign*. New York, Lippincott, 1968.

Hoopes, Townsend. *The Limits of Intervention*. New York, David McKay, 1970.

Jaworski, Leon. *The Right and the Power*. New York, Gulf, 1976.

Just, Ward. *Military Men*. New York, Knopf, 1970.

Kalb, Marvin and Kalb, Bernard. *Kissinger*. New York, Dell, 1975.

King, Lt. Col. Edward L. *The Death of the Army*. New York, Saturday Review Press, 1972.

Kissinger, Henry A. *White House Years*. Boston, Little, Brown, 1975.

Klein, Herbert G. *Making It Perfectly Clear*. Garden City, Doubleday, 1980.

Leckie, Robert. *Conflict: History of the Korean War*. New York, Putnam, 1962.

———. *The Wars of America*. New York, Harper & Row, 1981.

Loory, Stuart H. *Defeated: Inside America's Military Machine*. New York, Random House, 1973.

Lovell, John P. *Neither Athens Nor Sparta: The American Service Academies in Transition*. Bloomington, Indiana Univ. Press, 1979.

Lukas, J. Anthony. *Nightmare: The Underside of the Nixon Years*. New York, Viking, 1976.

Manchester, William. *American Caesar, Douglas MacArthur, 1880–1964*. New York, Dell, 1978.

Mollenhoff, Clark R. *The Man Who Pardoned Nixon*. New York, Giniger, 1976.

———. *Game Plan for Disaster*. New York, Norton, 1976.

Morris, Roger. *Uncertain Greatness: Henry Kissinger and American Foreign Policy*. New York, Harper & Row, 1977.

Mylander, Maureen. *The Generals*. New York, Dial, 1974.

Nessen, Ron. *It Sure Looks Different from the Inside*. New York, Playboy Press, 1978.

Newhouse, John. *Cold Dawn*. New York, Holt, Rinehart and Winston, 1973.

Nixon, Richard. *RN: The Memoirs of Richard Nixon*. New York, Grosset and Dunlap, 1978.

New York Times. *The End of a Presidency*. New York, Bantam, 1974.

———. *The Final Report of the Committee on the Judiciary, House of Representatives*. New York, Bantam, 1975.

———. *The Watergate Hearings*. New York, Bantam, 1973.

———. *The Pentagon Papers*. New York, Bantam, 1971.

———. *White House Transcripts*. New York, Bantam, 1974.

O'Hara, John. *Ten North Fredericks*. New York, Random House, 1955.

Phillips, David Atlee. *The Night Watch*. New York, Atheneum, 1977.

Pincus, Walter. "Alexander Haig." *The New Republic*, October 5, 1974.

Powers, Thomas. *The Man Who Kept the Secrets*. New York, Knopf, 1979.

Price, Raymond. *With Nixon*. New York, Viking, 1977.

Rather, Dan and Gates, Gary. *Palace Guard*. New York, Harper & Row, 1974.

Rees, David. *Korea: The Limited War*. New York, St. Martin's, 1964.

Reeves, Richard. *A Ford Not A Lincoln*. New York, Harcourt Brace Jovanovich, 1975.

Richardson, Elliot. *The Creative Balance*. New York, Holt, Rinehart and Winston, 1976.

Rogers, Lt. Gen. Bernard William. *Cedar Falls and Junction City: A Turning Point*. Vietnam Studies, Department of the Army, Washington, US Gov. Printing Office, 1974.

Safire, William. *Before the Fall*. New York, Belmont Tower Books, 1975.

Sebald, William J. *With MacArthur in Japan*. New York, Norton, 1965.

Schell, Jonathan. *The Village of Ben Suc*. New York, Knopf, 1967.

Shawcross, William. *Sideshow: Nixon, Kissinger and The Destruction of Cambodia*. New York, Simon and Schuster, 1979.

Shearer, Lloyd. "Keep Your Eye on Al." *Parade*, August 20, 1972.

Sirica, John J. *To Set the Record Straight.* New York, Norton, 1979.

Sullivan, William, with Brown, Bill. *The Bureau.* New York, Norton, 1979.

Szulc, Tad. *The Illusion of Peace.* New York, Viking, 1978.

Taylor, Maxwell D. *The Uncertain Trumpet.* New York, Harper & Row, 1960.

Thimmesch, Nick. "Chief of Staff." *Potomac* magazine, *The Washington Post*, November 25, 1973.

Truscott, Lucian K. IV. *Dress Gray.* New York, Doubleday, 1978.

Ungar, Sanford J. "Alexander Haig: Pragmatist at State." *The Atlantic Monthly*, March 1981.

White, Theodore. *Breach of Faith.* New York, Atheneum, 1975.

Woodward, Bob and Bernstein, Carl. *The Final Days.* New York, Simon and Schuster, 1976.

Zumwalt, Admiral Elmo R. Jr. *On Watch.* New York, Quadrangle, 1976.

INDEX